Why Nicaragua Vanished

Why Nicaragua Vanished

A Story of Reporters and Revolutionaries

ROBERT S. LEIKEN

ROWMAN & LITTLEFIELD PUBLISHERS, INC.
Lanham • Boulder • New York • Oxford

ROWMAN & LITTLEFIELD PUBLISHERS, INC.

Published in the United States of America
by Rowman & Littlefield Publishers, Inc.
A Member of the Rowman & Littlefield Publishing Group
4501 Forbes Boulevard, Suite 200, Lanham, Maryland 20706
www.rowmanlittlefield.com

PO Box 317
Oxford
OX2 9RU, UK

British Library Cataloguing in Publication Information Available

Library of Congress Cataloging-in-Publication Data

Leiken, Robert S., 1939–
    Why Nicaragua vanished: a story of reporters and revolutionaries / Robert S.
Leiken.
        p. cm.
    ISBN 0-7425-2341-1 (alk. paper) – ISBN 0-7425-2342-X (pbk.: alk. paper)
    1. Nicaragua—Press coverage—United States. I. Title.

070.4'4997285053—dc21   2002036607

Printed in the United States of America

⊖™ The paper used in this publication meets the minimum requirements of American
National Standard for Information Sciences—Permanence of Paper for Printed Library
Materials, ANSI/NISO Z39.48-1992.

To Katherine

Abbreviations

AJC — *The Atlanta Journal and Constitution*

BG — *Boston Globe*

CSM — *Christian Science Monitor*

CT — *Chicago Tribune*

DMN — *Dallas Morning News*

FBIS — Foreign Broadcast Information Service

HC — *Houston Chronicle*

LAT — *Los Angeles Times*

MH — *Miami Herald*

NYRB — *The New York Review of Books*

NYT — *New York Times*

NYTM — *New York Times Magazine*

SFC — *San Francisco Chronicle*

TNR — *The New Republic*

USAT — *USA Today*

WP — *Washington Post*

WSJ — *Wall Street Journal*

WT — *Washington Times*

Contents

Acknowledgments

This project could not have been undertaken without the generous and patient support of the Lynde and Harry Bradley Foundation as well as the Smith Richardson Foundation and the John M. Olin Foundation.

I thank Samuel P. Huntington for inviting me to the Harvard University Center for International Affairs (CFIA) to work on this project as a Visiting Fellow and a Research Associate for three years. At CFIA Jorge Dominguez looked in on my progress and was a source of encouragement. Malcolm Deas of St. Antony's College, Oxford University, pored over the manuscript and was extremely supportive. I wish to thank Stephan Thernstrom of the History department for his confidence and support. Sarah Chilton and Mary Fry of the Brookings Institution library gave me timely help. I am grateful to Dimitri Simes of the Nixon Center for his faith in my work.

At various points William Ratliff, Susan Kaufmann Purcell, Steven Solms, and Viron Vaky offered encouragement. Carl Gershman of the National Endowment for Democracy has been a steadfast friend and backer as has been Peter Skerry. Bruce Cameron and Tom Weisbuch, have been loyal supporters and friends. I wish also to thank David Flockhart, Spenser Schaeffer, and Allen Stone.

Stephen Kaplitt spent a summer helping to designing the quantitative analysis that appears in an appendix. Dan Amundson and Robert Lichter of the Center for Media and Public Affairs offered valuable tips. Mr. Kaplitt also compiled indices and then retrieved news items from the Lamont Library Microfilm Room before the time when many became available on LEXIS-NEXIS, redundantly, for us. Others who joined that mammoth safari included Leslie Cintron, for two long years, as well as Tim Graham, David Fazio, Carleton Dane, and Agelika Gissler. Kathy Long Rugg transcribed most of the interviews and typed in countless excerpts from news clips. Lee Harvey also helped on that huge task.

Thanks to Mike Tiorano and Janice Rand for their administrative help at CFIA and to Dorothy at the Vanderbilt Media Library for tracking down video tapes.

I cannot begin to list the many Nicaraguans who taught me about their country over the years, so those who follow must stand for all: Roger Guevara Mena, Marta Patricia Baltodano, the Cruz family, Jaime Wheelock, Rafael Solis, Pablo Antonio Cuadra, Fausto Amador, Violeta Chamorro de Barrios, Ernesto Palazio, Roger Miranda, Pepe Matus, Xavier Arguello, Justo, Rigoberto, and the valiant people of Chinandega.

Several people read the manuscript or parts of it. Their comments help eliminate at least some of the imprecision and clumsiness, though they bear no responsibility for what remains awkward or controversial. Those kind enough to read and help correct the manuscript were Malcolm Deas, Mark Falcoff, Leslie Hunter, Stephen Kaplitt, Katherine Leiken, and Nancy Llach. Others who helpfully read various segments of it in various forms were Bernard Aronson,

David Chanoff, Peter Collier, Arturo Cruz, Jr., Jorge Dominguez, Penn Kemble, John MacAward, Sam Leiken, Kent Shreeve, Robert Silvers, and Leon Weiseltier. Snippets of chapters 10 and 11 appeared in *The New York Review of Books* and *The New Republic* but are probably unrecognizable now. An earlier form of chapters 5 and 6 was awarded a prize in the 1991 Media Studies Essay Contest of the Woodrow Wilson International Center for Scholars in Washington, D.C.

Larry Harrison and Shirley Christian kindly offered me their Nicaragua memorabilia and Joshua Muravchik lent me the collection of Nicaragua press clips he utilized for the two periods covered in his excellent volume *News Coverage of the Sandinista Revolution*. Ron Maxwell gave me copies of the interview for his unfinished film on the Nicaraguan revolution. Dr. Alejandro Bolanos let me pore through his voluminous Nicaragua library in St. Louis and Colonel Edward Robbins lent me a bucolic place to assemble and write.

Among the journalists I interviewed or came to know, James LeMoyne, Sam Dillon, Gustavo Gorritti, Julia Preston, George Russell and Juan Tamayo were exceptionally generous with their recollections and insights.

At Rowman and Littlefield I am grateful to Mary Carpenter, Hedi Hong and Laura Roberts for their scrupulous attention.

No one was more indispensable to the production of this book than Randy Wells of the Library of Congress. His resourcefulness, trust and imagination, and his tireless work of formatting the manuscript and the book copy have been invaluable. The same could be said for Leslie Hunter's work on the indiex. Christine White edited the page proofs with her customary efficiency.

My mother, Gertrude Solin Leiken, my literary progenitor, lived only to see the birth of this project. My wife Katherine was inspired to make an unforgettable documentary film about many of the warriors in this tragic drama. She saw this volume through to the end with infinite kindness and patience, while raising our *sine qua non,* Benjamin and Samuel, who someday may care to learn of the battles over Nicaragua which not only crushed bodies but seared souls.

Robert S. Leiken
Washington, D.C.

Chapter 1
An Election Stunner

It seems incredible, but the Sandinistas might lose an election!
—Correspondent Frederick Thys from Managua
on *CBS Morning*, February 26, 1990

The Sandinistas' defeat in Nicaragua's February 25, 1990, elections made for one of those embarrassing but edifying occasions when the coverage itself becomes the story. On February 26 the *CBS Evening News* led with the admission that the election results were "a stunning surprise, at least to wide sections of the U.S. government and American journalism."[1] ABC's coverage acknowledged that the *ABC News–Washington Post* poll of Nicaraguan voters had proved "terribly wrong" prompting "a lot of explaining today about what happened."[2] The *NBC Nightly News*, which for the past month had been proclaiming that "Ortega will win the presidency by a wide margin," offered no explanation for treating a Sandinista victory as a foregone conclusion.[3]

The *Washington Post*'s ombudsman Richard Harwood remonstrated that NBC's several million election night viewers were not told of "any likelihood that the election might have a different outcome." Then Harwood indulged in yet one more media forecast and in a piercing analogy, "NBC will pay no price for that blunder because we in the news business ordinarily are sheathed in Teflon garments." The ombudsman did not fail to note that his own organization, whose February 21 front-page report forecast a landslide Sandinista victory, and put forth a belated and "brief explanation of the pratfall." Moreover, Harwood added, the *Post* placed the acknowledgment "in the fifteenth paragraph of a seventeen paragraph story on page seventeen." "Newspapers, like some physicians," Harwood commented mordantly, "bury their mistakes."[4]

Who Was Responsible?

If NBC and ABC went farthest out on the limb, they had plenty of company in the tree. A survey for this study of sixteen major news organizations found that on the forty-nine occasions where news stories cited public opinion polls to anticipate the outcome, forty-five [91 percent] favored Sandinista candidate Daniel Ortega, two considered the election too close to call, and only two favored opposition candidate Violeta Chamorro. The Center for Media and Public Affairs conducted a more limited survey of ten major media outlets, covering editorials and commentaries as well as news stories. That survey found that of "the eighteen occasions where opinion polls were cited to predict the outcome, sixteen (89 percent) favored the Sandinistas."[5]

In the months leading up to the vote, not a single news story foresaw a Sandinista defeat, still less a rout. The television networks were the most confident that, as NBC's Ed Rabel asserted, "Ortega will win the presidency by a wide margin."[6] NBC, along with CNN, repeated most insistently that Ortega was headed for an "overwhelming" victory, though CBS also stressed that Daniel Ortega was "comfortably ahead" as did ABC.[7] But if television news, with less room for nuance, was blunter in its assurance of a Sandinista triumph, the print media, with rare exceptions, raised similar prospects.

On February 1, alongside a large graphic showing the Sandinistas far ahead, *USA Today* declared "the almost certain defeat of U.S.-backed candidate Violeta Chamorro."[8] The *Miami Herald*, the American daily with the most thorough coverage of Latin America, reported on January 28 that "Ortega's lead appears to grow in polls . . . as the number of undecided votes dwindles," citing a European diplomat who did not "know a single person who is a neutral observer who predicts UNO [Nicaguan Opposition Unity] will win."[9]

ABC's *Nightline*'s usually careful Ted Koppel went further. He began his February 23 broadcast with the affirmation that the Sandinistas would win "almost certainly." Koppel's guest, former president Jimmy Carter, who was in Managua at the head of an official observer delegation, politely endeavored to remind Koppel that "the elections haven't been held yet." Unfazed, his host plunged on with what he termed "the real story": future relations between the U.S. and the newly re-elected Sandinista government.

The presumption of Sandinista victory permitted news organizations not merely to report but also to interpret and "explain" administration statements. A story in the January 25 *Washington Post* surmised that the Bush administration was harping upon Sandinista campaign abuses "to discredit a potential Sandinista victory in advance" or else perhaps "to mend . . . fences with Republican conservatives who believe Bush made a mistake in emphasizing elections over military efforts to oust the Sandinistas."[10] Whatever its motive, the authors concluded, "the administration also appears increasingly frustrated at the apparent failure of Chamorro to generate more voter support." On February 9 a *New York Times* Washington correspondent observed that:

the Bush Administration has already issued many statements declaring the
elections biased, possibly to lay the groundwork for dismissing the results if
Mr. Ortega wins.[11]

Two weeks later NBC's John Cochran claimed that the purpose of administration criticism of Sandinista campaign abuses was damage control: "the White
House is already preparing public opinion in this country for a Sandinista victory."[12]

The assumed Sandinista victory was also used to explain events which had
not yet occurred. Four days prior to the voting, *NBC Nightly News*, having concluded that "Ortega will be elected overwhelmingly this weekend," began focusing its coverage on the ramifications of a Sandinista victory.[13] Before the
polls closed Sunday, Rabel divulged that "the widespread belief that the
Sandinistas will prevail has shifted thinking far beyond the ballot box." The
Nightly News devoted the remainder of its "election day coverage" to the impending "normalization" of relations between the United States and Sandinista
Nicaragua. Jaime Gangel and Deborah Norwood revealed that NBC had
"learned" (from whom we were not told) that its "basic terms" had been worked
out in "secret high level talks" between the State Department and the immi-
nently re-elected Sandinistas. There was no mention of the State Department's
denial of any such talks.[14]

For Harwood the error was the consequence of straying from hard facts into
the domain of "widespread belief." Expressing the distaste of the veteran newsman toward an upstart generation, Harwood observed:

as the "media" grow wealthier and more ambitious, they more and more attract
people with sophisticated and creative minds, people who are not content to
deal merely with the "record" and those mundane things subject to verifica-
tion.[15]

The creative young journalist might have responded that fallacious election predictions were hardly the monopoly of youth, and that the American press' most
notorious election blunder had occurred in 1948, when readers and listeners
went to bed believing their next president to be Thomas Dewey. Our journalist
could claim that the fallacious predictions were based on numerous public
opinion surveys by reputable American polling organizations. As CNN's Latin
American correspondent Ronnie Lovler, who had been among those most confident of Sandinista victory, hastened to note the morning after the elections:
"pollsters, and Latin American specialists, most journalists, everybody, was predicting a Sandinista victory . . . everybody expected the Sandinistas to win."[16]

So the journalists were only following the pollsters. But the pollsters had
minded the "Latin American specialists" who told them that Nicaraguan voters
readily confided in inquiring strangers. And the specialists had fed on a steady
diet of newspaper clippings. If "everybody" was responsible, then no one was.

But, in fact, not "everybody" expected a Sandinista victory. For one, former Costa Rican President Oscar Arias, who had won the Nobel Peace Prize for his Central American peace plan, frequently reiterated his conviction that the "Sandinistas could not win a fair election."[17] Though, theretofore, Arias's opinions had enjoyed an almost oracular status with the American press, his unconventional prediction received no coverage at all.[18] Likewise liberal Congressmen Steven Solarz, a staunch opponent of Republican policy in Central America, returned from Managua a few days before the elections prognosticating a comfortable Chamorro victory. In addition, polls by Latin American organizations consistently had the opposition out in front, often by wide margins. While rarely mentioned by American journalists, and then only disparagingly, those surveys helped spur a number of Latin American journalists and at least one leading European newspaper to suspect an upset.[19]

There were substantial *prima facie* grounds to support that suspicion—information which ordinarily would make an incumbent candidate a long shot. President Ortega had presided over a world-record inflation, topping 35,000 percent annually, a fall in real wages of over 90 percent, a 30 percent decline in Gross National Product, an exodus of 15 percent of the country's population, the internal displacement of hundreds of thousands, and a civil war costing the lives of more than 25,000 of his countrymen.[20] What leveled this statistical mountain? How did the views of President Arias, *Le Monde,* and the Latin American pollsters become the aberrant ones?

After the election, and in sharp contrast to its previous perspective, *Time* wrote that the Sandinista loss "should not be so surprising."

> They had thoroughly mismanaged an economy that was one of Central America's more prosperous. . . . They wasted scarce resources backing other revolutionary movements in the region. They drove out Nicaragua's middle class with their quirky brand of Marxist economic dogma. . . . [T]hey severely repressed civil liberties.[21]

The more interesting question is not why others got it right, but how the Americans got it so wrong.

Notes

1. Dan Rather, *CBS Evening News,* February 26, 1990. In the day's final edition the *Miami Herald* sounded its retreat from embarrassing previous headlines. Based on informal exit polling before the returns came in, the vote now "seemed much tighter than anticipated by polls predicting a landslide Sandinista victory" (Christopher Marquis and Andres Oppenheimer, "Nicaragua's Elections Surprisingly Close," *MH* [final edition], February 26, 1990).

2. Peter Jennings, *ABC World News*, February 26, 1990.

3. Ed Rabel, *NBC Nightly News*, January 27, 1990.

4. Richard Harwood, "The Teflon Estate," *WP*, March 4, 1990, C6.

5. Our survey covered the six months leading up to the elections (August 26, 1989 to February 25, 1990). The Center's survey encompassed the period February 1 to March 31, 1990. For a more detailed discussion of the surveys, *see* chapter 14.

6. Rabel, *NBC Nightly News*, January 27, 1990.

7. See also for example Rabel on *NBC Nightly News*, February 21 ("[Daniel Ortega] is the man pollsters say who will be elected overwhelmingly this weekend"); Jim Miklaszewski reporting on *NBC Today*, February 23 (the Bush administration is preparing now "for what it once thought unthinkable—a victory by Daniel Ortega in a fair and free election"); Bryant Gumble on *NBC Today*, February 22 ("Ortega is holding a comfortable lead"); Tom Brokaw on *NBC Nightly News*, February 23 ("Now it appears that Ortega could win the Nicaraguan presidency in a fair and square election"). *NBC Nightly News* reports on February 23 and February 25 centered on how the Bush administration was "preparing public opinion" (John Cochran) for a Sandinista victory, and on "how will a freely elected Sandinista government be treated by the United States" (Rabel). Unfortunately transcripts for *CNN Headline News* are not available, nor were tapes of CNN news broadcasts available from the Vanderbilt Media Library. Our (parenthetical) assertion of CNN's mistakes is based on viewing live CNN coverage.

8. "Ortega Runs Skilled Campaign; Nicaragua's President is a crowd-pleaser," *USAT*, February 1, 1990

9. "Sandinista Hits Election Stride as Foe Falters," *MH*, January 28, 1990, A1, A17.

10. John M. Goshko and Al Kamen, "U.S. Accused of Overstating Managua Election Offenses," *WP*, January 25, 1990, A1.

11. Robert Pear, "End to Official U.S. Observer Role in Managua Vote Raises Debate," *NYT*, February 9, 1990, A6. See also Goshko and Kamen, "U.S. Accused," A1, A34.

12. *NBC Nightly News*, February 23, 1990. For another story explaining administration actions on the basis of an assumed Sandinista victory, see Doyle McManus, "U.S. Gets Ready for Likely Sandinista Election Victory," *LAT*, February 24, 1990, A1.

13. Rabel, *NBC Nightly News*, February 21, 1990.

14. *NBC Nightly News*, February 25, 1990. In an interview with this author subsequent to the broadcast that same evening, Bernard Aronson, the Assistant Secretary of State for Latin America, denied that there had been any conversations at all with the Nicaraguan government since the previous November.

15. Harwood, "Teflon Estate," C6.

16. CNN, February 26, 1990.

17. Oscar Arias, press conference, San José, Costa Rica, January 22, 1990. Arias also told a delegation of East European democrats and a Polish television interviewer that "The people of Costa Rica would not go to an election under these electoral circumstances."

18. According to a computer search of all news sources available through the Lexis "Omni" service, 342 news items mentioned President Oscar Arias between October 1, 1989 and February 25, 1990. None of them cited his prediction of a Sandinista defeat. A *Washington Post* article in which Arias was interviewed celebrated his role in helping to bring about the Nicaraguan elections but did not mention his prediction. The article did state that "those elections . . . seem likely to produce a Sandinista victory, according to

most diplomats and independent election observers in Nicaragua." (Lee Hockstader, "Oscar Arias's Legacy: Negotiation," *WP*, February 9, 1990, A20.) However, after the Sandinistas' electoral defeat, the same correspondent recalled that Arias "once assured President Reagan that . . . free elections . . . would spell the end of the Sandinistas' hold on power" (Hockstader, "Ortega Concedes Defeat in Nicaraguan Vote, Pledges to Abide by the 'Popular Mandate'; Chamorro Issues Call for Reconciliation," *WP*, February 27, 1990, A1).

19. For example, see Bertrand de la Grange, "L'hostilite au regime s'accentue au Nicaragua," *Le Monde*, February 20, 1990, 1.

20. These statistics from a 1989 Nicaraguan government report can be found in Mark Uhlig, "A Nicaraguan Study Reports Economy in Drastic Decline," *NYT*, June 26, 1989, A1. The death toll is from Clifford Krauss, *Inside Central America* (New York: Summit, 1991), 165. See also Uhlig, "A Sandinista Promise Gone Sour Alienates Nicaragua's Working Class," *NYT*, November 7, 1989, A10; Uhlig, "Nicaraguans Hope for Decisive Election," *NYT*, February 25, 1990, A14; and William Branigin, "Election Shattered Many Sandinista Myths," *WP*, March 2, 1990, A26.

21. Johanna McGreary, *Time* (March 12, 1990): 13—14.

Chapter 2
Nicaragua: A Test of the News

When Walter Lippmann began formulating his views on the press, it was the Russian Revolution which "aroused the kind of passion which tests most seriously the objectivity of reporting." The United States intervened overtly in support of anticommunist counterrevolutionary armies, providing not only financial and military aid but also, together with other Western powers, landing troops on Russian soil. In examining the reporting of the Russian Revolution, Lippmann and his colleague Charles Merz needed a standard to assess the reliability of the news, "definite and decisive happenings about which there is no dispute."[1] They chose to measure the news by its accuracy in anticipating the outcome of the major battles of the Russian Civil War.

Though it aroused similar passions, the war in Nicaragua produced no such standard. As with most guerrilla wars the hostilities went mostly unobserved. The results of the fighting remained shrouded in controversy until the war was terminated by diplomacy and elections. However, the internationally monitored election of 1990 did constitute a definite and decisive happening and furnished a solid standard by which to measure the news reporting.[2]

His study of the Russian Civil War provided the first systematic account of what Lippmann would label "the manufacture of consent" and "government by newspapers."[3] Lippmann and Merz found that forty-nine of the eighty-two sources used to support Western optimism "emanated directly from official sources."[4] The reporters "accepted and believed what they were told by the State Department." They acted as "passionate partisans in a great war" in which "the chief censor and the chief propagandist were hope and fear in the minds of the reporters and editors."[5]

"From the point of view of professional journalism," Lippmann and Merz found the Russian reporting "nothing short of a disaster." The coverage was "dominated by the hopes of the men who compose the news organization." The reporting was "a case of seeing not what was, but what men wished to see."[6] The authors were referring to the American journalists' wish "to win the war . . . to ward off Bolshevism."[7] It was a measure of the distance traveled in American culture since the Russian Revolution—and even since the Cuban Revolution— that in the Nicaraguan instance most journalists deplored the side their government supported and distrusted the State Department.

Was the news coverage of the Nicaraguan revolution nonetheless a case of "the manufacture of consent" by the U.S. government? Did the coverage somehow result from government influence? There is a strong *prima facie* case against such a hypothesis since the coverage contradicted and impugned U.S. policy at every turn. Nonetheless, an important strand of media study would lead us to that conclusion.

In his influential study of the *New York Times* and the *Washington Post* between 1949 and 1970, Leon Sigal found that over half of the sources for political reporting resulted from routinized contact with Washington officials.[8] These results were very much in line with what Lippmann and Merz found a half century earlier. In the year of the breaking Watergate story, Sigal reached the conclusion that "the routines and conventions of their work incline [newsmen] to accept the worlds of officials without probing beneath them on their own."[9] As a result of these habits the news was "less a sampling of what is happening in the world than a selection of what officials think—or want the press to report—is happening."[10]

The only government officials who were pleased with U.S. press coverage worked not for Washington but for Managua.[11] As we shall show, the view that the government manufactured the Nicaraguan news is inconsistent both with the reporting and the increasing independence and vigor of the media in the post-Vietnam era.

Next to the government, big business was the main culprit of the post-Vietnam media criticism. Michael Parenti sustained that there was no ambiguity about who dominated the ideology and politics of the news:

> As with any profit-making corporation, the chain of command in the media runs from the top down, with final authority in the hands of the owners.[12]

A 1978 textbook describes the contemporary situation more accurately as one of "tension between the editorial and business offices."[13] The newspaper business had been characterized by two different sorts of "profit-making corporations": family dynasties often dominated by autocratic individuals—Bennetts, Hearsts, Pulitzers, Scrippses, Ochses, and Sulzbergers—and anonymous corporations with mulitiple economic interests. But the latter came to predominate even before our period. Parenti's view of employer-staff relations ignores the trend of "newsroom autonomy" facilitated by the decline of the hands-on "press lord" but also by the unionization and professionalization of journalism.[14] As Richard Davis has pointed out:

The professionalization of the journalistic corps . . . has diminished the influence of publishers, and large media organizations are rarely dominated by a single individual who seeks to utilize the organization for political objectives.[15]

A survey of eighty-five editorialists found that in the 1984 election campaign publishers "had the last word on presidential endorsements but not on political issues." Though a majority of their papers endorsed Ronald Reagan, the balance was far different on the eight controversial issues that separated the presidential candidates and their platforms: an anti abortion amendment, a school prayer amendment, a tuition tax credit, the Equal Rights Amendment, a tax increase, a space defense system, restrictions of covert operations abroad, and aid to the *Contras*. On each issue the newspapers endorsed the liberal and Democratic position by a wide margin. One editorial page editor commented on the split between candidate and issue endorsements:

So many editorial pages carry a moderate-to-liberal tone for 47 months, and on the 48th month of reckoning turn conservative. Some call the presidential endorsements the publishers' four year itch, and others, the editorial writers' agony.[16]

Another study found

newspapers competing for the same geographic and demographic market will produce highly similar products due to the similarity of their professional values, beliefs and practices. The increasing professionalization of journalism . . . has resulted in a convergence of views among journalists about what is the news of the day.[17]

Though news organizations competed in style, especially televised production values, and most aggressively for "scoops," they "produced highly similar products"—thus, the overall form and general content of the news was remarkably homogeneous.

Commercial considerations—sales or ratings—always play a part, and in a given situation, on a given subject, may establish the character of the coverage. In another situation the availability of resources or information may be telling. Alternatively the professional ethos of the journalist may be the dominant influence. But in the case of a highly politicized subject in the last, mightily polarized, decade of the Cold War, it makes sense to pay close analytical attention to ideology.

Neither the government nor the newspaper owners dominated the news from Nicaragua. The journalists did, or, more precisely, the mind-set they shared did. Moreover, the Nicaraguan news frame changed radically over time, from a slant friendly to or tolerant of the Somoza government, to one that radically opposed it, and finally to a news frame that legitimized the revolutionary government and delegitimized the policies of the U.S. government.

At best the criticisms of the post-Vietnam school of media criticism applied to the news of an age that had passed or was passing, an age that had been transformed in part by the investigative activity and the public and corporate power of the media in postindustrial America.

A "Combination of Limitations"?

The U.S. media reported the 1968 "Tet offensive" as a breakthrough for the Vietcong and a disaster for U.S. backed South Vietnamese Army. The repercussions in the United States of this reporting were profound. The "Tet disaster" led many opinion leaders to speak out against the war, contributing to President Lyndon Johnson's decision not to run for re-election to the presidency. The image of an intrepid Vietcong routing "the leader of the Free World" made a signal contribution to the protests and demonstrations which would typify the late 1960s.

Later even reporters critical of the war came to acknowledge that Tet had been, in reality, a "grievous military setback" and a political blow to the Vietcong, and that Hanoi's "miscalculation" temporarily strengthened support for the government.[18] Nonetheless, Peter Braestrup's magisterial study of the U.S. reporting on the 1968 Tet offensive in Vietnam found "'ideological' explanations of media flaws gravely insufficient." In his view the distortions of Tet derived from "a *rare* combination of habits, incentives, economic constraints, and managerial and manpower limitations peculiar to each of the major U.S. news organizations"[19] (emphasis added). Staffs were too small, communications equipment deficient and sparse, and reporters had too little knowledge of the local language and topography. Competitive time pressures led to haste; travel was difficult; the war "invisible"; politics inevitably local.[20]

Be that as it may, most of those constraints did not affect the coverage of the Nicaraguan elections, yet the distortions were remarkably similar. The war was also "invisible." It was hard to reach the rural back country where much of the fighting occurred. From time to time the Sandinista government placed certain combat zones off-limits, and the CIA and Honduran government severely restricted news expeditions with the anti-Sandinista fighters. However, there was no lack of physical access to the Nicaraguan electorate or to Nicaraguan political life. In any case, this story was less about war than about the Nicaraguans' "hearts and minds."

Nor were geography and language major impediments. Nicaragua is about the size of Iowa. Most of its then 3 million people resided on or near the western or Pacific littoral, so that outlying urban centers could be reached in a two- to three-hour drive from the capital along paved highways. Most beat journalists spoke a serviceable Spanish, and the major news organizations retained resident staffs which included Nicaraguans.

The country reminded Pulitzer Prize winner Shirley Christian of "an extended small town where everybody seems to know everybody else or to be related." As early as 1979 several journalists

> had worked in Nicaragua off and on for years and had acquaintances there on all sides of the issue. The Hispanic-Indian, Roman Catholic culture of the country was not totally foreign to them.[21]

That did not mean that American correspondents caught all the nuances of Nicaraguan culture. The sluggishness in perceiving the growing importance of the Roman Catholic Church during the revolutionary period proved a major failure. But this and similar lapses stemmed from incomprehension of the nature of the Nicaraguan political regime more than unfamiliarity with the culture.

Compared to Vietnam, communications were superb. Reporters based in Managua generally had direct telephone access to their home offices and usually could file for the next day's papers. Copy was beamed by computer over phone lines from Managua to the central office which could remit for rewriting or supplementation. For television, portable video cameras and satellite hook-ups were available.[22] The American public was treated to a greater quantity and frequency of images and accounts, which were more vivid, immediate and, in many ways, more extensive than those of any previous revolutionary process.

Staffs were not sparse. Managua was host to thousands of journalists in the nearly eleven years of Sandinista rule. By the early 1980s most major news organizations had full time staffers and local aides in Nicaragua. The media took advantage of Sandinista hospitality to provide a decade of sustained coverage.

The combination of limitations held responsible for the defects of the Tet coverage certainly did not mark the Nicaraguan coverage. There the hypothesis of an "ideological explanation" is harder to dismiss.

Sources and Materials

Discussion and debate over the changes that originated in the 1960s and their impact on the media have been plentiful. But they have generally been untested, conducted without the empirical evidence that can provide a sound basis for drawing conclusions.

Beside "the test of news" that Lippmann and Merz proposed—definite, decisive, and indisputable events by which to "measure the objectivity of the news,"—the Nicaraguan coverage furnishes two further tests of what we shall call the post-Vietnam paradigm.

It provided a case in which, to use Lippmann's words, the "passions were aroused," and "the stereotypes" consistently invoked. In the 1980s Nicaragua was "the single most divisive issue in American foreign affairs since the Vietnam War," as a *New York Times* Central American correspondent observed in

Foreign Affairs.[23] Indeed, Nicaragua was more than a foreign policy issue, it became a bitter domestic controversy at a time when Americans were sharply divided over the role of the United States in the post-Vietnam world as well as on numerous domestic political and social issues. A tissue of feeling, if not of logic, connected these domestic and foreign positions. "Tell me your views on Nicaragua," declared Tom Farer, a human rights lawyer, active in the Central American policy debate, "and I'll tell you your views on affirmative action, the tax revolt, nuclear arms negotiations, abortion rights, gun control, the death penalty, and the Panama Canal Treaty."[24] But the *Foreign Affairs* piece stretched the Vietnam analogy in stating that Nicaragua yielded "the same kind of domestic dissatisfaction." In fact, the general public expressed little interest in the controversy over Central American policy that raged in Washington, in the universities and church hierarchies, and some congregations, in book store cafés and professional association meetings, in the prestige press, and on the nightly news and Sunday morning talk shows.[25] That policy, as the pollster Daniel Yankelovich observed, was an "elite not a mass issue."[26]

The so-called "Nicaragua obsession" cannot be entirely accounted for by geography or even geopolitics.[27] It formed a passionate subchapter of American cultural history. For one section of the American intelligentsia, U.S. policy was a reversion to the bullying "ethnocentrism" of Vietnam and the glory days of the Spanish Civil War; for another, the minority, it recalled postwar Communist takeovers after World War II. For the majority of what we may call the American cultural elite, Nicaragua constituted the primary example of the post-Vietnam paradigm: Once again a corrupt puppet-dictatorship, hated by the people, installed and propped up by the United States; another National Liberation Front falsely portrayed by the U.S. government as Communist; another newly independent country, led by such a "broad national front," besieged by the United States and its surrogates.

Secondly, Nicaragua exhibited U.S. press coverage over a prolonged period and from a broad range of outlets. The scope was sufficient to develop a longitudinal and latitudinal record against which to test the post-Vietnam paradigm.

Sensitized by thousands of U.S. sympathizers to the internal American divisions we have mentioned, the Sandinistas encouraged, rather than discouraged, media coverage, though they did so selectively when they could. Before the revolution, the Sandinistas, imitating Fidel Castro, sought to use the international press to their advantage. After the revolution, rather than block Western media access, as had been done by previous revolutionary regimes, the Sandinista government welcomed many Western journalists and sought to influence them.

What Paul Hollander has called "the techniques of hospitality" reached new levels of sophistication in Managua. The country hosted tens of thousands of visitors, ranging from church groups to East German security advisers and from revolutionary tourists to politicians from virtually every country on earth, but especially from the United States.[28] These visitors included every variety of journalist—both the disinterested and the "committed" professionals representing large media organizations and the romantic enthusiasts who often represented only their alumni bulletin but helped shape the environment at press conferences and other "media events."

Both print and television coverage of Nicaragua intensified dramatically as the revolutionary crisis spread in 1978. Stories devoted to Nicaragua on *ABC Evening News* rose from negligible in the mid-1970s to 2.6 percent of total coverage in 1978 when Nicaragua vaulted into the top twenty countries covered by ABC.[29] The Nicaraguan revolution and counterrevolution became the first really "big" foreign news story after Vietnam—in terms of numbers of stories and length of coverage. During the 1980s, according to our computer survey, Nicaragua placed among the top ten countries mentioned in news stories: eighth, ahead of Japan, Germany, Canada, China, Poland, South Africa, Mexico, Iraq, and Vietnam, and just behind Great Britain. Between January 1, 1981 and December 31, 1990, 9,492 stories mentioned Nicaragua in sixteen major news outlets.[30] The coverage was also unprecedented in a qualitative sense. Networks frequently led their nightly news programs with Nicaraguan stories, and Nicaragua often made front-page headlines.

Typical studies of U.S. foreign reporting cover a single episode, utilize one or two sources exclusively, and lack independent access to the events covered and the reporters covering them. An independent study is especially important since in the case of the Nicaraguan revolution no one who has followed it is without strong opinions, including the present author.

Focusing on a discrete episode, the election campaign, made possible an exhaustive view of the totality of the U.S. coverage—virtually all major national news outlets—print and television, daily and weekly and monthly. The election study is based on a systematic reading and viewing of the "prestige media" from the opening of the campaign in September 1989 through its aftermath in March 1990.[31] As a hedge against subjectivity, a computer search was employed to chart news articles using polls to predict an outcome in the election.

How representative was the coverage of the elections in the context of U.S. media coverage of the Nicaraguan revolution? If representative, when did it become so? To answer those questions it was necessary to review the entire U.S. press coverage of Nicaragua for the full revolutionary period, from 1977 to 1990. For the decades between the Cuban and Nicaraguan revolutions such comprehensiveness was not feasible.[32] The views of journalists covering Nicaragua were investigated in extensive interviews and via a rudimentary questionnaire.[33] A quantitative content analysis was also employed (see appendix C).

Before the 1990 election campaign, there were no "defining events" but rather passionate controversy over nearly every event. But the 1990 election results cast doubt on the long-held assumption of Sandinista popularity.

My own conclusions do not rest on the paradigm I brought to this subject. I came to the Nicaraguan Revolution with many of the assumptions which guided the reporters and professors. Like some of those reporters, what I learned shook those assumptions. I have written about this elsewhere.[34] Thus, where I cite the conventional stereotypes I have included my own among the references.

As suggested, this study differs from other studies of media coverage because it rests on independent field studies and a review of primary and secondary source material. Several former and current Nicaragua government officials, former members of the Sandinista National Liberation Front (FSLN), former members of the Nicaraguan *Contras*, and members of the political opposition have allowed the author access to personal archives containing internal documents, newsletters, letters, diaries, and news clippings. I conducted interviews with former and current Nicaraguan government officials, members of the Sandinista and various anti-Sandinista organizations, members of business organizations, political parties, church officials, journalists, peasants, workers; American officials past and present, journalists, media analysts, and media executives.

Deficiencies, Constraints, and Limitations

This work does not address U.S. policy toward Nicaragua or the significant effect of the media on U.S. policy. The second major area omitted in this volume is that of Sandinista foreign and military policy toward its neighbors and the Soviet bloc. The latter comprised a major portion of the media coverage. A longer book would have dealt extensively with this subject, especially with the matter of treatment of the U.S. "White Paper" on arms shipments to the Salvadoran guerrillas. In the light of the discovery, after the Sandinista election defeat, of more than two dozen arms caches in Nicaragua, many of which were used to transfer arms and ammunition to El Salvador, the treatment of the "discredited" White Paper deserves to be reviewed.[35]

Joshua Muravchik's *News Coverage of the Sandinista Revolution*, which treats the period from mid-1978 to mid-1980, should be consulted by those wishing to deepen their understanding of that coverage.[36] My own investigation, including extended interviews with members of the Sandinista government and of the *Contra* movement, necessarily form the background rather than the foreground of this study.

I did not see the need for an independent discussion of the contribution of editors and other "gatekeepers" to the final news product. Only two of the journalists interviewed reported that significant "gates" were erected by editors or producers. The two instances involved a network television correspondent whose investigations led him into conflict with a bureau chief sympathetic to the Sandinista regime, and a reporter who clashed occasionally with an editor over his findings that the *Contras* had popular support. Those exceptions tended to confirm our impression that, in general, editors and correspondents shared the same key assumptions. In this respect the Nicaraguan case differed from both the China reporting in the 1930s and 1940s, when reporters like Theodore White and John Hersey felt stymied by editors like Whittaker Chambers, and from the

Vietnam reporting of the early 1960s, when David Halberstam, Neil Sheehan, and Charles Mohr engaged in epic battles with their editors.[37]

Though hardly comprehensive, this study, to the best of my knowledge, is a departure. It analyzes a comprehensive, sustained, and representative body of media reporting. It attempts to document in a single consistent corpus how the dominant culture changed from 1958 to 1990. It ascertains when those changes occurred, precisely what those changes in outlook and approach were, and how they influenced the major media. In the conclusion, further studies that could complete the picture of the ideological evolution of the major media in our day are proposed.

Finally, the study of Nicaragua reporting puts to the test some of the principal theses presented by media scholars about the sources, focus, and standards of contemporaneous journalism. The reader will be able to judge how well both correspondents and critics fared in the test of the Nicaragua news.

Notes

1. Walter Lippmann and Charles Merz, "A Test of the News," *TNR*, August 4, 1920, 2.

2. Indeed, in the light of appraisals of the Russian Revolution not available to Lippmann, it could be argued that the 1990 Nicaraguan election formed the basis for a more solid standard. See for example Orlando Figes, *A People's Tragedy: A History of the Russian Revolution* (New York: Viking, 1997).

3. Walter Lippmann, *Liberty and News* (New York: Harcourt Brace and Howe, 1920; revised edition New Brunswick, New Jersey: Transaction, 1995), 55, 57. See also Walter Lippmann, *Public Opinion* (New York: Macmillan, 1922; revised edition New York: Free Press Paperback, 1965), 248.

4. Lippmann, *Liberty and News*, 6.

5. Lippmann and Merz, "A Test of the News": 3.

6. Lippmann and Merz, "A Test of the News": 3.

7. Lippmann and Merz, "A Test of the News": 3.

8. Leon V. Sigal, *Reporters and Officials: The Organization and Politics of Newsmaking* (Lexington, Massachusetts: D. C. Heath, 1973), 128-29.

9. Sigal, *Reporters and Officials*, 195. For a similar view, see W. Phillips Davison, *Mass Communications and Conflict Resolution* (New York: Praeger, 1974).

10. Sigal, *Reporters and Officials*, 188.

11. U.S. officials complained bitterly and regularly about press coverage in interviews with the author. Interviews included officials who served as Assistant Secretary of State for Inter-American Affairs in the Reagan and Bush Administrations (Thomas B. Enders, Eliott Abrams, and Bernard Aronson), Deputy Assistant Secretaries (William Walker and Crescencio Arcos), as well as the press officials for those offices (Otto Reich and Robert Kagan). The author also discussed press coverage with officials of the U.S. Embassy in Nicaragua. Sandinista officials often expressed their agreement with the tendency of the U.S. press and U.S. dispatches, which were regularly reprinted in the government and Sandinista press. Interviews and conversations were conducted in Washington, D. C. and Managua.

12. Michael Parenti, *Inventing Reality: The Politics of the News Media*, 2d edition (New York: St. Martin's, 1993), 50. For a similar perspective, see Ben Bagdikian, *The Media Monopoly* (Boston: Beacon, 1983), 20-21; Mark Hertsgaard, *On Bended Knee: The Press and the Reagan Presidency* (New York: Farrar, 1988), chapter V; Stanley Cohen and Jock Young, eds., *The Manufacture of News: A Reader* (London: Constable, 1973); Martin A. Lee and Norman Solomon, *Reliable Sources: A Guide to Detecting Bias in News Media* (New York: Lyle Stuart, 1990), chapter IV; Tom Koch, *The News as Myth* (Westport, Connecticut: Greenwood, 1990), 23.

13. Jon G. Udell, *The Economics of the American Newspaper* (New York: Hastings House, 1978), 64.

14. Though the 1990s saw the partial resurrection of the press lord in the persons of Ted Turner and Rupert Murdoch, such figures have been overshadowed by corporate mergers, the emergence of media conglomerates and the heightened competition of new media. In any event, our observations pertain to the period under discussion (1974-90).

15. Richard Davis, *The Press and American Politics* (New York: Longmans, 1992), 21.

16. F. Dennis Hale, "Editorial Diversity and Concentration," in *Press Concentration and Monopoly: New Perspectives on Newspaper Ownership and Operation*, ed. Robert G. Picard, James P. Winter, Maxwell E. McCombs, and Stephen Lacy (Norwood, New Jersey: Ablex, 1988), 169-70.

17. Maxwell W. McCombs, "Concentration, Monopoly and Content," in *Press Concentration and Monopoly: New Perspectives on Newspaper Ownership and Operation*, ed. Robert G. Picard, James P. Winter, Maxwell E. McCombs, and Stephen Lacy (Norwood, New Jersey: Ablex, 1988), 136.

18. Don Oberdorfer, *Tet* (New York: Doubleday & Company, 1971), 329-30; Neil Sheehan, *A Bright Shining Lie: John Paul Vann and America in Vietnam* (New York: Random House, 1988), 718; Arnold R. Isaacs, *Without Honor: Defeat in Vietnam and Cambodia* (New York: Vintage, 1984), 116. Even a journalist who sympathized warmly with the Vietcong acknowledged most of these facts; see Francis FitzGerald, *Fire in the Lake* (Boston: Little, Brown, 1972), 398. See also Peter Braestrup, *Big Story: How the American Press and Television Reported and Interpreted the Crisis of Tet 1968 in Vietnam and Washington* (Garden City, New York: Anchor Press, 1978; reprint New Haven: Yale University Press, 1983), ix-x.

19. Braestrup, *Big Story*, xi.

20. Braestrup, *Big Story*, especially chapters i and xiii. This last factor appears to suggest the presence of an ideological dimension: an "ethnocentrism" which allowed reporters to overlook the enemies' mistakes. But, according to Braestrup, "the ethnocentric emphasis placed by U.S. newsmen on American GIs reflected, above all, the wants of their editors at home" (Braestrup, *Big Story*, 169, 174, 337).

21. Shirley Christian, "Covering the Sandinistas: The Foregone Conclusions of the Fourth Estate," *Washington Journalism Review* (March 1982): 33-38.

22. Author's interviews with Sam Dillon of the *Miami Herald*, Christopher Dickey of the *Washington Post*, Stephen Kinzer and James LeMoyne of the *New York Times*, and Peter Collins of ABC-TV. See also AP Central American correspondent Bryna Brennan, "'The First Casualty'—Covering Central America," Occasional Paper No. 3 of the Media Studies Project, Woodrow Wilson International Center for Scholars, Washington, D.C., 20.

23. Mark A. Uhlig, "Latin America," *Foreign Affairs* 70 (no. 1, 1991): 103-4. Clifford Krauss of the *Wall Street Journal* agreed that "reporters covering Central America . . . serve[d] as the news filter for the most controversial foreign policy issue since Viet-

nam." ("Vietnam Generation Goes Centrist," *Media Studies Journal*, Gannett Media Studies Center, Columbia University [Fall 1989]: 35.) "For Congress, Central America, with Nicaragua leading the way, was the single most divisive foreign policy issue during the 1980s. Nearly forty floor votes in the House, and more than a dozen in the Senate were taken on aid to the anti-Sandinista contra rebels." ("Reagan-Era Zeal for Central America Fades," *WP*, October 16, 1990, A18.)

24. Conversation with author, February 1984.

25. Congressional votes on aid to the *Contras* became a focal point for the interested parties. Before one such vote a front-page *Washington Post* report described the massive lobbying campaigns by religious, human rights, and other policy advocacy groups, on both sides of the issue, utilizing "computers and postcards, sit-ins and videotapes, . . . and photos of bloody corpses, Nobel laureates, and Hollywood actors," as well as "bands, clowns, musicians, and balloons." Formats included television documentaries and spots, books, reports, articles, editorials, policy papers, newsletters, organized letter-writing campaigns, mass mailings, "thousands of speeches and probably millions of phone calls," as well as group and individual visits with Congressmen. The report quoted the comment of the chairman of the House Foreign Affairs Subcommittee on Western Hemisphere affairs: "If somebody wrote a novel about it, it would not be credible" ("Contra Aid Fight Nears: Hill Besieged from All Sides," *WP*, April 15, 1985, A1).

26. Daniel Yankelovich, presentation at the Western Hemisphere Forum, Carnegie Endowment for International Peace, Washington, D.C., January 16, 1986.

On July 1, 1983, the *New York Times* reported (on the front-page) that, "Despite months of controversy over U.S. policies on Central America, most of the American public does not know which side the Reagan Administration supports in either El Salvador or Nicaragua, according to the latest *New York Times*/CBS News poll."

The *Times* reported that only 13 percent of Americans knew that the United States "sides with the insurgents in Nicaragua." Only 8 percent were aware of United States positions in both El Salvador and Nicaragua. "Generally," the more informed strata was "more hostile" to the U.S.' involvement than the rest of those surveyed. The article quoted public opinion experts to the effect that these findings "were in marked contrast to the public's attitudes on foreign affairs before the Vietnam War" (Adam Clymer, "Poll Finds Americans Don't Know U.S. Positions on Central America," *NYT*, July 1, 1983, A1).

Those in the *Times*/CBS poll who could correctly identify alignments in Nicaragua rose gradually to 19 percent in April 1984, 26 percent in June 1985, and 38 percent in April 1986 (Clymer, "Most Americans in Survey Oppose Aid for Overthrow of Sandinistas," *NYT*, June 5, 1985, A8; *NYT*/CBS News survey April 6-10, 1986).

To the ABC News/*Washington Post* survey question: "Have you read or heard anything about the fighting between the Sandinista government in Nicaragua and rebels seeking to overthrow that government," positive responses rose from 59 percent in August 1983 to 78 percent in March 1986.

Majorities in the *NYT*/CBS poll continued to oppose aid to the Nicaraguan rebels but "support for administration policy [in Nicaragua]" tended to increase "especially among the growing numbers who know which side the United States backs" (Phil Gailey, "Polls Show Most Americans See Reagan Tax Plan as Fair," *NYT*, June 5, 1985, A1).

The high point of public awareness of the Nicaragua issue, and of support for the insurgents, came in the summer of 1987 after the testimony of Lt. Colonel Oliver North to the congressional committee investigating the Iran-*Contra* affair. At that time surveys found the public more or less evenly divided on aiding the Nicaraguan rebels (NBC/*WSJ* survey, July 12, 1987; ABC/*WP* survey, July 15, 1987; CBS/*NYT* survey, July 16, 1987;

LAT survey, July 1987). Subsequently public support for assistance to the rebels reverted to earlier levels. As always, of course, much depended on how the questions were framed. An article in *The Nation*, a publication hardly sympathetic to the rebels, acknowledged that "there is some validity to [the] argument" that the framing of *Contra* aid questions in most polls tended to underestimate support for the policy.

A CBS/*NYT* survey in April 1986 found only 25 percent supported "military and other aid to the contras trying to overthrow the government in Nicaragua." But that same month a *Time*/Yankelovich poll found 58 percent in agreement with the proposition that "the United States should aid the rebels in Nicaragua in order to prevent Communist influence from spreading to other countries in Central America." (William Bollinger and Daniel M. Lund, "Mixing Polls and Propaganda," *The Nation* [April 1986]: 636).

The general public continued to display ambivalence on the issue even as it became somewhat better informed. At the end of a decade of controversy, a review of the polling on the issue found that "most people in the United States are aware but not very knowledgeable or intensely concerned about these situations in Central America" (Richard Sobel, "Public Opinion about United States Intervention in El Salvador and Nicaragua," *Public Opinion Quarterly* [vol. 53]: 115). See also Robert S. Leiken, "Introduction" in *The Central American Crisis Reader*, ed. Robert S. Leiken and Barry Rubin (New York: Summit, 1987), 34-36; Everett Carll Ladd, "Where the Public Stands on Nicaragua," *Public Opinion* (September/October 1987); Howard L. Reiter, "U.S. Public Opinion of the Nicaraguan War and the Implications for Political Strategy," (paper delivered at the annual meeting of the American Political Science Association, September 5, 1987); and *Public Opinion in U.S. Foreign Policy: The Controversy over Contra Aid*, ed. Richard Sobel (Lanham, Maryland: Rowman & Littlefield, 1993).

27. "The Nicaraguan Obsession," Editorial, *NYT*, February 25, 1990, 18.

28. See Paul Hollander, *Anti-Americanism: Critiques at Home and Abroad, 1965-1990* (Oxford: Oxford University, 1992), 266-73; see also Hollander, *Political Pilgrims: Travels of Western Intellectuals to the Soviet Union, China and Cuba* (New York: Oxford, 1981), chapter 8. On the East German role, see John O. Koehler, *Stasi: The Untold Story of East Germany's Secret Police* (Boulder: Westview, 1999), and Leiken, "Fantasies and Facts: The Soviet Union and Nicaragua," *Current History* (October 1984).

29. James F. Larson, *Global Television and Foreign Policy* (New York: Foreign Policy Association, 1988): 182-83, and table F.1.

30. Based on a computer search covering major media available on NEXIS (see chapter 14 for a listing).

31. For the purposes of this study the "prestige" media in 1990 comprehended: the two major "agenda setting" newspapers: The *New York Times, Washington Post*; the three other "national" newspapers: The *Wall Street Journal, USA Today,* and the *Christian Science Monitor*; influential regional newspapers such as the *Los Angeles Times, Boston Globe,* and *Miami Herald*; the three major weekly news magazines: *Time, Newsweek,* and *U.S. News and World Report,* and weeklies and monthlies such as *The New Republic, The New Yorker, The Atlantic,* and the *New York Review* and, of course, the five national television networks: ABC, CBS, NBC, PBS, and CNN. This study was supplemented by a selective reading of several regional newspapers and of the other periodical journals of opinion.

32. For the period 1958-77 the study focused on the entire coverage of the *New York Times,* the *Washington Post,* and *Time* magazine, major portions of the coverage of the *Los Angeles Times, Wall Street Journal, Christian Science Monitor, Boston Globe, Miami Herald,* and *Newsweek,* as well as regional newspapers on an *ad hoc* basis. These sources were supplemented by a broad examination of the evening news transcripts of the

three major television networks between 1978 and 1990, along with a viewing of a selection of television news tapes provided by the Vanderbilt University Media Library. Tapes or transcripts of PBS and CNN news were obtained when available along with transcripts from "60 Minutes" and other television "news magazines" and special news programs on Nicaragua as well as entertainment programs which dealt with the subject. To collect transcripts and print articles, microfilm was selected and copied from the Microform Room of the Harvard University Library and the Library of Congress. In some cases transcripts could be obtained from the networks.

33. Unfortunately only eight of the twenty-five questionnaires were completed fully, although many of the respondents were kind enough to send extensive supplementary comments.

34. Leiken, "The Charmed Circle," and "Truth and Consequences" in *Second Thoughts: Former Radicals Look Back on the Sixties*, ed. Peter Collier and David Horowitz (New York: Madison, 1989), 25-34, 125-32; and Leiken, "Nicaragua's Untold Stories," *TNR*, October 8, 1984,.

35. See Clifford Krauss, "Sandinistas Admit Missiles Went to Salvador," *NYT*, December 31, 1990, A5; Tim Johnson, "Blast Shakes Nicaraguan Government," *NYT*, May 25, 1993, A1; "3 Years after Defeat of Sandinistas, Nicaragua Remains Terrorist Haven," *MH*, July 5, 1993, 1A; "Arms Cache Discovered in Nicaragua," *MH*, September 5, 1993, 18A; John M. Goshko, "Salvadorans Accused of Hiding Arms, Guerrilla Cache Said to be in Nicaragua," *WP*, June 17, 1993, A37; Douglas Farah, "Managua Blasts Rip Lid Off Secrets, Salvadoran Rebel Cache, Leftist Kidnap Data Exposed; Sandinistas Implicated," *WP*, July 14, 1993, A1. For links among the Sandinistas, Mideast terrorist groups and the 1993 bombing of the World Trade Center in New York, see Ralph Blumenthal, "Inquiry Traces Suspect to Occupied Territories," *NYT*, March 7, 1993.

36. Joshua Muravchik, *News Coverage of the Sandinista Revolution* (Washington, DC: AEI, 1988).

37. See Stephen R. MacKinnon and Oris Friesen, *China Reporting: An Oral History of American Journalism in the 1930s and 1940s* (Berkeley: University of California, 1987), 4, 7-22, 118-40; and William Prochnau, *Once Upon a Distant War: Young War Correspondents and their Early Vietnam Battles* (New York: Vintage, 1996), 178-79, 261-62, 316-17, 396-98, 425-26, etc.

Chapter 3
Cohorts: Vietnam and the New Foreign Correspondent

David Halberstam and Neil Sheehan were among "the small band of American newsmen" stationed in Vietnam in 1962.[1] "It was a small war then," Halberstam recalled.[2] "The foreign press corps," Sheehan remembered,

> had not yet burgeoned to the hundreds of both sexes and all nationalities— newspaper, television and radio correspondents, still photographers, television cameramen, sound technicians, and sundry war groupies posing as freelances— who were to descend on Vietnam to cover "the big war."[3]

Nor had the American media gained the prestige and the self-assurance which were to make it a powerful, autonomous social force at the time of the Nicaraguan conflict. When Sheehan and Halberstam first encountered the American adviser Lt. Colonel John Paul Vann in South Vietnam in 1962, the press was still a fairly compliant subsection of the Establishment. Though the half-dozen or so reporters in the field were beginning to file reports irritating to Washington, the press as a whole had not yet staked out an antagonistic position toward the war, still less toward the entire structure of U.S. foreign relations.[4]

This is not to say that at this early stage of the Vietnam War all was harmony between the administration—in this case the Kennedy Administration— and the press, or for that matter within the press itself and within the administration. If there was little public debate over Vietnam, there were plenty of "bitter behind the scenes conflicts."[5] But as Daniel Hallin observes:

21

As furious as these battles seemed to those involved, however, they all took place within the narrow confines of a tight consensus on the nature of world politics and the American role in it; none brought into question the premise that the preservation of an anti-Communist Vietnam was indeed a legitimate goal of American policy.[6]

Accordingly, in these years a journalist as notoriously critical as Halberstam could still "believe that Vietnam is a legitimate part" of the U.S. "global commitment" and "truly vital to U.S. interests."[7]

Sheehan stressed later that he and his colleagues had "shared the [American military] advisors' sense of commitment" to the Vietnam War:

> Our ideological prism and cultural biases were in no way different. We regarded the conflict as our war too. We believed in what our government said it was trying to accomplish in Vietnam, and we wanted our country to win this war just as passionately as Vann and his captains did.[8]

Contrast this stance to that of the first group of reporters to cover the Nicaraguan conflict for the American press. During the spring of 1979, during the final revolutionary offensive against Anastasio Somoza Debayle, a group of American press correspondents rather like Halberstam, Sheehan, Peter Arnett, and the other "Vietnam veterans" of 1962, pooled their efforts to track a fast-breaking story in a Third World country in which the United States was deeply involved. Alan Riding of the *New York Times*, Karen DeYoung of the *Washington Post*, Bernard Dietrich of *Time* and the *Washington Star*, later joined by Stephen Kinzer of the *Boston Globe*, like their predecessors in Vietnam, paved the way for those who followed.[9] Together with the Brazilian journalist Silio Boccanera, the Americans shared a house in Managua and a division of labor for covering the breaking news.[10] But, unlike their Vietnam predecessors, the group in Managua also shared a highly critical view of what the U.S. government "was trying to accomplish."

Riding and his companions considered the Carter Adminstration misguided in seeking to mediate on behalf of a coalition government that the Sandinistas would not dominate.[11] They believed that Washington failed to appreciate "the strength and popularity of the Sandinista guerrillas"[12] The views of the Carter Administration "bore frighteningly little resemblance to reality," partly because the U.S. government "operated . . . in a near-total vacuum of accurate information or worthwhile analysis about the country."[13] The reporters reckoned mediation misguided and futile, violence inevitable, Washington's views of Cuban influence "alarmist," the Sandinistas predominantly "patriots and democrats" and clear-headed pragmatists reconciled to the inevitability of U.S. regional dominance.[14] In other words, the government was misguided and the journalists knew better.

The contrast to Halberstam's colleagues was even sharper in the case of the "half-dozen American reporters" tracking the *Contras* in Honduras in March

1983. The Reagan Administration had abandoned all efforts at cooperation with the Sandinistas and approved funding of "covert actions" against Nicaragua in December 1981.[15] By 1983 reporters were engaged in a war of words—and of images and politically-charged stereotypes—with the president.[16] Among the Honduran group was Steven Kinzer, who had just left the *Boston Globe* for the *New York Times*, who later wrote as follows about his intentions:

> All of us had drifted to this part of the world with the same unstated ambition: to find a contra base inside Honduras and expose the truth that the contras were not indigenous rebels, but cross-border raiders under foreign protection.

Kinzer and a colleague did stumble on a *Contra* base, filed a hard-hitting story and "were jubilant, like high school ballplayers after winning a big game" at the prospect of "the people in Washington whose breakfasts would be ruined . . . the following morning. . . . When Congress reconvened Nicaragua was the topic of heated debate in both chambers."[17] Far from sharing with U.S. officials "a sense of commitment," these journalists were committed to exposing and even reversing government policies.

However one may appraise these two paradigms of journalism, it is hard to deny their considerable differences regarding the journalist's role, especially respecting the U.S. government, and in their "ideological prism and cultural biases."[18]

For Halberstam the Vietnam war had appeared "a test of two political systems." Halberstam and company "thought our system the better, our values exportable . . . and thought perhaps with luck and skill our side might win." But "events soon disabused" Halberstam leading him to determine that:

> The American optimism of the period was clearly mindless; the Viet Cong were infinitely stronger and more subtle than the [South Vietnam] government, their sense of the people far truer. . . . [T]he other side had captured the nationalism of the country. . . . I came to the conclusion that [the U.S. involvement in Vietnam] was doomed and . . . we were on the wrong side of history.[19]

In their emerging criticism of U.S. foreign policy, Halberstam and his colleagues were, as he wrote, "probably ahead of the society as a whole and our profession as a whole."[20] They can be regarded as harbingers of a cultural change which was to alter the climate of opinion surrounding American intellectuals, scholars, regional specialists, policymakers, and pundits as well as editors and reporters.[21]

Clifford Krauss, who had been the Central American correspondent for the United Press International, the *Atlanta Constitution* and the *Wall Street Journal*, remarked in 1989 that his generation of reporters "grew up with very different ideas about the use of American power abroad than Ernie Pyle's in World War II, or even David Halberstam's in Vietnam." Krauss and his contemporaries brought to this newest foreign adventure, one that clearly resonated with Vietnam parallels, new and critical assumptions that the vast majority of our older colleagues would have found unacceptable. We had grown up with the Kennedy and King assassinations, the Tonkin Gulf incident, the secret bombing of Cambodia and finally Watergate. Our first assumption was to doubt the word of U.S. officials and the justice of the American cause. Many members of this generation of reporters came to Central America to help stop the next Vietnam, and, if that were not possible, to see it and feel it.[22]

A New Foreign Correspondent

In 1974 Ben Bagdikian observed "a rapid change within news institutions in the last decade."

> The received conventions . . . are being rejected and reformed. Standards of "legitimacy" are being questioned. . . . A different kind of novice professional has entered the field.[23]

A sophisticated corps was forming in the "prestige press" which hailed from a higher social class, had received more formal education, and was better remunerated than its predecessors.[24] The profession was now esteemed socially, a source of pride to its members who expressed their opinions with increased self-assurance.

An American Society of Newspaper Editors (ASNE) study in 1987-88 showed a "dramatic increase" since 1971 in "the proportion of newsroom workers who are college graduates."[25] Of younger reporters under 30, 93 percent possessed college degrees and nearly 70 percent had majored in journalism. These percentages were higher at larger newspapers.[26] There was also a sharp increase in "the percentage of U.S. journalists with graduate degrees."[27]

Previously, "newspapering was one of those occupations that afforded working-class families . . . middle-class status or better," Bagdikian wrote:

> College educations were seldom required and were often at a disadvantage. . . . [This] produced . . . journalists whose only perceptions of the outside world after they left junior or high school were what they saw or heard in the newsrooms. . . . It also provided a simplistic view of society and . . . the strong strain of anti-intellectualism that characterized American newsrooms for generations.[28]

Bagdikian, a journalist turned professor of journalism, was doubtless correct about the training of journalists. However, our study will suggest that the university environment produced views which if less "anti-intellectual" were not always less "simplistic."

By 1979-80 the journalists at prestigious news organizations were drawn primarily from northern industrial states, were raised in upper-middle-class homes and drew upper-middle-class salaries.[29] Journalism had become a well-remunerated, genteel, and prestigious profession. In the case of U.S. foreign correspondents these trends were accentuated, Stephen Hess writes, because "news organizations that employ foreign correspondents are most likely to employ elites."[30] According to his 1992 survey, 98 percent of foreign correspondents had attended a university—70 percent went to "highly selective" colleges, nearly half had done graduate work, of whom 80 percent had received advanced degrees.[31] The correspondents typically earned annual salaries "between $50,000 and $90,000, with senior people earning still more," plus generous benefits.[32] But the "best indicator" of their "elite" status, according to Hess, was their parents' occupations which were predominantly managerial or professional.[33]

John C. Pollock's exhaustive, but little-noticed 1979-80 survey shows that Latin American correspondents had similar characteristics.[34] Pollock's entire sample had attended college, with only 2 percent failing to graduate.[35] About a quarter of the sample had master's degrees, half of those in journalism. Fifty-two percent had gone to "well-known universities"; 34 percent attended elite private universities.[36] Younger journalists had more years of schooling and more advanced degrees.[37] With few exceptions, virtually all of the correspondents who covered the Nicaraguan Revolution came from the younger group.

***

Several authoritative surveys of journalists conducted between 1971 and 1986 showed that along with their improved socioeconomic class situation and social status, not to mention the increased prestige of their profession, journalists developed a distinct set of cultural and political attitudes and opinions.[38] In 1985 the *Los Angeles Times* asked large and scientifically selected samples of journalists and the general public similar questions.[39] Eighty-four percent of the news staffers surveyed supported a nuclear freeze, 76 percent opposed aid to the anti-Sandinista rebels, and 82 percent supported legalizing abortion.[40] Fifty-five percent of the journalists surveyed called themselves liberal (17 percent conservative) while only 24 percent of the general public termed themselves liberal, 31 percent fewer than among journalists.[41] Moreover, newspaper journalists were also "markedly more liberal than others of similar educational and professional standing." Thirty-seven percent of other college-educated professionals said that they were liberal, 18 percent fewer than the journalists.[42] The *Times* survey also displayed a wide disparity between the journalists' views and those of the general public, with the former generally far more liberal on most questions. However, "[t]he pattern breaks down somewhat in the case of economic issues, with professionals on average slightly more conservative than the general public and journalists slightly, but not markedly more liberal.[43] This "exception," however, was quite consistent with the upward social and economic mobility of the journalistic profession.[44]

In the decade before the comprehensive *Times* poll, similar findings resulted from surveys conducted by the *Washington Post* and Harvard University, the Brookings Institution and the University of California State–Los Angeles, the Lichters and Stanley Rothman as well as the Indiana University School of Journalism.[45] The 1982–83 Indiana University survey found that journalists in more prominent news organizations were more likely "to identify themselves as left-of-center politically than those working for less prominent organizations . . . and considerably fewer journalists from the prominent organizations claim to lean to the right."[46]

Less relevant than where the journalists *placed themselves* on the political spectrum are the content of their views and their influence on the news product.[47] By 1982-83 views which in 1971 may have seemed leftist may well have appeared "middle-of-the-road" among the ranks of the journalists. That would only show that the ideas of the "adversary culture" had moved into the "mainstream." These surveys showed unmistakably that the dominant ideas of journalists in the prestige press reflect a distinct subculture or what the Lichters and Rothman call

> a largely homogeneous group that is cosmopolitan in background and liberal in outlook. And they are an elite in terms of economic status, public perception, and social influence.[48]

The subculture had become dominant in key sectors of the cultural establishment—the universities, the media, the publishing and entertainment industries, social, cultural, and human service professionals. As early as the late 1960s, observers such as Pulitzer Prize winning journalist Theodore H. White began to worry about the "breach in American culture" between the Manhattan-based national media and the heartland.[49] In 1981 the respected columnist Joseph Kraft lamented that his peers "no longer represent a wide diversity of views and ceased to be neutral in reporting events." In his view the new "Imperial Media" had been "taken in tow by the adversary culture."[50]

Pollock's study of correspondents covering Latin America for major U.S. news organizations uncovered similar cultural and political attitudes. However, Pollock's categories must be refined in order to yield useful data. They are muddied by the post-Vietnam paradigm. Pollock divides reporters into "examiners" and "chroniclers." The latter denotes "breadth, restraint, and 'technically efficient' journalism," while the "examiner perspective" signifies "investigative, analytical, and interpretative reporting."[51] At first glance this seems a helpful classification of the pre- and post-Vietnam journalistic paradigms we have been describing. But Pollock goes on to define the examiner orientation as more "professional" than the chronicler perspective. Those judged "highly 'professional' in reporting on social change abroad" are reporters who "cherish 'autonomy' from officials and who generally favor nonintervention and East West *détente*"—they are 'examiners." Conversely, the "chroniclers" who "cherish close contacts with officials, and customarily favor intervention generally and conflict with the Soviet Union specifically, will be judged in this study as less professional."[52] For our purposes, Pollock's "professionals" and "examiners" were those who in Nicaragua embraced the post-Vietnam paradigm.

By analyzing Pollock's sample we can correlate his findings with those of the surveys previously discussed.[53] Thus 72 percent of correspondents forty or younger tend to be "strong examiners." Examiners (or "new journalists") tend to earn advanced degrees and to have majored in humanities and journalism.[54] Examiners are generally "less experienced in journalism or reporting on Latin American"—most are unfamiliar with Castro's 1959 ascension to power—but "appear cosmopolitan and interested not simply in journalism as a profession."[55] By the same token, Pollock found that those reporters "more likely to favor *détente*" are younger, better educated and earn higher salaries than those who did not.[56] Pollock also found such "examiners" less likely to be "'organization' types." Conversely: "those who tend not to be examiners have spent many years as journalists, work in a team context, and lack master's degrees." Pollock supplies a "composite portrait" of his lackluster "unprofessional" "chronicler:" "the 'good soldier', the stable experienced reporter with many years of reporting on Latin America."[57]

Pollock also discovered that his "critical" or "examiner" journalist "tended to be found in substantial concentrations in . . . the *New York Times* and the *Washington Post*." With their "appeal to selected audiences," their influence in setting "foreign policy agendas," those prestige papers "nurture and encourage those types of newsmen most likely to challenge officials."[58]

Pollock's "professional"—an exemplary specimen of the "new correspondent"—who embraces the virtues of the adversary culture ("critical," "antiwar," "progressive," "pluralist," "antiauthoritarian," and "cosmopolitan") was not only more likely to be university-trained and successful—that is working for the prestige press. He was also less experienced, better paid, and younger.

Theodore Edward Kruglak's earlier study enables us to compare Pollock's Latin American reporter with U.S. correspondents working in Europe in the mid-1950s. In 1955, as today, Europe was a highly coveted assignment, unlike Latin America. The European correspondents' pay scale soared "well above the average of comparable newsmen in the United States."[59] So it is not surprising that nearly three-quarters of those correspondents sported B.A. degrees—73 percent—and that as many as 10 percent possessed master's degrees.[60] These figures easily exceeded those of reporters at home, yet were lower than those of Pollock's Latin American correspondents twenty-five years later.

By the same token, the political views of U.S.-European correspondents reflected those "of a cross section of American public opinion." Only 1.3 percent of the correspondents supported the third-party presidential candidacy of former Vice President Henry Wallace in 1948; less than the general public. In 1952 the Republican candidate General Dwight Eisenhower was more popular among the reporters in Europe than he was at home.[61] But in general, like their counterparts at home, the U.S. reporters "generally shunned politics."[62] Like their counter-parts at home, foreign correspondents did not represent a political sub-culture with highly demarcated views on a vast array of issues. If they had university degrees, the university had not stamped on them a political or ideological ethos different from that of the country's mainstream. They were college graduates, they lived in cosmopolitan Europe, they rubbed shoulders with the European journalist who "indulged in editorial opinion to make his point," but they re-tained the American fidelity to objectivity.[63]

The University and the New Journalist

The university played a central role in generating, training, and certifying the new correspondent. By the mid-seventies, with the advent of what Daniel Bell was to christen "postindustrial society" the university had become, according to Everett C. Ladd and Seymour Martin Lipset, the "legitimizing and certifying institution of contemporary secular societies."[64] They argued that prominent journalists sought "acceptance as intellectuals and . . . look to faculty as a pri-mary reference group."[65]

Ladd and Lipset found that the views of faculty members on the Vietnam War and on other social issues tended to parallel those of their students and to contrast sharply with the general public.[66] But Ladd and Lipset discovered a "divided academy": social sciences and humanities faculties most likely to be left or liberal, while business and engineering least likely to be so.[67] Steven Brint's 1994 study of American professionals found a similar "polarization of views *within* the professional stratum." Those employed in professions associ-ated with the "technical needs of American industry" such as applied science and engineering holding more conservative political views than their colleagues in the "social and cultural professions, the human service occupations and in the nonprofit sectors. Within professionals the more intellectual, social, and cultural professions were associated with greater liberalism."[68] These divisions corre-spond to Bell's notion of a basic cultural contradiction between the "cultural" and the "techno-economic" realms.[69] (See appendix B.)

Ladd and Lipset wrote that "academics can be seen as occupying a particu-larly ideological subculture in American life."[70] Ladd and Lipset's analysis of surveys revealed "an underlying ideological dimension . . . across a range of intramural as well as national issues." These issues included the causes of black urban riots, marijuana legalization, busing for racial integration, Vietnam policy, student radicalism, as well as political self-characterizations as left, right, and center.[71] The academy, unlike the general public, displayed an "underlying ideological perspective."[72] Across issues in faculty responses there was signifi-cant linkage or "constraint," to use sociologist Phillip Converse's term:

We depend implicitly upon such notions of constraint in judging, for example, if a person is opposed to the expansion of social security, he is probably a conservative and is probably opposed as well to any nationalization of private industries, federal aid to education, sharply progressive income taxation and so forth.[73]

We have already noted a similar level of "constraint" or linkage in the surveys of journalists taken in the 1980s. Among academics, as among journalists, radical and liberal views were more pronounced among those with the most eminent and politically influential positions.[74] These commonalties are one of the indicators that the emergence of adversarial attitudes among journalists cannot be comprehended as a generational shift or merely the entrance of new social strata into the profession. As John Pollock remarks, the "questioning perspective toward foreign affairs" drew power from a "cultural shift."[75] (See appendix B.)

The Ascendance of the Media

The new activism and self-confidence of the journalist in general, and the foreign correspondent in particular, derived in part from his social background and educational experience, but it was also a function of the profession he had chosen. With the advent of television and the decline of "intermediate institutions" (church, parties, unions, neighborhoods, extended families) the media occupies a far more prominent position in "the information society."[76] It has vanquished all rivals in the formation of public opinion, and its role in the shaping of policy has never been larger.

It was no accident that media organizations began insisting on a university training as a prerequisite for journalistic employment. "Postindustrial society is an information society," Bell observed. In part, this is due to "the sheer amount of information" that had to be absorbed. To be well-informed now meant following general developments in scores of countries and keeping up with unfolding events in several key areas at once.[77] Furthermore, in postindustrial society information becomes more technical—even in the realm of "international affairs," not to mention economic policy and the like. Given the need for a "selection from the vast flow of information," "there is a greater need for journalistic mediation, or journalistic translation."[78]

Samuel Huntington has pointed to the rationalization of authority, institutional differentiation, and increased political participation as three components of political modernization.[79] We might add that the mediation of information is a central feature of economic as well as of political modernization. The communications media have supplanted relatives, neighbors, gossips, correspondence, newsletters, messengers, and clergy as authoritative sources of information in modern society. The news media have grown from messengers and town criers into financially and politically independent institutions of incomparable influence. In the process political and economic life has become more extensive, complex, and indirect.

In 1959 Douglas Cater wrote

> the political scientist has so long neglected the study of the interaction between government and the press. The American Fourth Estate operates as a *de facto* quasi-official fourth branch of government.[80]

In 1963 Bernard Cohen reported that the press was not only the main source of information for the public but the vehicle through which the various regions of the government communicated.[81] For Cater the power of this fourth estate derived from "ability to select—to define what is news and what isn't."[82] Bernard Cohen elaborated:

> The press is significantly more than a purveyor of information and opinion. It may not be successful much of the time in telling people what to think, but it is stunningly successful in telling its readers what to think *about*.[83]

To Lippmann's "map-making function," Cohen was adding, in the parlance of social science—an "agenda-setting function."[84]

In 1963 television news began to supplant newspapers as the public's main source of information, becoming a more predominant source in the following decades.[85] Shanto Iyengar and Donald R. Kinder conducted a broad study testing the reaction of a cross section of American viewers. The authors concluded that

> the results vindicated Lippmann's original suspicion that news media provide compelling accounts of a political world that is otherwise out of reach. Our studies show specifically that *television news powerfully influences which problems viewers regard as the nation's most serious* (authors' emphasis).[86]

Iyengar and Kinder's experiment went further. They show that television influences viewers not only in what to think about but also what to think—"about governments, presidents, policies, and candidates for public office."[87] They describe as "priming" television's capacity to call attention to some matters and ignore others, evoking impressions "which influence the standards by which political judgments are rendered and political choices made."[88]

Iyengar and Kinder did not investigate whether television had a greater "priming" effect than newspapers. They did endorse P. H. Weaver's argument that the media conveys a mantle of authority to anchormen and correspondent alike.[89] If we take into account the "framing" effects discussed in the next chapter it was certainly the case in the 1980s that:

> To a degree that was hardly envisaged a generation ago, the major media stand at the center of the struggle for social influence. They act as gatekeepers for the messages contending groups and individuals wish to send to each other and to the general public.[90]

Notes

1. Peter Braestrup, *Big Story: How the American Press and Television Reported and Interpreted the Crisis of Tet 1968 in Vietnam and Washington* (Garden City, New York: Anchor Press, 1978; reprint New Haven: Yale University Press, 1983), 1-2; see also Neil Sheehan, *A Bright Shining Lie: John Paul Vann and America in Vietnam* (New York: Random House, 1988), 270.

2. David Halberstam, *The Best and the Brightest* (Greenwich, Connecticut: Fawcett, 1973), 813.

3. Sheehan, *A Bright Shining Lie*, 270.

4. For a discussion of this period in U.S. foreign corresponding, see William Prochnau, *Once Upon a Distant War: Young War Correspondents and Their Early Vietnam Battles* (New York: Vintage, 1996).

5. Daniel C. Hallin, *The Uncensored War: The Media and Vietnam* (New York: Oxford University Press, 1986), 34. Halberstam wrote that the press corps became "an outlet" for the complaints of officers like Vann who considered the South Vietnamese government and military corrupt and inept and were unhappy with U.S. strategy. (Halberstam, *The Best and the Brightest*, 253; see also Sheehan *A Bright Shining Lie*, 316.) Halberstam and others report that President Kennedy asked the publisher of the *New York Times* that Halberstam be withdrawn from Vietnam because his stories "raised doubts about the wisdom of American policy there." (Louis Heren, *No Hail, No Farewell* [New York: Harper & Row, 1970], 24; Halberstam, *The Powers That Be* [New York: Knopf, 1979], 445-46; see Kathleen J. Turner, *Lyndon Johnson's Dual War* [Chicago: University of Chicago, 1985], 56; and Hallin, *The Uncensored War*, 48; Sheehan, *A Bright Shining Lie*, 345-51; and Braestrup, *Big Story*, 2-3.)

6. Hallin, *The Uncensored War* 48.

7. Halberstam, *The Making of a Quagmire* (New York: Random House, 1965), 319.

8. Sheehan, *A Bright Shining Lie*, 271.

9. In point of fact Alan Riding of the *New York Times* was the son of British parents in Brazil and was educated in England, and *Time*'s Bernard Diederich hailed from Australia, as did Peter Arnett who worked for the Associated Press in Vietnam.

10. See Stephen Kinzer, *Blood of Brothers* (New York: Putnam, 1991), 45.

11. For accounts of U.S. aims during this period, I relied on conversations with former Assistant Secretary of State for Inter-American Affairs, Viron P. Vaky, Washington, D.C., during 1983-87; Anthony Lake, *Somoza Falling* (Boston: Houghton Mifflin, 1989), chapters vii-viii; and Robert Pastor, *Condemned to Repetition: The United States and Nicaragua* (Princeton: Princeton University, 1987), chapters iv-viii.

12. Alan Riding, "U.S. in Role of Key Nicaragua Arbiter," News Analysis, *NYT*, July 10, 1979, A3.

13. Kinzer, *Blood of Brothers*, 43; and Karen DeYoung, "Nicaragua from Carter to Reagan," *Washington Post Book World* (November 1987): 1.

14. Bernard Diederich, *Somoza and the Legacy of U.S. Involvement in Central America*, 2d edition (Maplewood, New Jersey: Waterfront Press, 1989): 148; other citations in order from Alan Riding, "Unable to Force Out Somoza," *NYT*, July 1, 1979, A3; Kinzer, *Blood of Brothers*, 43; DeYoung, "Nicaragua from Carter to Reagan"; and Alan Riding, "Sandinistas, Patriots First—Marxists Maybe Second," *NYT*, November 19, 1978, 4-1.

15. See Presidential Finding, September 1983, cited in United States, President's Special Review Board, *The Tower Commission Report* (New York: Times Books, 1987), 450. For background, see Robert Kagan, *A Twilight Struggle: American Power and Nicaragua, 1977-1990* (New York: Free Press, 1996), 196-207. The Reagan administration had placed Central America near the top of its foreign policy agenda and significantly raised the accompanying rhetoric. U.N. Ambassador Jean Kirkpatrick declared that "Central America and the Caribbean [is] the most important place in the world for us" (Speech delivered to the Conservative Political Action Conference," March 21, 1981, cited in Roy Gutman, *Banana Diplomacy: The Making of American Policy in Nicaragua, 1981-87* [New York: Simon & Schuster, 1988], 31).

16. In 1985 the president raised the rhetorical ante—the anti-Sandinista fighters were now the "moral equivalent of the founding fathers." The last phrase was coined by White House speech-writer Peggy Noonan and delivered by President Reagan in a speech to the Conservative Political Action Conference in Washington, D.C., on March 1, 1985 (United States, Department of State, *American Foreign Policy Documents* [1985, Doc. 540); see also *New York Times*, March 2, 1985, A1]. Five years later in an interview on National Public Radio (NPR) Noonan admitted that she regretted the phrase which "created problems for the President." She went on to explain that the White House Communications Director Patrick Buchanan and Reagan himself had asked her to compare the anti-Sandinista rebels with the founding fathers and with the French resistance. Noonan explained that she did not regard the comparison itself absurd since the "contras" were also fighting "against long odds." But she was sorry that her "wording" seemed to make the *Contras* "the equals of the angels who wrote the Declaration of Independence and the Constitution" ("Fresh Air," NPR, February 14, 1990).

17. Kinzer, *Blood of Brothers*, 101, 92, 108, 110-13.

18. Marvin Kalb, the veteran television correspondent who became the Director of the Shornstein Barone Center for Media Studies at Harvard University, commented in October 1986:

> As Moscow correspondent in the 1950s and 1960s, the feeling was that I was there as an American. My close friends . . . were with the embassy staff. I didn't think that was wrong. There was a feeling we were all in something together, us versus them. Soon after I returned to Washington in 1963, there came the Gulf of Tonkin Story. My instinct from being in Moscow was to suspect anything written in *Pravda* or said by Krushschev, but not to be suspicious of the U.S. government. . . . [After Vietnam] our collective attitude, and the attitude of the government, changed from innocence to constant testiness. (Cited in Simon Serfaty, "The Media and Foreign Policy," in *The Media and Foreign Policy*, ed. Simon Serfaty [New York: St. Martin's, 1990], 16.)

We do not wish to overstate this shift in attitudes. Even during the serenity of the Eisenhower administration, foreign correspondents, and foreign affairs reporters in Washington, could often be "suspicious and skeptical of the motives of officials." (Bernard C. Cohen, *The Press and Foreign Policy* [Princeton, New Jersey: Princeton University, 1963], 265, see also 77-79.)

19. Halberstam, *The Best and the Brightest*, 813-14.

The disillusionment of Halberstam and many of his cohorts had a major influence on subsequent American reporting of the Vietnam War. Young as most of them were, they were the veterans: "For a decade their views helped shaped the attitude of newly arriving U.S. newsmen toward U.S. officialdom, successive Saigon regimes, the South Vietnamese fighting man and the enemy" (Braestrup, *Big Story*, 2).

20. Halberstam, *The Best and the Brightest*, 813.

21. Cf. Prochnau, *Once Upon a Distant War*, 31, 450.

22. Clifford Krauss, "Vietnam Generation Goes Centrist," *Media Studies Journal*, Gannett Media Studies Center, Columbia University (Fall 1989): 35-36.

23. Ben Bagdikian, "Professional Personnel and Organizational Structures in the Mass Media," in *Mass Communications Research*, ed. W. P. Davidson and F. T. C. Yu (New York: Praeger, 1974), 134.

24. See chapter 2, fn. 31, for a description of the prestige press.

25. American Society of Newspaper Editors, Human Resources Committee, *The Changing Face of the News Room*, Report (May 1989): 31; see also David H. Weaver and G. Cleveland Wilhoit, *The American Journalist* (Bloomington, Indiana: Indiana University, 1991), 48.

26. American Society of Newspaper Editors, *Changing Face*: 31-32, 37.

27. Weaver and Wilhoit, *American Journalist*, 48.

28. Bagdikian, *The Media Monopoly* (Boston: Beacon, 1983), 135. See also Richard Davis, *The Press and American Politics* (New York: Longmans, 1992), 21.

29. S. Robert Lichter, Stanley Rothman, and Linda S. Lichter, *The Media Elite* (Bethesda, Maryland: Adler and Adler, 1986), 22-23.

30. Stephen Hess, *International News and Foreign Correspondents* (Washington, DC: Brookings, 1996), 12.

31. Hess, *International News*, 141, table A-15.

32. Hess, *International News*, 12.

33. Hess, *International News*, 13.

34. John C. Pollock, *The Politics of Crisis Reporting* (New York: Praeger, 1981), 46-47.

35. Pollock, *Politics of Crisis Reporting*, 51.

36. Pollock, *Politics of Crisis Reporting*, 51

37. Pollock, *Politics of Crisis Reporting*, 51-52.

38. By "class situation" we understand "the opportunities to gain sustenance and income that are primarily determined by typical, *economically* relevant, situations," e.g., property and skills. Class situation also comprises "the ensuing typical living conditions"; see Max Weber, "The Social Psychology of the World Religions," in *From Max Weber: Essays in Sociology*, ed. and trans. H. H. Gerth and C. Wright Mills (New York: Oxford University, 1960), 301; and Weber "Class, Status and Party" in *From Max Weber*, 181. For further discussion of class and class situation, see Lesek Kolakowski, *Main Currents of Marxism* (Oxford: Oxford University, 1987), vol. I: 352-58; Nicos Poulantzas, *Political Power and Social Classes* (London: Newe Left, 1973), 70-79; Ralf Dahrendorf, *Class and Class Conflict in an Industrial Society* (Stanford: Stanford University, 1959), 121 ff.; and Marta Harnecker, *Conceptos Elementales de Materialismo Histórico* (Buenos Aires: Siglo XXI, 1975), 189. "Status" refers to the social estimation of honor; see Weber, "Class, Status and Party," 189, 301. "Prestige" refers to social honor accorded to a profession which may or may not be a function of "standard-of-living" or "contribution to the community well-being" (Steven Brint, *In an Age of Experts: The Changing Role of Professionals in Politics and Public Life* [Princeton: Princeton University, 1994], 41); see also Weber, "The Chinese Literati," in *From Max Weber*, 416-44.

39. Nearly 3,000 newspaper reporters and editors, selected randomly from the staffs of more than 600 newspapers were canvassed. They were asked more than 100 questions; the same questions were put to a national random sample of some 3,300 adults—setting up a direct comparison with the attitudes of the journalists.

40. *LAT* Poll #94, questions #19, 20, 22, 23 (Survey results supplied to the author by the *Los Angeles Times*.) For an analysis of the poll, see William Schneider and I. A. Lewis, "Views on the News," *Public Opinion* (vol. viii, no. 4, August-September 1985).

41. For a similar survey of the Washington press corps, see Stephen Hess, *The Washington Reporters* (Washington, DC: Brookings, 1981), 88-89.

42. Schneider and Lewis, "Views on the News," 7.

43. Schneider and Lewis, "Views on the News," 7.

44. Lichter, Rothman, and Lichter, *Media Elite*, 41.

45. For an analysis of the results of these surveys, see Lichter, Rothman, and Lichter, *Media Elite*, chapter II.

46. Weaver and Wilhoit, *American Journalist*, 27. Accordingly, the Indiana study found a "much less pronounced" "left-leaning tendency" among a national sample "than found in the Lichter and Rothman's sample of Northeastern elite journalists" (Weaver and Wilhoit, *American Journalist*, 25).

47. As to readers' assessment, a 1989 survey conducted by Gallup found that 76 percent of the public saw "a great deal" or "a fair amount" of political bias in news coverage. Large majorities of those who characterized the bias found it to be liberal rather than moderate or conservative (Times-Mirror Center for the People and the Press, "The People and the Press, Part 5" [August 1989]).

48. Lichter, Rothman, and Lichter, *Media Elite*, 53. While one might wish to quarrel with the terminology, the point here is substantial if nebulous. The term "media elite" should be restricted to the upper echelon of the staff of the prestige press. Not every journalist or correspondent belongs to the elite in terms of income, social class, status, or prestige. When Steven Kinzer was filing copy on an occasional basis for the *Boston Globe*, he was not a member of the media elite. When he became the Managua bureau chief of the *New York Times*, he achieved that rank. In Weberian terms the "media elite" may be classified as an amorphous "status group," the focus of whose "community" are the news organizations themselves. As Weber observes, "class distinctions are linked in the most varied ways with status distinctions." If, for the sake of argument, we adopted the concept of the "new class," the media elite could be considered a status group linked to that class (Weber, "Class, Status and Party," 186-87). To the extent that members of the press constitute an amorphous status *group*, it is by virtue of their relationship to the media—to the power and prestige accruing to upper echelons of that profession.

49. White, "America's Two Cultures" *Columbia Journalism Review* (Winter 1969): 9-10, quoted in Lichter, Rothman, and Lichter, *Media Elite*, 91.

50. Joseph Kraft, "The Imperial Media," *Commentary* (May 1981): 42, cited in Lichter, Rothman, and Lichter, *Media Elite*, 33-34.

51. Pollock, *Politics of Crisis Reporting*, 29. Pollock's "chronicler" and "examiner" are elsewhere characterized as "neutral" or "observer," on the one hand, and "participant" on the other (see John W. C. Johnstone, Edward Slawski, and William Bowman, *The News People* [Urbana: University of Illinois, 1976], 118; Lichter, Rothman, and Lichter, *Media Elite*, 138-39).

52. Pollock, *Politics of Crisis Reporting*, 29, 31. One cannot help wondering how many of the "chroniclers" would have concurred that by virtue of their "agree[ing] somewhat" with the proposition: "Only a show of military strength can prevent the U.S.S.R. from trying to gain world domination" they thereby "favor conflict with the Soviet Union." Assent to that proposition indicates to Pollock membership in his "hegemonic" as opposed to his "pluralist" type. To be a "pluralist" one must "agree strongly" with the view that "Military considerations play too great a role in formulating U.S. foreign policy" (Pollock, *Politics of Crisis Reporting*, 106). The hegemonic per-

spective would regard "leaders calling for rapid change as 'unrepresentative'" (Pollock, *Politics of Crisis Reporting*, 104).

53. Pollock's findings do not generally distinguish between active and inactive journalists. Pollock's sample includes journalists who "for any appreciable time. . . covered Latin America in the past or present" for a major U.S. news organization. No specific coverage dates are attached to responses. Of the respondents 27 percent began working on Latin America before 1958, 39 percent before 1968, and 34 percent after 1968 (after the Tet Offensive in the early spring of 1968 to be precise) (Pollock, *Politics of Crisis Reporting*, 47, table 3, 49).

54. Pollock, *Politics of Crisis Reporting*, 73-74.

55. Pollock, *Politics of Crisis Reporting*, 83.

56. Pollock, *Politics of Crisis Reporting*, 113-53.

57. Pollock, *Politics of Crisis Reporting*, 143.

58. Pollock, *Politics of Crisis Reporting*, 101.

59. Theodore Edward Kruglak, *The Foreign Correspondents: A Study of the Men and Women Reporting for the American Information Media in Western Europe* (Geneva: Librairie E. Droz, 1955; reprinted Westport, Connecticut: Greenwood Press, 1974), 66 and appendix IV, table 2, 150-51.

60. Kruglak, *Foreign Correspondents*, 48-49.

61. Kruglak, *Foreign Correspondents*, 88-89.

62. Kruglak, *Foreign Correspondents*, 87.

63. Kruglak, *Foreign Correspondents*, 11.

64. Everett C. Ladd, Jr. and Seymour Martin Lipset, *The Divided Academy: Professors and Politics* (New York: McGraw-Hill, 1975), 3.

65. Ladd and Lipset, *Divided Academy*, 2.

66. Ladd and Lipset, *Divided Academy*, 36.

67. Ladd and Lipset, *Divided Academy*, 60, table 10.

68. Brint, *Age of Experts*, 5, 8, 13, 99, 100, table 5.3.

69. See Daniel Bell, *The Cultural Contradictions of Capitalism* (New York: Basic Books, 1976): 15, 33-34, 37.

70. Ladd and Lipset, *Divided Academy*, 198.

71. Ladd and Lipset, *Divided Academy*, 39, 40-42.

72. Ladd and Lipset, *Divided Academy*, 40.

73. Phillip E. Converse, "The Nature of Belief Systems in Mass Publics," in *Ideology and Discontent*, ed. David E. Apter (New York: Free Press, 1964): 207; see Ladd and Lipset, *Divided Academy*, 38.

74. Ladd and Lipset, *Divided Academy*, 134-48.

75. Pollock, *Politics of Crisis Reporting*, 139-40.

76. For a discussion of this decline, see Lipset, "American Democracy in Comparative Perspective," in *A New Moment in the Americas*, ed. Robert S. Leiken (New Brunswick, New Jersey: Transaction, 1994), 8 ff. See also Robert Putnam, "Bowling Alone: America's Declining Social Capital," *Journal of Democracy* (1995); and Theodore Caplow, *American Social Trends* (San Diego: Harcourt Brace Jovanovich, 1991).

77. Bell, *Cultural Contradictions*, 467.

78. Bell, *Cultural Contradictions*, 468.

79. Samuel P. Huntington, *Political Order in Changing Societies* (New Haven: Yale University, 1968), 34-35.

80. Douglass Cater, *The Fourth Branch of Government* (Boston: Houghton Mifflin, 1959), 13.

81. Cohen, *Press and Foreign Policy*, 210-11.

82. Cater, *Fourth Branch*, 14.

83. Cohen, *Press and Foreign Policy*, 12.

84. See M. E. McCombs and D. Shaw, "The agenda setting function of the mass media," in *Public Opinion Quarterly* (vol. 36, 1972): 176-87; M. E. McCombs, "The Agenda Setting Approach," in *Handbook of Political Communication*, ed. D. D. Nimmo and K. R. Sanders (Beverly Hills: Sage, 1981); and *More than News: Media Power in Public Affairs*, ed. M. Mackuen and S. L. Coombs (Beverly Hills: Sage, 1981).

85. See Prochnau, *Once Upon a Distant War*, 199; Robert T. Bower, *The Changing Television Audience in America* (New York: Columbia University, 1985); Stephen Ansolabehere, Roy Behr, and Shanto Iyengar, *The Media Game: American Politics in the Television Age* (New York: Macmillan, 1993), 44-45.

86. Shanto Iyengar and Donald R. Kinder, *News That Matters: Television and American Opinion* (Chicago: University of Chicago Press, 1987), 4, 111-13, and chapter 3. See also Iyengar and Adam Simon, "News Coverage of the Gulf Crisis and Public Opinion: A Study of Agenda-Setting, Priming, and Framing," in *Taken by Storm: The Media, Public Opinion, and U.S. Foreign Policy in the Persian Gulf War*, ed. W. Lance Bennett and David L. Paletz (Chicago: University of Chicago Press, 1994).

87. Iyengar and Kinder, *News That Matters*, 63.

88. Iyengar and Kinder, *News That Matters*, 114, 4; see also chapters 7-11.

89. P. H. Weaver, "Newspaper News and Television News," in *Television as Social Force: New Approaches to TV Criticism*, ed. D. Cater and R. Adler (New York: Praeger, 1975), 84, 90 (as cited in Iyengar and Kinder, *News That Matters*, 126).

90. Lichter, Rothman, and Lichter, *Media Elite*, x.

Chapter 4
Media Studies

Even as what Lionel Trilling dubbed the "adversary culture" was developing from an elite into a mass phenomenon, the college degree was becoming a prerequisite for an increasing number of employments, including journalism.[1] Journalism and media and communication studies were becoming academic fields as part of "a great surge in education for the professions and the so-called 'emerging professions' which now [1982-83] dominates undergraduate education."[2]

Vietnam War reporting became a critique of the war and media studies, in large part, a critique of mainstream reporting. By 1978, the year Nicaragua became a major news story, "a vast literature" had emerged

> which in various ways makes the point that the content of the news is a function of the social structure of news gathering and news organization. Most of this literature observes that the process of "newsmaking" favors official points of view.[3]

That literature made a strong case for the "ethnocentric" character of "American news values" (Herbert Gans) and that "official circles dominate press coverage" (Leon Sigal).[4] Much of it also sustained that not only the news but the process and practice of gathering and producing it reflect conceptions which "legitimate the status quo" (Gaye Tuchman).[5] Most shared the view that even more than the specific details reported the news frame itself, by its semblance of objectivity, assured "similar bureaucratically created and ideologically embedded accounts" (Todd Gitlin and Thomas Koch).[6]

Ethnocentrism

During the Vietnam period Herbert Gans investigated the "key assumptions" of four American news organizations.[7] Published in 1979, his *Deciding What's News* found U.S. reporting of foreign news dominated by an "ethnocentrism" which "judges other countries by the extent to which they live up to or imitate American practices and values" and which regards "democracy superior to dictatorship" especially "if it follows American forms."[8] Gans reported that stories on foreign dictators

> concern themselves mainly with the violation of American political values by dictators, and thus illustrate once more the extent to which American ideas and values dominate the reporting of foreign news.[9]

For a time after President Nixon's visit, the coverage of the People's Republic of China gave Professor Gans a rare opportunity to extol the media for reporting

> the economic and social benefits which the revolution had provided for ordinary Chinese people. They celebrated the enthusiasm and public-spiritedness of the Chinese citizens they observed, particularly their willingness to work hard and make personal sacrifices in the public interest. In fact, at the time, some commentators noted that these were virtues which had once existed in America, were now lost, and should be revived.[10]

Gans objected to what he regarded as typical headlines announcing "the Fall of South Vietnam," with scarcely a recognition that by other values, it could be considered a liberation, or in neutral terminology, a change of governments.[11] He found that the press labeled the North Vietnamese and the Vietnamese National Liberation Front "as 'the enemy,' as if they were the enemy of the news media."[12]

Gans noted that in the news:

> Conservative dictators are apt to be treated more kindly than socialist ones, either because they are American allies or because they maintain public order; however in recent years critical comments have been made about the economic policies of right-wing Latin American dictators such as Nicaragua's Somoza.[13]

Though Gans's account may be valid in describing earlier news stories, that last clause was as close as Gans came to noting the paradigm shift among journalists which was occurring even as he was at work. Gans visited the *CBS Evening News*, *NBC Nightly News*, *Newsweek*, and *Time* each for several months between 1965 and 1969. He updated his investigations in 1975.[14] To the extent that they reflect the Nicaragua reporting at all, Gans's observations apply to the

1950s and 1960s. That may be because Gans's principal observations appear to have been drawn from his fieldwork in the 1960s when the paradigm changes were barely underway.[15] But then Gans, like many of his colleagues, subscribed to the emerging paradigm himself.

The stereotype of the raffish, muckraking, fedora-fixed, cigarette-dangling "working stiff" derives from the Progressive Era in American history. By the 1970s the group it depicted was becoming a vanishing breed superseded by a new social type. Nonetheless, despite the opinion surveys summarized in the previous chapter, many academic investigators cleaved to the old image, upon which they focused a critical gaze. Gans saw "small-town pastoralism," together with "ethnocentrism," as central "enduring values" for journalists.

Gans thought that "the reliance on public officials, and other equally authoritative and efficient sources, is almost sufficient by itself to explain why the news drew the portrait" he described.[16] For the alleged reliance on public officials he counts heavily on evidence from Leon Sigal's *Reporters and Officials*. Sigal had analyzed "2,850 domestic and foreign stories that appeared in the *New York Times* and the *Washington Post* and found that public officials were the source of 78 percent of the stories."[17] Writing when he did, Gans saw no need to add that the stories Sigal analyzed were published between 1949 and 1969 and that "for economy of effort five-year intervals were chosen."[18] Thus fully 80 percent of the stories Sigal analyzed preceded the 1965 U.S. escalation in Vietnam and could not possibly reflect the new paradigm taking hold in universities and among journalists.

What Sigal calls "the routine channels for newsmaking" did indeed, "constitute the mechanisms for official dominance of national and foreign news in two papers" *for the sample he studied*—or for most of it. Sigal himself noted that "reporters' reliance on official sources declined over the period 1949-69." His tables provided documentation that reporters' use of "enterprise channels" (*i.e.*, independent research, interviews initiated by the reporter, spontaneous events, and reporter's own conclusions) rose 83 percent from 1949 to 1969 with most of the rise occurring in 1969.[19] Sigal himself acknowledges that the Johnson and Nixon administrations perceived "increased hostility in the press" that may have reflected "a change in newsmen's political attitudes" as well as "a manifestation of longer-term trends in newsgathering away from channels dominated by senior officials, trends resulting from an expansion of news staffs and a proliferation of news bureaus."[20] (We shall return to this point in chapter 15.)

The "Myth of Objectivity"

The information explosion led to increased staffs and bureaus and stimulated a demand for journalists who could synthesize data and present information in an accessible manner—hence the demand for a university degree and even advanced studies. The journalist was no longer simply a news provider but, to some degree, by necessity a news interpreter. In the process the very concept of news underwent a kind of revolution in the direction of interpretative, investigative, and feature journalism.

Many trends contributed to this revolution: the advent of television, the decline of press magnates, journalistic professionalization, and the impact of the "adversary culture."[21] The exigencies of the Cold War led to what James Reston, then vice president of the *New York Times*, criticized as the government's "growing tendency to manage the news."[22] Mainstream journalists began to chafe under the strictures of government news management. The now better educated, more urbane, more "interpretative" younger journalist bridled against the ethic of impartiality which had prevailed for nearly a century.[23] More erudite in his opinions, the journalist also felt more entitled to embody them in stories. Lewis Lapham, the editor of *Harper's*, observed from first-hand experience:

> Having enjoyed the privileges of both affluence and education the new generation of journalists felt inhibited by the older conventions. They thought of themselves as "creators," as the possessors of "the truth."[24]

Thus even as journalists became more sophisticated, their heightened status and the surrounding journalistic culture gave them greater license to inject those opinions into their stories.

Competition from television constituted another challenge to the chastity of news columns. As Sigal observed, if the news pages could not compete with the vividness and speed of television, they could certainly provide more depth and detail. For many, the solution was to add to the traditional news criteria of "who, what, where, and when" a much more "explicit concern with the 'why' of news."[25] The door to "interpretative journalism" was ajar.

In stepped the adversary culture—a powerful source of pressure on the standard of objectivity. Young journalists and media critics began denouncing objectivity as a "myth."[26] In taking arms against objectivity they were declaring war on the older generation of journalists even as antiwar activists were attacking the political establishment.

In his 1963 study Bernard C. Cohen stressed that the "bright thread of preference for objectivity" was widely characteristic among both readers and reporters.[27] In the United States objectivity as a news value was associated with the transition of the press from journals of partisan opinion to a commercially-oriented news medium. An ethic of impartiality was encouraged by the growth of advertising revenues and by competition for circulation—partisanship could offend readers or advertisers. The root of the ethic of objectivity may be found in both the inexpensive daily press, the "penny press," of the early nineteenth century and the prestige nonpartisan press of the early twentieth century. The rise of news gathering agencies supplying stories to a philosophically diverse clientele reinforced the tendency to avoid injecting opinion into news columns.

Fostered by a growing sense of professionalism and a philosophical preference, objectivity as a supreme news value reached its zenith during the 1950s.[28]

Despite their elevated status in the 1950s, U.S. European correspondents and editors took care not to allow subjective opinions enter news columns. Since their readers were less familiar with foreign than with domestic events, it was necessary to provide background and interpretation. U.S. editors in Europe solved this problem by granting foreign correspondence wider latitude in reporting. As we have seen in chapter 3, the correspondent for a European newspaper "frequently indulged in editorial opinion to make his point" but the custom was "frowned upon by American editors."[29] Instead the Americans "interpreted" events by supplying, in the words of Lester Markel, Sunday editor of *New York Times*, "setting, sequence, and above all significance."

Markel insisted on the "tremendous difference between interpretation and opinion: the first is objective, or as objective as human beings can make it; the second is subjective."[30] The sharpness of Markel's distinction was to grow muddled by the end of the next decade as "interpretation" tended to become a euphemism for opinion.

"In the 1960s 'objectivity' became a term of abuse," as historian Michael Schudson has observed—and not only among journalists but, even more so, among media academics.[31] Much of the subsequent media scholarship considered conventional reporting to be governed by a paradigm of objectivity, when it did not consider objectivity itself to be a paradigm. Leon Sigal starts from the premise of "the subjectivity of all knowledge" and that "all seeing is theory-laden."[32] Ben Bagdikian wrote that standards of objectivity

> contradict the essentially subjective nature of journalism. Every basic step in the journalistic process involves a value-laden decision. . . . "Objectivity" place[s] overwhelming emphasis on established, official voices and tend[s] to leave unreported large areas of genuine relevance that authorities choose not to talk about.[33]

For Parenti the idea of journalistic objectivity was a "myth" instructing journalists that, "they must not press too deeply into areas that might cause discomfort to those of power, wealth, and conservative ideology."[34]

"So-called objectivity" embodied institutionalized values: socially constructed decisions as to what is newsworthy, where news occurs, who is a reliable source, and what is the relevant time frame. In his study on "the mass media in the making and unmaking of the New Left," Todd Gitlin argued that "without calling attention to itself, the media divide movements into legitimate main acts and illegitimate sideshows, so that these distinctions appear 'natural,' matters of 'common sense.'" By this means, without overt comment or editorializing, "popular or radical" or revolutionary movements, were "rendered illegitimate."[35]

Though inspired by a variety of theoretical perspectives—the theory of "bureaucratic politics," structuralism, frame theory, social constructionism, Mannheimian sociology, and Marxism, the precursors of what today is called post-modernism—many practitioners of media and communication studies shared the view that the organization and practices of newsmaking inexorably produced news that promoted government policies and sanctioned and sustained the *status quo*.

For Gaye Tuchman the newsman's pursuit of an illusory standard of objectivity produced only an illusory "web of facticity" which camouflaged and legitimated the structure of power.[36] The intimate relationship between the media and government officials was for Tuchman a structural function of "objectivity." Tuchman, dubbed the purportedly objective structure of newsmaking a "strategic ritual," validating the news product and absolving the reporter of political responsibility.[37] Andrew Arno contended that reporters' "storylines" are simply "agreed conventional scenarios" which "cast facts into certain molds."[38] Robert M. Entman held that the ideal of objectivity actually "facilitates the manipulation of a news slant" and assists "elite news managers."[39]

Much of post-Vietnam media study wished to "deconstruct" the apparent naturalness, the givenness of the news, to expose its "common sense" as ideology legitimizing the *status quo*. In the case of Gitlin and Tuchman and others that meant seeking to "look at news as a frame."[40] If the media frame "makes the world beyond direct experience look natural," the "picture of the world" the reader receives is not a faithful reflection but "a constructed reality."[41] The very notion of a "frame," of synthetic border around the news, like a window or picture frame or, more precisely, a film frame, controverted the apparent naturalness of the putatively objective news report. "Largely unspoken and unacknowledged," Todd Gitlin explained, "Media frames 'organize the world both for journalists who report it and, in some important degree, for us who rely on their reports.'"[42] Frames are patterns of cognition, selection, interpretation, emphasis, and presentation "composed of little tacit theories about what exists, what happens, and what matters."[43]

The frame in itself, according to Tom Koch, may be more important than the specific details it surrounds because its very form makes for "similar bureaucratically created and ideologically embedded accounts."[44] Tuchman stressed how the news "frames," in Erving Goffman's film metaphor, "strips of everyday occurrences" and accordingly cannot be considered "a mere mirror of events."[45] News, she argued, is "a legitimating ideology."[46] According to Dan Schiller, throughout the history of the American press social conflict has been "disguised, contained, and displaced through the imposition of news objectivity, a framework legitimating the exercise of social power of the interpretation of reality."[47]

Tuchman is not speaking of a willful distortion but of a "structural pattern."[48] Tuchman's is not a philistine critique:

> I do not mean to accuse newsworkers of bias. The news professionals rightfully insist that those who shout 'bias' be able to define objective truth in a definitive manner. I do not claim that ability. But I do claim that it is valuable to identify news as an artful accomplishment attuned to specific understandings of social

reality. Those understandings, constituted in specific work processes and practices, legitimate the status quo.[49]

Tuchman's investigations belong to the "social construction" school influenced by such modern theorists as Goffman, Alfred Schutz, Ferdinand de Saussure, Paul Feyerabend, Claude Levi-Strauss, Roland Barthes, Thomas Kuhn, Jurgen Habermas, Jacques Derrida, and Michel Foucault. Christopher Lasch termed the social construction of reality—"the central dogma of postmodernist thought."[50]

Many of those who embraced the new paradigm appeared to have reconstructed the "dogmatic idealism" of George Berkeley who, in Immanuel Kant's words "degraded bodies to mere illusions." That is to say they regarded physical reality as an imaginative entity constructed by the perceiver.[51] If the scholar holds that objective reality is impervious to "definitive" characterization, he may deem it sufficient merely to show the institutional or ideological "structure" of the coverage in order to demonstrate that it is "reproducing the *status quo*." The media analyst thus could be absolved from independently investigating the events covered in the reportage he is examining. Much of the analysis of foreign reporting in the university which we shall review below tends to take for granted the academy's preferred conception of events without bothering to investigate independently. In criticizing the subjectivism of these trends John R. Searle observes trenchantly that it is

> somehow satisfying to our will to power to think that "we" make the world, that reality itself is but a social construct alterable at will. . . . Equally it seems offensive that there should be an independent reality of brute facts . . . utterly unaffected by our concerns.[52]

As it grew more powerful the American news media was tempted to reshape the events they portrayed, thus converging with emerging "postmodern" philosophical trends.

An associated tendency has been the "blurring" of the division between fact and opinion or reporting and editorializing. If contemporary journalists felt more entitled to introduce "interpretation" into the news, news itself was being seen increasingly not simply as a "social artifice" but as art. Tuchman has told us that "it is valuable to identify news as an artful accomplishment."[53] Though journalists might invoke scientific objectivity, for Tuchman what they produce is much closer to art.[54] Tuchman recognized in the "new journalism" school a kindred contemporary journalistic expression of her own perspective. "New journalism" wanted to break the "artificial" boundaries between fact and fiction. Tuchman lamented that the phenomenon was "largely confined to magazines and signed work by recognized columnists."[55] But as Schudson observed:

While "new journalism" did not have much direct impact on news-writing in daily papers it . . . fed the imaginations of daily reporters. . . . [The new trends reward] flair, personality, style, and insight and trains the tastes of journalists and their readers away from objective reporting.[56]

Bob Woodward who with Carl Bernstein broke the Watergate story in the *Washington Post* also helped create, along with Norman Mailer and others, the new genre of "docudrama."[57] Each of the three volumes on the Nicaraguan *"Contras"* produced by American journalists deployed the Woodward technique.[58] All of them featured fictionalized interior monologues, reconstructed "verbatim" conversations, and "real life" "novelistic" details.

Our study focuses on the news pages of the newspapers and the news segments of the television news broadcasts. Though more conducive to ideological analysis, editorial and commentary are less interesting to us. We are primarily concerned with opinion presented as fact. Opinion when it is embedded in news stories is far more powerful and influential than in an overt editorial. News stories, we assume, are objective. Yet the period we are studying saw not only the rise of "sound bite journalism" but the erosion of the distinction between interpreting the news and reporting it. Kiki Adatto discovered that in coverage of the 1968 U.S. elections

> newscasts . . . distinguished sharply between reporting and commentary. . . . Coverage still partook of an unadorned "wire-service" style of reporting, emphasizing description not interpretation. Opinions and analysis were reserved for explicitly designated commentary segments, which resembled spoken "op-ed" pieces.[59]

Studying the 1979 coverage of the Nicaraguan revolution another analyst was struck by

> the frequency with which stories' conclusions are made by unstated implication, by innuendo, and by unrefuted third parties. Rarely do the correspondents explicitly offer more than equivocal concluding remarks. They have, however, refined the art of making rhetorical questions sound like an obvious indictment.[60]

We shall show many examples of this blurring of commentary and reporting, of the artful introduction of opinion into news pages and newscasts. Adatto has noted another, related, "blurring." Her studies demonstrate how television coverage of each successive American presidential campaign after 1968 downgraded what the candidates were saying and accentuated how they looked, elevating image over content.[61] Adatto considers this part of a

> tendency, some would say a danger, implicit in the image-conscious culture we inhabit. This is the tendency to blur the distinction between the event and the image, between document and art.[62]

The presentation of the Nicaraguan elections as a series of "media events"—which we shall examine in the next chapter—can be understood as an example of the "post-modern" tendency to exalt technique, style, and form above content and information.

Studies of Foreign Correspondence and the Post-Vietnam Paradigm

For Tuchman the work of American news professionals was

> geared to maintaining the American political system as much as the work of a Soviet journalist is geared to preserving that nation's political system.[63]

The distance could hardly be greater from the distinction drawn in 1963 by Bernard Cohen between the media in a democratic system in contrast to a media under regimes "where political power is highly centralized." In the latter the media become "instruments of that centralization." The media are put to uses of the ruling group "in maintaining their power and advancing their policies" and in solidifying outward and downward "the lines of control." On the other hand, in democratic societies such as the United States where political power is widely dispersed

> the media may be used to sustain the position of any holder of power anywhere in the system; . . . as effectively against an administration as on behalf of one, as the late Senator McCarthy of Wisconsin demonstrated so clearly.[64]

When the United States and other liberal democracies are no longer seen as distinct regimes characterized by the rule of law, republican institutions, and democracy but subsumed under the concept of "power structures," a whole set of distinctions vanishes.[65] The media sustains the "political system;" officials "dominate the news." In the eyes of analysts such as Noam Chomsky and his followers, the kind of critiques made by Sigal and Tuchman were found especially pertinent to the West where "objectivity reinforces the *status quo*," and the media serves the interests of big business and expanding Western imperialism.

Studies of foreign reporting have been influenced strongly by this new paradigm. William Dorman and Mansour Farhang argue that the ideal of "objective journalism" encouraged reporters covering the Iranian revolution slavishly to follow the cues of American policymakers.[66] *China Reporting* summarizes a 1982 conference of journalists who had covered the Chinese Revolution. The contemporary academic authors of the volume concluded that the reporters

were "of the generation who consciously pursued 'objectivity' as journalists."
That meant that "inevitably" the news they reported was "severely limited" by
shortcomings in "language, access, background" as well as by "official lies, censorship, and . . . gatekeepers back home." The outcome was "a highly structured
news reality" which "meshed well with the interest of American policy and
opinions about China at home."[67]

Patrick O'Heffernan has pointed out that the adversarial component of the
media-government relationship "has grown significantly since [Bernard C.]
Cohen described the cooperation between media and government in 1963." He
notes that since then the media often had advocated "modifications or reversal"
of U.S. policy: "From forcing diplomatic negotiations into the open and revealing both embarrassing and injurious information, to actively opposing policies
such as *Contra* aid."[68]

Nonetheless, much of the academic literature on the media cites U.S. media
reporting on Central America as further evidence of supposed media subordina-
tion to government. Daniel Hallin argues that the media continued to play a
"'hegemonic' role," and thus contributed "to the maintenance of consent for a
system of power: the post–World War II *'pax Americana'*—the world capitalist
system dominated both politically and economically by the United States."[69]
Hallin acknowledges that the coverage of Central America has been "strikingly
different" from the coverage of Vietnam he studied but argues that the dominant
frame did not change. According to Hallin the Reagan "administration retained
the predominant power to shape the news."[70] In his view:

> Opposition political movements in the Third World, especially in areas like
> Central America . . . necessarily involve levels of political passion quite unfa-
> miliar to most North Americans. With a few exceptions, they appear in a
> harshly negative light.[71]

Hallin's notion of the ineffable and exotic political passions of the Third World
and Central America, in fact, was widely shared in the media. As we shall show
the presentation of the Sandinista movement was the reverse of "harshly negative." As with much of the academic criticism of foreign reporting, Hallin
weighs the coverage not against any independent research or field experience
but against his own, widely shared, stereotype of the region.

But Hallin at least grants that, unlike the coverage of the Vietnam War he
describes,

> there was in the 1980s a real political contest over the framing of the Central
> American story. This is not a case that can easily be assimilated to a model of
> the media that sees them essentially as a tool of a unified ruling elite. (Herman
> and Chomsky's propaganda model is close to this view.)[72]

After his work at the Massachusetts Institute of Technology created a new paradigm in the field of linguistics, Chomsky became a passionate critic of the war

in Vietnam and has remained a familiar and influential voice on college campuses. In the 1980s he and his followers turned their batteries on the news media's "manufacture of consent" about U.S. foreign policy, soon producing their own ardent version of Sigal's notion that "official circles dominate the news."[73]

"The media's purpose in a free society," as summarized by one of Chomsky's followers, "is to manufacture consent among the governed, rallying the population to endorse elite decisions."[74] In the late-1960s Chomsky began challenging "the general subservience of the articulate intelligentsia" in the United States "to the framework of state propaganda."[75] But notwithstanding his persistent denunciation of "the articulate intelligentsia," Chomsky and his followers assail the media for not paying more attention to the opinion of intellectuals and academics. Robert Sahr complains that although "most academic experts in the United States" rejected U.S. policy toward Nicaragua, "American media almost never utilized these experts as sources."[76] Here Sahr echoes Chomsky's charge that in the press coverage of Nicaragua's 1984 elections

> a careful study of the election by the U.S. Latin American Studies Association (LASA) was virtually ignored by the press as were the elections themselves.[77]

Chapters 10 and 14 show just how much attention the media did in fact pay to organizations such as LASA in the 1984 and 1990 elections and how profoundly these groups influenced the media's analysis and prognostications.

As if taking Sigal's work to its logical conclusion, Sahr argues that coverage of Nicaragua during the 1980s was dominated by "Reagan administration officials and Democratic leaders in Congress" along with the "small part of expert opinion" that failed to challenge the premises of these elites.[78] Another Chomsky disciple, Jack Spence, agrees that on Nicaragua "the press substantially replicated Washington's biases."[79]

In a study of commentaries in the *Washington Post* and the *New York Times* in early 1986 Chomsky claims to find that a "total conformity was maintained on the central issue" of Sandinista popularity. Chomsky reaches this conclusion because in his view "all 85 opinion pieces were critical of the Sandinistas, the overwhelming majority bitterly hostile."[80] Chomsky cites a British television correspondent who concluded that Daniel Ortega's "greatest achievement" was in persuading most Nicaraguans that the Sandinista revolution was "still worth fighting and suffering for."[81]

Yet Chomsky supplies no systematic citation from these opinion pieces or any other documentation in his "careful analysis." Moreover, he defines the "central issue" as Sandinista popularity with Nicaraguans and the viability of their agrarian and other social reform programs. But at this time and in these opinion pieces the central issue was not Sandinista popularity but an upcoming vote on aid to the *Contras*. The overwhelming majority of these opinion pieces opposed this funding, some shrewdly conceding Sandinista "mistakes."

As Chomsky points out, however: "The most effective editorializing is carried out within the news columns."[82] The latter, along with the editorial comment, shared Chomsky's view of the *Contras*, as we shall see in chapter 11. And, as we show in chapters 1, 12, and 14, when the issue *was* Sandinista popularity, as in the elections of 1990, both the news and the editorials foresaw certain Sandinista victory. If Nicaraguan coverage was an example of the "engineering of consent," as Chomsky claims, it was not consent to the anti-Sandinista program of the administration in power.[83]

Chomsky's study appeared in a collection of essays edited by Thomas W. Walker. Walker was one of the most prolific academic writers on Sandinista Nicaragua, and his views typified those prevailing in the academic community. Upon that stereotype of Nicaragua Chomsky, Hallin, and the others depended when arguing that the media was unsympathetic to the Sandinistas and other opposition movements and regimes. In Walker's view "unlike the Somozas . . . the Sandinistas drew their strength . . . from the mass of the people. The system of government that emerged . . . reflected this reality."[84] For Walker, compared to their nationalism, the Sandinista adoption of Marxism-Leninism was a minor detail of Third World sociological analysis:

> Accordingly the overriding concern of the young revolutionaries who governed Nicaragua . . . was to reconstruct the country, defend its hard-won sovereignty and dignity and uplift the condition of its popular masses.[85]

So ecumenical was the amalgam that Walker conceived to be the ideology of the Sandinistas that "in addition to being Marxists, many of the Sandinistas were also devout Catholics."[86]

Together with John Booth, Walker published a textbook widely used in college courses. Booth and Walker explained that "the Sandinistas created a pluralist system in which representatives of the upper-class minority were encouraged to participate."[87] According to these authors the Sandinista pluralist and democratic regime was also an observer of human rights:

> The major human rights organizations all concur that the practice of systematized [sic] torture, murder, and disappearance of political opponents—massively institutionalized in Guatemala and El Salvador—was not a problem in Nicaragua.[88]

Booth's own 1982 volume was the scholarly source on the Sandinista revolution most frequently cited by policymakers and became the standard college text.[89] Booth presents the FSLN as a peasant-based movement, ideologically pluralistic, indeed dominated by social democrats. Of these mainstream academic views Donald Hodges wrote that "eminent scholars" had presented a nationalist "populist image" of the Sandinista Revolution as "a third path promising the best of both the capitalist and socialist worlds," and one in which "the supposed perils of Communism represented by the FSLN are dismissed because of their 'patently bogus nature.'" But Hodges argued that such formulations "mistake the FSLN's appearance for reality."[90] Hodges describes the Sandinistas' "Machiavellian" use of the human rights issue as a political instrument, and, along with Dennis Gilbert, shows that the Sandinistas were unmistakably Marxist-Leninists.[91] We confirm the accuracy of this analysis and its divergence from the media depiction in chapter 9.

Booth and Walker tell us that even as late as 1988 "the public appeared badly alienated from the opposition" which it characterized as a wealthy, upper-class minority.[92] As for the anti-Sandinista "*Contra*" rebels:

> By the mid-1980s it was clear to most informed observers that the Contras could never rally enough popular support to overthrow the government. After the mid-1980s, the Contras became steadily less successful militarily and more isolated from the population.[93]

These conceptions of the anti-Sandinista opposition and of Sandinista pluralism, popular support, and tolerance comprised key assumptions and "fundamental stereotypes." They found little echo in the Reagan and Bush administrations, but they were hegemonic in the university, among professionals in general, in Hollywood, in the media, and quite influential in the U.S. Congress. It was on the basis of such views that Chomsky and other academic critics managed to find the media coverage unfavorable to the Sandinistas and supportive of U.S. government policy.

The Media's Objective Role

Chomsky, Hallin, Sigal, Tuchman, and the others tended to view the news from the subjective side, as an instrument for manufacturing consent, as "legitimating ideology." The closest many came to noticing the objective role of the news was to expatiate on journalists belonging to "a profit-making corporation." But this narrow economistic perspective ignored the objective function of the production of news in modern society. Invented to facilitate communication in a modernizing society, the news media are as essential to modern communication as wire and wave.

Unlike their predecessors, the early nineteenth-century "penny press" regularly printed impartial and independent accounts of local, national, and foreign events. These first U.S. mass newspapers derived their support not, as previously, from social ties or political allegiances, but, as Michael Schudson notes, from "market-based income from advertising and sales."[94] The product of urbanizing America, the penny press signified that the newspaper could reflect not only "the affairs of an elite in a small trading society" but also "the activities of an increasingly varied, urban and middle-class society of trade, transportation, and manufacturing."[95]

The "news" was invented to abet the communication of a diverse society. The impartiality and independence of the penny press established the American newspaper's claim to "stewardship of the pursuit of enlightened reason in the public sphere," as Dan Schiller writes, and "the enduring foundation upon which news objectivity was built."[96] The prestige press, the focus of our attention, was the direct descendant of the popular commercial press. Publisher Arthur Ochs promised that even as the *New York Times* competed with the popular press, it would "tell promptly and accurately the happenings and occurrences that were not sensational but of real importance in the affairs of the people."[97]

After World War I, as Walter Lippmann was culminating "one of the first truly systematic analyses of journalistic performance" with the publication of *Public Opinion*, Ochs' *Times* was already acquiring the character of a national newspaper as well as one "more generally read all over the world than any other American paper."[98] Now "practically everywhere it is assumed." Lippmann wrote, that the press "spontaneously" each day would "present us with a true picture of all the outer world in which we are interested."[99] Lippmann pointed out, however, that, even putting aside the distortions of ideology and prejudice, there were "structural" limitations, so to speak, in the very mission of news-gathering. What generates news stories is not the search for truth but an event assumed to be interesting to the reader. Not reality's mirror, the press is more "like the beam of a searchlight that moves restlessly about, bringing one episode and then another out of darkness into vision."[100] That searchlight is powered by commercial and bureaucratic demands, not scientific ones. Like Tuchman, Lippmann emphasized the structure of newsgathering: time constraints, the institution of "reliable" sources, and the central sites where what is called "news" emerges (such as the police blotter, the press conference, the daily briefing). These structural elements condition the news product.[101]

Even with the best of intentions, the journalist cannot be guided always by a truly objective standard or an exact test for determining what is important. Recording market fluctuations, births and deaths, baseball scores, and election results requires no wizardry. But the reader will usually want to know how the market will behave tomorrow, or which candidate is likely to win, or how he or she managed to prevail. As for foreign reporting, as Bernard Cohen pointed out a generation ago,

> the subject matter . . . has become so complex that most people do not understand the news unless the bare facts about developments are clothed with explicit statements of their significance.[102]

These matters, Lippmann noted, fall under the journalist's own discretion.

> And the more he understands his own weaknesses, the more ready he is to admit that where there is no objective test, his own opinion is in some vital measure constructed out of his own stereotypes, according to his own code, and by the urgency of his own interest.[103]

Thus, even in the absence of overtly commercial criteria—"selling papers," the "ratings"—the news generally brings to our attention only those "events" which take a conventional form, which conform to the journalist's idea of relevance, often a stereotypical one. Even in the rare case when the journalist has been assigned to a particular beat long enough to acquire expertise (and perhaps to transcend his own prejudices), his decisions are also subject to the judgment of editors as to what will interest the readers. That means his news decisions are also subject to the conventions, customs, prejudices, and pressures of the opinionmakers and of society at large.

But does all this signify that "news is myth" as Koch argues or that "objectivity is a myth," as one well-placed young reporter, Kerry Gruson, announced in 1969?[104] Does the ideal of objectivity, as Tuchman argued, produce only an illusory "web of facticity" that camouflages and legitimates the structure of power? Is it, at best, as Schudson avers, a "response" to the "relativism, the arbitrariness of values, a sense of the 'hollow silence' of modernity"?[105]

While recognizing the ideological and structural limitations of the news—"news and truth are not the same thing, and must be clearly distinguished" — Lippmann never degraded news to the status of "myth."[106] He understood its signal and objective role in a modern commercial economy and a modern democratic polity. The code of objectivity is not objectivity itself. To his daughter Kerry's proclamation that objectivity was "a myth," Sidney Gruson, the assistant to the publisher of the *New York Times* in Markel's day, conceded that "pure objectivity might not exist." But, he insisted, "you have to strive for it anyway."[107] To draw an analogy from philosophy, conceptual relativity—the fact that we have different systems of representation (languages, philosophies)—in no way refutes the independent objectivity of external reality or discharges the responsibility of attempting to depict it.[108]

Preconceptions

"The major obstacle to objectivity in contemporary American journalism," it has been argued, "is not unyielding partisanship but unavoidable preconceptions."[109] In Gans's view those preconceptions are unavoidable because:

> Values enter the news most pervasively in the form of reality judgments, the assumptions about external reality associated with the concepts which the journalists use to grasp it.[110]

"Many reality judgments," Gans continues, "are stereotypes."[111] Gans devised the locution "paraideology" to depict that aspect of the news which embodies or reflects ideology, values and normative beliefs. Whereas "ideology" suggested, to Gans, something systematic and doctrinaire, "paraideology" is "only partially thought-out," an elastic and sometimes inconsistent "aggregate of values and reality judgments."[112]

Gans believes that his notion of paraideology "bears some resemblance to what Thomas Kuhn has called the dominant paradigm in the sciences."[113] But Gans's "paraideology" stands closer to Lippmann's "pattern of stereotypes" or "system of stereotypes" than to Kuhn's concept.[114] As Gans acknowledges, it was Walter Lippmann who first pointed out that "news depends on and reinforces stereotypes."[115]

As the term suggests, Lippmann's "system of stereotypes" implied a *relationship* among stereotypes. The stereotypes form part of an ideology, like patches in a quilt which form a pattern. In Phillip Converse's terms the individual items are "constrained" in a "belief system."[116] Ideology functions as if it were "a logically or quasilogically interrelated system of ideas."[117] But ideologies inhabit a realm not of truth or science but of attitude and opinion. They reflect the *zeitgeist* or "the climate of opinion."[118] Which is not to say that stereotypes may not contain more than "a grain of truth."

Wittgenstein might have said that there was a "family resemblance" among ideologies, paraideologies, belief systems, world pictures, systems of stereotypes, and paradigms: a "network of similarities, overlapping and crisscrossing."[119] These loose organizations of moral and cognitive elements combine, like religious symbols, a world view and an ethos. As "cultural symbolsystems," they function as "templates," "extrinsic sources of information." And, as Clifford Geertz points out,

> they come most crucially into play in situations where the particular kind of information they contain is lacking, where institutionalized guides for behavior, thought or feeling are weak or absent. It is in country unfamiliar emotionally or topographically that one needs poems and road maps.[120]

For our purposes "system of stereotypes" and "paradigm" will be employed almost interchangeably. Paradigm is used in its root sense, with only glancing notice of Kuhn's application of the term to the philosophy of science. There was, as the Nicaraguan election results showed, little scientific about the reporting that derived from the paradigm we are examining. Here paradigm signals "model" or "pattern." (To illustrate the basic underlying meaning of the term "paradigm" Kunh notes that in grammar "hablo, hablas, habla" is " a paradigm because it displays the pattern to be used in conjugating a large number of other [Spanish] verbs."[121])

By the same token we shall utilize the concept of a "media frame" apart from its questionable ideological and epistemological affiliations, discussed above. By examining earlier Nicaragua coverage, we identify and analyze what Gitlin calls the "hegemonic frame" which governed reporting on the Nicaraguan elections a decade later.[122] That is:

> By looking closely at that coverage, we can discover the original frames and watch them hardening into the taken-for-granted conventional wisdom, the hegemonic definitions of how things are.[123]

Notes

1. Lionel Trilling, *Beyond Culture* (New York: Viking, 1965), xii-xiii. On the adversarial culture as a mass phenomenon, see Daniel Bell, *The Cultural Contradictions of Capitalism* (New York: Basic Books, 1976), 40-41, 123.

2. David H. Weaver and G. Cleveland Wilhoit, *The American Journalist* (Bloomington, Indiana: Indiana University, 1991), 43; see also William R. Lindley, *Journalism and Higer Education: The Search for Academic Purpose* (Stillwater, Oklahoma: Journalistic Services, 1975).

3. Michael Schudson, *Discovering the News: A Social History of American Newspapers* (New York: Basic Books, 1978), 218, fn. 52. Besides the books mentioned in the text immediately below, see *inter alia* David L. Altheide, *Creating Reality: How TV News Distorts Events* (Beverly Hills: Sage, 1976); Lou Cannon, *Reporting: An Inside View* (Sacramento: California Journal, 1977); Stanley Cohen and Jock Young, eds., *The Manufacture of News: A Reader* (London: Constable, 1973, and Beverly Hills: Sage, 1973); Stuart Hall, "Culture, the Media, and the 'Ideological Effect,'" in *Mass Communication and Society*, ed. James Curran, Michael Gurevitch, and Janet Woollacott (London: Edward Arnold in association with the Open University Press, 1977); Edward J. Epstein, *News from Nowhere* (New York: Random House, 1973); Epstein, *Between Fact and Fiction: The Problem of Journalism* (New York: Vintage, 1975); Bernard Roshco, *Newsmaking* (Chicago: University of Chicago, 1975); Gaye Tuchman, ed., *The TV Establishment* (Englewood Cliffs, New Jersey: Prentice Hall, 1974); P. H. Weaver, "Newspaper News and Television News," in *Television as Social Force: New Approaches to TV Criticism*, ed. D. Cater and R. Adler (New York: Praeger, 1975).

4. Herbert Gans, *Deciding What's News* (New York: Vintage, 1980), 42; Leon V. Sigal, *Reporters and Officials: The Organization of Politics and Newsmaking* (Lexington, Massachusetts: D. C. Heath, 1973), 70.

5. Tuchman, *Making News: A Study in the Construction of Reality* (New York: Free Press, 1978), 216.

6. Todd Gitlin, *The Whole World is Watching* (Berkeley: University of California, 1980); Tom Koch, *The News as Myth* (Westport, Connecticut: Greenwood, 1990), 20; see also Allan Rachlin, *News as Hegemonic Reality* (New York: Praeger, 1988), 13; and Stephen Ansolabehere, Roy Behr, and Shanto Iyengar, *The Media Game: American Politics in the Television Age* (New York: Macmillan, 1993), 146.

7. Gans, *Deciding What's News*, 65, 66.

8. Gans, *Deciding What's News*, 42-43.

9. Gans, *Deciding What's News*, 37.

Gans's own "paraideology" may be illustrated by his complaint that the American-centered coverage by U.S. news organizations paid little attention to the "successes" of Soviet Russia and to détente between the United States and the U.S.S.R., instead featuring "in great detail Soviet violations of civil liberties, the ill-treatment of Jews and intellectuals, or the protest activities of dissidents. Since these phenomena are interpreted as signs of government weakness or immorality, the victims of Russian totalitarianism are treated as heroes or martyrs; and unlike American dissidents, Soviet dissidents are always reported favorably" (Gans *Deciding What's News*, 33).

10. Gans, *Deciding What's News*, 34
11. Gans, *Deciding What's News*, 43.
12. Gans, *Deciding What's News*, 42.
13. Gans, *Deciding What's News*, 37.
14. Gans, *Deciding What's News*, xi-xii.
15. Gans, *Deciding What's News*, 4.
16. Gans, *Deciding What's News*, 145.
17. Gans, *Deciding What's News*, 19, 145, citing Sigal 1973: table 6-5, 124.
18. Sigal, *Reporters and Officials*, 120.
19. Sigal, *Reporters and Officials*, table 6-11, 129 (*my calculations*).
20. Sigal, *Reporters and Officials*, 129.
21. See Schudson, *Discovering the News*, chapter 5; S. Robert Lichter, Stanley Rothman, and Linda S. Lichter, *The Media Elite* (Bethesda, Maryland: Adler and Adler, 1986), 142-48.
22. House of Representatives, Committee on Government Operations, *Availability of Information from Federal Departments and Agencies*, part I (hearings before a subcommittee) November 7, 1955: 25, cited in Schudson, *Discovering the News*, 216, fn. 14.
23. For a view of journalistic objectivity consistent with the approach of this volume, see Stephen Klaidman and Tom L. Beauchamp, *The Virtuous Journalist* (New York: Oxford, 1987), 32-56, esp. 44-50.
24. Lewis Lapham, "Gilding the News," *Harper's* (July 1981): 35, as cited in Lichter, Rothman, and Lichter, *Media Elite*, 147.
25. Sigal, *Reporters and Officials*, 68.
26. Schudson, *Discovering the News*, 161, citing Kerry Gruson; see also Michael Parenti, *Inventing Reality: The Politics of the News Media*, 2d edition (New York: St. Martin's, 1993), 51; and Koch, *News as Myth*.
27. Bernard C. Cohen, *The Press and Foreign Policy* (Princeton, New Jersey: Princeton University, 1963), 51.
28. See Fred S. Siebert, "The Libertarian Theory of the Press," in *Four Theories of the Press*, ed. Fred Siebert, Theodore Peterson, and Wilbur Schramm (Urbana: Univeristy of Illinois, 1956), 60-61; Theodore Peterson, "The Social Responsibility of the Press," in *Four Theories of the Press*, 88; Sigal, *Reporters and Officials*, 66; Schudson, *Discovering the News*; Bernard A. Weisberger, *The American Newspaperman* (Chicago: University of Chicago, 1961), 89 & chapters 3-4; Elmer Davis, *History of the New York Times* (New York: New York Times, 1921).
29. Theodore Edward Kruglak, *The Foreign Correspondents: A Study of the Men and Women Reporting for the American Information Media in Western Europe* (Geneva: Librairie E. Droz, 1955; reprinted Westport, Connecticut: Greenwood Press, 1974), 11.
30. Schudson, *Discovering the News*, 161.
31. Schudson, *Discovering the News*, 160; see also Lichter, Rothman, and Lichter, *Media Elite*, 142-43.
32. Sigal, *Reporters and Officials*, 2.
33. Ben Bagdikian, *The Media Monopoly* (Boston: Beacon, 1983), 181-82.
34. Parenti, *Inventing Reality*, 51.
35. Gitlin, *Whole World*, 6.
36. Tuchman, 1978: chapters v, x, and 160-61.
37. Tuchman, "Objectivity as Strategic Ritual," *American Journal of Sociology* (January 1972): 660-79.

38. Andrew Arno and Wimal Dissarayake, eds., *The News Media in National and International Conflict* (Boulder: Westview, 1984), 7, 9.

39. Robert M. Entman, *Democracy without Citizens* (New York: Oxford, 1989), 37.

40. Tuchman, *Making News: A Study in the Construction of Reality* (New York: Free Press, 1978), 1.

41. Gitlin, *Whole World*, 6; Tuchman, *Making News*, 182; see also Koch, *News as Myth*, 19 ff.

42. Gitlin, *Whole World*, 7.

43. Gitlin, *Whole World*, 7.

44. Koch, *News as Myth*, 20 (Koch was a Kiplinger Scholar in Public Affairs Journalism at Ohio State University); see also Rachlin, *News as Hegemonic Reality*, 13. Tuchman and Gitlin and the other innovators of this critique were strongly influenced by the sociological theorist Erving Goffman. Tuchman tell us, "I have tried to take Goffman's work to its logical conclusion." (Tuchman, *Making News*, 216; see also Gitlin, *Whole World*, 6; Tuchman, *Making News*, 7; and Erving Goffman, *Frame Analysis* (Boston: Northeastern, 1986).

45. Tuchman, *Making News*, 7 n.; Goffman, *Frame Analysis*, 10-11.

46. Tuchman, *Making News*, 14.

47. Dan Schiller, *Objectivity and the News* (Philadelphia: University of Pennsylvania, 1981), 196.

48. Koch, *News as Myth*, 29.

49. Tuchman, *Making News*, 216.

50. Christopher Lasch, *Revolt of the Elites* (New York: Norton, 1995), 20.

51. Immanuel Kant, *Critique of Pure Reason*, translated by Norman Kemp Smith (New York: St. Martin's, 1961), B70, 275, 89, 244. V. I. Lenin would have called their denial of the "objective content of experience" a form of "subjectivism" and a "reactionary philosophy." See V. I. Lenin, *Materialism and Empiro-Criticism: Critical Comments on a Reactionary Philosophy*, vol. xiv of *Collected Works of V. I. Lenin* (Moscow: Foreign Language Publishing House, 1972), vol. xiv, 9-30, 135-46. It would be crass—if not entirely unwarranted—to identify the new paradigm with Marxism; to call it a precursor of postmodernism would be closer to the mark. Along with William James, Edmund Husserl, Jurgen Habermas, Schutz, and Goffman, Friedrich Nietzsche's radical historicism, Martin Heidegger's existentialist critique of "metaphysics," Feyerabend's attack on science and Western rationalism, Derrida's "deconstructionism," the linguistics of Saussure, Edward Sapir, and B. L. Whorf (which suggests that language shapes the perception of reality), Thomas S. Kuhn's *The Structure of Scientific Revolutions* (Chicago: University of Chicago, Phoenix edition, 1964), and Foucault's genealogy of "the social construction of reality" are equally pertinent modern philosophical sources. An influential application of Schutz, thinking is Peter L. Berger and Thomas Luckmann, *The Social Construction of Reality* (Garden City, New Jersey: Doubleday, 1966).

52. John Searle, *The Construction of Social Reality* (New York: Free Press, 1995), 158.

53. Tuchman, *Making News*, 216; see above.

54. Tuchman, *Making News*, 203-4.

55. Tuchman, *Making News*, 204.

56. Schudson, *Discovering the News*, 188.

57. One Woodward volume dealt with Nicaragua: Bob Woodward, *Veil: The Secret Wars of the CIA* (New York: Simon & Schuster, 1987).

58. Christopher Dickey, *With the Contras: A Reporter in the Wilds of Nicaragua* (New York: Simon & Schuster, 1985); Sam Dillon, *Commandos* (New York: Henry Holt,

1991); Glenn Garvin, *Everybody Has His Own Gringo: The CIA and the Contras* (Washington: Brassey's, 1991).

59. Kiki Adatto, *Picture Perfect: The Art and Artifice of Public Image Making* (New York: Basic Books, 1993), 15. See also Daniel C. Hallin, "Sound Bite News: Television Coverage of Elections," (mimeograph paper, Woodrow Wilson Center for International Scholars, Washington, 1991).

60. Waltraud Queiser Morales, "Revolutions, Earthquakes and Latin America: The Networks Look at Allende's Chile and Somoza's Nicaragua" in *Television Coverage of International Affairs*, ed. William C. Adams (Norwood, New Jersey: Ablex, 1982), 91-92.

61. See Adatto, *Picture Perfect*, chapter 2; and Adatto, "Sound Bite Democracy: Network Evening News Presidential Campaign Coverage, 1968 and 1988," (Research Paper R-2, John F. Kennedy School of Government, Harvard University, June 1990). See also Hallin, "Sound Bite News."

62. Adatto, *Picture Perfect*, 165. For a provocative discussion of these "postmodern" tendencies in the theory and practice of fine arts, see Thomas McEvilley, *Art and Discontent: Theory at the Millennium* (New York: McPherson, 1991).

63. Tuchman, *Making News*, 99.

64. Cohen, *Press and Foreign Policy*, 15-16.

65. When the liberal internationalist consensus broke down over Vietnam, the consensus on press/official relations also dissolved and so did the code of objectivity. The broad bipartisan unity around liberal internationalism decomposed into liberal anti-interventionism on the one hand and neoconservative internationalism on the other; media-government relations became adversarial. Philosophically, objectivity gave way to what has been called alternatively antirealism, relativism, or subjectivism. (For these terms see Searle, *Construction of Social Reality*, 149-97; Alan Bloom, *The Closing of the American Mind* (New York: Simon & Schuster, 1987); Sydney Hook, *et al.*, *On the Barricades: Religion and Free Inquiry in Conflict* (Buffalo, New York: Prometheus, 1989), 127.

66. William Dorman and Mansour Farhang, *The U.S. Press and Iran: Foreign Policy and the Journalism of Deference* (Berkeley: University of California, 1987), 220.

67. Stephen R. MacKinnon and Oris Friesen, *China Reporting: An Oral History of American Journalism in the 1930s and 1940s* (Berkeley: University of California, 1987), 193. For another, more critical perspective on China reporting in this period, see Steven W. Mosher, *China Misperceived: American Illusions and Chinese Realities* (New York: HarperCollins, 1990), 49-69.

68. Patrick O'Heffernan, *Mass Media and American Foreign Policy* (Norwood, New Jersey: Ablex, 1991), 87; James F. Larson makes the contrary case in *Global Television and Foreign Policy* (New York: Foreign Policy Association, 1988).

69. Hallin, *We Keep America on Top of the World: Television Journalism and the Public Sphere* (London: Routledge, 1993), 150.

70. Hallin, *We Keep America*, 147.

71. Hallin, *We Keep America*, 153-54.

72. Hallin, *We Keep America*, 147.

73. See especially Noam Chomsky, *Turning the Tide* (Boston: South End, 1985); *Necessary Illusions* (Toronto: CBC, 1989); and (with Edward S. Herman), *Manufacturing Consent: The Political Economy of the Mass Media* (New York: Pantheon Books, 1988).

74. Martin Middlestaedt, "Is it Really All the News that's Fit to Print?" *Toronto Globe and Mail*, October 8, 1988, D3 (cited in Koch, *News as Myth*, 17).

75. See Chomsky, *American Power and the New Mandarins* (New York: Pantheon, 1969) and Chomsky and Herman, *After the Cataclysm* (Boston: South End, 1979), 29.

76. Robert Sahr, "Credentialing Experts: The Climate of Opinion and Journalist Selection of Sources in Domestic and Foreign Policy," in *Media and Public Policy*, ed. Robert J. Spitzer (Westport, Connecticut: Praeger, 1993), 163.

77. Chomsky, *Turning the Tide*, 137; see also Chomsky and Herman, *Manufacturing Consent*, 117, 140.

78. Sahr, "Credentialing Experts," 162.

79. Jack Spence, "The U.S. Media: Covering (Over) Nicaragua," in *Reagan versus the Sandinistas*, ed. Thomas W. Walker (Boulder: Westview, 1987), 199.

80. Spence, "U.S. Media," 203; see also Chomsky, "U.S. Policy and Society: The Lessons of Nicaragua," in *Reagan versus the Sandinistas*, 292.

81. *The Listener* (February 26, 1987) in Chomsky, *Culture of Terrorism*, 207.

82. Chomsky, "U.S. Policy and Society."

83. Chomsky, "U.S. Policy and Society," 290.

84. Walker, "Introduction," in *Nicaragua: The First Five Years*, ed. Walker (Westport, Connecticut: Praeger, 1985), 22.

85. Walker, "Introduction," 23-24.

86. Walker, "Introduction," 24.

87. John A. Booth and Thomas W. Walker, *Understanding Central America* (Boulder: Westview, 1989), 66.

88. Booth and Walker, *Understanding Central America*, 106.

89. Booth, *The End and the Beginning: The Nicaraguan Revolution*, 1st edition (Boulder: Westview, 1982), 116-20. In the footnotes to his account of the period, Anthony Lake, the Carter administration State Department's Director of Policy Planning (later Bill Clinton's National Security Adviser), writes that Booth's book was "the best account . . . of events in Nicaragua throughout 1978-79." In his conclusion he adds that "most of the data here about the Nicaraguan revolution is drawn from [Booth's] excellent study" (Anthony Lake, *Somoza Falling* [Boston: Houghton Mifflin, 1989], 298, 301).

90. Donald C. Hodges, *Intellectual Foundations of the Nicaraguan Revolution* (Austin: University of Texas, 1986). 194-95. Hodges is citing Walker and Booth in particular.

91. Hodges, *Intellectual Foundations*, 264-68; 161 ff; Dennis Gilbert, *Sandinistas* (Oxford: Basil Blackwell, 1990). Hodges himself believed that both Fidel Castro and the Sandinistas adopted an "ideologically enriched Marxism." In the end, "Sandinismo is Sandino's revolutionary legacy impregnated with the new Marxism" (Hodges, *Intellectual Foundations*, 176, 196). But Hodges own research shows just the opposite. Sandino was rehabilitated by the group of dissident communists, Marxist-Leninists impatient with the Communist PSN's tactics and impatient to conquer power through violence. Hodges confuses the Cuban and Sandinista rejection of the "reformist" policies of the traditional Latin American Communist parties with a repudiation of orthodox Leninism.

92. Booth and Walker, *Understanding Central America*, 129.

93. Booth and Walker, *Understanding Central America*, 129.

94. Schudson, *Discovering the News*, 18. See also Frank Luther Mott, *American Journalism*, revised edition (New York: Macmillan, 1950), 215; and Henry King, *American Journalism* (New York: Arno, 1970), 5-6.

95. Schudson, *Discovering the News*, 22.

96. Schiller, *Objectivity and the News*, 75.

97. Davis, *History of the New York Times*, 198-200.

98. Davis, *History of the New York Times*, 389; Weaver and Wilhoit, *American Journalist*, 8; see Ronald Steel, *Walter Lippmann and the American Century* (Boston: Little, Brown and Company, 1980), 171-81.

99. Walter Lippmann, *Public Opinion* (New York: Macmillan, 1922; revised edition, New York: Free Press, 1965), 320.

100. Lippmann, *Public Opinion*, 364.

101. Lippmann, *Public Opinion*, 127; Tuchman, *Making News*, chapter II.

102. Cohen, *Press and Foreign Policy*, 26-27.

103. Lippmann, *Public Opinion*, 359-60.

104. Koch, *News as Myth*; Schudson, *Discovering the News*, 161.

105. Schudson, *Origins of the Ideal of Objectivity in the Professions* (New York: Garland, 1990), 269.

106. Lippmann, *Public Opinion*, 358.

107. Schudson, *Origins of the Ideal of Objectivity*, 161.

108. For an extensive discussion of this point, see Searle, *Construction of Social Reality*, 151, 160-67.

109. Lichter, Rothman, and Lichter, *Media Elite*, 63.

110. Gans, *Deciding What's News*, 201.

111. Gans, *Deciding What's News*, 201.

112. Gans, *Deciding What's News*, 68.

113. Gans, *Deciding What's News*, 68.

114. Lippmann, *Public Opinion*, 96, 119. Whatever its value for the history of science, Kuhn himself hardly endorsed transporting his theory of paradigms from the natural to the social sciences. Kuhn's paradigm was "a set of recurrent and quasi-standard illustrations of standard theories in their conceptual, observational, and instrumental applications" whose revolutionary renovation was "the usual developmental pattern of mature science" (Kuhn, *Structure of Scientific Revolutions*, 43, 10, 12). For Kuhn the appearance of paradigms signaled the emergence, after considerable fact-gathering and discussion of a relatively "mature discipline" (Kuhn, *Structure of Scientific Revolutions*, 10-15). Kuhn considered it "an open question what parts of social science have acquired such paradigms at all" (Kuhn, *Structure of Scientific Revolutions*, 15). Nonetheless, it soon became fashionable for social scientists to invoke Kuhn's paradigms. In our case, Gans's "paraideology" more closely resembles what Kuhn called "preparadigm schools" made up of "beliefs and preconceptions" (Kuhn, *Structure of Scientific Revolutions*, 17).

115. Gans, *Deciding What's News*, 201; see Lippmann, *Public Opinion*, part III.

As Elisabeth Noelle-Neuman pointed out, Lippmann was the first to examine "what journalists consider 'news values' in their selection," thereby "anticipating a major research branch of the science of communication in the fifties, sixties, and seventies" (Noelle-Neumann, *The Spiral of Silence* [Chicago: University of Chicago, 1984], 220).

The debts of modern media scholars to Lippmann sometimes go unacknowledged. One illustration: Todd Gitlin does not cite the inventor of the phrase and concept "manufacture of consent" either in his text or in his "Selected Bibliography." Gitlin seems to borrow directly from Lippmann in passages which begin "People directly know only tiny regions of social life," and "The media bring a manufactured public world into private space." (Gitlin, *Whole World*, 1-2). Compare these passages with those in Lippmann's *Public Opinion* which begins "Each of us lives and works on a small part of the earth's surface, moves in a small circle," and "For the most part we do not first see, and then define," and "That the manufacture of consent is capable of great refinements." (Lippmann, *Public Opinion*, 79, 125, 248).

116. Phillip E. Converse, "The Nature of Belief Systems in Mass Publics," in *Ideology and Discontent*, ed. David E. Apter (New York: Free Press, 1964), 206-7.

117. Everett C. Ladd, Jr. and Seymour Martin Lipset, *The Divided Academy: Professors and Politics* (New York: McGraw-Hill, 1975), 38; and Converse, "The Nature of Belief Systems," 210-11 For other relevant discussions of ideology see Karl Mannheim, *Ideology and Utopia* (New York: Harcourt Brace, 1985), 55-97; Clifford Geertz, "Ethos, World View and the Analysis of Sacred Symbols" in *The Interpretation of Cultures*, ed. Clifford Geertz (New York: Basic Books, 1973), 126-41; Geertz, "Ideology as a Cultural System" in *Interpretation of Cultures*, 193-233; Francis Fukuyama, "The Primacy of Culture," *Journal of Democracy* (January 1995): 7-8; *Selections from the Prison Notebooks of Antonio Gramsci*, eds. Quintin Hoare and Geoffrey Nowell Smith (New York: International Publishers, 1971), 323-77; Louis Althusser, *For Marx* (London: Allen Lane, 1969; and New York: Pantheon, 1969), 49-86, 164-75, 182-93, 231-36, 252; Althusser, "Ideology and Ideological State Apparatuses," in *Lenin and Philosophy* (New York: Monthly Review, 1971), 127-87; Althusser, *Essays in Self-Criticism* (London: New Left Books, 1976), 153-56; Althusser and Etienne Balibar, *Reading Capital* (New York: Pantheon, 1976), 125-44; Jurgen Habermas, *Toward a Rational Society* (Boston: Beacon, 1970), 95-101; Alvin W. Gouldner, *The Dialectic of Ideology and Technology* (New York: Oxford University, 1982), 3-90, 210-28; Samuel P. Huntington, "Conservatism as an Ideology," *The American Political Science Review*, vol. LI, no. 2 (June 1957): 454-73; David W. Minar, "Ideology and Political Behavior, *Midwest Journal of Political Science*, vol. V, no. 4 (November 1961): 317-31; Ladd, *Ideology in America: Change and Response in a City, a Suburb, and a Small Town* (New York: Norton, 1972), 6-8; Arthur O. Lovejoy, "The Historiography of Ideas," in *Essays in the History of Ideas* (New York: Capricorn, 1960), 1-13. See also Karl Marx and Frederick Engels, *The German Ideology: Collected Works*, vol. 5 (New York: International Publishers, 1976), 28-48, 59-62; Engels, "Letters to C. Schmidt and F. Mehring," in Marx and Engels, *Selected Works*, vol. II (Moscow: Foreign Language Publishing House, 1958), 486-88, 490-99; Lesek Kolakowski, *Main Currents of Marxism*, vol. I (Oxford: Oxford University, 1987), 153-55; Vaclac Havel, *Living in Truth* (London: Faber and Faber, 1989), 37-40; Max Weber, *The Protestant Ethic and the Rise of Protestantism* (New York: Scribner, 1958); Benedetto Croce, *History of Europe in the Nineteenth Century* (New York: Harbinger, 1963), 3-19; Ron Rosenbaum, *Explaining Hitler* (New York: Random House, 1998), 288).

118. Alfred North Whitehead, *Science and the Modern World* (New York: Macmillan, 1925), 4-5; and Mannheim, *Ideology and Utopia*, 1985: 55-56. For another modern usage of "climate of opinion," see Carl Becker, *The Heavenly City of the Eighteenth Century Philosophers* (New Haven, Connecticut: Yale University, 1965), chapter I; and Peter Gay's critique in *The Party of Humanity: Essays in French Enlightenment* (New York: Knopf, 1964), 191-93.

119. Ludwig Wittgenstein, *Philosophical Investigations* (New York: Macmillan, 1989), 31-32.

120. *The Interpretation of Cultures*, 218; see also 126-27.

121. Cf. Kuhn, *Structure of Scientific Revolutions*, 23.

122. Gitlin, *Whole World*, 51.

123. Gitlin, *Whole World*, 303.

Chapter 5
An "All-American-Style Election"

"It is a star-spangled all-American-style election" NBC's Ed Rabel told viewers of the *Today* show from Managua, voicing-over "campaign visuals."

> See the candidate autograph the baseball, see him toss it to the crowd [Ortega autographing and tossing]. See him hug the baby [Ortega hugging]. Watch the other candidate give the victory sign [Chamorro]. Watch the masses roar their approval.[1]

The U.S. television networks presented the 1990 Nicaraguan election campaign as they had grown accustomed to presenting American campaigns—as a succession of artful, self-conscious media performances.[2] This orientation, akin to postmodernist philosophical trends mentioned in the previous chapter, led many reporters to a false and fatal assumption. Even print journalists, such as the *San Francisco Chronicle* correspondent, assumed that for "both sides . . . the crux of their popular appeal lies with the medium rather than the message."[3]

If media sophistication was the crucial element, the conclusion was foregone. A month before the vote, the *Washington Post*'s chief corrspondent, Lee Hockstader, citing unnamed "analysts," pronounced that a Sandinista victory was assured by virtue of their "huge financial edge and superior political instincts." The opposition had been "outsmarted, outmanned, and outspent by the well-organized Sandinistas."[4] The Sandinistas agreed: "It's a populist, media image campaign that has worked on all levels," their spokesman, Paul Oquist, told Hockstader as the campaign drew to a close. "It was put together by research, the way it's done in the United States or France."[5]

By contrast the National Opposition Union [UNO] campaign was poorly organized even by Nicaraguan standards, not to mention "the way it's done in

the United States or France." Nonetheless, Chamorro's campaign team exuded a
confidence that bemused foreign observers. Citing Ortega's "growing lead" in
the polls, the *Miami Herald* quoted conclusively an "unidentified" U.S. official:

> A lot of the UNO campaign people are convinced that [Nicaraguans] are so fed
> up with the Sandinistas that they are condemned to win . . . I think that's wish-
> ful thinking.[6]

The opposition was pursuing what seemed a hopelessly passé campaign
strategy. UNO did not seek to match the Sandinistas onslaught of TV advertising, billboards, direct mail, and giveaways. Instead the opposition concentrated
on training sufficient poll watchers to expose fraud and on getting their candidate to as many towns as possible. The opposition believed that the key to success was neither the medium nor the message but overcoming the voters' hesi-
tance to cast an opposition ballot. "We had to convince them that their vote is
secret," said Alfredo Cesar, a former *Contra* leader advising the Chamorro campaign. "We had to get them to lose their fear of the dictatorship."

> It is difficult to lose your fear watching a TV ad. But seeing Doña Violeta
> challenge the (Sandinista) Front in your town makes you lose fear.[7]

Accordingly many UNO strategists regarded the modern American campaign paraphernalia as irrelevant. Acknowledging *post hoc* the accuracy of the
UNO "referendum" analysis, Hockstader recalled that UNO strategists had told
him that anti-Sandinista sentiment ran so deep that it "could not be erased with
words . . . no matter how glitzy the Sandinista campaign."[8] For the opposition,
the Nicaraguan voter was not a sovereign customer exercising consumer choice.
He was constrained by what pollsters dubbed retrospectively "the fear factor."
Opposition strategists saw their campaign task not in luring fence-sitters, but in
conquering fear.[9]

That theory of the campaign and of the Nicaraguan voter, and the practice
that followed from it, could not have been further from the Sandinista view. The
opposition campaign never gained the attention of the American journalists. The
artful correspondent, who focused on the "American-style" media events in order to send "better pictures" home, was also choosing, albeit often uncon-
sciously, a theory of the campaign, one laden with political implications.

Thus from the outset Americans learned that while opposition candidate
Violeta Barrios de Chamorro "got off to a pathetic start," her rival was nominated "in a splashy party convention" and launched a "surprisingly effective
grass-roots campaign."[10] As the Sandinista campaign climaxed with a parade
through Managua, ABC's Ensor reported over corresponding visuals that the
Ortega campaign

> is slick and sexy. Talking to first time voters, their poster says, "When you do
> it for the first time with love, it's beautiful." And they've hired a popular Co-

lombian rock band to draw a crowd. The message: Daniel Ortega and the
Sandi-nista voters have more fun. Despite the miserable state of this country's
economy . . . voter polls suggest the campaign tactic may be working.[11]

None of the many dispatches reporting the fun-loving *comandante*'s alleged
allure for young voters mentioned that the Ortega government had unilaterally,
and in the face of opposition protests, lowered the traditional voting age from
eighteen to sixteen. The Sandinistas assumed that soldiers in the Sandinista
Popular Army would form a captive voting bloc, especially since the opposition
was barred from campaigning on army bases.[12] As it happened, Ortega ran behind Chamorro in several restricted military voting precincts. American accounts also failed to note that Nicaraguans might resent the lavish campaign
spending by a party presiding over economic collapse. Nor was attention drawn
to the possibility that in this most Catholic of Central American countries some
voters might not welcome invitations to their sixteen-year-olds to "do it for the
first time."[13]
    On the contrary, many journalists found further grounds for skepticism in
Mrs. Chamorro's devout Roman Catholicism. They poked fun at her veneration
of her late husband: "she said she 'consults' with him—as she does with God
and the Virgin Mary."[14] But though such sentiments might have encumbered
American candidates, they were less likely to inflict damage in a country where
the Virgin Mary is ardently venerated, every village commemorates its patron
saint with celebrations lasting for days, relatives commune with their departed in
their prayers, and even the Sandinistas choose to represent their fallen leaders as
martyrs and saints.
    To the American press, the indisputable deficiencies of the Chamorro cam-
paign appeared ruinous. UNO campaign posters were hard to find even in Managua; its television presence was negligible; Chamorro rallies were smaller
than Ortega rallies. In contrast to the pervasive Sandinista presence, UNO was
"practically invisible."[15] During one opposition rally Chamorro's campaign
manager-cum-son-in-law got into a shoving match on the speaker's podium with
her running mate's chief of staff in full view of the appalled audience.[16]
    The problems of the fractious fourteen-party UNO coalition were com-
pounded by government harassment. Equipment as well as funds donated by the
U.S. Congress were delayed for months, often until too late. As an example,
Hockstader cited twenty-two jeeps held up for weeks by the customs director,
who was conveniently out of town. Meanwhile UNO campaign workers bick-
ered over their eventual disposition: "the jeeps are a symbol of the state of
Chamorro's presidential campaign—lacking momentum, tangled in red tape,
beset by squabbles, and paid for by Washington."[17] For Hockstader, all this illustrated how the Sandinistas had "outsmarted" their opponents. It was only
after the elections that a number of journalists concluded that such trickery ("*en-
gaño*") served only to confirm popular suspicions.

***

Many journalists depicted the Sandinista party-cum-government-cum-army combine as a modern Latin version of an American "political machine." Even Mark Uhlig of the *New York Times*, whose election reports generally excelled, wrote that the Sandinistas' "sophisticated favor-granting machinery" was cashing in on Ortega's new "image of excitement and personal celebrity." The *comandante*-turned-candidate was fusing "the language of revolution with the patronage politics of an old-fashioned party boss."[18] American political machines, however, have never enjoyed a government television monopoly or deployed partisan armies and state security agencies.

The Sandinistas made lavish campaign use of government funds, offices, phones, personnel, vehicles, and media.[19] Government television and radio coverage was extravagantly pro-Ortega. The observer mission from the Organization of American States described government broadcasts as filled with "flagrant distortions, derogatory remarks, and misrepresentations."[20] The United Nations observer mission found references to UNO on government news programs "nothing short of slanderous."[21] Thanks to its television monopoly and vastly superior resources, the government party was usually free to assail the opposition as "Somocista" or "Yankee puppets," without fear of much rebuttal from UNO.

Efforts to establish a nongovernmental television channel were rebuffed by the authorities. UNO was allotted twenty minutes per week on the weaker of the two government channels, which was reportedly "unwatchable" even in parts of Managua.[22] Approximately 70 percent of the radio stations were controlled by the government or the FSLN, and the principal government radio stations possessed ten times, and the Sandinista party stations five times, the power of even the most robust private station.[23] Moreover, that private station was forced to suspend UNO campaign advertising at a crucial point of the campaign until UNO could pay its overdue bills. Government red tape and tariffs on outside funding had put UNO in arrears.[24]

Newspapers were the only segment of the media where UNO could compete. Three Sandinista daily newspapers—a new pro-Ortega daily, featuring color photos, was brought out during the campaign—confronted the Chamorros' *La Prensa*. Due to continued high rates of illiteracy despite a much ballyhooed earlier Sandinista "literacy campaign," print was the least effective campaign medium.[25] Moreover, *La Prensa* had certainly seen better days. By election time, it had become as one-sided as its rivals, often yielding to the temptation to sensationalize while maintaining a curious silence about the personal corruption of Sandinista officials. Thanks to shortages and government strictures, *La Prensa* had been reduced to twelve pages while the Sandinista newspapers ranged between eighteen and twenty-four. Many of the best staffers had fled the country, though some returned for the elections. The paper's circulation could not match the Sandinista press which was routinely dispensed *gratis* to state employees, but its sales were greater. Its prestige managed to survive despite regular attacks on the paper in the Sandinista press as "the organ of the National Guard and the CIA."

Nicaragua's most visible campaign poster read "GN-1," or [Somoza's] National Guard-UNO.[26] The few posters the opposition could muster were systematically removed by Sandinista militants. For the large number of Nicaraguans who worked in state enterprises, or counted on government credits, refusing to attend Sandinista rallies could mean an army call up or the loss of job or land in "a country where the government holds the keys to everything from college scholarships to bank loans."[27]

A *Los Angeles Times* editorialist, like many journalists, commentators, and area specialists, equated Sandinista campaign "irregularities" with those of "incumbent governments . . . all over the world." To the American reader, what Hockstader of the *Washington Post* called "the Sandinista's edge as an incumbent party" might suggest a congressman abusing his "franking privilege," or, at worst, behavior that, according to a *Los Angeles Times* editorial, "may not have been any more irregular—and perhaps less—than the kind common not so very long ago in underdeveloped places like Cook County, Illinois."[28] How many readers would be helped by that analogy to imagine the kind of encounter described in the following William Branigin *Post* dispatch?

> [T]hree armed state security agents . . . threatened, among other reprisals, to confiscate [an UNO supporter's] land after the elections unless he withdrew as a poll watcher.[29]

"Incumbency" denotes a regime characterized by alternation of power, impermanence in office, separation of powers and the rule of law, not one whose police, military, and security forces were controlled by a dominant party. In this light the real differences between the Nicaraguan and American campaigns were hinted at in a Uhlig piece surmising "that the election may come down to a test of strength between the Sandinistas' impressive political machinery and opposition voters acting largely on their own."[30]

***

The American press discovered, not for the first time, a new "moderate" and "pragmatic" Sandinista man. "Perhaps the most striking aspect of the campaign" for Uhlig was *comandante* Ortega's evolution "from an unsmiling, often strident revolutionary leader to a polished, upbeat political performer" and a "teen idol." The *Post*'s Hockstader found "a kinder, gentler Daniel Ortega."[31] No journalist saw in this "transformation" signs of a budding personality cult or of the union of family and party that had attended the middle-age of Third World revolutionary vanguards in Vietnam, North Korea, Romania, Iraq, and Cuba. Nor did reports discern echoes and omens of the dynasticism that had marked Nicaraguan history.[32]

For the American journalist naked eye and scientific survey alike seemed to corroborate Sandinista success. The ubiquitous Ortega television commercials, signboards, banners, posters, and T-shirts, the offices in almost every city and town, the banners and flags on public buildings, the Sandinista graffiti sprayed, willy-nilly, on private homes, the massive and ardent rallies, the polls and supporting survey statistics, led inescapably to *USA Today*'s conclusion that "Ortega . . . is wildly popular here."[33]

In querying liberal Democratic Congressman Steven Solarz who returned from a visit to Nicaragua just before the elections, Public Broadcasting's Robert MacNeil summarized the then conventional view:

> What do you say Congressman to the many reports that I have seen that in this election . . . whatever his past reputation and whatever he may have done, . . . Daniel Ortega himself has run a brilliant campaign; that he has changed his image and that he has moved away from Marxism Leninism, that he is extremely flexible and that he has become a really American style candidate and just run a good campaign?[34]

Solarz, who had come back with the unconventional view that Ortega would lose, replied that "one of the mistakes that American journalists and political analysts are making is to apply American political constructs to Nicaraguan realities." That might sound familiar, but Solarz was sounding a different chord in the critique of ethnocentrism:

> In our country, where the differences between candidates are often quite marginal, money and organization can indeed make the difference. But in a country like Nicaragua, where the Sandinistas have been running the show for ten years, where they have had 37,000 percent inflation, where young men are dragooned from their homes or shanghaied off street corners in order to serve in the army, where people are thrown in jail for criticizing the government, where the Church in the most Catholic country in Central America has been continually harassed, I think that people have pretty much made up their minds.[35]

Solarz had put his finger on the very point that the U.S. media so often ignored. The choice in Nicaragua was not between personalities or campaign styles, or even about where the candidates "came down on" a few determinate "issues." It was a choice between regimes.

A CBS report by Juan Vasquez reflected the media's own very different assumption. The report accented the judgment of former Sandinista official Father Xavier Gorostiaga that:

> This country had ten years of a real ideological fight. These elections are anti-ideological.[36]

In other words, the elections would be, in Fidel Castro's famous phrase, "within the Revolution." Or, to echo a refrain from the 1988 American presidential campaign, these elections were "about competence not ideology." In this view the contest was about the qualifications of the candidates, not the nature of the government. That formulation was exactly what UNO officials challenged in asserting that the elections were a "referendum" or a "plebiscite on Sandinista rule."[37]

Was Solarz warranted in asserting that the "journalists and political analysts" were mechanically applying "American political constructs?" If so, they were guilty of the very ethnocentrism so many of them deplored. The journalists and analysts might have concurred with the congressman that between Ortega and Chamorro there was a difference in principle, but in their view it was precisely that difference which condemned Chamorro to defeat. Indeed, many believed that Nicaraguans saw things quite differently even from relatively enlightened Americans like Mr. Solarz—undoubtably insufficiently purged of ethnocentrism. But, then, if Nicaragua was so different, and ethnocentrism such a danger, why present the Nicaraguan campaign as if it were taking place in the United States?

The ironies abound: anti-imperialist Sandinistas running "an American-style" campaign, anti-ethnocentric journalists presenting it in American terms and pictures, with apparent contempt for Nicaraguan culture and customs. The Nicaraguan elections tested the assumptions of the new American intelligentsia.

Here is a relevant definition of "ethnocentrism" from a collection widely cited in the anti-Vietnam war movement:

When William Graham Sumner published his classic *Folkways* in 1906, he coined the term 'ethnocentrism.' He defined it as the tendency of every group or nation to nourish its own vanity, boast its own superiority, exalt its own divinities, and to look with contempt on outsiders. A modern form of ethnocentrism is to deny the relevance, or even the existence, of the historical experience of peoples with which we become involved.[38]

One aspect of the coverage had an indisputably ethnocentric caste. In the course of demonstrating the reduction in the size of the typical "sound-bite" from actual campaign speeches in recent television coverage of American election campaigns, Kiki Adatto observed:

As television news has grown impatient with political speech in recent years, it has become preoccupied with political image-making, with the efforts by campaigns to produce pictures that will play on the evening news.[39]

This transformation of political reporting into theater criticism not only set the tone of American television coverage of elections at home, but in the case of our foreign election the similar preoccupation with the formal and technical aspects of the campaign, with "image" versus "message," was as pronounced in print as in television. The space between theater and reality, between art and life, is being narrowed, almost as if in illustration of the theories of Goffmann, Tuchman, and the other precursors of postmodernism. The weakening of this distinction flows from the notion that "objectivity" is itself a Western, ethnocentric construct.

Notes

1. *NBC Today*, February 22, 1990.

2. See Kiki Adatto, *Picture Perfect: The Art and Artifice of Public Image Making* (New York: Basic Books, 1993), 24-27, and Adatto, "Sound Bite Democracy: Network Evening News Presidential Campaign Coverage, 1968 and 1988," (Research Paper R-2, John F. Kennedy School of Government, Harvard University, June 1990), 6-7. See also Daniel C. Hallin, "Sound Bite News: Television Coverage of Elections," (mimeograph paper, Woodrow Wilson Center for International Scholars, Washington, 1991), 29. Accordingly, NBC's Rabel would narrate over "media events" displaying President Ortega dancing and jogging *ad modum* Bush or Dukakis; Daniel Ortega on the campaign trail; Ortega the marathon runner; Ortega in designer jeans and wildly patterned shirts (*NBC Nightly News*, February 23, 1990). Employing the same technique, ABC's David Ensor would accent the efficacy of Ortega's "new-age political marketing and image making" (*ABC World News*, February 2, 1990).

3. Robert Collier, "More Medium Than Message in Nicaragua: Ortega and Chamorro Campaigns Pit *Machismo* vs. Virginity," *SFC*, February 21, 1990, A14.

4. Hockstader, "Nicaraguan Opposition: Outsmarted and Outspent," *WP*, January 25, 1990, A29.

5. Hockstader, "Crowds Cheer Nicaraguan Opposition: Anti-Sandinista Coalition Holds Final Election Rally in Managua," *WP*, February 19, 1990, A1.

6. Christopher Marquis, "Sandinista Hits Election Stride as Foe Falters," *MH*, January 28, 1990, A1.

7. Richard Boudreaux, "Political Novice Winding Up Bid to Dislodge Daniel Ortega," *LAT*, February 19, 1990, A18.

8. Hockstader, "Chamorro Issues Call for Reconciliation," *WP*, February 27, 1990, A1, A19.

9. Author's interviews with UNO candidate Violeta Chamorro, campaign manager Antonio Lacayo, and press spokesman Ernesto Palazio, November 1989, New York City. Author's interviews with Ernesto Palazio, February 24, 1990 and June 18, 1993, Washington, D.C., and with Roger Guevara Mena, UNO advisor and president of the Nicaraguan Bar Association, January 23, February 14, and February 21, 1990.

10. "Playing Politics with Peace: Headed toward Elections, Ortega Blows His Cool," *Time*, November 13, 1989, 49.

11. *ABC World News Tonight*, February 21, 1990.

12. Author's interview with Major Roger Miranda Bengoechea, former chief of the Nicaraguan Defense Ministry Secretariat, May 1989.

13. Journalists did acknowledge some of these complications after the elections. For example:

> By massively outspending UNO, distributing thousands of "Daniel for President" T-shirts and caps, and plastering his image on billboards across the country, the Sandinistas might have alienated poor voters who viewed the campaign as a waste of money (Miller and

Boudreaux, "Sandinistas Conclude They Lost Touch With Populace," *LAT*, March 4, 1990, A12).

The eminent Peruvian novelist Mario Vargas Llosa wrote that Nicaragua was "one of the most Catholic countries I know" (*NYTM*, April 28, 1985, 45). Humberto Belli, a former Sandinista and editor of *La Prensa* and later Minister of Education in the Chamorro government, had a similiar view: "Nicaragua, according to many observers, is one of the most religious countries in Latin America. . . . In some ways, Nicaragua resembles Poland, where Catholic faith is also deeply rooted in the lives and traditions of the people" (Belli, *Breaking Faith* [Garden City, Michigan: Puebla Institute, 1985], 139). For illustration of the latter, see Edward R. F. Sheehan, *Agony in the Garden* (Boston: Houghton Mifflin, 1989), 87-95, 240-41; Belli, *Breaking Faith*, chapters i, ix; Shirley Christian, *Nicaragua: Revolution in the Family* (New York: Random House, 1985), 203. See also Arturo J. Cruz Sequira and Mark Falcoff, "Who Won Nicaragua?" *Commentary*, vol. 89, no. 5 (May 1990): 36.

14. Boudreaux, "Political Novice Winding Up," *LAT*, February 19, 1990, A1. See also MacPherson, *WP*, February 20, 1990, C1 ("Even though he's dead, Pedro is with me in my heart and he's helping me. He talks to me . . .").

15. Hockstader, "Nicaraguan Opposition Operating on a Shoestring," *WP*, October 13, 1989, A1.

16. Uhlig, "Opposition Gaining a Bit in Nicaragua: Despite Some Scuffles, Public and Private, the Coalition Picks Up Momentum," *NYT*, February 9, 1990, A6; Boudreaux, *LAT*, February 19, 1990, A1.

17. Hockstader, *WP*, January 25, 1990, A29, A34.

18. Uhlig, "Ortega on the Campaign Trail: Designer Glasses Give Way to a Humble Face," *NYTM*, February 14, 1990, A4.

19. Bertrand de la Grange, "Le Front Sandiniste Mobilise ses Partisans," *Le Monde*, February 23, 1990, 6; Council of Freely-Elected Heads of Government, *Report on Fourth Observer Delegation* [Carter mission], January 26-28, 1990, 3.

20. Organization of American States, *Third Report on the Observation of the Nicaraguan Electoral Process*.

21. OAS, *Second Report to the Secretary-General by the United Nations Observer Mission*, December 7, 1989, 24.

22. John McAward, *Mission to Nicaragua: The First Stage of the Electoral Process* (New York: Freedom House, 1989), 4. See also OAS, *Second Report*, 22.

23. Consejo Supremo Electoral de la Republica de Venezuela, "Informe de la Mission Electoral a Nicaragua," Caracas (March 1989), section III; McAward, *Mission to Nicaragua*. See also OAS, *Second Report*, 24-25.

24. "Carter Warns Nicaragua to Free U.S. Election Aid," *Atlanta Journal and Constitution*, January 27, 1990, A17; Uhlig, "Nicaragua Approaches an Election That May Rise or Fall on Its Fairness," *NYT*, January 28, 1990, 3.

25. On the literacy campaign, see Robert Leiken, "Nicaragua's Untold Stories," *TNR*, October 8, 1984.

26. For one citation of these posters, see Hockstader, "Crowds Cheer Nicaraguan Opposition," *WP*, February 19, 1990, A1.

27. Uhlig, "For the Devoted Sandinista, An Item to Fit Every Mood," *NYT*, February 11, 1990, 28. *La Prensa* reported often during the campaign of such government pressure on state employees, farmers, coffee growers, members of artisan cooperatives, etc.

28. "And If the Sandinistas Win?" *LAT*, February 25, 1990, M6. For other reports stressing the "advantages of incumbency," see Hockstader, "Nicaraguan Campaign Seen

as Relatively Free and Open: Observers Find Most Threats, Violence to be Minor," *WP*, February 17, 1990, A1, A26, A27; see also Uhlig, "For the Devoted Sandinista," *NYT*, February 11, 1990; for a post election interpretation that "the advantages of incumbency" backfired on the Sandinistas, see Michael Kinsley, "In Office Too Long," *WP*, March 15, 1990, A27.

29. William Branigin, "Nicaraguan Neighbors Feud as Election Nears," *WP*, February 24, 1990, A21, 23.

30. Uhlig, "The Sandinista Machine vs. Avid Opponents," *NYT*, February 6, 1990, A11.

31. Uhlig, "Ortega on the Campaign Trail: Designer Glasses Give Way to a Humble Face," *NYT*, February 14, 1990, A4; and Hockstader, "Nicaraguan Opposition: Outsmarted and Outspent," *WP*, January 25, 1990, A29. Predictably television was even less nuanced and more categorical. For ABC's Ensor, "Gone is the Commandant Ortega, who wore glasses and military fatigues and talked about Karl Marx. The President's new image: Daniel the swinger" (ABC *World News Tonight*, February 21, 1990). Ed Rabel of NBC was similiarly impressed: "Daniel Ortega has undergone a dramatic transformation, taking on a fresh persona just as his government enters a brand new political era . . ." (*NBC Nightly News*, February 23, 1990).

32. For both of these, see Leiken, "Old and New Politics in Managua," *Journal of Democracy* (Summer 1990); see also Arturo J. Cruz Sequeira and Consuelo Cruz Sequeira, "Crisis of the Clans," *TNR*, May 21, 1990.

33. "Ortega runs skilled campaign: Nicaragua's president is a crowd-pleaser," *USAT*, February 1, 1990; see also Hockstader, "Nicaraguan Opposition Operating on a Shoestring," *WP*, October 13, 1989, A1.

34. "Focus—Vote on Change," *MacNeil Lehrer News Hour*, February 23, 1990.

35. "Focus—Vote on Change," *MacNeil Lehrer News Hour*, February 23, 1990.

36. The chiron on Juan Vasquez' report identified "Father Xavier Gorostiaga" solely by his affiliation with the "Social Research Center." Viewers could conclude that he was an independent analyst, representing, if anything beyond a research institute, the Church. After the elections, Julia Preston somewhat more accurately identified him as "a Jesuit academic who sometimes contributes ideas to the Sandinistas" ("The Defeat of the Sandinistas," *NYR*, April 12, 1990, 27). Gorostiaga, born in Spain, was a "liberation theologian" who moved to Nicaragua from Panama when the Sandinistas took power. He had served as the revolutionary government's first Director of National Planning from 1979 to 1981. Gorostiaga continued to collaborate with the Sandinistas in his subsequent role as director of Managua's National Institute of Social Studies (INIES), later known as the Regional Center for Economic and Social Research (CRIES). Ardently supportive of Sandinista policies, the Center's periodicals, monographs, and seminars were dedicated to explaining and defending those policies and "the advances of the Revolution" to foreign audiences. Preston reported that Gorostiaga had offered an UNO adviser "ten-to-one odds that the Sandinistas would win, with a minimum bet of $100." According to a State Department publication before the 1984 elections Gorostiaga stated that "the internal dynamics of this country don't require us to have elections. The elections are much more for external benefit. They are a symbolic gesture." U.S. Department of State, *Nicaraguan Biographies: A Resource Book*, January 1988, 34.

37. Christopher Marquis, "Sandinista hits election stride as foe falters," *MH*, January 28, 1990, A1; see also Hockstader, *WP*, February 27, 1990, A1.

38. *Vietnam: History, Documents, and Opinions on a Major World Crisis*, ed. Marvin E. Gettleman (Greenwich, Connecticut: Fawcett, 1965), 9.

39. Adatto, "Sound Bite Democracy," 6; see also Adatto, *Picture Perfect*, 24-26.

Chapter 6
The "Authentic Expression of Nationalism"

Besides stressing its American form, the media affirmed the campaign's nationalist, anti-American content. The media reached a consensus that Violeta Chamorro would be tripped up by Nicaraguan nationalism. Anti-Americanism had been stimulated by three U.S. "mistakes": invading Panama, funding the anti-Sandinista "*Contra*" rebels, and donating to the UNO campaign. So this is how NBC presented matters as the campaign closed:

> This is the man pollsters say who will be elected overwhelmingly this weekend [shows Ortega on white horse, waving hat; then kissing beauty queens]. . . . The man president Reagan said would "cry uncle".
>
> The United States spent hundreds of millions of dollars on the contras, the so-called "freedom fighters," to do the job. They failed. Election observers say the Bush administration may have itself to blame for Daniel Ortega's rise in popularity among the voters. . . . Ortega opponents realized too late that failure to criticize the invasion [of Panama by the U.S.] hurt them. [1]

The *San Francisco Chronicle*'s correspondent considered "resentment against the U.S. invasion of Panama" a "major factor in the Chamorro slump."[2] In an early on-the-spot network campaign report NBC's Rabel stressed that: "Recent polls show Daniel Ortega will win the presidency by a wide margin, in large part because many Nicaraguans, leftists, and conservatives alike, openly oppose the invasion."[3] Even the *New York Times*' Mark Uhlig agreed that "the Sandinista Front . . . has benefited from public outrage over the American invasion of Panama."[4] On election day the veteran Latin American correspondent and pundit Tad Szulc wrote in a *Los Angeles Times* commentary: "The Panama invasion may have played right into Sandinista hands. It rearoused nationalism."[5]

Journalists were virtually unanimous that Mrs. Chamorro's failure to criticize the "wildly unpopular" invasion was suicidal.[6] But the Chamorro team thought the invasion would embolden its supporters.[7] *New York Times* columnist Tom Wicker provided the only echo of this view. Wicker reported a talk at the Americas Society in New York by the Nicaraguan intellectual Arturo Cruz, Jr. who had been a Sandinista official and then a *Contra* adviser. Cruz had argued that the invasion might help rather than hurt Chamorro:

> It could encourage her supporters to vote, in the belief that if the election were stolen the U.S. would come to her rescue as it claims to have done for Guillermo Endara in Panama.[8]

Indeed, the Sandinistas' own postelection surveys and vote analysis were to confirm the view that the invasion in fact helped the opposition.[9]

The *Los Angeles Times* correspondent cited not only the Panama invasion to explain Mrs. Chamorro's decline in "all five" recent polls. He also cited "increased activity by the *Contras*, who are highly unpopular among Nicaraguans."[10] Here again the conventional wisdom was that the *Contra* connection hurt Chamorro's chances.

Early in the campaign when Daniel Ortega, alleging renewed *Contra* attacks, suspended a cease-fire agreement, the Sandinistas were seen to reap electoral advantage.[11] The *Post* correspondent observed "the Sandinistas have taken full propaganda advantage of the situation to paint UNO and the rebels as two prongs of a concerted Yankee attack on Nicaragua's sovereignty."[12] By the end of the campaign it was commonplace to assert that "the CIA-backed Contras remain vastly unpopular" and that Chamorro was damaging herself by "her refusal to denounce marauding attacks by Contras."[13]

The polls sponsored by U.S. organizations appeared to corroborate *Contra* unpopularity. To support its front-page thesis that *Contra* support for Chamorro was hurting her campaign, the *Los Angeles Times* cited a survey by the Washington polling firm Greenberg-Lake that showed 56 percent of Nicaraguan voters viewed the *Contras* negatively and that 67 percent believed UNO was "too close" to the *Contras*. The poll gave Ortega a wide lead.[14] On the basis of an ABC/*Washington Post* poll Peter Jennings reported that "72 percent [of Nicaraguans] are angry the United States has supported the *Contras*."[15] None of these reports were tempered by reflections as to how much candor could be expected on this subject. According to human rights groups, even suspicion of support for the *Contras* had for many years been grounds for imprisonment.[16]

The greatest onus Mrs. Chamorro bore, in the view of the U.S. media, was the simple fact of U.S. support. ABC's David Ensor judged that:

> There's nothing [Chamorro] can do about what has turned out to be a
> major liability: President Bush's support, U.S. money for her cam-

paign. Those have hurt her with the many Nicaraguans who resent what they see as U.S. interference.

[Professor Richard Fagen] "They feel they cannot back the candidate that is in their eyes a creature of the United States."[17]

As Robert Kagan points out, the opposition probably "spent a little more than half of what the Sandinistas spent" without including the "advantages of incumbency" enumerated in chapter 5.[18]

If U.S. backing violated national independence, the Sandinistas "for all their Marxist orthodoxy and Castro-style muscle," the editors of the *Christian Science Monitor* explained, "are the authentic expression of Nicaraguan nationalism."[19] The *Washington Post* correspondents agreed. The Sandinista campaign had "further cemented their image as the legitimate bearers of nationalism in Nicaragua." On the other hand, Chamorro's "perceived link with Washington has hurt, polls have shown" because "resentment of armed interventions by the United States early this century [remains] deep."[20] The ABC/*Washington Post* poll of Nicaraguan voters led Peter Jennings to conclude that the Sandinistas would win because "more than half think the opposition takes orders from Washington." So bitter was Nicaraguan resentment of the United States that:

> while a majority of people in Latin America usually say they would like to move to the US for better economic opportunities, seven out of ten Nicaraguans say they would never come here.[21]

Jennings apparently had not been briefed on the copious news reports in the past eighteen months attesting to Nicaraguans having become the largest Hispanic refugee group seeking entrance to the United States.[22]

Disabled by her current alliances, Mrs. Chamorro was also hampered by her social origins. Announcing her nomination the *New York Times* Stephen Kinzer described her as "a product of the Nicaraguan aristocracy," who was "certain to be attacked as representing an unjust past."[23] The *Los Angeles Times* cited the Hemisphere Initiatives/Greenberg-Lake poll which found that 69 percent of voters surveyed considered Chamorro "too close to the rich and big commercial interests."[24] NBC's Garrick Utley depicted Chamorro as "a matriarch of the elite . . . "; Richard Boudreaux of the *Los Angeles Times* called her "an aristocratic widow"; and Lee Hockstader of the *Post* "one of the wealthiest members of Nicaraguan society."[25] A profile of "the conservative Chamorro" for the Style section reflected the view of the *Post* staff that she was "[b]orn into a wealthy family" and grew up "rich and conservative." Seeking an American counterpart for the young Chamorro, the writer chose "a young Gloria Vanderbilt."[26]

The comparison was not felicitous. Violeta Chamorro herself, as opposed perhaps to some of her relatives and associates, was unpretentious. She was the daughter of a cattle rancher from the frontier state of Rivas, historically a kind of colony of Granada. Her late husband's oldest friend remarked that her family appeared to the Granadine elite "the way a self-made Texas rancher would to a

Cabot or a Vanderbilt."[27] Chamorro's blunt, plebeian patois was definitely a campaign asset. Her common touch proved an effective counterpunch:

> The Sandinistas are handing out gifts to buy votes. Take them. Your vote is secret. I say take the T-shirt, dip it in chloride, take Daniel's name off and put your own name on if you want. . . . How can anyone forget 10 years of misery for a T-shirt? [28]

After a year in an American college "studying to be an executive secretary," in 1950 Violeta married Pedro Joaquín Chamorro, the son of a newspaper publisher from the illustrious, yet hardly plutocratic, Chamorro clan. Social and income disparities were less pronounced in Nicaragua than in her neighbors in northern Central America. Unlike, for example, in El Salvador, land in Nicaragua was abundant, the internal "frontier" extensive and dotted by settlements and homesteads. Modern agri-business based on wage labor was confined mainly to the cotton growing regions of the Pacific coast. Land elsewhere was cultivated by middling campesinos who were more like yeomen farmers than plantation peons, as well as by dirt-poor yet independent peasants.[29] Eight months after their wedding, an old friend and colleague remembers, "Violeta and Pedro rented a small house on Candelaria Street. They lived modestly on Pedro's salary and with the help of the rent from a house . . . that Violeta received from her mother."[30] Several years later, Mrs. Chamorro recalled, "we were able to buy a car." Pedro Joaquín became the Somozas' foremost opponent, and Violeta grew accustomed to visiting him in jail. A crusading journalist, publisher and politician, Pedro Joaquín Chamorro's assassination under mysterious circumstances in January 1978 set off the insurrection which eventually toppled the dictator.

Mrs. Chamorro was less "conservative" than she was "wealthy." Beginning students learn that the terms "Liberal" and "Conservative" designating traditional Latin American political parties do not correspond to American usage. Somoza was the leader of the "Liberal" Party; his principal opposition were the "Conservatives." Chamorro's husband was the founder of the social-democratic (or liberal) faction of the Conservative Party. In an American context the Chamorros' political views would have put them in the neighborhood of Jimmy Carter. In 1979 when she was named to the first revolutionary junta, the press described her in terms very different from those of 1989, as in this lapidary sketch in the *New York Times*:

> Was active in anti-Somoza coalition, founded by her husband, that was a precursor of moderate Broad Opposition Front. . . . When named to junta last month was vice-president of the Inter-American Press Association's Freedom of the Press Committee.[31]

Likewise the *Post* noted that Mrs. Chamorro

took up not only [her late husband's] political banner, becoming a sort of ma-
triarchal symbol to the moderate opposition, but also an active participant in the
family-owned newspaper *La Prensa*. . . .

She is a close friend of former Venezuelan [Social Democratic] president
Carlos Andrez Perez, whose government provided moral and material support
to the Sandinistas. . . .

[at press conferences] She speaks generally of Nicaragua nationalism and
liberal democracy and is considered the representative of those who followed
her husband's moderate political line.

Moreover, she had proved a "surprising hard-liner in resisting U.S. pressure."[32]
But ten years later, Chamorro's political history and nationalistic attitudes
were overlooked in the *Post*'s campaign coverage which stressed U.S. assistance
to the UNO campaign, "money that may have done little more than deepen voter
suspicions about her dependence on Washington."[33] Noting that the Sandinista
government was able to block the arrival of U.S. contributions to UNO, another
Post report observed:

The Sandinista campaign was especially successful when it hammered UNO,
calling it Washington's "rented opposition." UNO, unable to muster an effective response, was tainted by money it had not received.[34]

Post readers had to wait until after the returns were in for Julia Preston to point
out that "although the Sandinistas paint her as a puppet of Washington,
Chamorro has long shown an abhorrence of U.S. interference in Nicaraguan
affairs."[35]
The only sizable *New York Times* story on the opposition campaign in the
two months following its announcement of Chamorro's nomination focused on
her solicitations in Miami, "mostly from a $100-a-plate fund-raising dinner to-
night organized in concert with the Cuban American National Foundation, a
conservative anti-Castro group."[36] *Time* agreed that the candidate was too much

out of the country, raising funds among wealthy exiles and testing the world
stage. This has made little impression on an electorate more worried about the
price of food in Matagalpa.

By that date the Chamorro campaign had held large and enthusiastic rallies in
Jinotega, Jalapa, Chontales, Masaya, Chichigalpa, Matagalpa, and Managua.
Journalists like Hockstader of the *Post* believed that poorer Nicaraguans
had special reasons for preferring Ortega to the "wealthy, aristocratic"
Chamorro:

the Sandinistas can . . . count on support from Nicaraguans who have benefited
from social programs enacted during their 10-year rule, including a nationwide
literacy drive and efforts to improve housing for the poor.[37]

His colleague from the Style section stressed the government's "free health programs—which remain the Sandinista's strong suit for many voters."[38] The articles provided no evidence that these highly publicized programs, which were
regularly denounced by opposition candidates as fraudulent, had actually benefited the poor. The breakdown of election results were to show that the Sandinistas fared worst in the country's most impoverished districts.

The prevailing media wisdom was that though economics might favor
UNO, politics favored the Sandinistas.[39] Politics would prevail because, as Hendrick Hertzberg of the *New Republic* explained: "The Sandinistas have national
pride on their side. They have stood up to the colossus of the north."[40] Lindsey
Gruson of the New York *Times* reported that the Sandinistas had

much more support than might be expected in the face of depression, widespread unemployment and growing hunger.[41]

Daniel Ortega would prevail despite everything that would make such a vote
inconceivable were this truly "an all-American election." That judgment seemed
to be validated by massive Sandinista demonstrations overflowing with chanting
supporters apparently prepared not just to vote but to die for the Sandinistas.
Such displays succeeded in assuring many journalists that Ortega was indeed
"wildly popular."

For more resourceful reporters those demonstrations disclosed radically different news. At one of them, Mark Uhlig asked a woman for whom she would
vote. "You can see for yourself," she declared. "You can see the people have
come to hear the *comandante*."

The subject was dropped for a quarter-hour of small talk. Then the woman, a
barefoot child clasping her cotton dress, quietly led the reporter away from the
crowd. "I am here because they know I live here," she confided, indicating the
Sandinista militants in red-and-black scarfs standing nearby. "But in this barrio
we are voting for Violeta. Things can't go on like this."[42]

Uhlig was not the only journalist who vouchsafed such testimony.[43] By
election day two *Washington Post* correspondents found:

The survey results [favoring Ortega] seem at odds with reporters' random interviews on the streets, where discontent and resentment directed at the
Sandinistas and their management of the economy are commonplace.[44]

Uhlig noted the same "consistent contrast" between the polling forecasts "and
observations from almost any set of random interviews in the street." The contradiction, he wrote, caused "deep uncertainty" among "diplomats and journal-

ists" as to "the willingness of Nicaraguan voters to describe their true political feelings to journalists or to poll takers on a first encounter."[45]

After the elections several journalists recalled interviews whereby they "became convinced that the polls were misleading."[46] But none of them had seen fit before the elections to share that conviction with their readers. None had afforded those interviews such prominence as to suggest a Sandinista defeat in the offing. Before the returns themselves provided shelter, not a single journalist openly broke with the established consensus. Afterwards they all did, forming a new consensus.

At most those close encounters with Nicaraguans produced comments on the lack of transparency and the difficulty of making predictions. Uhlig, the most skeptical and bold, went no further than equivocation:

> After years of political conflict, most Nicaraguans remain deeply reluctant to discuss their personal views, and few experienced diplomats and foreign experts here have dared to predict how the public will [behave] at the voting booth.[47]

For a news dispatch the language is circumspect and euphemistic. Why would "political conflict" discourage Nicaraguans from voicing their views? Why should we not expect just the opposite? After six years without elections, some would say decades, years of economic crisis and war, here at last was a clear choice before the public. A spirited, polarized, doubtful contest turning into the home stretch—that sounds like a recipe for outspokenness. Why were so many Nicaraguans instead "reluctant to discuss their personal views?" And why was Uhlig's description so guarded? Would another, better, name for "political conflict" be "fear?"

The reticence of the Nicaraguans is easier to account for than that of the journalists. To be sure, the press corps was in the midst of a breaking story with competitive pressures further intensified by the presence of hundreds of general assignment reporters. Perhaps this was not the moment to explore the political environment, those "years of political conflict," although if not then, when? Instead the journalist retreated to the conventional "mental picture" or "pseudo-environment," in Lippmann's terminology.[48] For more than a decade the major news organizations had been reporting that the Sandinista regime was wildly popular.

Figuring prominently in that mental picture or paradigm was Nicaraguan nationalism. The Sandinista appeal to nationalism was capable of transcending mundane facts like economic collapse, political repression, civil war, and mass exodus. And if nationalism was so powerful, then an "American-style campaign" could only be a form disguising a radically different content. For if this campaign were taking place in the United States, the press corps could be counted upon to ask whether a candidate raising the cry of national betrayal was trying to avoid blame for failed policies. But the Sandinista recourse to nationalism was treated not as the desperate ploy of a demagogic "incumbent" but as the authentic and defensive protest of a small, victimized nation. If the Sandinistas' "American-style campaign" was succeeding brilliantly, it was not because Nicaraguans were just like Americans; it was because they profoundly disliked America ("seven out of ten Nicaraguans say they would never come here").

***

Two very different images of Nicaragua were superimposed in the American election coverage. One was the "star-spangled all-American style election" featuring a "splashy party convention," "media events," "incumbent advantages," and polls on "the issues." Overlapping this picture, however, was another model, an ancient one, that presented Nicaragua as a place so different that the usual assumptions did not hold. This was a people driven by noble and primal sentiments—a nationalism inspiring extraordinary sacrifices. The Sandinistas incarnated the authentic, ineffable Nicaragua. They were Nicaragua standing up for itself, Nicaragua standing up against America—the America that intervened, occupied, bullied, and that imposed itself. The Sandinistas were the antithesis of, and the nemesis of, ethnocentric America. Thus, Nicaragua was actually Vietnam even though it could look like America.

If these two approaches coexisted despite their contradictions, that does not mean they were harmonious. But both led to the conclusion that the Nicaraguan people would re-elect the Sandinistas—whether as the authentic expression of Nicaraguan nationalism, of the Nicaraguan general will, or as a more effective political party in a modern democratic election. One approach assumed Sandinista popularity on Rousseauian, the other on Jacksonian grounds.

"Shattered Myths"

A few days after the elections William Branigin, who had reported occasionally from Nicaragua since the mid-1980s, though he was never the *Post*'s man in Managua, observed that "the election outcome has served to explode a number of myths that the Sandinistas have built up over the years."[49] That same week *Newsweek*'s Charles Lane, used the identical term. Their "shattered Sandinista myths" included:

- "The myth of the Sandinistas' popularity"[50]
- "The idea that the voters would not hold the Sandinistas responsible for the economic debacle, blaming instead the United States"[51]
- "that the Sandinista revolution had at least been of benefit to the poor"[52]

- "that the *Contras* had no support, and embodied no widespread peasant grievances"[53]
- "The implication that many interviewees lied to pollsters shattered another myth: That the Sandinistas were not associated with widespread repression"[54]
- "Other myths were . . . Sandinista support among the young people . . . as well as the front's powerful machine and modern campaign tactics"[55]

According to Branigin and Lane the election results and postelection interviews disproved each of these myths or stereotypes. With respect to the notion "that the Sandinistas enjoyed broad public backing" Branigin recalled a passage in a pre-election critique of U.S. press coverage by a "media-monitoring group" called *Fairness and Accuracy in Reporting*:

> "While dire economic situations have toppled governments across Latin America, experts across the spectrum have noted the Sandinistas' remarkably strong support."[56]

"In fact, as shown by interviews with voters and the vote result," Branigin rejoined, "Nicaraguans were seething with resentment." "The myth of the Sandinistas' popularity," he added, "was punctured when they lost Sunday in eight of Nicaragua's nine administrative regions, winning only in the remote Rio San Juan 'special zone' of 15,000 voters in the southeastern corner of the country."

Actually, the bald official election count probably exaggerated Sandinista "popularity." For example, in that isolated San Juan "special zone" there was little international observation. Moreover, those opposition poll watchers who were induced or coerced to resign could not be replaced as they could elsewhere. Furthermore, because of forced wartime relocations, a significant portion of the local population now lived across the Costa Rican border.

Scrutiny of the election returns reinforces the impression of diminished Sandinista popularity:

- Over 6 percent of the ballots were declared "illegible" or otherwise nullified by the Supreme Electoral Council. Opposition leaders charged that these were mostly UNO votes fraudulently annulled.
- An estimated 15,000 Nicaraguans were not afforded the possibility of registering (nearly all in areas considered opposition strongholds).
- Nicaraguans living abroad, estimated at 15 to 20 percent of the population, could not vote. Overseas Nicaraguan communities, made up primarily of refugees and exiles, could be expected to vote overwhelmingly against the government.
- Although in October about 1.75 million Nicaraguans had taken pains to register despite long delays, on election day some 241,000 (14 percent) of them abstained, many apparently unconvinced that the secrecy of their ballot would be

respected. This was another set of predominantly antigovernment voters lost to the opposition.

Contrary to the standard picture, the opposition sweep won by wide margins in many of Managua's poorest barrios. One of the successful Latin opinion surveys found that "richer people were stronger supporters of the incumbent regime."[57] Lane concluded that "the people knew who had made them poor by wasting resources on unproductive state enterprises, not to mention mansions and custom automobiles for the *comandantes*."[58]

The most stunning reversal of expert opinion concerned the peasants and the *Contras*. Lane noted that "Chamorro's UNO coalition rolled up its biggest margins in mountainous rural areas where the *Contras* were most active."[59] Branigin provided more detail:

> Another myth was that the anti-Sandinista rebels, or contras, portrayed for years as widely reviled in Nicaragua, would drag UNO to defeat because the coalition was too closely identified with them and included former contra leaders. As it happened the two regions where the contras have been most active showed among the most lopsided results in favor of UNO. In the central provinces of Chontales and Boaco, UNO won with 67.9 percent of the vote compared to 27.7 for the Sandinistas. In the northern provinces of Matagalpa and Jinotega UNO got 57.7 percent of the vote to the Sandinistas 37 percent.
>
> In both areas independent farmers and ranchers have long supported the contras. Many of the rebels are sons of these peasants. [60]

The final returns showed wider Chamorro victories: 74.8 percent in Boaco and Chontales, 63.9 percent in Matagalpa and Jinotega. In these areas UNO won all the local offices, installing mayors who were to prove themselves supporters of the *Contras*.[61] Later, Sandinista Vice President Sergio Ramirez acknowledged: "It was the peasants, not the oligarchs, that voted us out of office."[62]

After the Sandinistas, the biggest losers at the Nicaraguan polls were the pollsters themselves. Branigin commented acidly:

> Helping to fool foreign observers and the Sandinistas themselves about the election were polls that gave new meaning to the term "margin of error." Several, including one for The *Washington Post* and ABC News, showed more than a 30-point difference. [63]

Everything suggested to Branigin "that many interviewees lied to pollsters" and that conclusion "shattered another myth: the Sandinistas were not associated with widespread repression." It became obvious to Branigin that many Nicaraguans

> clearly feared to express their true sentiments to strangers. "I think people were scared," said Marvin Ortega, director of Itztani. "They thought we were Sandinistas."[64]

At the outset of his analysis Branigin had asked how it was that the opposition which the Sandinistas had "tarred" as an extension of the hated pre-1979 Somocista National Guard and of CIA-backed *Contras* could have won in a landslide? What had happened to "the almost mystical force" of Sandinismo?

> One answer is that for years now, and especially during the latest election campaign, the Sandinistas have been fooling a good portion of international public opinion and, not least of all, themselves.[65]

But then the journalists were also deceived, or were a party to the deception. Branigin was the rare exception who went undeceived. Not, perhaps, wanting to be seen as crowing, he spared his colleagues. But since a "media-monitoring group" is given as the source for the idea of strong Sandinista support, Branigin's reader might have gotten the impression that the "myths" were held not by the media but rather by their critics. That was not the case, as we have seen.

"Reporters like myself," observed the *Post*'s Julia Preston in the *New York Review* after the elections,

> who had long experience in Sandinista Nicaragua (I have been covering the story for more than seven years) were, I think, less able than others to imagine such a vast change.[66]

No more than Branigin or Lane did Preston expand on the failure of the media's "imagination." However, Branigin's piece, and Lane's, implicitly acknowledged that more was involved than a mistaken election assessment. Something was wrong with the way the media "imagined" Nicaragua. The myths shattered were not the exclusive property of the Sandinistas. They were just as much the product of the "system of stereotypes" or paradigm which had framed a decade and a half of intensive American media coverage of Nicaragua.

Notes

1. *NBC Nightly News*, February 21, 1990.
2. "U.S. Firm's Nicaragua Poll Gives Ortega Wide Lead," *SFC*, January 25, 1990. For a similiar West Coast view, see "Ortega Increasing Pre-election Lead," *Seattle Post-Intelligencer*, January 25, 1990.
3. *NBC Nightly News*, January 27, 1990. An academic specialist explained in a *New York Times* op-ed: "The U.S. invasion of Panama . . . turned the . . . elections . . . into a referendum on whether the U.S. will once again dominate the country. . . . George Bush . . . decisively strengthened . . . Ortega's hand" (Elizabeth Dore, "Panama, Key to Ortega's Campaign," January 30, 1990, A23).
4. Mark A. Uhlig, *NYT Sunday Magazine* (February 11, 1990): 35, 62, 65, 67.
5. Tad Szulc, "Nicaragua Votes Today, U.S. Agonizes Tomorrow," *LAT*, February 25, 1990, M1.

6. Christopher Marquis, "Sandinista hits election stride as foe falters," *MH*, January 28, 1990, A1; *Washington Post*'s Style section piece echoed the consensus that "many, outraged at the United States' invasion of Panama, may now shy away from the U.S.-backed Chamorro" (Myra MacPherson, "In Nicaragua, a Widow's Calling: Violeta Chamorro, Taking Up Her Husband's Cause as an Opposition Presidential Candidate," *WP*, February 20, 1990, C1, C4).

7. Author's interviews with Chamorro's campaign manager Antonio Lacayo and spokesman Ernesto Palazio, January and February 1990.

8. Tom Wicker, "In the Nation," *NYT*, February 22, 1990, A23. After the elections Cruz wrote that "the U.S. invasion of Panama in late December, far from hurting the opposition in Nicaragua, was perhaps crucial to its victory" (see Arturo J. Cruz Sequiera and Mark Falcoff, "Who Won Nicaragua?" *Commentary* 89, no. 5 (May 1990): 36; see also Cruz, *Memoirs of a Counter-Revolutionary: Life with the Contras, the Sandinistas, and the CIA* (New York: Doubleday, 1989).

9. Paul Oquist, "Sociopolitical Dynamics of the 1990 Nicaraguan Elections," in *The 1990 Elections in Nicaragua and Their Aftermath*, ed. Vanessa Castro and Gary Prevost (Lanham, Maryland: Rowman & Littlefield, 1992), chapter I.

10. Richard Boudreaux, "Chamorro is Losing Ground in Nicaragua," *LAT*, February 15, 1990, A9.

11. *Time* explained that "Nicaraguans resent dying in this long-drawn-out conflict, and more of them blame the *Contras* than the Sandinistas for the latest surge in countryside attacks" ("Playing Politics with Peace: Headed toward Elections, Ortega Blows his Cool," *Time* [November 13, 1989]: 52).

12. "In Rural Nicaragua War Dominates Politics," *WP*, November 12, 1989, A31, 33.

13. MacPherson, "In Nicaragua, a Widow's Calling," C1, C4.

14. Boudreaux, "*Contras'* Campaign Tactics Could Boost Sandinistas," *LAT*, February 17, 1990, A1.

15. *ABC World News*, February 20, 1989.

16. For example, see Amnesty International, *Nicaragua, The Human Rights Record, 1986-1989* (London: Amnesty International Publications, 1989), 4.3, 20-24; and *Report on Human Rights Defenders in Nicaragua* (New York: International League of Human Rights, 1986), chapter ix.

17. *ABC World News Tonight*, February 22, 1990. After the elections the Sandinistas, and a few in the media who echoed them, dropped the view that Chamorro was crippled by U.S. support and adopted the position that voters backed Chamorro only because the United States did. In postelection speeches Daniel Ortega claimed that: "The United States succeeded . . . in influencing a large sector of the population" with a policy of "blackmail, pressure, aggression, and death." "We held elections with a gun, with a gun barrel pointed at the head of the Nicaraguan people." (Foreign Broadcast Information Service, FBIS-LAT 90-042 [March 2, 1998]: 21, 24.)

CNN provided an egregious example of the tenacity of stereotypes in its 1998-99 24-part documentary *Cold War*. Episode 18, "Backyard," closed with the assertion that "Violeta Chamorro . . . narrowly [*sic*] won a surprise victory. Washington spent nearly $10 million backing her campaign."

18. Robert Kagan, *A Twilight Struggle: American Power and Nicaragua, 1977-1990* (New York: Free Press, 1996), 701.

19. "The Vote in Nicaragua," *CSM*, February 22, 1990, 20.

20. Lee Hockstader and William Branigin, "Sandinistas Seem Changed by Election Campaign," *WP*, February 25, 1990, A1, A19.

21. *ABC World News*, February 20, 1989.

22. For examples, see *NYT*, October 16, 1988, A1; *NYT*, January 14, 1989, 1; *NYT*, February 27, 1989, A14; *BG*, March 10, 1989, 1; *CT*, April 23, 1989, 23C.

23. "Anti-Sandinistas Choose Candidate," *NYT*, September 4, 1989, 1, 4.

24. "Bitter Workers Hold Fate of Sandinistas in Election," *LAT*, January 29, 1990, A1, A9.

25. *NBC Sunday Today*, February 25, 1990; Boudreaux, "Delays in U.S. Aid Hamper Opposition in Nicaragua," *LAT*, January 22, 1990, A1; Hockstader, "Crowds Cheer Nicaraguan Opposition: Anti-Sandinista Coalition Holds Final Election Rally in Managua," *WP*, February 19,1990, A1.

26. MacPherson, "In Nicaragua, a Widow's Calling," C1, C4. *Washington Post* staff writers often pointed out that "The opposition includes many of the wealthiest members of Nicaraguan society, including Chamorro." (Hockstader, "Crowds Cheer Nicaraguan Opposition") The candidate herself was "Violeta Chamorro, head of one of the nation's wealthiest families, conservative publisher." ("Nicaraguan Candidate Nominated: Widow of Slain Hero of 1979 Revolution to Oppose Ortega," *WP*, September 3, 1989, A1.) The freelance reporter and later *New York Times* editorialist Tina Rosenberg would depict the Chamorro election victory as "turning power over to the oligarchy." But as James LeMoyne pointed out, unlike El Salvador and Guatemala, "there were rich families in Nicaragua, but there never was real 'oligarchy.' (See Tina Rosenberg, *Children of Cain: Violence and the Violent in Latin America* (New York: Morrow, 1991), and James LeMoyne, "Brothers in Arms," *Washington Monthly* [November 1991]: 50.)

27. Biographical data on Violeta Chamorro from author's interviews with Violeta Chamorro Barrios, Pedro Joaquín Chamorro Barrios, Jaime Chamorro Cardenal, Enrique Alvarez Montalvan, and Arturo J. Cruz; see also "Violeta Chamorro," in *Life Stories of the Nicaraguan Revolution*, ed. Denis Lynn Daley Heyck (New York: Routledge, 1990); Arturo Cruz, Jr. "Nicaragua's Family History . . ." *NYT*, March 4, 1990, IV, 3; and Jaime Chamorro, *The Republic of Paper* (New York: Freedom House, 1988), chapter I.

28. Boudreaux, "Delays in U.S. Aid Hamper Opposition," A1.

29. See Cruz, "Somocismo and the Sandinista Revolution," in *Conflict in Nicaragua*, ed. Jiri Valenta and Esperanza Duran (Boston: Allen & Unwin, 1987), 139; but see also Forrest D. Colburn, *Post-Revolutionary Nicaragua: State Classes and the Dilemmas of Agrarian Policy* (Berkeley: University of California, 1986), 31–32, 48, 66, 86; and Phillip Warnken, *The Agricultural Development of Nicaragua* (Columbia: University of Missouri, 1975), 16-19, 24.

30. Mario Cajina-Vega, "La Semblanza de Pedro," in Pedro Joaquín Chamorro C., *La Patria de Pedro: El Pensamiento Nicaragüense de Pedro Joaquín Chamorro* (Managua: *La Prensa*, 1981), vi.

31. "Sketches of the Nicaraguan Junta's Five Members," *NYT*, July 18, 1979, A10.

32. Karen DeYoung, "Uneasy Alliance of Rebels, Businessmen to Rule Nicaragua," *WP*, July 22, 1979, A14; Chamorro's "conservatism" proved more enduring. Announcing her inauguration on April 26 the *WSJ* labeled Mrs. Chamorro "a conservative elected in February."

33. Richard Morin and Hockstader, "Pre-Election Poll Shows Ortega Leads: Surveys Influence Nicaraguan Politics," *WP*, February 21, 1990, A1, A17.

34. Hockstader, "Nicaraguan Opposition: Outsmarted and Outspent," *WP*, January 25, 1990, A29, A34. The *Post* appeared to echo a *Los Angeles Times* story which made the same observation. Ironically, UNO was damaged by three months of Sandinista propaganda that accused it of being a "rented opposition" while in reality it was not get-

ting a penny from Washington (Boudreaux, "Delays in U.S. Aid Hamper Opposition in Nicaragua," *LAT*, January 22, 1990).

35. Julia Preston, "Chamorro, Familial Conciliator, Faces a Wider Task," *WP*, February 27, 1990, A16.

36. George Volsky, "Anti-Sandinista Candidate Seeks Aid Among Exiles in Miami," *NYT*, September 19, 1989, A18.

37. Hockstader, "Sandinistas Stage Last Rally in Capital: Managua Seen as Crucial Battleground in Nicaraguan Election," *WP*, February 22, 1990, A26.

38. MacPherson, "In Nicaragua, a Widow's Calling," C1, C4.

39. For example, see *NBC Nightly News*, January 27, 1990; Boudreaux, "Delays in U.S. Aid Hamper Opposition," A6; and "Chamorro is Losing Ground in Nicaragua," A9; Uhlig, "A Sandinista Promise Gone Sour Alienates Nicaragua's Working Class," *NYT*, November 7, 1989, A10.

40. Hendrick Hertzberg, "Civics, Nicaragua-style," *TNR*, December 25, 1989, 23-25. This was not the magazine's editorial position. See "Sandinista Fix?" *TNR*, February 19, 1990, 9-11.

41. Lindsey Gruson, "Sandinistas Mount Mammoth Rally," *NYT*, February 22, 1990, A10. See also David Ensor on ABC *World News Tonight*, February 25, 1990.

42. Uhlig, "Secretive Nicaraguan Voters Leave Election Hard to Call," *NYT*, February 18, 1990, 1, 14.

43. See also Kwame Holman's report in "Focus—Vote on Change," *The MacNeil-Lehrer Newshour*, February 23, 1990; Gruson, "Sandinistas Mount Mammoth Rally"; and Boudreaux, "Political Novice Winding Up Bid to Dislodge Daniel Ortega," *LAT*, February 19, 1990, A16.

44. Hockstader and Branigin, "Sandinistas Seem Changed," *WP*, February 25, 1990, A1, A19.

45. Uhlig, "Secretive Nicaraguan Voters."

46. Uhlig, "Ortega Pledges He Will 'Respect and Obey' Voters' Mandate," *NYT*, February 27, 1990, A1. See also Hockstader, "Ortega Concedes Defeat in Nicaraguan Vote, *WP*, February 27, 1990, A1; and Preston, "The Defeat of the Sandinistas," *NYR*, April 12, 1990, 25.

47. "Nicaraguans Hope for Decisive Election, *NYT*, February 25, 1990, 14. See also Uhlig, "Secretive Nicaraguan Voters," 1; and "Fear of Disorder Shadows the Opposition Campaign in Nicaragua," *NYT*, February 20, 1990, A6.

48. Walter Lippmann, *Public Opinion* (New York: Macmillan, 1922; revised edition, New York: Free Press Paperback, 1965), chapters i, ii (*e.g.*, 15, 43).

49. Branigin, "Election Shattered Many Sandinista Myths," *WP*, March 2, 1990, A26.

50. Branigin, "Election Shattered Many Sandinista Myths," A26.

51. Branigin, "Election Shattered Many Sandinista Myths," A26.

52. Charles Lane, "Who 'Won' Nicaragua?" *Newsweek* (March 12, 1990): 14.

53. Branigin, "Election Shattered Many Sandinista Myths," A26.

54. Branigin, "Election Shattered Many Sandinista Myths," A26.

55. Branigin, "Election Shattered Many Sandinista Myths," A26.

56. Branigin, "Election Shattered Many Sandinista Myths," A26.

57. Felipe Noguera, "South Polls," *Campaigns & Elections* (April-May 1990): 36.

58. Lane, "Who 'Won' Nicaragua?"

59. Lane, "Who 'Won' Nicaragua?" According to an analysis by a pro-Sandinista team, in the countryside Ortega did best among "collectivized peasants" and "state agricultural workers," Chamorro with the poorer and middling peasants. See Vanessa Castro,

"Electoral Results in the Rural Sector," in *The 1990 Elections in Nicaragua and Their Aftermath*, ed. Castro and Prevost, 137.

60. Branigin, "Election Shattered Many Sandinista Myths," A26.

61. See *The 1990 Elections in Nicaragua and Their Aftermath*, ed. Castro and Prevost, appendix 3, 224-25; and Castro, "Electoral Results in the Rural Sector," in *The 1990 Elections in Nicaragua and Their Aftermath*, ed. Castro and Prevost, 132.

62. Douglas Farah, "Ex-Rebels Find Unity Imperiled," *WP*, September 4, 1993, A17.

63. Farah, "Ex-Rebels Find Unity Imperiled."

64. Farah, "Ex-Rebels Find Unity Imperiled." On Itztani, a leftist think tank, and other pollsters, see chapter 14.

65. Branigin, "Election Shattered Many Sandinista Myths," A26.

66. Julia Preston, "The Defeat of the Sandinistas."

Chapter 7
Shaking the Imperial Frame

Nemo repente fuit turpissimus [No one ever became a villain all at once].

—Juvenal

On Sunday, June 28, 1959, a small dispatch on page twenty of the *New York Times* in a tone suited to peripheral subjects told that "rebels intent on invading Nicaragua from Honduras" had been crushed by Honduran troops.[1] The Honduran government explained that it had acted by virtue of an agreement in which the two countries had pledged "not to allow their soil to be used as a base for invasion." The "would-be-revolutionary band" was composed of "Nicaraguans, Cubans, and Hondurans," and led by Rafael Somarriba, "a former Nicaraguan National Guard lieutenant." Several days later the *Times* reported from Havana that an airliner had deposited "twenty-eight Cubans captured by Honduran authorities last week in an aborted attempt to invade Nicaragua."[2] The *Times* later reported that an Organization of American States fact-finding commission submitted evidence that "a close associate of Premier Fidel Castro lent aid to last month's unsuccessful invasion" and that the aide's name "was Major Ernesto (Ché) Guevara."[3]

His army's action was popular neither with Honduran President Dr. Ramón Villeda Morales, nor with the Honduran press. The latter denounced "the massacre at El Chaparral," in which nine rebels died, an extravagant appellation which would be invoked by a generation of revolutionary descendants.[4] Dr. Villeda, who was a Liberal in more than name and who abhorred the Somozas and admired Ché Guevara, then looked the other way as another small band of Nicaraguans set up camp, with the assistance of Cuban advisers and arms. When they

87

sallied across the border, President Luis Somoza Debayle retaliated by foment-
ing a military coup against Villeda.[5]

A former National Guard officer leads cross-border raiders based in Honduras, trained and armed in revolutionary Cuba, intent on overthrowing Somoza!
For those familiar with the drama that unfolded a generation hence, our episode
might seem more like a summer's rehearsal performed by Nick Bottom's moon-
struck company.

There is another refrain in our haunting, if discordant, overture. Two Sun-
days earlier the *Times* had reported that a "Señor Chamorro and fifteen other
rebels . . . surrendered today near Santo Tomas . . ." in southern Nicaragua.[6] The
ill-fated "invasion of Olama y Mollejones," as it would be known, had originated in Costa Rica with the assistance of leaders of the social democratic National Liberation Party. Violeta's husband supervised the training of over a hundred Nicaraguans and the acquisition of the C-46 which transported his
detachment of sixty-three into the Chontalean hills overlooking the plains of
Mollejones on May 31. On June 2 the *Times* divulged that after downing
Chamorro's plane, "the Nicaraguan pilots said the 'mercenaries,' wearing unknown uniforms, fled."[7]

The same report summarized a "lengthy message" from the rebels "ad-
dressed to Herbert L. Matthews, a member of the *Times* editorial board"—of
whom more later—calling on the Nicaraguan people to "join the uprising by
strikes and military activity to establish democracy." The *Times* dispatch carried
evenhandedly and without comment both government and rebel accounts of the
episode.

The rebel incursion was accompanied by what the *Times* called "the first
large-scale act of civil disobedience" since the beginning of the Somozas' rule in
1933. The "general strike" had "closed most commercial activity" in Managua.
But "Señor Somoza said . . . it had failed completely." According to Somoza
"only a few stores owned by 'reactionary conservatives' failed to open." He also
predicted that the rebels would be "completely annihilated by tomorrow."[8]

Certainly the confidence of the second-to-last Somoza did not prove unwarranted. As soon as he and his comrades landed, Chamorro wrote later in the
prologue to his *Prison Diary*, "we were pursued, bombarded, machine-gunned,
and attacked by the infantry of the National Guard. After two weeks of this we
were forced to surrender."[9] Indeed, less than two weeks after his landing, a
front-page photo showed Pedro Joaquín in guerrilla fatigues, his face downcast,
beside two gloomy comrades, all three standing downwind from General
Anastasio Somoza Debayle, all four facing the camera. The accompanying article explained that the President's brother, chief of the armed forces, "General
Somoza disdained to address the prisoners directly. He ordered them to about-
face and delivered a scathing jeering tongue-lashing to their backs."[10]

Karl Marx wrote that history repeats itself "the first time as tragedy, the
second as farce."[11] In our story the order was reversed. These misadventures
constituted the initial skirmishes of a thirty-year war in the course of which the

carbine and the boxy Costa Rican C-46 would give way to surface-to-air missiles and Soviet MI-24 attack helicopters.[12]

***

A *Time* magazine report observed that Chamorro's rebels

> had overestimated their own toughness and underestimated the Somoza boys strength. . . . Most Nicaraguans apparently are not interested in overthrowing President Luis, who has been liberalizing the dictatorship he inherited from his assassinated father, tough old Anastasio ("Tacho") Somoza.[13]

A *New York Times* editorial attributed the failure of the rebellion to "lack of popular support." The *Times* observed that: "The successful revolutions in . . . Venezuela and Cuba were all made possible by the willingness of the people to fight for liberty." Then the *Times* editorial added categorically that:

> The father of the present rulers, Anastasio (Tacho) Somoza, who was dictator from 1936 to 1956, always had support from the peasants and workers. His sons have done nothing to alienate the people.[14]

It is unclear how the *Times* measured the level of "peasant and worker support." The first Somoza's populist period, when he was supported by the labor unions and the Communist Party, terminated well before the dictator was assassinated in 1956. Certainly by the summer of 1959 the sympathies of Nicaraguan students did not appear to favor the self-styled reform administration of his eldest son Luis Somoza Debayle. A quarter of a century later one of those students still recalled vividly his first day at high school:

> Suddenly the whole high school was in the central court yard, chanting slogans. We burst open the gates of the school and went marching down the main street of Managua, a thousand-strong, capsizing vehicles and burning police cars. Soon students from the other schools joined in. After two hours of this I still did not know what it was we were protesting. Finally I learned there'd been a student massacre in León. University students were shot by the Somoza National Guard, and there was a reaction (a bit like your Kent State during Vietnam). The students in León protested because guerrilla fighters had been captured or killed up north in a place called El Chaparral in the first major guerrilla encounter of the new type that was developing in Nicaragua. The 23rd of July, the commemoration of the student massacre in León, became a permanent annual event as the student movement developed.[15]

The Herbert L. Matthews to whom the Nicaraguan revolutionaries sent their "lengthy message" was, of course, the *New York Times* journalist whose sensational February 1957 interviews with Fidel Castro from his mountain headquarters in the Sierra Madre had, according to some accounts, provided a crucial spark for the rebel movement, by affirming that "the old corrupt order in Cuba is being threatened for the first time."[16]

"The sixties" in Latin America began in the late fifties. By 1958 students were hurling rocks at Vice President Richard Nixon's motorcades in the streets of Caracas and Lima and drawing bearded revolutionary visages on walls. In August Nicaraguan students prevented Milton Eisenhower, dispatched on a fact-finding tour by a now worried Eisenhower Administration, from receiving an honorary degree at the National University in León. The previous month, according to Carlos Fonseca Amador, the founder of the FSLN and a survivor of El Chaparral, those same students "organized massive acts of solidarity with the popular struggle in Cuba when for the first time since his assassination the name of . . . Augusto César Sandino, was publicly acclaimed."[17]

For some in the United States "the sixties" also started in the fifties. Fidel Castro and Ché Guevara became the first New Left heroes. David Horowitz, an early New Left publicist, recalls that he and his comrades welcomed the Cuban revolution "as a liberation not only from American capitalism but from Stalinism as well." Suddenly the New Left, unlike the old, could criticize the ills of American society without having to answer for the evils of the Soviet Union.[18]

"We were all children of the Cuban revolution," recalls our high school freshman, whose illustrative political career included stints as Christian Democrat, Sandinista, *Contra* activist, vice minister in Violeta's Chamorro government, and fugitive from justice.[19]

> But we were also children of the blood of our comrade students. The Cuban revolution and our own awakening of the student massacre were related intimately. From those events rose the leadership of the student movement that would organize the Sandinista National Liberation Front.[20]

✳✳✳

In the United States it was still the stolid fifties. The *Times*, with the exception of Herbert Matthews, remained aloof toward Latin rebels, though not hostile. Like Matthews, though far less ardently, his newspaper was willing to take at face value Castro's democratic declarations. From a front-page article in April 1959 headlined "Castro Rules Out Role as Neutral; Opposes the Reds" we learn that "the bearded soldier said that his heart lay with the democracies and that he did not agree with communism."[21]

As the revolution turned radical and repressive and Castro's assurances less credible, the tone of the *New York Times'* coverage remained detached even as it began to accent geopolitical factors and U.S. security concerns. If the headlines now sometimes bluntly characterized Castro himself as "Red," the body of the text still carried his own disclaimers without comment.

During the crisis that eventually climaxed at the Bay of Pigs, the news coverage in both the *Times* and the *Washington Post*, then hardly a rival for the *Times*, was broadly compatible with, when not directly dependent on, State Department releases, and sources and editorials did not impugn government policy. On Sunday, November 20, 1960, the *Times* devoted the bulk of its "News of the Week in Review" to the "Hemisphere Duel/U.S. vs. Castro." This was after a month of headlines consistent with State Department charges that Cuba had been receiving "substantial quantities of arms" originating "exclusively in Iron Curtain countries."[22] Amidst reports of "considerable evidence of clandestine support by the Cuban regime for revolutionary movements in Latin America" the *Times'* Sunday unsigned lead summary/analysis observed that:

> At the heart of the duel is Premier Castro's determination to "export" to the rest of Latin America a revolution which has become increasingly Communist-oriented and has allied itself firmly with the Communist bloc. The immediate critical area is Central America.

But, the summary concluded, the long range

> stakes for the United States are huge. . . . Cuban policies threaten to open the doors of Latin America to Soviet influence. . . . Washington regards such a development as a direct threat to the security of the United States.

The "stakes" included

> not only vast U.S. economic holdings in Latin America, but U.S. prestige and influence in the area. The repercussions would be felt on the U.S. standing throughout the under-developed areas of the world.[23]

Opposition to communism and to Soviet expansionism was combined with, indeed apparently indistinguishable from, what, in a later day, would be considered not general U.S. interests but those of "the multinational corporation."

A companion article, what today would be called a "news analysis," took what might appear to be a different view. "The instability in Central America," it contended,

> is a legacy of old wrongs—of peonage, exploitation, police brutality, suppressions of liberty, and the postponement of economic reforms by the small ruling classes. . . . In the popular Latin American mind, the United States has become associated with old social and economic grievances.[24]

However, the linkage is attributed not to the inherent character of the United States but rather to its "inevitably [having] to deal with the governments in power, whatever their complexion." And, in another unexpected twist, the piece noted:

All this makes fertile ground for "fidelismo." Fidel Castro has defied the United States. . . . He has proclaimed himself the champion of the aspirations of the masses throughout Latin America. It takes a good amount of political sophistication to see through the speciousness of the Castro claims, to realize that fidelismo means the substitution of a dictatorship of the left for the hypocritical oligarchy of the right.[25]

Before "the sixties" it was no contradiction for the *Times* to impugn the "legacy of old wrongs" of "the small ruling classes" on the one hand and to oppose "fidelismo" and support U.S. political and business interests on the other. Events in Central America were being viewed from a standpoint distinct from the one that would later become customary—after the shift in terrain or paradigm or *problematique*.[26] U.S. "stakes" are in the foreground, the stuff of Latin America in the background. There is a distance between the reader—unquestionably an *American* reader—and events "south of the border." The stakes are "huge," but our interest is engaged less than our "interests."

Nonetheless, the old paradigm is not as its critics have it. To be sure, these reports subscribe to what Daniel Hallin calls "the key assumptions" of the "Cold War consensus on foreign policy."[27] Yet, the frame differs from what we would expect from reading Hallin, Herbert Gans, and other critics of pre-Vietnam reporting. If there is something of what would come to be called "ethnocentrism," the perspective is not provincial. If there is no hesitation in embracing the U.S. interests or in denouncing editorially the "speciousness of the Castro claims," there is also a clear recognition of "social and economic grievances." The "American puppets" catch as much criticism as their Cold War adversaries. "Political sophistication" sees through "oligarchies of the right" as clearly as "dictatorships of the left." In that news world a geopolitical perspective in which Central America is "critical" and the U.S. stakes "huge," could combine with denunciation of "exploitation, police brutality, and suppressions of liberty." Let us call this frame "imperial democratic."

The Position Changes, the Frame Remains the Same

Whether through indifference or inadvertence, the traditional frame survived in American reportage on Nicaragua well into the 1970s. Yet that frame and perspective permitted ample room for mounting criticism of the Somoza dynasty. By February 1963 the editors of the *Times* began noticing some serious defects in a regime which three and a half years earlier they had depicted as enjoying "support from the peasants and workers."

No Latin American nation, not even Nicaragua, is going to put up indefinitely with a dynasty that owns a great part of the country's land and industries, that controls the armed forces, picks members of the government from top to bottom, represses any serious opposition, and runs everything inefficiently by bribery, tolerance of corruption and where necessary, by force.[28]

At this point U.S. expeditionary forces in Vietnam barely had reached eleven thousand, and the Buddhist crisis, which would eventually topple South Vietnamese President Ngo Dinh Diem, was only starting to simmer.[29] But Neil Sheehan remembers that David Halberstam's critical reporting already was forcing the *Times* "into a consistently adversarial position with the Kennedy administration."

> The decade of Vietnam was to change the attitudes of [*Times* senior news editors] [Turner] Catledge and [Clifton] Daniels. Both men were to become advocates of an aggressive and rigorously independent press, but in 1963 the adversarial role was new and they did not like it at all. The *Times* executives were also still feeling the pain of the controversy over Herbert Matthews's sympathetic reporting of the pre-Communist phase of Castro's revolution in Cuba. They were afraid that Halberstam might be bringing a similar scandal upon them. . . . In early September the *New York Journal-American* and the other Hearst newspapers began to accuse Halberstam of being naive about Communism and preparing the way for a Vietnamese Fidel Castro.[30]

The *Times* editors made it clear that they did not see a leftist Cuban-style regime as the solution to the defects of the Somozas: "The great assets of the Somozas are that they are anti-Communist, anti-*Fidelista* and pro-United States, including American business."[31]

The *Times* continued to share the fear of Cuban expansionism in Central America which had led President Kennedy to sponsor the Alliance for Progress. But now the *Times* began hoping that Kennedy would

> talk to the Nicaraguans about the democratic ideals of the Alliance for Progress and Mr. Kennedy's firm belief that the continuation of feudalism in Latin America . . . paves the way for Communism and Fidelismo.[32]

The Somoza dynasty had lost its benevolent and populist image in the *New York Times* and began to look more like the aforesaid "hypocritical oligarchies of the right"—without inspiring any sympathy for "dictatorships of the left."[33]

Reporting on the February 1963 elections, the generally more conservative *Time* magazine bared disgust with Somoza hypocrisy and some impatience with Washington:

> The opposition loudly cried fraud, said that the ballot boxes were stuffed before the polls opened, that the government had printed thousands of duplicate registration cards. In the new regime . . . the only genuine opposition will have no voice in the legislature. Nevertheless, the U.S. chose to regard the election as a small evolutionary step toward representative democracy.[34]

If the American journalistic perspective was evolving, so was Nicaragua herself. "Times have changed," wrote *New York Times* correspondent Henry Giniger from Managua in January 1967, "and naked brutal dictatorship has changed with it . . . Nicaragua is not what it was twenty-five years ago when old General Anastasio Somoza García was ruling."[35]

For two years Henry Giniger's spot reporting framed the political crisis which would climax in 1967 and revive the Sandinista movement. In November 1965 Giniger filed a lengthy report on the changing Nicaraguan economy. The signal regional achievement of the Alliance for Progress was the Central American Common Market, which was promoting economies of scale. "The introduction of large-scale and efficient cotton production" was, Giniger wrote, "sparking a boom that has brought with it a high rate of industrial expansion." Consequently the wages of factory and government workers were "rising an average of 6 per cent a year." The expanded consumption of sugar and meat "and increasing purchases of radios and motorcycles are considered indications of slowly improving living standards."[36] By early 1967 Giniger could report that over the past decade the country had regularly registered annual increases of 8 percent or more in the gross national product, and that "Nicaragua has less unemployment than any other country in Central America."[37]

However, many remained underemployed. As Giniger noted in an earlier article "much of the country's population is living at or near the subsistence level," surviving on "the corn and beans they can raise. . . ." Industry accounted for no more than 14 percent of the gross national product while 70 percent of the people still lived off agriculture, where, "critics say, the wealth is filtering down too slowly." Nicaragua, Giniger pointed out, was the largest country in Central America with 57,000 square miles, but with only 1.6 million people it was also the most thinly populated. Land was abundant but food and social services were scarce.[38]

Still the social profile of the country was changing with the economy:

> The country used to be contemptuously dismissed as "Somozaland". . . . The Somozas are still a power, but the base of wealth is broadening, the middle class is growing stronger and a young dynamic group of entrepreneurs, notably in cotton, is making its weight felt.[39]

These entrepreneurs and middle management of Nicaragua's developing light industry would swell the ranks of the opposition.

Nonetheless, Nicaragua remained a patrimonial society:

> Families, and the loyalties they produce, are powerful factors and Nicaragua has for a long time been dominated by one family or another bearing such names as Somoza, Chamorro and Sacasa.[40]

But the appurtenances of modernity began to transform Nicaragua's medieval landscape: "Illiterate peasants are less ignorant of political affairs . . . thanks to transistor radios bought for a few cents a week."[41] Electricity and machinery, but also labor unions and large relatively cosmopolitan universities with their contagious student movements were making a patrimonial monarch seem out of place.

Giniger had traveled to Managua in November 1965 to report on the development of a civilian opposition movement against the Somoza dynasty. And while he noted that the first Somoza had ruled "more benevolently than most other dictators in Latin America until he was assassinated in 1956," it was evident that "a desire has grown for a break with the Somoza-dominated past."[42] Fifteen months later a popular civic movement manifesting this desire culminated in a bloodbath which would become, Giniger wrote, "an indelible part of the country's history."[43] His reporting on the January 1967 *dénouement* was the only sustained U.S. media coverage Nicaragua would receive during the 1960s.

The episode began when an opposition rally tried to turn itself into a kind of voters' coup. The result was what Giniger called "some of the bloodiest street fighting in Central American history."[44] Somoza's second son, Anastasio Somoza Debayle, had replaced his reformist older brother Luís as Nicaragua's strongman and was running for the presidency. The civilian opposition presented a serious challenge to Somoza's ambitions. Like their predecessors in 1962, and their successors of the 1970s and 1980s, the opposition presidential candidate, an eye doctor named Fernando Agüero Rochas, and his principal lieutenant, Pedro Joaquín Chamorro, believed a government-orchestrated electoral fraud was in the making. To thwart it they urged supporters to converge on Managua with "little packages of food," a thinly-veiled euphemism for arms.[45] On Sunday, January 22, two weeks before election day, Agüero and Chamorro led a march to the National Guard headquarters. There Agüero called for a general strike to "demand electoral guarantees" and "appealed to the army to join his forces against Somoza."[46] The guardsmen drew bayonets and slugged demonstrators with the butts of their rifles. Then, "shots were fired. Who fired first is in dispute. Well over a thousand of the demonstrators, mainly peasants who had come into Managua for the rally, took refuge in the Gran Hotel."[47]

The Sandinista Fausto Amador, a half-brother of founding member Carlos Fonseca Amador, thought the rally "stupid. A supposedly peaceful movement in which those in the rear were armed with rifles? A peaceful movement doubling as an armed insurrection?" Since the FSLN had declared that "there was no point in supporting the rally," Amador, attended "more as a curiosity-seeker than as a participant." He was swallowed up by what was "probably the biggest demonstration in the history of Nicaragua until the fall of Somoza":

> I went with my wife, who was pregnant. . . . There I ran into [another clandestine Sandinista] Humberto Belli, right at the head of the demonstration. "Look, this is nuts," I said to him: "What are you planning to do when the firing starts?"

There was a permit until 4 in the afternoon. At 4:05 [the authorities] said: "Your permit has lapsed. Fire!" and they began to shoot over the heads of the crowd. Probably the first shots went into the air. . . . But then the guns started to dip slowly toward the people. There was a general stampede, and I began to see scenes out of Dante—someone fleeing with his stomach open, people in the streets running without their arms, people falling, a carpet of blood over the ground. I ran quickly to try to find a refuge for us in one of the houses near the avenue with the inglorious name of Roosevelt.[48]

For the next twenty-four hours the Gran Hotel became a fortress where the Agüeristas held hostage some 125 foreigners, including eighty-nine Americans. Throughout that Sunday night snipers with automatic weapons exchanged fire with the National Guard. To overwhelm the snipers the Guard brought up tanks, which fired 37-mm cannons at the Gran Hotel and other outposts. Two fires burned through the night as fighting continued around Managua's telegraph office into the morning. "By then," Giniger recounted, "hundreds were dead or wounded on both sides."[49]

The *Times* estimated the number of dead as "at least thirty-two persons and as possibly as many as sixty."[50] But the opposition insisted that many more were killed. "It was said that 300 died," Amador recalled:

That there were 13,500 wounded . . . many corpses were simply thrown into a common ditch, because they were just campesinos who came from far away. . . . It was never possible to know for certain how many people died.[51]

The Nicaraguan Church, together with the Papal Nuncio and finally the U.S. ambassador, succeeded in negotiating an agreement for the safe conduct of the rebels in exchange for the release of their foreign hostages. "But," Giniger concluded, "the more basic political struggle and its accompanying rancor continued."[52]

At a press conference a few days later Agüero acknowledged that he had "tried to stage a coup during the shooting Sunday." The candidate explained that he had sought "to convince the National Guard . . . to join him in setting up a provisional civilian-military junta" whose object would be "to organize 'honest' elections."[53] On the following day, "Pedro Joaquín Chamorro, publisher of *La Prensa*, the principal opposition newspaper, was taken into custody . . . by forces of the National Guard."[54] The *Times* expressed solidarity with its colleague:

Although Dr. Agüero was allowed to remain at liberty, his associate, Pedro Joaquín Chamorro, publisher of La Prensa, was arrested and maltreated and his respected newspaper was closed. All of which provides a foundation for Dr. Agüero's charge of "robbery by brute force."[55]

But the *Times* editorialists chose not to replicate the explosive term in which the editor of *La Prensa* had described his ordeal to Giniger.

Yesterday [Chamorro's] wife and mother were allowed to visit him [along with] several newsmen. . . . He looked well, but he said he was tortured when he entered the prison.

Col. Ernesto Ruzama Nuñez, Managua's chief of police, said pouring a bucket of water on the editor did not constitute torture. Mr. Chamorro retorted that one bucket might not, but 25 or 30 did.[56]

Even if Giniger did not mean his reader to smile at this exchange, it is hard not to do so today. Notwithstanding, the substantial increase in body-count from "the massacre at El Chaparral" to the Agueristas' bloody debacle, "torture" and "massacre" in Nicaragua would acquire far graver meanings.

The irrepressible Pedro Joaquín Chamorro had engaged repeatedly in protests, plots, and rebellions against the regime, occasionally receiving rather more severe treatment in Somoza's jails than what he complained of in 1967.[57] Yet the Somozas usually let his newspaper appear—even though, in Giniger's words, "the kind of blasts it issued every day against the Somoza family would keep libel lawyers working overtime in the United States."[58] The Somoza brothers, both educated in the United States, realized that Americans tended to view a "free press" and "free elections" as sure signs of democracy. The last Somoza noted in his *apologia*:

When dignitaries from various parts of the world came to me, they were always amazed at the contents of *La Prensa*. To all of them I could point to it and say, "Perhaps now you can believe that we do have freedom of the press in Nicaragua."

To those who called me "dictator" and worse, I could always point to Chamorro and *La Prensa* as obvious evidence of our free press policy.[59]

Somoza was also careful to observe electoral niceties. When asked why he remained free, though the same accusations had been lodged against him as against Chamorro, Agüero responded: "Because I am a presidential candidate. The Somozas have always had, as a tactic to give the appearance of legality." Meanwhile, Giniger added, "the walls and streets of Managua eloquently tell who has the upper hand. Somoza posters, billboards, and streamers are everywhere. One has to look hard to find anything favoring Dr. Agüero."[60] The Somozas, like all Nicaragua's modern rulers, understood the prevailing conventions for operating within the U.S. "sphere of influence." A former adviser to Sandinista *comandante* Bayardo Arce has stated that his chief acknowledged these persistent resemblances by observing: "We learned from a master."[61]

The Somozas also worked the American press but with less skill than their successors. Anastasio ended the tragic campaign of 1967 with "a noisy, colorful rally of about 50,000 people in Managua's main square" during which Somoza "called on the crowd to wave flags 'so the foreign press may see it,'" Giniger noted wryly.[62] The Somozas presented Nicaragua to Americans as an active partner in the struggle against communism and as an emerging democracy. They regularly claimed that "terrorism . . . was leading up to a Cuban invasion of Nicaragua."[63] Together with pointing to *La Prensa*'s freedom, they would boast to visitors of their "regular elections," in which the opposition received a quota of about 30 percent of the seats in the National Assembly.

The 1967 events marked a milestone in the declining efficacy of Somoza "spin." In 1965 Giniger wrote:

> If there is a dictatorship, it is probably the most freely discussed one in the world. The opposition controlled paper, La Prensa, has the biggest circulation in the country and an outspoken editorial line against the Somozas and the regime in general. Few complaints are heard of repression of any kind.[64]

Giniger's account of the 1967 confrontation sympathized with the opposition. Agüero attempted his self-confessed coup "because he felt there was no other recourse."[65] The aim of the coup was "to organize 'honest' elections, a kind now impossible in Nicaragua. . . ."[66] Rather than condemn the taking of innocent Americans as captives, the *Times'* editors commiserated that the opposition "must have been desperate to face such hopeless odds and to hold foreign guests in a hotel as hostages."[67]

A postelection *Times* editorial, sardonically entitled "The Somozas Forever," endorsed the opposition charge of election "robbery by brute force."[68] That verdict contrasted with the correspondent's account that, for all its irregularities,

> most neutral observers felt that General Somoza's victory was nonetheless a genuine one and represented the present balance of force in the country.[69]

Somocista circles complained about his treatment by the U.S. press. Giniger wrote that:

> The single-minded supporters of Maj. Gen. Anastasio Somoza Debayle have at times been exasperated by the less-than-total commitment among foreign observers to the general's presidential candidacy. "Why do you want to bring Communism to Nicaragua?" one Somoza man asked American correspondents in Managua just before the elections. He was rather angry but in the end he had the last laugh. Last Sunday, the election gave General Somoza something approaching a three-to-one victory, thus thwarting "international communism" and its journalistic accomplices.[70]

On January 26 Somoza had told Giniger that Agüero's movement was "linked . . . with communist youth groups trained in Cuba."[71] In fact, the Sandinistas, many of whom had indeed trained in Cuba, repudiated the *Agüeristas*. The FSLN condemned the "criminal irresponsibility of the opposition bourgeoisie" in organizing the demonstration and published the first leaflet signed by the FSLN national directorate *"con nombres y appellidos"* [without pseudonyms].[72] Sandinista leader Carlos Fonseca Amador was to boast that the Sandinistas had been "the only political force opposing the new electoral farce."

> The bourgeois opposition played along by presenting a candidate: Fernando Agüero, latifundist from the cattle-growing region.

> One so-called revolutionary sector unfortunately also went along—in what can definitely be called a case of following the masses' butt [*"cularse"*]. We believed that it was not necessary to tail any candidate just to connect with the masses and that . . . we could take advantage of the mobilization that the electoral process could generate.[73]

But between the Conservative opposition and the armed revolution, the Sandinistas did see a "link," albeit one quite different from that asserted by Somoza. Tomás Borge, along with Carlos Fonseca Amador, perceived in the failure of the movement "the collapse of the traditional parties. . . . "[74] Giniger, while conceding that it was "undeniable that the Somozas have a popular following," declared that "a continuation of Somoza control may be actually encouraging the growth of extremism."[75] Several days later Giniger noted

> reports that a few opposition people with arms have taken to the mountains in northern Nicaragua near the Honduran border. Doctor Agüero indicated he would not participate in such activities.[76]

After the calamitous Agüerista rally, the accidental participant, Sandinista Fausto Amador, sought out the family of his comrade Humberto Belli:

> I wanted to let his family know that . . . maybe [Belli] was hurt. So after crossing town stealthily, . . . I got to his house. But the one who came to open the gate was Humberto!

> Yet those who were in that demonstration felt the jolt in our souls for the rest of our lives. . . . That shock formed the necessary background to the real beginning of the guerrilla movement in Nicaragua. . . . It began in Pancasán.[77]

✳✳✳

But that was over the horizon—for the *Times* as well as for most Nicaraguans. The *Times* editors continued to hold that meaningful change south of the border could only happen through evolution, not revolution. The repression, the illegitimate elections were all residue "from an older Latin America that has gone into history except in a few other countries like Paraguay and Haiti."[78] For the whole of the decade of the 1960s, armed revolution, not to mention the FSLN, remained offstage. To the extent that it was part of the *Times* frame, it was as a distant if disquieting prospect. On October 7, 1962, the *Times* reported that government control of election procedures had fostered in the beleaguered opposition a "conviction that the Somoza family . . . will never be displaced from power peacefully."[79]

Though violence figured prominently in the coverage of Nicaragua, and though sporadic, if in Sandinista hagiography, "historic," guerrilla forays persist into the 1960s, revolutionary guerrillas remain far off in the background of the *Times'* picture. After El Chaparral, Carlos Fonseca spent the next few years consolidating his group from a base in Havana and endeavoring to launch guerrilla movements from Honduras. Their failure led Fonseca's Sandinistas in 1963 to retreat into a "legalist interim"[80] where fleetingly they crossed the view of the *Times*:

> Nicaraguan Students Protest Managua. . . . University students here and in Leon staged sit-ins today and warned of a general strike unless the Government freed a National Liberation Front leader, Carlos Fonseca Amador. The Government identified him as a Communist terrorist.[81]

This was the group's sole appearance in the American media until 1967. That year the FSLN's "legalist interim" ended when the small group launched their most ambitious guerrilla campaign to date in a remote mountainous area of the *Cordillera Dariense* of Matagalpa called Pancasán. In August the *Times* carried a wire service dispatch from Managua citing *La Prensa*'s report that some twenty-five guerrillas "had died in combat with the Government's National Guard in the Matagalpa Mountains, ninety miles north of here. . . ."[82]

The *Times* covered the subsequent rout of the Sandinistas somewhat more fully, but only within the framework of Cuban expansionism. On September 11 a column-length Giniger article datelined Managua summarized the failure of the latest efforts to foment "violent Castro-style Communism throughout Latin America."

> These included Ché Guevara's fatal final adventure in Bolivia.

> Intelligence reports indicate that the Castro-aided guerrillas are not receiving substantial or consistent popular support in Bolivia, Venezuela or Nicaragua. Without massive popular support, the informants stress, the guerrillas must inevitably lose out to the local security forces.

> The informants said that the third "anti-Castro" success in the last month was in Nicaragua. The national guard was said to have killed 14 insurgents of about 40 believed to be operating in the hilly north-central area of the country. No losses were reported on the Nicaraguan side.[83]

"Intelligence reports" enjoy a credibility here which would have been considered unseemly a decade later. Only the most perfunctory confirmation, and no on-the-spot reportage, is considered necessary. Giniger does not visit the northern mountains.

Nicaraguan events were viewed from the capital and within a geopolitical context, at a greater distance and a palpably different angle from the one later used to observe the revolution. The U.S. stakes remained in the foreground, Latin American matters in the background, decidedly "South of the Border."

For all that, Giniger's account of the *Fidelistas'* failure ran counter to conventional wisdom among U.S. and Latin American area experts and proved generally correct.[84] A month later, on the very day that the *Times* announced that "Cuba Ends Silence On Guevara Report"—his capture and execution in Bolivia—Giniger could chime in from Managua that: "An attempt to prepare a new Communist guerrilla front in Central America appears to have been smashed in the northern mountains here."

> National guard units have ambushed a group of would-be fighters east of Matagalpa and have killed 15 of them. . . . Of the 15 would-be fighters who were killed, 10 are said to have been identified. Eight were reported to have . . . undergone training in Cuba. Two major leaders are in flight. One, Tomás Borge, is a long-standing activist. . . . The other is Carlos Fonseca Amador, also an active leftist for several years.

This was to be the most thorough-going description of the Sandinistas until the mid-1970s:

> The organization that these leaders helped build is called the Sandinista Front of National Liberation. It represents an effort to capitalize on the name and reputation of a legendary pioneer in guerrilla tactics, Gen. Augusto Sandino, who rose to prominence by fighting against the occupation of Nicaragua by United States Marines from 1927 to 1933.[85]

The appellation "Sandinista" turns up in the pages of the *Times* for the first, and from its account of the disaster at Pancasán, ostensibly the last, time. But Giniger made it clear that "the danger had not completely passed."

While his report seemed to accept Somoza's claim that the Sandinistas were linked with Cuba, Giniger was far from ascribing all Nicaraguan dissent to Castro's interventions:

> General Somoza . . . said that since Premier Fidel Castro came to power in Cuba, Nicaragua had experienced 27 attempts to mount extremist attacks on the regime. But the Somoza-dominated regime has also had to contend with strong and sometimes violent non-Communist opposition.[86]

Moreover, for the first time a *Times* report from Nicaragua accented what would later be known as "human rights violations." In language that now begins to anticipate "post-Vietnam" reportage Giniger cites "the agreement of most observers" that

> much would depend on how quickly the Government could move to alleviate rural poverty and how well national guardsmen were able to distinguish between peasants and guerrillas. There were reports of cases in which such distinctions had not been made, but the [Nicaraguan] President belittled these.[87]

We are left at this level of generality. There is no evidence of any investigation to determine whether in fact the guerrilla movement had been "smashed" or only disabled.

Peasants and guerrillas remained minor players even in the late sixties, relegated to the background while powerful families continued to occupy main stage. Giniger concluded his coverage of the events of 1967 with a note about the Somoza-Chamorro "feud":

> One of the most enduring feuds in Latin America has become more bitter than ever as a result of renewed Communist activity here. . . . The Government and the country's leading newspaper are harassing each other. . . . Somoza . . . and the editor of *La Prensa*, Dr. Pedro Joaquín Chamorro, have long and intensely disliked each other. In the background is a Communist movement trying to establish itself as a viable force. The two men accuse each other of fostering the movement, each in his own way.[88]

The Sandinistas did not formally reenter the pages of the *Times* in the sixties. But they can be heard off-stage in the very last *Times'* Nicaragua article of the sixties, a piece describing the inauguration of the *Rubén Dario* theater in Managua. During the "social cultural 'week of the decade' " as the theater was being inaugurated, a group of "students enacted a satirical play about the family of a typical Nicaraguan landowner and his old-fashioned Roman Catholic wife, facing moral issues and a son with revolutionary ideas."[89]

The *Times* attributed the guerrilla theater to the "student federation of the University of Nicaragua." The students were protesting illiteracy with signs which read "We have a theater and we can't read." Shouting 'Death to the Somozas!' and '*Viva, Fidel*!' and '*Viva, Ché*!' the students marched off into the night followed by three jeep loads of policemen."[90] At that time the student federation of the University of Nicaragua (the *Federación Estudiantil Revolucionaria* or FER) was controlled by the FSLN.

Notes

1. *NYT*, June 28, 1959, 20.
2. *NYT*, July 4, 1959, 5.
3. "Castro Aide Linked to Nicaraguan Raid," *NYT*, July 28, 1959, 2.

4. The *New York Times* said that the split between the Honduran army and the ruling Liberal Party surfaced "when 'the massacre of El Chaparral' was reported" by the Honduran press. "Nine rebels were killed, fifteen wounded, and twenty-seven captured in the hour-and-forty-five-minute fight," the dispatch continued disparagingly. "The band consisted of Cubans, Salvadorans, Guatemalans, Mexicans, Hondurans, and Nicaraguans." *NYT*, July 12, 1959, 14.

5. Tomás Borge is one of those who tells of Villeda's "complicity" which he attributes his admiration for Ché (Tomás Borge, *La paciente impaciencia* [Mexico: Diana, 1989], 149, 51). See also Victor Tirado López, "El FSLN: un producto y una necesidad históricos," in *Nicaragua: una nueva democracia en el tercer mundo* (Managua: Vanguardia, 1986), 25; and Victor Bulmer-Thomas, "Honduras Since 1939," in *Central America Since Independence*, ed. Leslie Bethell (Cambridge, England: Cambridge University, 1991); James Morris, *Honduras: Caudillo Politics and Military Rulers* (Boulder: Westview, 1984); Stefania Natalini del Castro, Maria de los Angeles Mendoza Saborio, and Joaquín Pagan Solorzano, *Significado histórico del gobierno del Dr. Ramón Villeda Morales* (Teguciagalpa: 1985); Edelberto Torres Rivas, *Sandino y sus Padres* (Managua: Editorial Nueva Nicaragua, 1981), 762-63; author's interview with Manuel Gamero, editor of *El Tiempo*, Tegucigalpa, August 1981.

6. *NYT*, June 14, 1959, 29.

7. Paul P. Kennedy, "Nicaragua Fights Armed Invaders," *NYT*, June 2, 1959, 1.

8. Kennedy, "Nicaragua Fights Armed Invaders," 1.

9. Pedro Joaquín Chamorro C., *Diario de un Preso* (Managua: Pez y Serpiente, 1981), 15.

10. *NYT*, June 15, 1959, 1.

11. Karl Marx, "The Eighteenth Brumaire of Louis Bonaparte," in Marx and Frederick Engels, *Selected Works* (Moscow: Foreign Language Publishing House, 1958), vol. I, 247.

12. The fullest accounts of El Chaparral and of Pedro Joaquín's landing in Chontales, the episode known as the "invasion of Olama y Mollejones," are to be found in Miguel Jesús Blandon, *Entre Sandino y Fonseca Amador* (Managua: Impresiones y Toqueles, 1980), 82-113. My discussion of El Chaparral also benefited from "Las Notas Autobiograficas de Alejandro Martinez," the unpublished memoirs of a Nicaraguan survivor of the 1959 expeditions. See also Torres Rivas, "El Crimen de El Chaparral," *Despertar* (Organ of the *Frente Revolucionario Nicaraguense*), Mexico (July 1959); Claribel Alegría and D. J. Flakcll, *Nicaragua, la revolución sandinista: una crónica politica, 1859-1979* (Mexico: ERA, 1982), 153-56; Borge, *La paciente impaciencia*, 147-51; and Tirado López, "El FSLN: un producto y una necesidad históricos," 25. A brief account in English of Olama y Mollejones can be found in Bernard Diederich, *Somoza and the Legacy of U.S. Involvement in Central America* (1st edition, New York: E. P. Dutton, 1981; 2d edition, Maplewood, New Jersey: Waterfront Press, 1989), 58-59.

13. "Nicaragua: Calling-Card Surrender," *Time*, June 22, 1959, 33-34.

14. *NYT*, June 16, 1959, 34.

15. Antonio Ibarra Y Rojas, interview with author, Washington, D.C., April 17, 1987.

16. Herbert L. Matthews, "Old Order in Cuba is Threatened By Forces of Internal Revolt," *NYT*, February 26, 1957, 13.

17. Carlos Fonseca, *Bajo la bandera del sandinismo* (Managua: Editorial Nueva Nicaragua, 1981), vol. I, 46, 356.

18. David Horowitz, *Radical Son* (New York: Free Press, 1997), 102, 107.

19. Antonio Ybarra-Rojas was vice minister to the president from 1990 to January 1992. He was implicated in a wide-ranging corruption scandal and fled the country. On Ybarra's adult adventures, see U.S. Senate, Committee on Foreign Relations, "Sworn Affidavit of Dr. Antonio Ybarra-Rojas," March 15, 1993, unpublished; and *The Economist Intelligence Unit* (February 23, 1994).

20. U.S. Senate, "Sworn Affidavit of Dr. Antonio Ybarra-Rojas," 3; and *The Economist Intelligence Unit* (February 23, 1994).

21. *NYT*, April 20, 1959, 1.

22. "US Text on Arming Cuba," *NYT*, November 19, 1960, 2.

23. "Hemisphere Dual—U.S. vs. Castro," *NYT*, November 20, 1960, E1.

24. E. W. Kenworthy, "IN WASHINGTON: Dispatch of Naval Vessels Still Leaves Future Actions Uncertain" *NYT*, November 20, 1960, E3.

25. Kenworthy, "IN WASHINGTON," E3.

26. On such shifts, see Michael Foucault, *Madness and Civilization* (London: Tavistock, 1967), Introduction; Thomas S. Kuhn, *The Structure of Scientific Revolutions* (Phoenix edition, Chicago: University of Chicago, 1964); Louis Althusser and Etienne Balibar, *Reading Capital* (New York: Pantheon, 1970), 26-28.

27. Daniel C. Hallin, *We Keep America on Top of the World: Television Journalism and the Public Sphere* (London: Routledge, 1993), 127.

28. "The Nicaraguan Election," *NYT*, February 6, 1963, 2.

29. Neil Sheehan, *A Bright Shining Lie: John Paul Vann and America in Vietnam* (New York: Random House, 1988), 270; David Halberstam, *The Best and the Brightest* (Greenwich, Connecticut: Fawcett, 1973), 307; also Halberstam, "The Bhuddist Crisis in Vietnam," *NYT*, September 11, 1963; and Halberstam, "The Coup in South Vietnam," November 6, 1963, reprinted in *Vietnam: History, Documents, and Opinions on a Major World Crisis*, ed. Marvin E. Gettleman (Greenwich, Connecticut: Fawcett, 1965), 262-81.

30. Sheehan, *Bright Shining Lie*, 348.

31. Editorial, *NYT*, February 6, 1963, 2.

32. Editorial, *NYT*, February 6, 1963, 2.

33. In October 1962 the *Times* reported that any opposition hope that the Somoza family could be "displaced from power peacefully . . . virtually vanished last week when the all-powerful Supreme Electoral Commission was heavily weighted in favor of the Somoza party." In another echo, or foreshadowing, the piece continued that both opposition and pro-Somoza "political observers" agreed that Somoza "could win a free election. The administration party has a disciplined national machine. The Conservative Party, until recent years was barely able to maintain a skeletal structure because of Government harassment." *NYT*, October 7, 1962, A11.

34. "Nicaragua: Evolutionary Election," *Time* (February 15, 1963): 29.

35. Henry Giniger, "Nicaragua's 'Dynasty' Digs In," *NYT*, January 29, 1967, section IV, 4.

36. Giniger, "Nicaragua Gains in Economic Area," *NYT*, November 28, 1965, 12F.

37. Giniger, "To the Somozas, 'Dynasty' Is a Nasty Word," *NYT*, February 12, 1967, section IV, 3.

38. Giniger, "Nicaragua Gains in Economic Area."

39. Giniger, "Nicaragua Gains in Economic Area."

40. Giniger, "To the Somozas, 'Dynasty' Is a Nasty Word."

41. Giniger, "Nicaragua Split on Somoza's Role: Former Dictator's Son May Seek Presidency in 1967," *NYT*, November 5, 1965, A14. For further discussion of patrimonialism, see Max Weber, *Economy and Society: An Outline of Interpretive Sociology* (Berkeley: University of California, 1978); Richard Morse "The Heritage of Latin America,"

in *The Founding of New Societies*, ed. Louis Hartz (New York: Harcourt Brace and World, 1964); and Octavio Paz, *Sor Juana* (Cambridge, Massachusetts: Harvard University, 1988), 11-33.

42. Giniger, "Nicaragua Split on Somoza's Role."

43. Giniger "To the Somozas, 'Dynasty' Is a Nasty Word."

44. Giniger, "Somoza Confident of a Victory in Today's Nicaraguan Election," *NYT*, February 5, 1967, 20.

45. "50 Hostages Freed, Nicaragua Calmed," *NYT*, January 24, 1967, A1; Giniger, "Rival of Somoza Still in the Race," *NYT*, January 25, 1967, A14. See Richard Millet, *The Guardians of the Dynasty* (Maryknoll, New York: Orbis, 1977), 229; and Eduardo Crawley, *Dictators Never Die* (New York: St. Martin's, 1979), 133-35.

46. Giniger, "Fighting Flares Again in Managua," *NYT*, January 26, 1967, A16.

47. Giniger, "Rival of Somoza Still in the Race."

48. From unpublished text of filmed interview in Spanish for "In the Land of the Poets," directed by Ronald Maxwell, Person to Person Films, October 1987, translated by the author.

49. Giniger, "Nicaragua's 'Dynasty' Digs In." Also *NYT*, January 23, 1967, 1, 14; *NYT*, January 24, 1967, 6; *NYT*, January 25, 1967, 14.

50. *NYT*, January 25, 1967, A14.

51. *NYT*, January 25, 1967, A14. Antonio Ybarra-Rojas, claims that "more than three hundred peasants were killed in the city of Managua on the twenty-second of January 1967" (Interview with Ronald Maxwell in "In the Land of the Poets").

52. Giniger, "Nicaragua's 'Dynasty' Digs In."

53. *NYT*, January 26, 1967, 16.

54. *NYT*, January 27, 1967, 12.

55. "The Somozas Forever," *NYT*, February 6, 1967, 28.

56. Giniger, "Somoza Confident of a Victory."

57. Chamorro claims that brutal beatings were carried out in the notorious "sewing room" where the Somozas detained prisoners within a stone's throw of the Presidential Palace. See Chamorro, *Estirpe Sangriente* (Mexico: Diogenes, 1980), chapter IX.

58. "Nicaragua's 'Dynasty' Digs In."

59. Anastasio Somoza and Jack Cox, *Nicaragua Betrayed* (Boston: Western Islands, 1980), 28.

60. Giniger, "Somoza Confident of a Victory."

61. Arturo Jose Cruz, Jr., author's interview, Oxford, England, November 12, 1991.

62. Giniger, "Somoza Campaign Ends with a Rally," *NYT*, January 30, 1967, A23.

63. Kennedy, "Nicaragua Fears Cuba Will Invade," *NYT*, October 11, 1961, E3. See also "Somoza Charges Red Plot," *NYT*, March 23, 1961, 4; "Nicaragua Sees Red Revolt Peril," *NYT*, July 10, 1962, 10; *NYT*, September 25, 1964, 16.

64. *NYT*, November 5, 1965, A14.

65. Giniger, "Somoza Confident of a Victory."

66. Giniger, "Rival of Somoza Still in the Race."

67. *NYT*, January 25, 1967, 32.

68. *NYT*, February 5, 1967, 28.

69. Giniger, "To the Somozas, 'Dynasty' Is a Nasty Word."

70. Giniger, "To the Somozas, 'Dynasty' Is a Nasty Word."

71. *NYT*, January 25, 1967.

72. Jacinto Suarez in *Nicaragua: Revolución: Relatos de combatientes del frente sandinista*, ed. Pilar Arias (Mexico: Siglo XXI, 1980), 40; after the repression, "It seemed that the opposition had died" (Suarez in *Nicaragua: Revolución*, 41).

73. Fonseca, "Entrevista, 1970" in *Bajo la bandera del sandinismo*, 223. "Tailing the masses" is a Leninist term denoting a vanguard's opportunistic failing of "bowing to the spontaneity of the masses" instead of leading them in a revolutionary way. See V. I. Lenin, *What Is to be Done*, volume v in *Collected Works* (Moscow: Foreign Language Publishing House, 1961), chapter II. For a highly critical account of the *Agüerista* demonstration by a veteran Sandinista, see Borge, *La paciente impaciente*, 282-83. Some members of the FSLN, as we have seen, participated in the demonstration, but the organization as such boycotted it. Giniger wrote: "Hard-core Communists in Nicaragua amount to only a few hundred, and sympathizers perhaps a few thousand. A good many of them are students at the National University and it appeared that they took an active part in the bloody disturbances that broke out in Managua January 22," *NYT*, February 12, 1967, section IV, 3.

74. Borge, *La paciente impaciente*, 283.

75. *NYT*, January 29, 1967, section IV, 4.

76. Giniger, "Somoza Is Victor; Calls For Unity," *NYT*, February 7, 1967, 14.

77. Interview with Ronald Maxwell in "In the Land of the Poets."

78. *NYT*, February 6, 1967, 28.

79. "Rivals Losing Hope for a Peaceful End of Somozas' Rule," *NYT*, October 7, 1962, 11.

80. See *Nicaragua: Revolución*, chapter 2.

81. "Nicaraguan Students Protest," *NYT*, July 2, 1964, 3.

82. "Guerrilla Toll in Nicaragua," *NYT*, August 21, 1967, 27.

83. "Latin Guerrillas Said to be Losing," *NYT*, September 11, 1967, 13.

84. Jorge Dominguez, Professor of Government, Harvard University, emphasized this point in comments on earlier draft of this manuscript, June 11, 1992.

85. Giniger, "Nicaragua Rebels Believed Crushed," *NYT*, October 12, 1967, 22.

86. Giniger, "Nicaragua Rebels Believed Crushed."

87. Giniger, "Nicaragua Rebels Believed Crushed."

88. Giniger, "Nicaraguan Political Feud Growing More Bitter," *NYT*, December 10, 1967, 33.

89. "Managua's 'Week of the Decade' Is Socially Hectic with Overtones of Protest," *NYT*, December 10, 1969, A15.

90. *NYT*, December 10, 1969, A15.

Chapter 8
A New Correspondent in Nicaragua

Through the fifties and sixties the *New York Times* seemed to report with assurance to a reader confident of his place in the world. His Communists are unmistakable, as are their arms, activities, and allies such as Cuba. Revolutionaries threaten an established order which, though it contains noticeable flaws regarding justice and equity, is nonetheless stable, certain, and slowly improving. There is an air of imperial and ethnocentric self-assurance against which events in peripheral places like Nicaragua may be reported with a detachment which borders on indifference. The characters in the drama—the Somozas, Chamorro, Agüero, Fonseca, *et al.*—do not have strongly charged moral presences. Though some may be preferable to others, none represent unmitigated good or evil. There is little percussive or persuasive force in this reporting. There is a universe of news which one does not feel the reporter challenging or seeking to alter. We are dealing with the kind of news which provoked the criticisms of Sigal, Gans, Gitlin, Tuchman, and company. Persuasion and commentary are left to the editorial page. The line of demarcation between editorial and reportage is clear although there is room for summary and interpretation. These are contained in articles which have the evident character of what today would be called "news analysis," though they are not so titled.

This manner of presenting Nicaragua changed sharply in the mid-1970s as did Nicaragua itself. Though the country continued to enjoy sustained, albeit uneven, economic growth after 1967, the third Somoza was unable to halt the political erosion. A broader professional and business class had emerged to manage a diversifying economy. Their children went to universities and joined a student movement fanned by the breezes of the sixties. Anastasio Somoza Debayle, the last and least able of the Somoza dynasty, seemed oblivious to the permutations beneath the surface of Nicaraguan politics.

Disaster struck the old Nicaragua in the midst of Christmas weekend 1972. Having driven home through the celebrating city, Pedro Joaquín Chamorro, or the hero of his semifictional semiautobiographical account of the earthquake, climbed into bed with his wife after an evening of revelry.

> It was as if we were in Pompeii when . . . the butlers were surprised by catastrophe as they served the wine and the butchers weighed out the meat and others made love in their beds.[1]

Like the Chamorros, though in a very different locale, Juvenal, the Sandinista hero of Xavier Arguëllo's novel *Las Delicias del Volga*

> awoke suddenly to a rough jolt and a long, ominous volcanic roar from the bowels of the earth.
>   The lights of the cell went out. . . . The prisoners shrieked in the darkness, crowding against the bars. He felt the pressure of bare feet on his head. Sweaty and foul-smelling bodies trampled him. . . . The ground moved nearly half a foot three or four times a second and bounced upward perhaps eight times.[2]

An earthquake was ripping through the city. Anastasio Somoza, who was awake "looking out over our capital city of Managua and thinking that Christmas is really here," tells us he "sensed immediately that this was no tremor. Managua was literally being torn apart. In those few short minutes, some 10,000 people died in Managua."[3]

The eruption split hills, demolished factories, and broke open El Hormiguero penitentiary, Somoza's notorious "Anthill." Arguëllo's suddenly liberated Sandinista saw it coming

> in rather shallow concentric waves. . . . In its path the quake left cracks in the earth like broken mirrors. Sidewalk bricks shook out of place. Automobiles swerved out of control on the zigzagging road, undulating like the surface of a stormy sea.[4]

The front-pages of both the *Times* and the *Washington Post* favored the story even over accounts of Nixon's "Christmas bombing," in which "U.S. planes continued the heaviest assault of the war on North Vietnam through a sixth day Saturday, as Hanoi accused the United States of waging an 'extermination' bombing campaign against populated areas."[5]

The *Times* headlined "Thousands Dead as Quakes Strike Nicaraguan City," and the *Post*'s lead story began:

> A series of sharp earthquakes followed by uncontrolled fires reduced most of Managua, Nicaragua, to rubble Saturday.[6]

The *Times* recounted:

In Managua, survivors fled in panic, jamming all roads around the city, which is on a lake east of the Pacific coast. Hundreds of mutilated bodies were strewn along the streets, some still wrapped in bedsheets, some missing heads, hands or feet, said one witness fleeing the city.

[One Managuan] described the scene as "like the end of the world."[7]

But before long, all that most Americans would recall of the earthquake would be the death of World Series hero Roberto Clemente, a Puerto Rican, who perished attempting to deliver aid to Managua on New Year's Day. Already two days earlier Marvine Howe of the *New York Times* reported from Managua:

Life began to return to normal in this earthquake-stricken capital today as the Conservatives and Liberals resumed party disputes that have characterized political life in this country for more than a century.[8]

Things never "returned to normal." Managua was never rebuilt and Nicaraguan political life was never the same. Somoza, reportedly with the encouragement of the Nixon Administration's ambassador to Managua, Turner Shelton, discarded the pretense of sharing power and shoved aside his two partners in government and began to rule by decree.[9] Somoza appeared most inspired by the opportunity to pilfer international relief funds and to corner reconstruction work. Businessmen under the leadership of Alfonso Robelo Callejas and others began organizing countrywide meetings and conventions demanding honesty in government and social reforms. The Church publicly denounced government corruption. In February 1974 the *Times* reported that Somoza had alienated the business community by his peculation of relief monies, monopolization of reconstruction work, and the "sharp increases in the price of cement—an industry largely owned by the Somoza family." The report added that:

The Conservative party split last year over the issue of special powers granted by the Constituent Assembly to General Somoza to sign foreign loans for rebuilding the capital.[10]

The schism originated in the outrage of Pedro Joaquín Chamorro and other Conservatives at Agüero's 1972 decision to participate with Somoza in a cogoverning arrangement, caustically dubbed the "*kupia kumi*," Miskito Indian for "two hearts beating as one." The Conservative breach was never healed, not even with Violeta Chamorro's 1990 presidential victory. Many sons and daughters of leading Conservatives joined the Sandinistas, providing information which would ignite in December 1974 in a spectacular raid.

In that year the dictator announced his intention to "run" for re-election. Pedro Joaquín Chamorro formed a broad political coalition known as UDEL, Democratic Union for Liberation. UDEL and most of the opposition refused to support the official Conservative candidate and branded the election a farce. The Somozas' "democratic" facade had been irreparably breached.[11]

Somoza's figure in the U.S. media also would be marred past mending. In the first of a series of columns on the Nicaraguan autocrat in 1975-76, Jack Anderson painted an enduring portrait: "The world's greediest ruler is Anastasio Somoza, the potbellied potentate who runs Nicaragua as if it were his private estate."[12] Anderson's syndicated exposés drew attention to the corruption of the Somoza regime and to its human rights abuses.[13] They prompted Congressional investigations into U.S. Nicaragua policy. Anderson put Somoza indelibly within the post-Vietnam paradigm:

> His enormous wealth has been squeezed out of his impoverished subjects, whose average pay is 30 cents an hour. They live in shacks and teeming slums and eke out a living as best they can while the Big Banana stashes his millions in foreign banks. . . .
> Not only do American officials let him get away with this but they have subsidized the Somoza regime for 40 years with a steady flow of foreign aid.[14]

The Sandinistas considered Chamorro's UDEL the most worrisome sign of an emerging "bourgeois alternative of a new type," according to Sandinista *comandante* Jaime Wheelock. UDEL might succeed in "rejuvenating the system."[15] At that time Wheelock was putting the finishing touches on the FSLN's principal theoretical work which sustained that both Somoza and the opposition bourgeoisie were "local agents of U.S. imperialism."[16] Something dramatic was required "to evade the passage to a bourgeois democratic stage with bourgeois hegemony."[17] In the fall of 1974 the Sandinistas gathered themselves for a spectacular operation.[18] It was to be, in the words of *comandante* Wheelock, who became a severe critic of the operation, an attempt to "recompose the historical forces in one single act," to "deliver a stinging blow to the dictatorship and . . . take in a lot of pesos."[19]

The plan was to kidnap the U.S. Ambassador, Turner Shelton, during a Christmas party at the home of a wealthy Nicaraguan, José María ("Chema") Castillo. Shelton, a Somoza crony and a symbol of U.S. complicity, had already departed when the revolutionaries arrived, but other guests, including Somoza's foreign minister, were snared. Through their chosen mediator, Archbishop Miguel Obando y Bravo, the Sandinistas obtained the release of some eighteen political prisoners, publication of two communiqués denouncing Somoza, and a flight to Havana, where the liberated prisoners would receive further training.[20]

The Christmas raid hit a public relations bull's-eye, but the repression which followed not only immobilized the civic opposition, a Sandinista goal, but also nearly exterminated the FSLN itself. Carlos Fonseca and other Sandinista leaders were killed, while the survivors blamed one another. Repudiating the Christmas raid as *"petit-bourgeois* adventurism," Jaime Wheelock formed a rival faction. Months after the Christmas raid the FSLN had split into three feuding groups who accused one another of "sectarianism," "populism," "Trotskyism," and "class collaboration."[21]

If the Christmas raid produced mixed results for the Sandinistas, for American press coverage it is a buried landmark. Wrapping up a period of reporting prompted by the raid, Alan Riding of the *New York Times* wrote:

> An unusual combination of popular movements is transforming Central America from a forgotten mosaic of "banana republics" into an area of political unrest.[22]

The piece reflected a change in the region but even more in its coverage. "This was a time," Stephen Kinzer, who succeeded Riding at the *Times*, recalled, "when Nicaragua was perceived by Americans, if it was perceived at all, as remote and peaceful."[23] Riding, more than any single journalist, was to change that perception. Riding pioneered a generation of "participant" correspondents who viewed Central America from a "post-Vietnam" perspective.

In his coverage of the Christmas raid Riding took large note of "the great disparity between rich and poor in Central America" which he found "nowhere more apparent than in Nicaragua."[24] The Sandinistas, he declared, had

> almost overnight . . . emerged as a political force capable of inflicting a stinging defeat on the Government and proving the vulnerability of the long-ruling Somoza regime.[25]

Riding conceded that the FSLN was "an extreme leftist organization," though more often he describes them simply as "leftist guerrillas," and a small one, generously estimating them to have "perhaps 150 active members." The group had "been only sporadically active over the last three years."[26] "But," he contended:

> Nicaraguan political observers believe the sympathy for the organization is growing particularly among the repressed peasants of northern Nicaragua, the students of the cities of Managua and Leon and even middle-class professionals.[27]

Neither the Nicaraguan "observers" nor their affiliations or sympathies are identified. Riding provides no evidence that the Sandinistas were recruiting among "the peasants of northern Nicaragua." Riding's articles were an important source of the notion that the Sandinistas were composed of peasants, as well as students and professionals, that indeed they were something of a "peasant movement," one of the earliest and most enduring "Sandinista myths."

Riding's style and approach was a departure from both past coverage and contemporary coverage in rival newspapers. A *Washington Post* feature on the Christmas raid described the Sandinistas as "leftist Nicaraguan terrorists."[28] The government characterization of the FSLN figured prominently in *Post* dispatches:

Nicaraguan officials say the Sandinistas are extreme leftists dedicated to overthrow of the Somoza regime, removal of American influence in Nicaragua and
establishment of a Marxist-Socialist form of government. They claim that some
received guerrilla training in Cuba and the Soviet Union.

Riding reported in the *Times* that:

Although the group has been responsible for several important actions, such as
bank assaults, kidnappings and aircraft hijackings, over the last decade, it had
been quiet since four of its members were killed by National Guardsmen in
Nandaime in September 1973.

The *Post* placed these "important actions" in a far less sympathetic light, making
no mitigating mention of National Guard killings and including damaging details about the FSLN:

Between 1967 and 1974, the Sandinistas were believed to be responsible for a
number of bank robberies and for two attacks on helicopters transporting
money to factory workers and plantations in remote areas.[29]

The *Post*'s report on the raid's aftermath was equally unromantic about the
Sandinistas' most recent adventure:

The guerrillas, who shot their way into a cocktail party honoring U.S. Ambassador Turner Shelton Friday night, had pledged to kill their hostages at 12-hour
intervals beginning Tuesday if the government did not meet their demands.

That story was headlined "Nicaragua Flies Guerrillas to Cuba."[30]
If there was a "contest over the framing of the Central American story"
within the American press, it occurred not in the mid-1980s, as Daniel Hallin
argues, but in the mid-1970s.[31] It was over almost before it started. By 1978, as
we shall see, uniformity prevailed in the presentation of the struggle between
Somoza and the Sandinistas in the American news media, although the American political contest over Nicaragua was just beginning.
Several months later Riding took the trouble to travel to "northern Nicaragua," to Matagalpa, and investigate—at least as far as one could from the departmental capital. If Riding's article lacked the rich documentation of Matthews's pieces on the guerrillas in the Sierra Madre, it was nonetheless the first
report in the American media to provide some sense of Nicaraguan life beyond
the capital:

The [Sandinista] guerrillas, mostly from middle-class urban families, appear to
be succeeding in recruiting growing numbers of peasants to their cause. Witnesses said that most of the 40 or so rebels who temporarily occupied the town
of Rio Blanco, 65 miles east of here on March 21 were peasants.[32]

Riding relied on the information of "doctors, lawyers, and priests who regularly visit the mountain areas and enjoy the trust of the peasants." No peasant interviews are cited. Who are these "witnesses" and confidants of the peasants? What is their relation to the FSLN? All we are told is that these are "sources, who asked that their names not be mentioned but whose versions coincided." Could their stories have coincided because they were coordinated?

The notion of numerous peasant Sandinista recruits and "the support and loyalty of the peasantry in key zones" became a fundamental stereotype both in the press and in scholarly writings.[33] No direct evidence of major peasant participation was ever adduced, and it was subsequently denied by several participants, including the Sandinistas' martyred founder in the official text of his works. In his last notes, Carlos Fonseca complained that "campesinos . . . do not even know the name of our organization" and of the "absence . . . of representatives of the exploited." At most, the Sandinista "preguerrilla nuclei" had learned to "adapt urban cadre to the life of the mountains" and had created "the conditions for the consolidation of the campesino combatants."[34] As for Rio Blanco, Henry Ruiz, who was the Sandinista commander in the zone, wrote later of the highlands as a "crucible" in which to remake his "egocentric" urban cadre, predominantly of *"petit-bourgeois* and student origin."[35] *Comandante* Jaime Wheelock, who directed Sandinista agrarian policies, stated in a 1989 interview that the Sandinista cadre working in Matagalpa in 1984 were unfamiliar with the customs and social-makeup of the peasantry. As we discuss in chapter 11, Wheelock thought that the stereotyped attitudes of these militants served to alienate the farmers and "created a crisis in the countryside."[36]

Through the 1960s the American media frame widened to encompass a diversifying economy, a broadening middle-class, opposition political protests, the conditions of workers and peasants and the restriction of civil liberties. But it is Alan Riding who brings a full-fledged post-Vietnam *zeitgeist* to Central American reporting. The revolutionary exploits of the "leftist guerrillas" move from the perimeter to the center of the picture, displacing the "feuds" between the Somozas and their prominent rivals. U.S. geopolitical "stakes" recede from view. The perspective is closer to the ground and the style, matching the growing unrest in the region, is no longer aloof but intense. Statements from Nicaraguan government officials are viewed with immense skepticism—this of course would change again when the Sandinistas became the government; those from revolutionary sources, including "sources, who asked that their names not be mentioned," are accepted at face value. The point of view is no longer that of the detached imperial observer, but of the Nicaraguan people, or rather of those who, we are told, enjoy their "trust." The opinions of the peasants themselves, as before, are known only through intermediaries.

Well before its revolutionary crisis, Nicaraguan news was being reported within a new "paradigm." If a paradigm shift can be called a "revolution," the revolution in the coverage preceded the revolution itself.[37] Doubtless revolutionary conditions were developing in Nicaragua in these years quite independently of American reporting. But the Sandinistas did not begin to seize the initiative until the fall of 1977. When Riding first began reporting from Nicaragua the Sandinista movement was ebbing. Riding might well have concluded, as Giniger did in 1967 at another low tide, that the 1975 repression of the Sandinistas was an "anti-Castro success." But Riding's standpoint and paradigm, directed his gaze elsewhere, producing a very different assessment. Two years later, events would show that the Sandinistas had not been crushed by Somoza's offensive as many assumed. The views of the journalists and those events developed on different planes, American and Nicaraguan, each with their own histories and trajectories. Their "*encuentro*" gives our story its savor.

The lineage of U.S. journalistic sympathy with twentieth-century Latin American revolutionaries dates back at least to John Reed's travels with Pancho Villa.[38] The tradition encompasses the fascination of Lincoln Steffens, Carleton Beals, and John Dos Passos with the Mexican Revolution, and of course, Herbert Matthews's meeting with Fidel in the Sierra Madre.[39] Unlike his predecessors, Riding created what would become a "hegemonic media frame."[40] Within that frame Nicaragua would be presented to American audiences on television and in print. That could happen because these still nearly anonymous guerrillas and their antagonists would make much more news. Events they would shape and the reporting on them by Riding and his colleagues would bring the Sandinistas from the back pages to the headlines and to the center of the U.S. political debate.

Notes

1. Pedro Joaquín Chamorro C., *Richter 7* (Managua: Pez y Serpiente, 1976; reprinted 1981), 72.

2. Xavier Arguëllo, *Las Delicias del Volga* (unpublished); translated by Gladys Segal and Robert S. Leiken, in *The Central American Crisis Reader*, ed. Leiken and Barry Rubin (New York: Summit, 1987), 142-143.

3. Anastasio Somoza and Jack Cox, *Nicaragua Betrayed* (Boston: Western Islands, 1980), 4-5.

4. Arguëllo, *Las Delicias del Volga*.

5. "B-52s Pound N. Vietnam for 7th Day," *WP*, December 24, 1972, A1.

6. "Quakes, Fires Level Capital of Nicaragua," *WP*, December 24, 1972, A1.

7. "Thousands Dead as Quakes Strike Nicaraguan City," *NYT*, December 24, 1972, 1.

8. Marvine Howe, "Managua Parties Resume Politics," *NYT*, December 31, 1972, 11.

9. Richard Millet, *The Guardians of the Dynasty* (Maryknoll, New York: Orbis, 1977), 237-38.

10. "Somoza Widening His Control but Foes Vow No Letup," *NYT*, February 17, 1974, 14.

11. For this period, see Eduardo Crawely, *Dictators Never Die* (New York: St. Martin's, 1979), chapters xx-xxi; Bernard Diederich, *Somoza and the Legacy of U.S. Involvement in Central America* (1st edition, New York: E. P. Dutton, 1981; 2d edition,

Maplewood, New Jersey: Waterfront Press, 1989), 101-3; Claribel Alegria and D. J. Flakoll, *Nicaragua, la revolución sandinista: una crónica politica, 1855-1979* (Mexico: ERA, 1982); Millett, *Guardians of the Dynasty*, 241-43.

12. Jack Anderson, "Nicaraguan Ruler Is World's Greediest," *WP*, August 18, 1975.

13. Anderson's columns on Somoza appeared in the *Washington Post* on August 18-19, 1975, and March 19, July 6, August 26, September 11, and December 8, 1976.

14. Jack Anderson and Les Whitten, "U.S. Subsidizes Nicaragua's Dictator," *WP*, August 26, 1975, C9.

15. Doris María Tijerino, *Inside the Nicaraguan Revolution (As told to Margaret Randall)* (Vancouver: New Star, 1978), 161.

16. Wheelock added that Nicaragua had entered the stage of monopoly capitalism, that the rural proletariat was the main social class in the countryside and that social progress required a "proletarian vanguard." Later Wheelock acknowledged: "We said at the time that we were going to fight against Somoza for democracy but really we were fighting against imperialism." (Wheelock Román, *Nicaragua: Imperialismo y Dictadura* [Havana: Ciencias Sociales, 1980], 196; and Wheelock interview in Pilar Arias, *Nicaragua: Revolución: Relatos de combatientes del frente sandinista* [Mexico: Siglo XXI, 1980], 108.)

17. Arias, *Nicaragua: Revolución*, 186.

18. See for example Henry Ruiz, "La Montana era como un Crisol donde se forjaban los mejores cuadros," *Nicaráuac*, no. 1, Managua (May-June 1980): 17.

19. *Comandante* Jaime Wheelock in Arias, *Nicaragua: Revolución*, 106-8; Plutarco Hernández S., *El FSLN Por Dentro: Relatos de Un Combatiente* (San José, Costa Rica: 1982), 74.

20. Shirley Christian, *Nicaragua: Revolution in the Family* (New York: Random House, 1985), 32.

21. For a sample of the Sandinista factional polemics at this time, see *Central American Crisis Reader*, ed. Leiken and Rubin, 158-68; see also FSLN-TP, "La Crisis Interna Y Las Tendencias," Los Angeles, California, 1976.

22. Alan Riding, "Change, Even In Central America," *NYT*, September 14, 1975, section IV, 6.

23. Kinzer reflecting on his first trip to Nicaragua in November 1976 (Stephen Kinzer, *Blood of Brothers* [New York: Putnam, 1991], 18).

24. Riding, "Even Somoza Has His Rebels," *NYT*, January 5, 1975, section IV, 4.

25. Riding, "Nicaragua Jolted by Guerrilla Raid: Mass Kidnapping Reveals New Strength of Leftists—Regime's Move Awaited," *NYT*, January 3, 1975, A4.

26. Riding, "Guerrillas Kill 3 at Party, Seize Key Nicaraguans," *NYT*, December 29, 1974, A4; Riding, "Nicaragua Jolted," A4.

27. Riding, "Nicaragua Jolted," A4.

28. Dorothy McCardle, "Sevilla-Sacasa: 60 Hours of Terror," *WP*, January 22, 1975, B1.

29. "Nicaragua, Guerrillas Talk on Plan to Free Hostages," *WP*, December 30, 1974.

30. "Nicaragua Flies Guerrillas to Cuba," *WP*, December 31, 1974, A7.

31. Daniel C. Hallin, *We Keep America on Top of the World: Television Journalism and the Public Sphere* (London: Routledge, 1993), 147; see chapter 4, 46 *supra*.

32. Riding, "Ranks of Nicaraguan Guerrillas Appear to Grow," *NYT*, August 6, 1975, A11.

33. See John A. Booth, *The End and the Beginning: The Nicaraguan Revolution* (1st edition, Boulder: Westview, 1982), 137-38; see also 116-20, 140-41.

34. Carlos Fonseca, "Notas sobre la montana," in *Obras*, vol. I (Managua: Nueva Nicaragua, 1982), 132, 140, 136. See also Omar Cabezas, "A Small Insurgency," in *Central American Crisis Reader*, ed. Leiken and Rubin, 155-57; Cabezas, *Fire in the Mountains* (New York: Crown, 1985), 48, 63, 81-82 and *passim*; Ruiz, "La Montaña era como un Crisol." Also, author's interviews with former Sandinistas Edén Pastora (August 1983), Arturo Cruz, Jr. (July 1983), Roger Miranda (January 1988).

35. Ruiz, "La Montaña era como un Crisol," 18; see also Alegria and Flakholl, *Nicaragua, la revolución sandinista*, 248. The one exception to the general rule that peasants played a marginal role was the group formed in 1978-79 in Nueva Segovia. They were called MILPAS—Anti-Somicista Popular Militias—and in 1980 revolted against the Sandinista government (see chapter 11, 152).

36. Author's interview with *comandante* Jaime Wheelock, Managua, April 21, 1989.

37. Thomas Kuhn describes paradigm shifts as revolutions in Thomas S. Kuhn, *The Structure of Scientific Revolutions* (Chicago: University of Chicago, 1964), 12, 91–92.

38. The Mexican Revolution attracted the attention of radical journalists such as Frank Tannebaum and Ernest Gruening of *The Nation* and liberals such as Herbert Croly at *The New Republic* as well as Communists such as Bertram Wolfe at *The New Masses* (see Eugenia Meyer, *Conciencia histórica norteamericana sobre la revolución de 1910* [Mexico: Instituto Nacional de Antropología, 1970], 67-124; and John A. Britton, *Carleton Beals: A Radical Journalist in Latin America* [Albuquerque: University of New Mexico, 1987], 34-38).

39. See Britton, *Carleton Beals*, for a comprehensive account of Beals's Latin American reporting. See also John Reed, *Insurgent Mexico* (New York: International, 1969); Lincoln Steffens, *The Autobiography of Lincoln Steffens* (New York: Harcourt Brace and World, 1958), part IV, chapters ix-xi; and Justin Kaplan, *Lincoln Steffens* (New York: Simon & Schuster, 1974), 200-3.

40. Cf. Todd Gitlin, *The Whole World Is Watching* (Berkeley: University of California, 1980).

Chapter 9
The Media Presentation
of the Sandinistas, 1978-79

> Whoever fights monsters should see to it that in the process he does not become
> a monster. And when you look long into an abyss, the abyss also looks into
> you.
>
> —Nietzsche, *Beyond Good and Evil*

In 1981 the *Miami Herald*'s Central American correspondent Shirley Christian
became the first woman to win outright the Pulitzer Prize in International Reporting. Before joining the *New York Times* in 1985, she published a favorably
reviewed account of the Nicaraguan Revolution.[1] Ms. Christian, however, was
less popular with her colleagues. In a 1982 article in the *Washington Journalism
Review* she wrote that U.S. journalists had covered the Sandinistas "through a
romantic haze."[2] Her criticisms centered on the reporting on CBS and in the
Washington Post and the *New York Times*. The correspondents responsible for
most of that reporting, Karen DeYoung, by then the *Post*'s foreign editor, and
Alan Riding of the *New York Times*, answered with lengthy and indignant re-
joinders.[3]

As we have seen, Riding (and to a lesser extent DeYoung) pioneered the
modern press coverage of Nicaragua. In October 1977, after the Sandinistas re-
claimed attention with several surprise attacks on army barracks, Riding secured
the first on-the-record interview with a top FSLN leader. Though less sensational, the article was in some respects reminiscent of Herbert Matthews' well-
remembered interview with Fidel Castro. On the front-page of the *New York
Times*, "above the fold" on the right-hand side, the first of Matthews' three part
series began:

Fidel Castro, the rebel leader of Cuba's youth, is alive and fighting hard and successfully in the rugged, almost impenetrable fastness of the Sierra Madre.[4]

Beneath the accompanying photo was Castro's signature, confirming the article's claim that:

This is the first sure news that Fidel Castro is still alive and still in Cuba. No one connected with the outside world, let alone with the press, has seen Señor Castro except this writer.

The series went on to affirm the guerrilla leader's commitment to "liberty, democracy, social justice . . . elections." Matthews reported that "there is no communism to speak of in Fidel Castro's 26th of July Movement":

The 26th of July Movement talks of nationalism, anti-colonialism, anti-imperialism. I asked Señor Castro about that. He answered: "You can be sure we have no animosity toward the United States and the American people."[5]

In his concluding piece Matthews' enthusiasm carried him beyond Castro's avowals and beyond the customary tone of the *Times* news pages:

At last one gets the feeling that the best elements in Cuban life—the unspoiled youth, the honest business man, the politician of integrity, the patriotic Army officer—are getting together to assume power.[6]

In contrast to Castro's guerrilla hide-out in the Sierra Madre, Riding's setting—a hotel room in San José, Costa Rica—was too prosaic to mention. But Riding did manage to inject a touch of romance by pointing out that his article was the product of "a series of secret interviews with leaders of the FSLN."[7] Furthermore, the piece was "the first attributable interview given by a top Sandinist leader." The leader was Plutarco Elias Hernández, "previously known only by the alias of 'Alfonso.' "

The air of intrigue was a bit stale. Hernández, a well-known Costa Rican, and the son of a prominent politician, spoke publicly and regularly in Panama and Mexico where he met frequently with Riding. But in Costa Rica, where he was wanted for participating in a Sandinista jailbreak, he avoided public appearances for fear of provoking the indulgent authorities. Riding had been meeting with Hernández and other Sandinistas for several years.[8]

This first full presentation in the major American media of the new Sandinista image raised and ostensibly provided answers for all the questions that were to dominate the coverage and the American political debate for the next several years: Were the Sandinistas Castro's disciples striving to establish a Communist-type government, as Henry Giniger had presented them, or nationalists fighting for democracy? Were they Marxist-Leninists or left-wing social democrats? Were they terrorists, as Somoza claimed, or revolutionaries with popular support?

Steven Kinzer acknowledged in 1991 that the Sandinistas had carried off "a masterful deception," beguiling outsiders, "including journalists," as to their Marxist-Leninist ideology, their "close ties" with "foreign Marxists like Fidel Castro, North Korea's Kim il Sung, and the Palestine Liberation Organization," their comprehensive drilling in "training camps in Cuba" and "extensive periods of training in the Middle East and in North Korea."[9] Much of this information was available at the time Riding was writing. We shall consider his presentation of the Sandinistas not in the light of later revelations but on the basis of the materials then at hand. In 1991 Kinzer wrote that:

At the moment of the dictatorship's collapse, no outsiders knew the true story of the Sandinista Front. Only after the years that followed were we able to piece it together. Whenever I met or interviewed people who had been part of the Sandinista underground, I asked them to tell me their stories.[10]

However, by 1978 there were several former Sandinistas who had broken with the organization and could have provided much of the information Kinzer discovered later.

Alan Riding's introduction of the Sandinistas to the American reader led with:

Nicaragua's leftist guerrillas say that the objective of their new offensive is not to install a Communist government here but merely to overthrow the long-ruling Somoza regime and establish democracy.[11]

Riding explained that Sandinista leaders had "indicated" that they had

abandoned their struggle for a Marxist victory through "prolonged popular war" in favor of a more immediate popular insurrection.

The phrasing here is ambiguous and confusing. Insurrection is a staple in the Marxist panoply of tactics: that is how the Bolsheviks claimed to have taken power. So why should adoption of insurrection suggest abandonment of Marxism? Perhaps because, as the article continues,

'After the insurrection, we will hold the first free elections in Nicaragua's history,' said Plutarco Elias Hernández, one of six members of the front's national directorate.

Riding presents the guerrillas as converts to democracy, though Hernández is quoted only as supporting a "stage" of democracy since "socialism cannot be built overnight." As for Communism, that was just another red herring, as Hernández explains: "Those who think we'll be going straight to Communism are wrong. Our basic program is not Communist. It is a threat to no one who favors a just society." But again, the matter is far more equivocal than Riding indicates. The democratic stage, sometimes called popular or new democracy, was a staple of orthodox Communist strategy. Nonetheless, on the basis of his discoveries Riding's article appears to reverse his predecessor Giniger's judgment that the Sandinistas were "Communists," part of an international movement centered in Havana:

> Although Mr. Hernández recognizes that the front enjoys the moral support of Cuba today, he insisted that it receives no money or weapons from the Castro regime and that no Nicaraguan guerrillas have been trained in Havana since President Fidel Castro stopped "exporting revolution" around 1970.

Riding's account takes us considerably closer to the Sandinistas than those of his predecessors. The reporting is far more intimate and detailed than that of Giniger and brings the internal life of the movement into the news frame.

> Founded in 1962 in the wake of the Cuban revolution, the front has also long stood out among Latin American guerrilla groups, not only because of its ability to survive years of repression, but also because of its emphasis on political work among peasants, workers and students over isolated terrorist actions.[12]

Riding could even report on the inner workings of the Sandinista movement that "until recently" had been

> dominated by Marxists willing to fight a "prolonged popular war" in order to achieve a Communist victory here. This year, however, the Sandinistas revised their strategy—the committed Marxists broke away from the main organization in protest—and began working more closely with "bourgeois" opponents of the regime. . . . The guerrillas' new objective was . . . to overthrow General Somoza through a "popular insurrection" and to call free elections.[13]

As we have seen, since 1975 the Sandinistas had been involved in a three-way factional struggle. Riding was correct in pointing to dramatic changes espoused by one Sandinista faction. However, the innovations involved tactics, not goals or basic ideology. Moreover, the new group could hardly be characterized as the official organization from which the "committed Marxists broke away." On the contrary, Hernández's faction was the second breakaway from the original leadership. For that reason, it was branded *"Tercerista,"* the "third" FSLN faction.[14] Tomás Borge's "Prolonged Popular War" (*Guerra Popular Prolongada* or GPP) contended that it alone represented historical *Sandinismo* while the *Terceristas* were a "deviation." The GPP incorporated most of the old guard, upheld Sandinista orthodoxy on policy questions and was led by the only active surviving Sandinista founder. Carlos Fonseca expressly sided with them before his death.[15]

More importantly, the *Tercerista* or insurrectional faction was neither more official nor less Marxist than its rivals. The group had recently published a *General Platform*, written primarily by Humberto Ortega, which proclaimed the group the authentic "Marxist-Leninist vanguard detachment" which would dedi-

cate itself to "political-ideological formation under Marxist-Leninist guidelines."
The *Platform* also had stated: "our cause [is] the sacred and historical cause of
Marx, Engels, Lenin, and Sandino."[16]

Though Riding found the tactics of the new group an innovation, the language of its platform was a reversion to the orthodoxy of the Communist International, or Comintern, of the 1930s. If Riding waded beyond phrases like "our
Sandinista vanguard welds solidly together in one elite, the advanced fistful, the
finest representatives of the Nicaraguan working people,"[17] he might have been
bemused by such others as "the glorious October Revolution," "the advanced
detachment of the proletariat," or "democratic centralism." These terms were
coined by Lenin and popularized by Stalin.[18]

The *Tercerista* faction did depart from reigning Sandinista orthodoxy by arguing that conditions were ripe for an insurrection in Nicaragua if the "revolutionary vanguard" was willing to pursue an alliance with "progressive" sectors
of the "bourgeoisie." But one should recall that the Communist International, led
by Stalin and Georgi Dimitrov, had developed "the strategy and tactics of the
united front" which the group's new "anti-Somoza Front" closely resembled.[19]

The group's proclaimed alliance with the civic opposition was only "tactical
and temporary":

> The present struggle against tyranny should lead us to a true people's democ-
> racy (not a bourgeois democracy) that will be an integral part of the struggle for
> socialism. . . .[20]

This was what the new Sandinistas meant by democracy. "The term 'People's
Democracy,'" Zbigniew K. Brzezinski has pointed out, served as "policy plank"
for post-World War II East European Communists who viewed terms like "dictatorship of the proletariat" as not only "theoretically inapplicable but also a
political liability."[21]

Riding's articles established the frame for subsequent coverage of the
Sandinistas in the American media. Henceforth the Sandinistas who really
counted belonged to the faction which had allegedly "abandoned" Marxism for
democracy. The other factions were treated as marginal sects. Riding's influence
was most obvious in the case of his wife, Marlise Simons, who frequently covered Nicaragua for the *Washington Post*. In January 1978 Simons wrote that the
Sandinista "political line [had] changed from fighting for socialism in Nicaragua
to fighting for democracy."[22] Several months later, Karen DeYoung, who had
become the *Post*'s Latin American bureau chief and reported regularly from
Managua, described the anti-Somoza opposition as an "unlikely" alliance of
"conservative and liberal politicians, businessmen, farmers, students, and Marxist guerrillas."[23] By August 1978 DeYoung was describing the Sandinistas themselves as historically "hazy in ideology."[24] Yet the very next day the *Post* ran a
story based on wire service reports which described the Sandinistas as seeking to
"install a Marxist government in Nicaragua."[25]

As Joshua Muravchik noticed:

After August 1978, however, the *Post* ceased referring to the FSLN as Marxist. From then on, it was invariably characterized as only partly Marxist or as a group that was termed "Marxist" by its adversaries. After having called the Sandinistas "Marxist" in June and August of 1978, Karen DeYoung shifted in September. She then wrote of "the Sandinistas, who at various times in their 16-year history have espoused Marxist ideology." [September 30, 1978, A4.] In December, *Post* correspondent Marlise Simons wrote that the "*Tercerista*" faction of the FSLN "controls the Sandinista army" and is "largely non-Marxist."[26]

DeYoung came away from a visit to a Sandinista training camp with the impression that there was "a recognition by the bulk of [the Sandinistas] that a socialist revolution would not succeed in Nicaragua." In a passage that echoes Riding, DeYoung continued:

> That realization resulted in a three-way split in the Sandinista organization among the mountain fighters, the Marxist propagandists, and the insurrectionists, by far the largest and most active group. It is the third group whose national leadership for all practical purposes runs the Sandinista National Liberation Front.[27]

This was the sort of reporting that prompted Shirley Christian's central criticism:

> Neither the *Times* nor the *Post* denied or ignored the FSLN's Marxist roots and Cuban ties. There was a distinct tendency, however, to stress the reassuring impression that the Sandinista movement had been taken over in recent years by non-Marxists. Many were children of elites who had become guerrillas after seeing their parents frustrated in their efforts to defeat Somoza peacefully. Accordingly, the Marxist old-timers . . . had supposedly given up their plans for installing a socialist state immediately after taking power.[28]

Of course, the *Terceristas*, as we have seen, did not plan to establish a socialist society "immediately after taking power." But they did intend a Sandinista-dominated regime—"a socialist state" in Christian's terms—which would be, as the *Platform* proclaimed, "an integral part of the struggle for socialism."[29]

Christian faulted Riding and DeYoung for paying insufficient attention to the "radical" "Marxist old-timers." However, the "*Terceristas*" (who were hardly "non-Marxist") did gain the upper hand in a very real factional fight eventually settled by none other than Fidel Castro. During the 1980s the *Terceristas* were to prevail against "the Marxist old-timers"—precisely because they were more "pragmatic."

Christian, Riding, and DeYoung all assumed that Sandinista pragmatism and Sandinista socialism were at odds. Clifford Krauss's later survey reiterates this assumption, shared by nearly everyone who wrote about the Sandinistas:

From the very beginning the FSLN displayed two faces: one ideological, inspired by Socialist dreams and hatred for the United States; the other pragmatic, capable of molding its tactics to whatever political and economic realities it faced.[30]

All of these reporters seemed to assume that what they called Marxism was zealotry incapable of calculation. However, the *Tercerista* platform considered Marxism-Leninism "the *scientific* doctrine of the proletariat" (italics added). Marx and Engels often denounced the "childish impatience" of radical communists in passages that Lenin would cite in his classical critique of "infantile leftism," a tract often cited by Stalin, the supreme "pragmatist."[31] Lost on many reporters was the meaning of the core *Tercerista* slogan, based on Lenin's and Stalin's formulations: "flexible in tactics but intransigent in strategy."

$$* * *$$

The view of the Sandinistas now dominating mainstream reporting was shared, and reinforced, by university-based area experts. One influential and respected specialist was Richard Millett. His June 1979 Congressional testimony asserted that the dominant *Tercerista* faction had "never been officially Marxist" and had never "suggested that they want a Sandinista government."[32] Millett believed that the Sandinistas were seeking a nationalistic third way between capitalism and communism. Furthermore, he contended, although the Sandinistas had an understandable fear of U.S. interference, they were not motivated by ideological anti-Americanism and would welcome U.S. help in promoting constructive change.[33] Stanford University's Richard Fagen reported that the *Terceristas* helped to

> forge links between the FSLN and middle class and business groups, and their leadership and statements tended to reflect social democratic ideas as opposed to the more Marxist orientations of the other two [tendencies].[34]

Fagen also perceived an "unerring capacity of the U.S. government to be months and even years late in recognizing Nicaragua realities." "Cold War perspectives" in the Carter Administration and "the presence of Marxists in the Sandinista movement" had "congealed into a pervasive fear of an other-than-pro-U.S. post-Somoza regime—a 'second Cuba.' "[35]

Ohio University's Thomas W. Walker considered those worries unfounded. Though the Sandinistas

> logically felt a bond of friendship and found much in common with the only real revolutionary government in Latin America, the Nicaraguan revolutionaries, above all, were nationalists.[36]

Several years later Walker acknowledged that it was "true, most of the leaders of the Sandinista Revolution were Marxists or Marxist-Leninists." But, he wrote: "They never tried to deny that fact."[37]

***

In 1978 correspondents from other major news organizations began keeping Riding and DeYoung company. As the revolutionary crisis developed, U.S. print and television coverage of Nicaragua increased sharply. The news magazines augmented their staffs and the television networks started covering the more spectacular events. Stories devoted to Nicaragua on the *ABC Evening News*, negligible in the mid-1970s, rose to 2.6 percent of total coverage in 1978 when Nicaragua vaulted into the top twenty countries covered by that network.[38] By and large the newcomers followed the lines that the veteran Riding had established.

To the question "who are the Sandinistas" the media answered: they are a loose coalition of patriots backed by all sectors of the population waging a popular rebellion against a corrupt and brutal tyranny. While they have a small Cuban-influenced "radical" section, the majority are social-democratic "moderates" committed to pluralistic democracy, preserving private enterprise, and pursuing national development and independence from both superpowers. During the final Sandinista offensive, American newspapers reported the group was "hazy in ideology" (*Washington Post*[39]) and "politically ill-defined" (*New York Times*[40]), and at most "left-leaning" (*Wall Street Journal*[41]). The FSLN was characterized as "social democratic," as predominantly "moderate," "pragmatic," and "pluralist," and as "largely non-Marxist." They were above everything else nationalists, or in the words of the telling headline over a Riding piece in the *New York Times*: "Sandinistas, Patriots First—Marxists Maybe Second."[42] The press rarely challenged or probed Sandinista spokesmen's democratic credentials or professed goals.

Nonetheless in the case of the *Times* and the *Post* these unexamined goals—"pluralism, mixed-economy and nonalignment"—and the Sandinista promises of free elections, free press, respect for human rights, and "land to the tiller" were to become the badges by which the Sandinistas were identified.[43] In arriving at their sanguine characterization journalists placed little weight on previous or current Sandinista affiliations and programs and nearly all of it on assurances extended by Sandinista spokespersons.[44] There was an inclination to take these professions at face value.

As for television, Waltraud Queiser Morales's comparative study of the network treatment of the governments of Salvador Allende and Anastasio Somoza found:

The Marxist Sandinista guerrillas were projected as so many common people who had become courageous freedom fighters . . . There was only limited attention to the ideology, funding, and international connections of the Sandinistas. The tenor of the coverage on the networks was remarkably similar. . . .

    Coverage of Nicaragua refuted the claim that the networks take a conservative status-quo bias and are inherently hostile to the left in coverage of Latin America. Somoza's dictatorship was hardly the beneficiary of favorable stories. The ambivalence that characterized much of the coverage of Allende—wonderment over the elected, moderate Marxist, but qualms about the ultimate consequences of his rule—was rarely present in reports from Nicaragua. Unlike Chile, the intricacy of democratic versus Marxist ideology was not an important factor in the coverage of Nicaragua. The issue was clear: Dictatorship.[45]

***

Here is how Bob Schieffer introduced the CBS report from Nicaragua the day the Sandinistas took power:

> The five members of Nicaragua's new provisional government arrived today in Managua and were hailed as conquering heroes. Their first announcement: it will be three or four years before new elections were held. But that did not dampen the spirit of the people who have been embroiled in war for 16 years.[46]

However, the only celebrating Nicaraguans actually to have been "embroiled in a war for sixteen years" were the Sandinistas, the "conquering heroes" not "the people." To the extent that the latter joined the war, it was only in the past year and a half. Even then direct popular participation in the insurrection involved primarily urban youth.[47] During this period the Sandinistas repeatedly promised early elections. There was no way of knowing how many Nicaraguans were disappointed to learn of their postponement, but the CBS video from Managua did show great cheering as one junta member, Violeta Chamorro, proclaimed "Nicaragua is becoming a republic"—the perennial slogan not of the Sandinistas but of the "Conservative" anti-Somoza opposition of Pedro Joaquín Chamorro. The other resounding applause in the accompanying video was when a speaker declared that the country would have "democracy."

    That Nicaragua was in the process of installing a democratic republic was the universal impression left by the next morning's American reports. Karen DeYoung found "little to sustain fears shared by the United States and conservative Nicaraguans that the country will move far to the left."[48] Stephen Kinzer, then a cub reporter at the *Boston Globe*, anticipated a "presidential system similar to that of the United States."[49] Years later he was to learn from a Sandinista junta member that "the idea was to form a party along Marxist-Leninist lines . . . . There was never any intention of creating a pluralist project."[50]

    This need not have come as a surprise. That was the burden of all Sandinista programs. The FSLN made it quite clear on Nicaraguan television within two

weeks after taking power. On August 1, 1979, Charles Krause, temporarily replacing DeYoung who had returned to Washington to become deputy foreign
editor, reported:

> In two sessions in the last four days, televised for the nation . . . the top
> Sandinista leaders . . . showed that they know what kind of society they want to
> create and that they have every intention of retaining sufficient control—
> through the army, national police and trusted lieutenants in each key ministry—
> to ensure that their revolutionary ideas are carried out by the civilian junta
> government they placed in power.

Sandinista leaders stipulated that the FSLN was in charge, promises of elections
notwithstanding. They intended, in Daniel Ortega's words "to stay until our program is fully accomplished." In addition "Ortega warned that those who dis-
agreed with the decisions made by the junta and the Sandinistas might fall into
the category of traitors." The remarks of the Sandinista *comandante* in charge of
communications media were equally bracing:

> Bayardo Arce, a former journalism professor and a member of the Sandinista
> directorate, explained that until now the new Government of National Recon-
> struction and the Sandinista directorate thought it best to allow only one news-
> paper, one radio station and one television channel—all controlled by them—to
> operate.
> "We support freedom of the press," Arce continued. "But, of course, the
> freedom of the press we support will be a freedom of the press that supports the
> revolution."
> "Those who did not understand the revolution," Arce said, "thought that
> half an hour after Somoza's fall there would be absolute liberty."[51]

The nature of the regime the Sandinistas intended to establish had been ad-
umbrated live on national television for several hours. Obtaining the story required neither privileged access nor bounteous resources. However, the sessions
were not mentioned in other newspapers, nor did they seem to have much of an
impact on other journalists, not even those from the *Post*. Perhaps this was because Krause's piece was relegated to page A16.[52]
    Krause's editor, Karen DeYoung, returned to Nicaragua three months later
and prepared three reassuring front-page features. The first—"Government
Eludes Political Definition"—presented Sandinista rule as a "jumbled semi-
socialism that is administered by a blend of leftist militants and U.S.-trained
technocrats."[53] However, the "technocrats," who generally felt little allegiance
to the United States, were merely administrators; the FSLN's National Directorate made policy and that body was composed of a very definite kind of "leftist."
    DeYoung's timing was unfortunate. Within days the cabinet was restruc-
tured, the remaining "technocrats" replaced by Sandinistas. The next spring the
FSLN stacked the quasi-legislative Council of State, signed a party-to-party accord with the Soviet Communist Party and refused to condemn the Soviet inva-

sion of Afghanistan. In April 1980 these actions led to the resignations of the two non-Sandinista members of the revolutionary junta—Alfonso Robelo and Violeta Chamorro.[54]

Another motive for Chamorro's resignation was the increasing pressure on her newspaper.[55] In August 1979 the first restrictive press laws were passed. Of the country's two independent newspapers, one was abolished during the first months of 1980, the other subjected to increasing harassment and threats of confiscation. Television became a Sandinista monopoly, many independent radio stations confiscated, the rest prohibited from broadcasting "news detrimental to the revolution." By the end of 1980, according to the editor of *La Prensa*: "All independent media in Nicaragua had either been censored, closed, or destroyed."[56]

Nonetheless, according to Joshua Muravchik's study, "during the first year of Sandinista rule, few news reports focused on these issues," on "the all-important question of whether elections would be held," censorship of the media and the throttling of other civil liberties. Meanwhile "the TV networks carried nothing at all on these subjects."[57] Muravchik found:

Notable in the *Times*'s coverage was the almost total absence of reporting on these issues by its major Nicaragua correspondent, Alan Riding. . . . [58]

Notes

1. Shirley Christian, *Nicaragua: Revolution in the Family* (New York: Random House, 1985).

2. Christian, "Covering the Sandinistas: The Foregone Conclusions of the Fourth Estate," *Washington Journalism Review* (March 1982): 33-38.

3. *Washington Journalism Review* (April 1982): 6-7, 56-58.

4. Herbert L. Matthews, "Cuban Rebel Is Visited in Hideout," *NYT*, February 24, 1957, A1.

5. Matthews, "Cuban Rebel Is Visited in Hideout"; Matthews, "Rebel Strength Gaining in Cuba," *NYT*, February 25, 1957, 1.

6. Matthews, "Old Order in Cuba Is Threatened by Forces of an Internal Revolt," *NYT*, February 26, 1957, 13.

7. Alan Riding, "Nicaraguan Rebels Deny Marxist Aim," *NYT*, October 26, 1977, 9.

8. Telephone interview with Plutarco Hernández from San Jose, Costa Rica, July 28, 1989.

9. Stephen Kinzer, *Blood of Brothers* (New York: Putnam, 1991), 59-66.

10. Kinzer, *Blood of Brothers*, 59.

11. Kinzer, *Blood of Brothers*, 59.

12. Kinzer, *Blood of Brothers*, 59.

13. Riding, "In Nicaragua, This May Be the Twilight of the Somozas," *NYT*, October 30, 1977, section IV, 3.

14. According to a former FSLN militant Arturo Cruz, Jr.: "This new group claimed they could mediate the conflict between old and new [factions]. They were called the

Terceristas—the third way—by Jaime Wheelock and the name stuck." See Arturo J. Cruz Sequiera, *Memoirs of a Counter-Revolutionary: Life with the Contras, the Sandinistas, and the CIA* (New York: Doubleday, 1989), 63. It is important to note that the name *Tercerista* did not arise from any putative nonalignment ("third way" or "third option") between capitalism and socialism. It signified neither a third way between the U.S.S.R. and the United States nor between capitalism and socialism but a third alternative inside the Marxist-Leninist FSLN.

15. See "El último documento de Carlos Fonseca," in Plutarco Hernández S., *El FSLN Por Dentro: Relatos de Un Combatiente* (San José, Costa Rica: n.p., 1982), 118-31; see also *The Central American Crisis Reader*, ed. Robert S. Leiken and Barry Rubin (New York: Summit, 1987), 164-68.

16. FSLN, *Plataforma General Político-Militar de FSLN: Para el Triunfo de la Revolución Sandinista* (Algún lugar de Nicaragua, May 4, 1977), 32, 42-43. An English translation of the *Platform* (FSLN c.1977) is available in *Conflict in Nicaragua*, ed. Jiri Valenta and Esperanza Durán (Boston: Allen & Unwin, 1987), appendix A; however, this and other quotations are the author's translation. Riding's source, Plutarco Hernández, indicated that he provided Riding with a copy of the *Platform* when it was published (Telephone interview with Plutarco Hernández from San José, Costa Rica, July 28, 1989).

17. FSLN, *Plataforma General*, 42.

18. See for example Joseph Stalin, *The Foundations of Leninism* (Moscow: Foreign Language Publishing House, 1927).

19. See Stalin, *Foundations of Leninism*, chapter vii; and Georgi Dimitrov, "Report" and "Closing Speech" in *Seventh Congress of the Communist International, Abridged Stenographic Report* (Moscow: Foreign Language Printing House, 1938), 125-94, 557 ff.

20. FSLN, *Plataforma General*, 32, 34.

21. Zbigniew K. Brzezinksi, *The Soviet Bloc: Unity and Conflict* (Cambridge, Massachusetts: Harvard University, 1967), 26.

22. Marlise Simons, "Nicaraguan Publisher, Critic of Somoza, Killed by Gunmen," *WP*, January 11, 1978, A20.

23. Karen DeYoung, "'The Twelve': Nicaragua's Unlikely Band of Somoza's Foes," *WP*, July 23, 1978, A26.

24. DeYoung, "Nicaraguan Rebels Gaining Support," August 24, 1978, A21.

25. "Rebels are Flown from Nicaragua," *WP*, August 25, 1978, A1, A14.

26. Joshua Muravchik, *The Uncertain Crusade: Jimmy Carter and the Dilemmas of Human Rights Policy* (Lanham, Maryland: Hamilton, 1988), 11.

27. DeYoung, "Sandinistas Disclaim Marxism," *WP*, October 16, 1978, A1.

28. Christian, "Covering the Sandinistas," 36.

29. FSLN, *Plataforma General*, 32, 34.

30. Clifford Krauss, *Inside Central America* (New York: Summit, 1991), 135.

31. V. I. Lenin, *Left-Wing Communism, An Infantile Disorder* (Moscow: Novosti Press Agency Publishing House, 1975); see Stalin, *Foundations of Leninism*, chapter vii-viii.

32. U.S. House of Representatives, *United States Policy toward Nicaragua*, Hearings before the Subcommittee on Inter-American Affairs of the Committee on Foreign Affairs, 96th Congress, 1st session, June 21, 1979, 18.

33. U.S. House of Representatives, *United States Policy Toward Nicaragua*, 3.

34. Richard Fagen, "Dateline Nicaragua: The End of the Affair," *Foreign Policy*, no. 36 (Fall 1979): 183.

35. Fagen, "Dateline Nicaragua," 188.

36. *Nicaragua in Revolution*, ed. Thomas W. Walker (New York: Praeger, 1982), 20-21.

37. Walker, "Introduction," in *Nicaragua: The First Five Years*, ed. Walker (Westport: Praeger, 1985), 23. Walker's colleague John Booth also was eventually discreetly to acknowledge the Marxist-Leninist character of the *Terceristas*, and he did so with the same bad faith. In the first edition of his *The End and the Beginning: The Nicaraguan Revolution*, he presented the *Terceristas* as "ideologically heterodox" and characterized by "ideological pluralism" (page 143); in the second edition that characteristic is only "apparent" (page 144). In the first edition Booth argues the *Terceristas'* "reduction of Marxist-Leninist principles was truly substantive and not merely cosmetic. A true ideological pluralization had occurred . . ." (page 147). The second edition, though still claiming a "profound" "ideological evolution," states that the *Tercerista* program had "retained such Leninist features as a mobilizing vanguard party . . ." (page 147). The first edition claimed the *Terceristas* "relaxed the *Marxist* rigor of the original FSLN." In the second edition the *Terceristas* only had "relaxed the original FSLN's requirement for *Marxist-Leninist* orthodoxy . . . although the leaders remained Marxist-Leninists" (page 144) (italics added). In the second edition Eden Pastora, who broke with the FSLN in 1981 and formed an anti-Sandinista rebel group, is no longer included among these leaders. (See 1st edition John Booth, *The End and the Beginning* (Boulder: Westview, 1982), 143-47; 2d edition Booth, *The End and the Beginning* (Boulder: Westview, 1985), 144-47.)

38. James F. Larson, *Global Television and Foreign Policy* (New York: Foreign Policy Association, 1988), table F.1, 182-83.

39. DeYoung, "Nicaraguan Rebels Gaining Support," A21.

40. "Politically Ill-Defined Sandinista Guerrilla Movement," *NYT*, November 21, 1978, A20.

41. "What's News," *WSJ*, September 18, 1978, 1.

42. See appendix C for a quantitative analysis of the coverage of the Sandinistas in the *Washington Post* and the *New York Times* during this period.

43. See Muravchik, *The Uncertain Crusade*, chapter 1.

44. Muravchik, *The Uncertain Crusade*, 24.

45. "Revolutions, Earthquakes and Latin America: The Networks Look at Allende's Chile and Somoza's Nicaragua" in *Television Coverage of International Affairs*, ed. William C. Adams (Norwood, New Jersey: ablex, 1982), 102, 111-12.

46. *CBS Evening News*, July 20, 1979.

47. See Orlando Nuñez, "La ideología como fuerza material y la juventud como fuerza ideológica," in *Estado y clases socials en Nicaragua* (Managua: ANICS/CIERA, 1982); Carlos M. Vilas, *Perfiles de la Revolución Sandinista* (Managua: Neuva Nicaragua, 1987), 167-68; Humberto Ortega in *Central American Crisis Reader*, ed. Leiken and Rubin, 191-95; Humberto Belli, *Breaking Faith* (Garden City, Michigan: Puebla Institute, 1985), 38; Christian, *Nicaragua. Revolution in the Family*, 67.

48. DeYoung, "Nicaraguan Junta Assumes Rule in Jubilant Managua," *WP*, July 21, 1979, A1.

49. Kinzer, "Nicaragua: A Look Ahead," *BG*, July 11, 1979, A3.

50. Kinzer, *Blood of Brothers*, 78.

51. "Sandinistas Indicate They Will Keep Power in Nicaragua," *WP*, August 1, 1979, A16.

52. Carter Administration officials shared the media's perspective on the prospects for Nicaragua despite these professed intentions. Viron Vaky, the Carter Administration's

highly respected Assistant Secretary for Inter-American Affairs told a House sub-committee that the Nicaraguan government had shown

> generally moderate pluralistic tendencies in its initial policies. It is not distinguishably moderate in orientation, although Marxist figures are present in key positions. . . . The leadership is an amalgam . . . and no ideological current yet predominates.

Vaky pointed to the "moderate, democratic responsible bankers and professionals" who held seemingly important cabinet positions. (U.S. House of Representatives, *Central America at the Crossroads*, Hearings before the Sub-committee on Inter-American Affairs of the Committee of Foreign Affairs, first session, September 11-12, 1979, 3-4, 25.) Lawrence Pezzullo, the Carter Administration's able and experienced ambassador to revolutionary Nicaragua, told the same committee that while the Sandinista "rhetorical approach . . . will offend," the "real evidence of their direction" was in their "pragmatic" policies not "in the speechmaking and breast beating." (U.S. House of Representatives, *Central America at the Crossroads*, 28-29.)

53. The second stressed that they labored under "Somoza's Legacy: Plundered Economy"; the third was headed "U.S., Nicaragua Easing Mutual Suspicions," (DeYoung, *WP*, November 29-30, December 1, 1979, A1).

54. See Leiken, "Tangled Nicaragua," *NYRB*, December 5, 1985.

55. See Christian, *Nicaragua: Revolution in the Family*, 150-54; and Jaime Chamorro, *The Republic of Paper* (New York: Freedom House, 1988), 26-27.

56. Chamorro, *Republic of Paper*, 31. A few days after the Sandinista electoral defeat, the government abolished all restrictions on the press.

57. Muravchik, *The Uncertain Crusade*, 70, 67.

58. Muravchik, *The Uncertain Crusade*, 70.

Chapter 10
Sandinista Popularity and the Nicaragua News Frame, 1979-89

> There is no philosopher in the world so great but that he believes a million things on the faith of other people and accepts a great many more truths than he demonstrates.
>
> —Alexis de Tocqueville, *Democracy in America II*, ii

When noting that veteran Nicaragua reporters were unable "to imagine such a vast change" as the Sandinista election defeat, Julia Preston was not calling attention to what her colleague William Branigin termed "the myth of Sandinista popularity."[1] She was referring not to the durability of a stereotype but to the speed with which, she thought, the Nicaraguans had deserted the Sandinistas. That would explain why so many seasoned reporters failed to anticipate the election results. "As a result of the electoral campaign" Nicaraguan politics had "changed more radically than at any time since the early years of the Sandinista revolution," leaving in the lurch veteran journalists impressed by the solidity of the regime's support.[2]

Did the Nicaraguans really change their opinion of the Sandinistas so suddenly? It is certainly true that Sandinista popularity was hardly a "myth" when the guerrilla army triumphantly entered Managua in July 1979, to what CBS described as "a gigantic celebration . . . a coming-out party . . . a Mardi Gras."[3] Some Nicaraguans claim that public approval promptly began to decline, while others believe it survived far longer. In the absence of public opinion polls or elections, we are left with suppositions.

There is evidence that Sandinista charisma was routinized or, more often, dissipated.[4] In July and August 1981, soon after the government, in a highly controversial decision, prohibited the Archbishop of Managua from televising

131

his weekly mass, *La Prensa* conducted a survey among 900 Nicaraguans in the country's principal urban centers. It found that thrice as many Nicaraguans identified with the Archbishop Obando y Bravo as with his antagonist, Daniel Ortega, the coordinator of the revolutionary junta. Only 36 percent felt that the revolution had brought them some benefit. But while the survey showed a falling-off in Sandinista support, more than half of those interviewed continued to be in substantial agreement with the FSLN. And by a two-to-one margin the country's economic problems were attributed to "the legacy of the previous regime" rather than to "the incapacity of the present government."[5]

Though these survey results were mixed, the government forbade their publication in *La Prensa*, which it had now begun to censor regularly and to close down occasionally. Nevertheless in November, taking advantage of a visit by a commission from the Inter-American Press Association, *La Prensa* succeeded in publishing the results. When the commission departed, revolutionary decree #888 was issued banning all public opinion polls not authorized by the government, an action difficult to reconcile with the image of a government confident of its popularity.[6] A story on the survey and the government prohibition went out over the UPI wire, but it was not picked up by any major U.S. news organization.[7]

***

The long-delayed 1984 elections might have provided a clear answer to the question of Sandinista popularity. However, the episode was inconclusive, though once again illustrative.[8]

The main opposition group was a coalition very similar to that which was to nominate Violeta Chamorro in 1990. Like UNO, the Nicaraguan Democratic Coordinating Committee (CDN) chose as its standard-bearer a moderate, former member of the revolutionary junta who had broken with the Sandinistas. The candidacy of Arturo Cruz was supported by Mrs. Chamorro and her colleagues at *La Prensa* as well as by most of the labor unions, business and professional associations, and political parties that later backed Mrs. Chamorro. However, in 1984 the opposition feared that without impartial, official international observation of the sort that was to be established for the 1990 elections, there would be nothing to prevent the Sandinistas from intimidating opposition voters or perpetrating wholesale fraud. At that time the Sandinistas proscribed such supervision as interference in Nicaragua's internal affairs. Accordingly, several CDN leaders preferred to boycott the elections, rather than risk becoming known as "*zancudos*" (mosquitos)—the stigma attached to politicians who had acquiesced in the Somozas' fraudulent elections. Some of these recalcitrant opposition leaders also hoped that a boycott would strengthen the hand of the *Contras*, a posture reportedly bolstered by some CIA and White House officials though opposed by the State Department.[9] So the CDN attached conditions to its participation, some of them quite improbable. The consequence of this impasse was that the election campaign was overshadowed by several rounds of negotiations between the Sandinistas and the CDN mediated by the leaders of the Socialist International and a regional peace group, Contadora.

Before the deadline for registering candidates Cruz's CDN was allowed to campaign. In early August Cruz rallies began to grow. Upwards of 7,000 opposition supporters turned out in the historically pro-Sandinista city of Chinandega. The event was disrupted by armed "activists" covertly organized by the Interior Ministry and local Sandinista police and dubbed *turbas divinas*, or "divine mobs," by Daniel Ortega. It was the last open-air CDN meeting allowed by the government.[10] Cruz concluded that the Sandinistas feared the rally would set off "a chain reaction" in other cities.[11] (Indeed, as we shall see, something like that did happen in late January 1990 as citizens became increasingly emboldened by successively bigger Chamorro rallies.) *La Prensa* was prevented from carrying reports of the events.[12] Though an NBC camera crew taped the rally, there was no story on the episode in major American media.[13]

Eventually, the Sandinistas terminated negotiations with the CDN, casting the blame on the opposition. A minority of opposition leaders did, in fact, obstruct Cruz's efforts to work out a compromise. However, Stephen Kinzer, who covered the elections for the *New York Times*, concluded in a detailed reconstruction of the negotiations for his subsequent memoir that "Sandinista leaders bore ultimate responsibility for breaking off the talks . . . and, by extension, for the failure of the election."[14]

Kinzer's research confirmed at least one previous investigation.[15] Nonetheless, as often happened with the Nicaragua coverage, the false impression survived refutation by direct reporting. Thus, a few months after he replaced Kinzer as Managua bureau chief, Uhlig wrote that the opposition had "boycotted" the 1984 elections and thereby "fueled the *Contra* war."[16] Just before the 1990 elections the *Los Angeles Times* correspondent observed that "the main U.S.-backed anti-Sandinista coalition spoiled the 1984 election by pulling out."[17] When Clifford Krauss of the *Wall Street Journal* wrote his account of the period, he too noted that the opposition "dropped out."[18] So general was this belief that, for example, the arch-conservative editorial page editor of the *Boston Herald* could affirm that "in 1984, the major opposition candidate withdrew from the presidential race to protest gang attacks on his campaign."[19] Indeed Kinzer himself, though he already had completed his memoir, upon reporting Chamorro's nomination for the *Times*, only recalled that in 1984:

> The main opposition candidate that year, Arturo Cruz, refused to register his candidacy and left the country before election day to protest what he said were unfair conditions.[20]

The standard press view, in spite of the surge in CDN rallies and its subsequent banning, was that, as Julia Preston wrote:

The Sandinista Front confirmed its dominance as a majority party in November 1984 national elections which, though intensely controversial, were described as clean by most observers.[21]

However, this 1986 story failed to specify that "most observers" represented nongovernmental organizations sympathetic to the Sandinistas. The only official Western observers were from the Dutch government, one quite friendly to the Sandinistas but whose report hardly stamped the elections as "clean."

Colombia's president Belisario Betancur, at the time of the elections also President of the Contadora group, explained that he had shown his "disappointment" with campaign violence and election procedures by declining to send observers.[22] Other Contadora countries followed suit. As might have been expected the Reagan Administration did not send an observer delegation, but neither did Canada nor any of the members of the European Community with the exception of The Netherlands.

The Dutch government was an important donor of foreign assistance to Nicaragua. Nonetheless, its observer team reported that late in the campaign they

> repeatedly heard people remark that they did not want to vote but feared that to abstain would be interpreted by the CDS [Sandinista Defense Committees] as support for the counter-revolutionaries. . . . This social control is not conducive to a free election process.[23]

The records of the Supreme Electoral Council indicate that typical authorized observers included delegates from the Belgian Socialist Party, the British Labour Party, the Spanish Communist Party, the Portuguese Communist Party, the Italian Communist Party, and Petra Kelly of the Green Party. U.S. observers included representatives of left-leaning advocacy groups such as SANE, Physicians for Social Responsibility, the New York chapter of the ACLU, and the League of United Latin American Citizens (LULAC), unofficial dissident labor unions like the Arizona Association of Agricultural Workers, left-wing funders like the Samuel Rubin and Field foundations, similarly inclined religious groups such as the United Methodist Church's Office for the U.N., left-liberal politicians such as Julian Bond, socialist celebrities like folk singer Pete Seeger, and scholars such as Frank Brodhead (Noam Chomsky's collaborator). Those whom the mainstream press described as neutral observers were actually virtually all sympathizers.

Left-liberal interest groups such as the Washington Office on Latin America issued reports praising the elections as did the similarly-inclined Latin American Studies Association (LASA). The LASA report concluded that this had been "an electoral process which by Latin American standards was a model of probity and fairness."[24] LASA also found that

> the FSLN did little more to take advantage of its incumbency than incumbent parties everywhere (including the United States) routinely do. . . .

Chomsky himself was later to complain that Kinzer's coverage in the *New York Times* had ignored the foreign observers ("some with superb credentials") and had failed to accord the LASA report its "proper weight."[25] As one might expect in such a politicized environment the fact-finding mission of an organization with a conservative perspective, the European Democratic Union, strongly condemned the campaign procedures.[26]

What is most striking about the retrospective journalistic verdict on the 1984 elections was its contrast with most of the direct reporting at the time. Julia Preston, then of the *Boston Globe*, wrote of voters who

> said they feared Sandinista block organizations would withhold their food rationing cards or deny them exit visas if they failed to vote.

Preston also spoke with Nicaraguans who

> sometimes in defensive whispers, told of fears and aggravations for those who didn't want to vote at all or wished to vote against the FSLN. . . .
>
> "If I ever want to get out of this country again, or buy a meal for my family, I have to vote," said Jose Nuñez, 43, a Managua factory security guard. Voting is not obligatory in Nicaragua but the FSLN waged a noisy campaign in recent weeks describing those who would abstain as "traitors."[27]

The *Miami Herald* reported that

> Witnesses said Sandinista sympathizers made house-to-house sweeps of many neighborhoods Sunday afternoon, urging everyone to vote.[28]

The *Los Angeles Times* added that before the vote:

> Rumors circulated that people who did not vote would be blacklisted for government jobs, passports and other benefits.[29]

Chris Hedges of the *Dallas Morning News* noted that

> The CDS committees, located on nearly every block in any Nicaraguan town, have worked diligently to turn out voters for the government. Residents in the towns of Granada, Masaya and San Juan del Oriente said they feared that if they did not participate in the elections they would lose their government-issued food rationing cards. [30]

According to another *Miami Herald* dispatch "[Daniel] Ortega said an abstention was the same as a vote for CIA-backed anti-Sandinista guerrillas."[31] Indeed, though not cited in major press accounts, Ortega told a closing campaign rally:

The only ones who will not vote will be the enemies of Nicaragua, the traitors, the turncoats. We will wait for you to cast your votes. . . . Those who will not vote on 4 November are those who will stay at home waiting for the Yankee intervention and bombings. They will be voting for treason, for the turncoats. They will be turning themselves into turncoats and will expose themselves to the fury of the people at the moment of intervention.[32]

Hedges and Kinzer revealed that two weeks before the elections candidates in six "opposition" parties "signed a secret document agreeing to curtail their criticism of the unpopular military draft and encourage a massive voter turnout."[33]

From San Rafael del Norte the *Los Angeles Times* reported: "Morning lines at polling places were short. Many early risers seemed more intent on delivering fresh milk to market or buying meat for a Sunday meal than on marking ballots. Pool halls were packed."[34] Julia Preston wrote that "many observers noted that in some key cities, lines had dwindled to nothing by 10 a.m."[35] The present author, who was an official observer, reported in the *New York Review of Books:*

In the eleven voting places I visited in Masaya, Monimbo and Managua, the turnout averaged 40 percent. Voting appears to have been lighter in outlying districts. In small rural villages, residents later told me that between 20 and 35 percent had voted . . . In the late afternoon there was a small flurry of voting activity after Sandinista activists made house to house visits in many neighborhoods.[36]

None other than Julia Preston went so far as to raise a question about the validity of the vote count:

The thousands of volunteer election police, who will carry the ballots from local stations to be tallied by the council, wore Sandinista police and army uniforms.[37]

Official returns showed 25 percent of the voters abstained and 6 percent of the ballots were annulled, with Sandinista candidate Ortega winning 63 percent of the vote.[38] The turnout fell short of the Sandinistas goal of 80 percent, already downwardly revised from 90 percent as election day approached.[39] And, as Preston wrote,

the FSLN's margin of victory was much tighter than Sandinista leaders had hoped. Late last week . . . comandante Carlos Nuñez said the FSLN hoped Ortega would sweep 90 percent of the valid votes. Interior Minister Tomas Borge said recently that a victory with anything less than 70 percent would worry the Sandinistas.[40]

By their own count the Sandinistas received only 47 percent of the registered votes—against a majority consisting of those who abstained, annulled their ballots, or voted for the opposition. But even the disappointing official numbers may have been inflated.

Those "international observers" who did not depart the day after the vote eagerly awaited disclosures of partial and final results. They acted for all the world as if they were sitting out an "election-night vigil," tropical-style. Meanwhile nongovernmental Nicaraguan journalists, academics, and opposition leaders described the waiting period in terms more reminiscent of a smoked-filled room at a by-gone party convention.[41]

No one, to be sure, produced documentary evidence of a preelectoral pact or of tampering with the ballots. Opposition poll watchers were present at fewer than 20 percent of the polling sites. As Kinzer wrote years later, after leaving Nicaragua:

> There was no way for outsiders to determine if vote counts were genuine, but the Sandinistas showed themselves unusually sensitive to allegations of fraud. The newspaper of the Communist party, *Avance*, was ordered shut indefinitely after it published a statistical analysis purporting to prove that returns from several provinces had been falsified.[42]

Jaime Chamorro, the editor of *La Prensa*, later published abroad a detailed statistical analysis of the official registration and election figures, comparing them with the partial figures released during the "election night vigil." He noted numerous discrepancies and came to the conclusion that the FSLN had padded the registration count by 400,000. These votes, he argued, were later added to the FSLN election totals.[43] Sandinista censors prevented Chamorro from publishing his findings in his own newspaper. In the aftermath of the incident Kinzer recounts, directors of Nicaraguan communications media were summoned to a private meeting with government Communications Media Director Lieutenant Nelba Blandon and issued a new postelection "orientation." The first guideline stipulated:

> Absolute prohibition to refer to 4 November elections in terms that directly or indirectly express or suggest citizens' abstention, fraud, manipulation of figures, or lack of confidence in the electoral authorities.[44]

A *New York Times* editorial concluded that "only the naive believe that Sunday's election in Nicaragua was democratic or legitimizing proof of the Sandinistas' popularity."[45]

The *Washington Post* news pages stood as an exception to the generally critical coverage. Robert J. McCartney of the *Post* found "long lines at many polling places in Managua" and his associate John Lantigua also found "long lines . . . in Ocotal in Nueva Segovia."[46] McCartney dismissed out of hand any suggestion that "the Sandinistas somehow had manipulated figures to inflate the turnout."[47] Moreover, as we have seen above, despite on-the-spot press reports of intimidation and other abuses, the press, including some of those who filed those reports, eventually arrived at the verdict that the 1984 elections were a legitimate test of Sandinista popularity.

The Sandinistas themselves, however, viewed the election not as a submission to the popular will but rather as means of consolidating their revolution and legitimizing their rule. In announcing the postponement of the "early elections" promised during the revolutionary war, Humberto Ortega had declared at a public ceremony in August 1980:

> For the Sandinist Front, democracy is not . . . confined merely to participation in elections. . . . The revolutionary process . . . cannot go backward, . . . it will continue onward to the ultimate consequences. . . . The elections we are talking about are very different from the elections sought by the oligarchs and traitors, the conservatives and liberals. . . . They are elections to improve the power of the revolution . . . not a raffle to see who has power, because the people have power through their vanguard, the Sandinista National Liberation Front.[48]

Another *comandante*, Bayardo Arce, spoke in plainer terms in May 1984. "Elections are a nuisance as are a lot of things which make up the reality of the Revolution," lamented Arce, one of the most powerful Sandinista leaders, when he represented the National Directorate in a meeting with the Communist Nicaraguan Socialist Party (PSN). "If it were not for the state of war forced on us . . . elections would be absolutely inappropriate," he continued. Thus the Sandinista *comandante* refuted the widespread view that military pressure had stopped the Sandinistas from fulfilling their commitments to pluralism. The need was not "bourgeois formalities but the dictatorship of the proletariat." "Nonetheless," he argued, these "bourgeois details" can become "arms of the revolution," just as it has been "useful . . . to point to an entrepreneurial class and private production in a mixed economy while we got on with our strategic goals."[49] Tactical flexibility, strategic intransigence.

***

After the 1984 elections Archbishop Miguel Obando y Bravo emerged as the Sandinistas' paramount opponent. Returning in June 1985 from Rome, where he had been elevated to cardinal, Obando was welcomed by several hundred thousand rejoicing Nicaraguans.[50] That week the Sandinista press had furiously denounced Obando y Bravo for meeting with *Contra* leaders in Miami *en route* to Managua.[51] But his reception was so overwhelming that it took the "Cardinalmobile" nine hours to manage the six miles from the airport to the Cardinal's home. The crowds cried "Christianity yes, Communism no" and "the [Sandinista] Front must go"—the very same slogans heard at Cruz rallies the year before and at Chamorro rallies four years hence (except that "Democracy" replaced "Christianity"). Sandinista police were jeered, foreign journalists covering the event were assailed as government sympathizers and "encountered hostile shouts of 'tell the truth.'"[52] When the government tried to dispel the crowds by switching off street lights, torches were fashioned by the roadside from burning tires. As the "Cardinal-mobile" passed, the crowds sang the national hymn, the popular alternative to the official Sandinista anthem.

Neither the television networks nor the *New York Times* covered this event, and it was consigned to the back pages of the *Washington Post* and *Los Angeles Times*.[53] Kinzer of the *New York Times* stated several months later that he had filed a story but that it had arrived too late for early editions of the *Times* and then had been "crowded out of the paper by Lebanon."[54] On June 14, the day of the Cardinal's arrival in Managua, TWA Flight 847 was hijacked en route from Athens to Rome and forced to land in Beirut. Nevertheless, the Saturday, June 15, 1985 Late Edition of the *Times* ran thirteen major foreign news stories besides the two stories on the hijacking. The following day's (Sunday) edition ran seven major international stories besides those on the hijacking, but there was no story on the Nicaraguan Cardinal. How much importance did Kinzer or his editors attach to the story? By contrast, a prominent Spanish-speaking daily in the United States, the conservative *Diario Las Americas* gave the story a banner front-page headline.[55]

The Cardinal held open air masses the remainder of the year that continued to attract unprecedented crowds and whose political content was unmistakably anti-Sandinista. Clifford Krauss observed that during the decade of Sandinista rule "opposition priests drew far larger congregations to their churches than did the progovernment liberation theology priests" and Chamorro's *La Prensa* "far outsold two Sandinista newspapers."[56]

"The myth of Sandinista popularity" also survived press investigations into the nationwide resistance to the military draft. Two stories on draft resistance were rare exceptions to the general rule that investigative journalism in Nicaragua was limited to exposing the abuses and deficiencies of American foreign policy and of the anti-Sandinista forces. After a two-week June 1984 investigation in six Nicaraguan provinces, Stephen Kinzer found that "draft evasion is widespread," and that "school attendance has plummeted in many Nicaraguan high schools because of fear that recruiters will come."[57] The draftees and their parents—"most of them poor and frightened"—agreed to meet Kinzer "only after elaborate security measures were arranged."

Several months later an ABC camera crew led by correspondent Peter Collins managed to film and interview "draft dodgers literally on the run . . . in the hills where they've been hiding." Collins estimated that only 65 percent of eligible young men registered for the draft and that "desertions from the army are running at 20 percent." Nicaraguan youths were not being called up to fight a foreign war—as in the case of the United States during the Vietnam War—but for what the government described as "patriotic defense of the homeland against Yankee aggression." Yet Collins reported:

The young draft resisters say one thing over and over. They don't want to fight in what they see as a civil war among Nicaraguans for the interest of one political party—the Sandinistas.[58]

Nonetheless these on-the-spot reports failed to shatter the "myth of Sandinista support among the young people" or to raise lasting questions as to how the Nicaraguans apportioned blame for the war. Consequently neither mass demonstrations, draft resistance, nor widespread anecdotal evidence of Nicaraguans's disaffection penetrated the invincible conventional image of Sandinista popularity, an image which was to lead to so much "stunned surprise" and dismay the day after the 1990 elections.[59] Thus, leading American academic authorities, who took for granted the accuracy of the judgment of the 1984 elections presented by LASA, would later speak of the "silent erosion" of support for the Sandinistas.

There was as we now know, a silent erosion of the FSLN's political strength during 1985-89 (Oquist 1992). Several mass organizations were crumbling, and the political base of the revolution was shrinking.[60]

The parenthetical source reference is to an essay by Paul Oquist, the confident Ortega campaign spokesman we met in chapter 5, published in the principal U.S. academic account of the elections.[61]

In January 1989 Mark Uhlig replaced Kinzer as the *Times* Managua bureau chief. Uhlig's first "News Analysis," provided a glimpse of the assumptions he inherited:

In their scope and severity, the cutbacks announced by the Sandinista Government this week were just what its opponents had been waiting for: a signal of economic distress.

But the measures also bore the mark of a Government that is still deeply confident of its popular support.

"There are only a handful of countries where you could even consider something like this," said an American with long experience in the region. "If you tried this in most of Latin America there would be riots in the street."[62]

In the maiden analysis of his first assignment in the region, Uhlig concluded that "Nicaragua is not like most of Latin America." This sweeping judgment made no mention of Cuba. The newcomer was not drawing attention to the Sandinistas' more pervasive security apparatus but to the government's "Marxist *oratory*" and "powerful enemies" [italics added]. Still less was Uhlig anticipating what he would later describe as "a turnover that parallels to some degree the changes in Eastern Europe, where Communism has little by little given way to democratic change."[63] No, what Uhlig then thought distinguished the Sandinista regime was its "popular support," nourished by hostility to its "powerful enemies." If, unlike the rest of Latin America, dissent could not be found on Nicaragua's streets, that was because the anti-U.S. government was better liked, not because it was worse feared.

The fledgling *Times* correspondent's skeptical, even reticent, coverage of the elections suggests that, unlike many of his colleagues, Uhlig soon realized how shaky these myths were. Walter Lippmann insisted that when the press becomes the arbiter of "popular support" it puts itself "in the position of the umpire in the unscored baseball game":

> If that game were reported in the newspapers it would consist of a record of the umpire's decisions, plus the reporter's impression of the hoots and cheers of the crowd, plus at best a vague account of how certain men . . . moved around for a few hours on an unmarked piece of sod.

Uhlig appeared to have concluded with Lippmann that:

> All news about state of mind is of this character: so are all descriptions of personalities, of sincerity, aspiration, motive, intention, mass feeling, national feeling, of public opinion. . . . So is much news about what is going to happen.[64]

The *Post*'s Julia Preston, though one of the most thoughtful journalists who covered Nicaragua, was slower to learn that lesson, perhaps, as she suggested, because she had been following the story longer. Preston, who began filing from the region in the 1970s for publications like *Report on the Americas* of the leftist North American Congress on Latin American (NACLA) and the left-leaning *Seven Days* , later covered Central America for the *Christian Science Monitor*, the *Boston Globe*, National Public Radio, and the *Washington Post*. In July 1989 she wrote a farewell article as she completed her three-year stint for the *Post*. The occasion was the tenth anniversary of the Sandinistas' "uniquely ambiguous revolution." Preston found a firm core of support for "the Sandinistas' populist nationalism." Two months before the start of the election campaign which she would later claim had "radically changed" Nicaragua, she concluded that in regarding the opposition as "history's leftovers," "the Sandinistas may be right." Her "eight years covering Central America" along with what she described as "independent polls" led the *Post*'s veteran correspondent to suggest that "Ortega is . . . at least three times as popular as any single opposition figure."[65]

Notes

1. See chapter 6, 81 *supra*.
2. Julia Preston, "The Defeat of the Sandinistas," *NYRB*, (April 12, 1990), 25. Preston's "last trip to Nicaragua before the elections was in May 1989." She was preparing a commemorative piece on the tenth anniversary of the revolution which was to em-

phasize the continuing popularity of Daniel Ortega and the fractured nature of the opposition (*WP*, July 2, 1989, A1).

3. *CBS Evening News with Walter Cronkite*, July 20, 1979.

4. On Max Weber's concept of the "routinization of charisma," see *From Max Weber: Essays in Sociology*, ed. and trans. H. H. Gerth and C. Wright Mills (New York: Oxford University, 1958), 51-54, 262-64. Charisma can be routinized into traditional rule or its message and ideas may "fail to influence the conduct of everyday life or those whom they do influence" may "remain enclosed in a special way of life and alien to the larger social body" (*From Max Weber*, 54).

5. Nicaraguan Information Center, "Encuesta de Opinion: Análisis de Métodos, Resultados y Conclusiones," Agosto, 1981, 7-8.

6. *Decretos-Leyes Para Gobierno de Un Pais A Traves de Una Junta de Gobierno de Reconstrucción Nacional*, Managua 1981, Tomo V, 234-38; Jaime Chamorro, *The Republic of Paper* (New York: Freedom House, 1988), 35; Douglas Payne, *The Democractic Mask* (New York: Freedom House, 1985), 34.

7. Louis Garcia, UPI, November 12, 1981, AM cycle. The story was not picked up by any of the organizations archived by NEXIS. The *Boston Globe, Chicago Tribune*, the *Los Angeles Times*, the *New York Times, Washington Post, Newsweek, Time*, and the television networks were double-checked without discovery of any mention of the incident.

8. A private poll conducted for the FSLN by the Statistic Institute of Spain in November 1983, one year before the elections, showed that the Sandinistas could obtain only 35 percent of the vote unless they ran as part of an alliance with other parties and lowered the voting age to 16. They succeeded in doing the latter, but not in constituting the former. See Dennis Volman, "Free Elections in Nicaragua?" *CSM*, March 2, 1984, 8.

9. For the divisions in the Reagan Administration see Constantine Menges, *Inside the National Security Council* (New York: Simon & Schuster, 1988), chapter v.; Robert S. Leiken, "Tangled Nicaragua," *NYRB*, December 5, 1985, 58; and Roy Gutman, *Banana Diplomacy: The Making of American Policy in Nicaragua, 1981-87* (New York: Simon and Schuster, 1988), chapter xi.

10. See Leiken, "Nicaragua's Untold Stories," *TNR*, October 8, 1984.

11. Author's interview with Arturo Cruz, San José, Costa Rica, August 26, 1984.

12. The August 6, 1984 edition of *La Prensa* contained several articles and photographs relating to the Chinandega incident as well as stories about a similar event in Matagalpa the previous day and the CDN's declaration of its intention to "continue the struggle" despite having been declared "illegal." All of these articles were expunged. Copies of the proofs were obtained by the author. The articles on Chinandega were titled: "Chinandega estalló de jubilo: Entusiasta recimiento a la fórmula de triunfo: Cruz-Fletes"; "Las turbas no pudieron con los chinadeganos"; "Hallaron a las turbas rindiendo su informe"; "Policía detuvo a dos jóvenes socialdemócratas"; and "Muerte electoral pero vida moral."

13. NBC bureau chief Elena Caldera allowed me to view the NBC tape at the bureau in Managua. The rally was mentioned in an interview with Cruz in the *Christian Science Monitor* (Dennis Volman, "Cruz: 'Sandinistas Must Talk,' " *CSM*, August 17, 1984, 1); and in a short AP clip which was carried in the *New York Times* ("Main Opposition Parties Lose Legal Standing in Nicaragua," *NYT*, August 7, 1984 (Late City Final): A3; see also Leiken, "Nicaragua's Untold Stories," 21–22. A description of the Chinandega event can be found in Gutman, *Banana Diplomacy*, 242–43.

14. Stephen Kinzer, *Blood of Brothers* (New York: Putnam, 1991), 244.

15. See Leiken, "Tangled Nicaragua" and "The Nicaraguan Tangle: Another Exchange," *NYRB*, June 26, 1986.

16. Mark A. Uhlig, "Managua and Its Rivals Sparring Over Vote Rules," *NYT*, May 14, 1989, 18.

17. Richard Boudreaux, "Sandinistas Pull Levers of State Power to Woo Votes," *LAT*, February 22, 1990, A10.

18. Clifford Krauss, *Inside Central America* (New York: Summit, 1991), 157.

19. Don Feder, "Democracy Sandinista-style Teaches even Liberals a Lesson," *BH*, December 18, 1989, 31.

20. Kinzer, "Anti-Sandinistas Choose Candidate: Newspaper Publisher to Run for President in February," *NYT*, September 4, 1989, 4.

21. "Nicaraguan Legislator Flees To Embassy," *WP*, July 17, 1986, A1.

22. Conversation with the author, El Cerrejon, Colombia, December 1984.

23. Thom Kerstiens and Piet Nelissen, "Report on the Elections in Nicaragua," November 4, 1984, 23. The observers went on to say that "only parties of the left took part in the elections, and the fact that there were no great differences between these parties engendered a certain sluggishness in the electorate."

24. Latin American Studies Association, *The Electoral Process in Nicaragua: Domestic and International Influences*, Report of the Latin American Studies Association Delegation to Observe the Nicaraguan General Election of November 4, 1984, 32.

25. Noam Chomsky and Edward S. Herman, *After the Cataclysm* (Boston: South End, 1979), 117, 140; see also Chomsky, *Turning the Tide* (Boston: South End, 1985), 137.

26. "Report on the Election Process in Nicaragua," September 4, 1984.

27. Preston, "Nicaragua Voting Called Peaceful," *BG*, November 5, 1984, 1.

28. Juan O. Tamayo, "Sandinistas Surging Ahead in Early Presidential Returns," *MH*, November 6, 1984, 1A.

29. William R. Long and Dan Williams, "Nicaraguans Mustered to Polling Places," *LAT*, November 5, 1984, A1.

30. Chris Hedges, "Nicaraguan Election Orderly," *DMN*, November 5, 1984, 1A.

31. Juan O. Tamayo, "Tally Slows but Sandinistas Keep Big Lead in Nicaragua," *MH*, November 7, 1984, 2A.

32. Foreign Broadcast Information Service, *Central America*, VI, November 2, 1984, 18.

33. Hedges, "Margin is the Only Mystery in Today's Nicaragua Vote," *DMN*, November 4, 1984, 1A; and Steven Kinzer, "Nicaraguan Opposition Parties Cite Sandinista Aid and U.S. Pressure," *NYT*, October 31, 1984, A1.

34. Dan Williams, "Serenade Awakens Nicaraguans to Vote," *LAT*, November 5, 1984.

35. *BG*, November 6, 1984, 4.

36. Leiken, "Tangled Nicaragua."

37. Preston, "Nicaragua Voting Called Peaceful," *BG*, November 5, 1984, 1.

38. Kinzer, "Opposition in Nicaragua Vows Strong Challenge," *NYT*, November 18, 1984, A20; Robert J. McCartney, "Vote Said to Change Little in Managua," *WP*, December 28, 1984.

39. See McCartney, "Nicaraguans Go to Polls," November 5, 1984, A1; Leiken, "Tangled Nicaragua."

40. Preston, "Ortega Claims Victory in Nicaragua," *BG*, November 6, 1984, 4.

41. Leiken, "Tangled Nicaragua."

42. Kinzer, *Blood of Brothers*, 247. The Communist Party had refused to ally with the Sandinistas for the vote.
43. Jaime Chamorro C., "Farsa electoral en números, datos estadisticos y porcentajes," undated.
44. Chamorro, *Republic of Paper*, 93.
45. "Nobody Won in Nicaragua," *NYT*, November 7, 1984.
46. McCartney, "Nicaraguans Go to Polls," A1. See also McCartney and John Lantigua, "Sandinistas Winning in Nicaragua," *WP*, November 6, 1984, A1. Reports in the *Christian Science Monitor* also tended to be somewhat less critical than others. See Dennis Volman, "Nicaragua Vote Seen as Better Run than Salvador's," *CSM*, November 5, 1984, 13; and Volman, "After Election, Sandinistas Remain Under Pressure to Keep Yalking with Opposition," November 6, 1984, 36.
47. McCartney, "Sandinistas Winning in Nicaragua," A1.
48. "FSLN: Statement on the Electoral Process" (at a ceremony marking the end of the National Literacy Campaign, August 23, 1980) in Leiken and Barry Rubin, *The Central American Crisis Reader* (New York: Summit, 1987), 227-28.
49. Arce's secret speech was printed in the Spanish newspaper *La Vanguardia* on July 31, 1984. Sandinista authorities acknowledged the speech and PSN officials confirmed its authenticity. See Leiken, "Tangled Nicaragua;" and for the text of this speech see Leiken and Rubin, *Central American Crisis Reader*, 289-97.
50. Interview with Peter Collins of ABC, Miami, July 12, 1989 who supplied many of the following details of this episode as well as the number: "The population of Managua at that time I would guess was around 750,000 and if there weren't 350,000 people out in the streets, you know, I'd have to eat this tape recorder."
51. See *Barricada* and *El Nuevo Diario*, June 7-13, 1985.
52. Interview with Peter Collins; see also William Gasperini, "On the eve of the sixth Anniversary Sandinistas face troubled times," *In These Times*, June 26, 1985, 9; Pamela Constable, "Nicaraguan Cardinal's First Act Apolitical," *BG*, June 16, 1985, 7.
53. McCartney, "Nicaraguans Welcome Cardinal; Sandinistas, Meanwhile, Revive Threats to Buy Migs," *WP*, June 15, 1985, A14; Dan Williams, "Nicaraguan Cardinal Returns Home to Enthusiastic Welcome," *LAT*, June 15, 1985, A8.
Peter Collins of ABC recalled:

It was an incredible demonstration. And because it happened . . . on a Friday night, it would only make it into weekend news reports the following Saturday . . . so . . . I was only able to use some but not all of the tremendous . . . outpouring of emotion that we had seen the night before. I got it on the *ABC Saturday World News Tonight*, but the impact of what happened was diluted by the fact that there had been an event, a Mass, in between which was relatively poorly attended and organized. And some of the other journalists seized upon that as evidence that, "You see, the Catholics really aren't concerned about this," when in fact the previous night's demonstration had exhausted the city. (Interview with Peter Collins.)

54. Interview with author, Managua, February 13, 1986.
55. "200 mil Nicaraguenses le dan la bienvenida al Cardenal Obando," *World News Tonight*, June 16, 1985: A1.
56. Krauss, *Inside Central America*, 166.
57. Kinzer, "Military Draft in Nicaragua Is Meeting Wide Resistance," *NYT*, June 26, 1984, A1-6.
58. *ABC World News Tonight*, February 27, 1985.

59. For anecdotal evidence, see Leiken, "Nicaragua's Untold Stories" and "Tangled Nicaragua."

60. Rose J. Spalding, *Capitalists and Revolution in Nicaragua: Opposition and Accommodation 1979-1993* (London: University of North Carolina, 1994), 210. On pages 261–62 (note 52) and 209. Spalding cites the 1984 LASA election report as the source for her discussion of the elections. In the note, however, she does observe that the high absentee rate "suggested that some element of popular dissatisfaction was already there."

61. Paul Oquist, "Sociopolitical Dynamics of the 1990 Nicaragua Elections," in *The 1990 Elections in Nicaragua and Their Aftermath*, eds. Vanessa Castro and Gary Prevost (Lanham, Maryland: Rowman & Littlefield, 1992); for more on this essay see chapter 15 *infra*.

62. Uhlig, "Sandinistas' Medicine," *NYT*, February 1, 1989, A1.

63. Uhlig, "Chamorro Elected," *NYT*, February 27, 1990, A1.

64. Walter Lippmann, *Public Opinion* (New York: Macmillan, 1922; revised edition New Brunswick, New Jersey: Transaction, 1995), 342–43.

65. Preston, "Nicaragua's Ruler's Live by Revolution," *WP*, July 2, 1989, A1; her comment about the campaign is cited at the beginning of this chapter.

Chapter 11
The Media Presentation of the *"Contras,"* 1981-87

Washington created the *Contras* to fight the Sandinistas.

—CBS Evening News[1]

I have a dream. I dream that someday the United States will be on the side of the peasant in some civil war. . . It would be nice for once if our side did not wear gaudy military uniforms and hide their eyes behind dark glasses.

I would love it if our guys wore the suspenders and the wide hats and slept at night in the countryside instead of behind the guarded walls of some villa with a wife and a mistress and a Mercedes Benz.

I would like us once to be on the side of history. It would have been nice to have won in Vietnam and China before that.

— Richard Cohen, *Washington Post* columnist opposing U.S. support of *Contras*[2]

"When I told him that *Contra* activity was hurting the UNO campaign, he looked at me as if I were from another planet," said an American observer who met recently with [*Contra* leader] Galeano.

— Los Angeles Times[3]

The "system of stereotypes" which focused journalistic attention on the human rights abuses of Somoza's rule and on the promise of the Sandinista movement was less helpful in depicting the abuses of Sandinista rule and the character of the anti-Sandinista movement. The journalists' spotlight was focused so narrowly on the conflict between the United States and the Sandinista government that it obscured the domestic opposition to the latter. If the Sandinista government was a genuine, if flawed, attempt at national independence and social prog-

147

ress, it followed that armed resistance was an illegitimate attack by reactionaries and foreigners. The *Contras* and the journalists covering them inherited a frame.

That frame soon hardened into conventional wisdom supported by a set of fixed ideas. Thus, armed conflict in Sandinista Nicaragua derived solely from the Reagan Administration's hostility to the regime. The Reagan Administration unilaterally cut off aid to Nicaragua, compelled international lending organizations to restrict credit, put diplomatic and political pressure on the regime, and countenanced the training of anti-Sandinista guerrillas in Florida. The U.S. Central Intelligence Agency started the war by covertly funding remnants of the Somoza dictatorship's National Guard in their renewed effort to thwart the now governing Sandinistas. These remnants, the *Contras*, were bent on overthrowing the Sandinista revolution. They were trained initially by the Argentine military, funded by the CIA and based next door in pliant, colonial Honduras. The covey of former Guardsmen was essentially an external, mercenary intervention into Nicaraguan politics. The war itself perpetuated both U.S. interference in Latin America on behalf of right-wing client regimes and Somoza's repression of a nationalist and democratic movement.

This conventional wisdom held that because the Sandinistas enjoyed overwhelming popular support, the *Contras* had to resort to terrorism against civilians, schools, hospitals, and cooperatives. These assaults obliged the government to take admittedly harsh defensive measures such as forced resettlement and censorship, measures often excused by comparisons with U.S. wartime measures such as President Abraham Lincoln's censorship during the U.S. Civil War and the resettlement of Japanese citizens during World War II. But external pressure only heightened Nicaraguan patriotic ardor in support of the Sandinistas against surrogate cross-border raiders and terrorists. Far from overthrowing or modifying a revolutionary regime, that began as open and moderate, the *Contras* forced it to close ranks in defense of national sovereignty against superpower intervention.[4]

Lippmann stressed that "systems of stereotypes" were subject to "blind spots."[5] A big "blind spot" here was the widespread domestic backing for the *Contras*. Especially in the countryside, the rebels were called "the Resistance"— a term that evoked civilian anti-Nazi combatants, not counterrevolutionary officers. It was a challenge for this set of ideas to explain how the Resistance or the *Contras* became, as Sam Dillon of the *Miami Herald* calculated after the war, "the largest guerrilla force in Latin America since the Mexican revolution." The *Contras* were four times larger than the Salvadoran guerrillas in a country with fewer than two-thirds the people.[6] Officials from the United Nations and the Organization of American States who supervised the demobilization of *Contra* combatants were surprised at their numbers: between 22,000 and 28,000 fighters.[7]

After their electoral defeat Sandinista leaders themselves acknowledged publicly that it was false "that the *Contras* had no support, and embodied no widespread peasant grievances."[8] *Comandante* Luis Carrión told a meeting of Sandinista leaders: "The *Contras* ended up being a campesino movement with its own leadership."[9] Analysis of the election returns had shown the Sandinistas that the *Contras* were anything but an onus for the opposition, as the American press had supposed. In the regions where the rebels reportedly had terrorized the local peasantry, the opposition, led by *Contra* and former *Contra* campaigners, gained its widest majorities. Rival Sandinista factions started blaming each other for their unpopularity in the countryside. Orlando Nuñez, a top adviser to *co-mandante* Jaime Wheelock, stated that the *Contras* had "a large social base in the countryside."[10] In an analytical essay accompanying a revealing collection of Sandinista-conducted interviews with former *Contras*, Alejandro Bendaña, formerly the Sandinista government spokesperson and a close associate of Daniel Ortega, argued that "the integration of thousands of peasants into the counter-revolutionary army" was not the work of the CIA but the product of "the policies, limitations, and errors of *Sandinismo*."[11]

Bendaña's interviewees described a derangement of traditional peasant life: the intrusion of troops and block committees into villages and hamlets, arbitrary confiscations of the land and stock of small proprietors in order to enlarge government "cooperatives," driving peasants into "mass" organizations and "popular" militias, attacks on traditional religion in the name of a state-sponsored "Popular Church," and the jailings of nonconformists and bystanders as "counterrevolutionaries."[12] Bendaña's campesino subjects also pointed out that the poorest, most "proletarian" campesinos were the strongest supporters of the *Contras*.[13]

Even before the elections some Sandinista officials acknowledged that the *Contras* had "grass roots support" and that peasant leaders became *Contras* "in the first years of the war because of errors that might have been committed."[14] These "errors" included, according to the official Sandinista self-criticism after the elections:

> Indiscriminate confiscation of land from large, medium and even some small private farmers. . . . Forced purchase of basic grains at official prices . . . general hostility towards traders . . . confrontation . . . with the Catholic and some Protestant Churches.

Probing the source of these mistakes, the official document acknowledged the reproduction of "practices from socialist countries" that led to "a one-party style in the political leadership of society" and an excessive emphasis on "control and centralization of public administration." As a result government policies were carried out "in a coercive and bureaucratic fashion."

> The model we began to build under the banner of socialist orientation conflicted in practice with the program of reconstruction and national unity. That was the very criticism the "bourgeois" opposition had made from the beginning.

Following this model led to "abuses and violations" by Sandinista Army and Security Forces, government officials, and Party leaders that "distanced some social sectors from the Sandinista Revolution."[15] In 1986 the Sandinista Vice Minister of Interior had divulged the nature of some of these abuses:

> Criminals were among those who mobilized themselves [into Sandinista organizations]. These people often would [cut off] the hands of the peasants, treat them badly.[16]

In an interview a year before the 1990 elections, Sandinista Agrarian Reform Minister *comandante* Jaime Wheelock recalled his dismay in April 1984. He had been put in charge of developing "a comprehensive counter-insurgency strategy." Upon visiting the rural battle zone he discovered that urban party cadre had "divided the society into two classes":

> We were the proletarians and the rest were bourgeoisie. It was a dogmatic and mechanical Marxism-Leninism that prevailed among us.

When he reached the capital of the main battle front,

> Matagalpa looked like a militarized city—with spikes, barricades, roadblocks and a great martial deployment everywhere. In every route there were three or four road blocks where the campesino had to get off the bus to be searched.

Wheelock realized that Sandinista agrarian policy, which he had designed, was "too schematic." "We had not distributed land" to the campesinos but instead

> forced the campesinos to sell their grains exclusively to the State at fixed prices even as prices for their purchases were skyrocketing. We had overlooked the needs of the campesinos, forgetting the necessity to import medicines, nails for horseshoes, seeds.[17]

In short, *comandante* Wheelock' s verdict coincided with that of Bendaña's poor peasants: "We created a crisis in the countryside. The campesino viewed the state as something evil."[18]

Wheelock failed to mention that it was his own analysis dating back to his 1974 volume and his early leadership of the Agrarian Reform Ministry that initially divided rural Nicaragua into "proletarians and bourgeoisie."[19] A careful study of early Sandinista agrarian policy, conducted by an American scholar sympathetic to the revolution, concluded that the "crisis in the countryside" was a reality before the United States began funding the *Contras*. By 1981-82 agricultural workers had lost nearly 50 percent of their real income.[20] Production of basic grains and exports had fallen dramatically. The study found "many rural Nicaraguans sharply critical of the Sandinistas":

> When discussing their life since the revolution, peasants often make such comments as "Estamos jodidos" (We are screwed.) [and] "La misma mierda, solamente las moscas son diferentes" ("The same shit; only the flies are different")[21]

The combination of "crisis in the countryside," "confrontation . . . with the Catholic and some Protestant Churches," and the "abuses and violations" of the Sandinista police and army helped *Contra* recruitment in the early years of Sandinista rule. As early as July 1980, a group of eighty peasants who had fought alongside the Sandinistas occupied the northern town of Quilalí, Nueva Segovia in an act of protest against "the betrayal of the revolution" and began the first armed campaign against the Sandinista government.[22]

The American media tended to focus exclusively on two aspects of the *Contra* phenomenon: their CIA backing by the United States, and concomitantly, the presence of former Somoza National Guardsmen in the ranks of the principal *Contra* group.[23] The *Washington Post* provided the most extensive and the most influential reporting in these first *Contra* years, decisive ones in framing that conflict. In late 1981 Managua was facing food shortages, spiraling inflation, growing unemployment, dissent from the independent labor unions, the business sector and the Catholic Church, the defection from the Sandinista government of prominent civilian supporters like Violeta Chamorro, and the desertion of the best known Sandinista leader, Eden Pastora. On the foreign front, in the wake of the collapse of negotiations with Washington, it faced a now decidedly hostile U.S. Administration.[24] Of these two dimensions of conflict, the *Post* placed the great bulk of its attention on the external. The *Contras* were framed from the beginning not as a product of the internal contradictions of Sandinista rule, but as an exterior force.[25]

The *Contras* are from outside Nicaragua, from a previous time, Somoza's, another place—Honduras, Florida. From the beginning *Post* reports datelined Miami and Honduras presented the "counterrevolutionary groups" as part of "the invasion-plan picture."[26] That initial impression never fades from the *Post*'s coverage. Nor does the notion that the *Contras* are "former soldiers of Somoza's National Guard."[27] The first direct reports drew an analogy with "exiles from Fidel Castro's Cuba" who received "no popular support . . . only humiliating defeat at the Bay of Pigs."[28]

Just before the first of these stories were filed, the *Post* had noted that:

> The Nicaraguan economy is plummeting toward disaster. Bitterness, even hatred, has grown up among what were once the unified supporters of the revolution . . . shortages are becoming common place.[29]

Then, it is added, almost in passing, that:

> Some of the Sandinistas, as they are forced to cut back on the dream they once offered the Nicaraguan people, seek to blame the situation on outside forces or internal "counterrevolutionary" threats.[29]

At this time the *Post* was reporting that "Sandinista Mob Action Thwarts Rally by Opposition"[30] and that "a high ranking Nicaraguan Justice Ministry official has fled the country with his family, charging that communists are running the

Sandinista revolutionary government."[31] During 1980 and 1981 the *Post* also reported, even if generally on back pages, the suppression of the largest "bourgeois" civic opposition group in the revolutionary government and that leading Sandinistas were defecting. Nonetheless *Post* reports never raised the question whether the emergence of armed resistance was linked to this discontent, if "bitterness" and "hatred" among former "supporters of the revolution" had led them to join "the counterrevolution." Instead the *Contras* are exclusively the product of "pressure being applied by Washington."[32]

The *Contra* movement derived from five sources: former National Guardsmen, former Sandinistas, non-Sandinista members of the anti-Somoza opposition, Miskito Indians, and, by far the largest group, peasants.[33] Nevertheless, the National Guardsmen were virtually the sole focus of the *Post*'s accounts in the first several years of the war. Generally *Post* reports simply identified the main *Contra* organization, the Fuerzas Democraticas Nicaraguenses (FDN), as "former soldiers of Somoza's National Guard"[34] or as "U.S.-backed counterrevolutionary guerrillas."[35] No reports in the *Post* mentioned the Anti-Sandinista Popular Militias (MILPAS) who were composed of peasants and led by former anti-Somoza and Sandinista guerrillas. Even in the early days of the war most battlefield commanders were MILPAS. By the end of the war, even the top officers were MILPAS. The bulk of the leadership group that eventually negotiated the end to the war was MILPAS.[36]

By 1983 the war in Nicaragua had become an angry political dispute inside the United States. Republican President Ronald Reagan called the *Contras* "freedom fighters" and "the moral equivalent of the founding fathers"; Democratic Speaker of the House Thomas ("Tip") O'Neill referred to them as "butchers and maimers." The reality was more complex. The *Contras* in this period did commit serious human rights offenses in what had become a vicious internecine war, and yet most fought for personal liberties if not for freedom in general. But in the *Post*, whose coverage was more extensive but not less nuanced than other news organizations, the picture of the *Contras* was starkly drawn. They were a group of mercenary cross-border raiders, organized, armed, and financed by the CIA, composed of remnants of the Somoza regime, motivated by vengeance, intent on restoring the prerevolutionary order, capable of wreaking terror against a local population essentially loyal to the regime but not of challenging the Sandinista armed forces.[37]

Although the stereotypical character of the *Post*'s reporting on the *Contra* owed much to the preestablished system of stereotypes in the Nicaragua coverage, the early *Contra* leadership and especially its CIA patrons were at least equally responsible for the persistence of the *Contra* stereotype. The U.S. Congress and large sectors of American public opinion balked at policies reminiscent of previous interference in countries such as Vietnam or Chile. So the CIA sought to keep its program of assistance secret. Argentine military trainers, bred in an atmosphere responsible for the term "disappearances," could be even more furtive and restrictive. Enterprising American reporters set out to uncover the existence of *Contra* camps in neighboring Honduras, a staunch U.S. ally but one sensitive to the opinion of congressional and Western European donors.[38] The reaction in Congress and in Honduras only strengthened the agency's determination to ban the journalists. The lack of contact fostered stereotypes and the air of secrecy only confirmed previous impressions.

On-the-spot coverage of the *Contras* was rare because of the policies of the *Contra* leadership and its Argentine and American sponsors, the difficulty of the terrain, and the structural demands of the news organizations whose competitive pressures discouraged lengthy time commitments. Most of the fighting occurred in the central highlands and the eastern coast. The latter was declared off-limits by the government. Until October 1987, travel with the *Contras* themselves required a long arduous march. As a result there were only two occasions when press pools from major American media accompanied the *Contras*.[39]

At the end of March 1983, just as the *Post*'s Edward Cody found "No sign of broad popular support for the counterrevolutionaries," one of his colleagues was traveling with the *Contra* rebels and finding very different signs.[40] For six days and ninety miles Christopher Dickey of the *Post* and James LeMoyne, then at *Newsweek*, later of the *New York Times*, accompanied units of the main group of anti-Sandinista rebels, the FDN, on three expeditions inside Nicaragua.[41] These were the first correspondents from major U.S. publications to travel with the *Contras* and their stories were for many years the only ones to provide Americans with concrete information about the makeup and motives of the Nicaraguan resistance and the extent of their support in rural Nicaragua.

The on-the-spot reports contrasted sharply with previous accounts. Dickey discovered that the *Contras* were "small land-owners and local country people for the most part."[42] LeMoyne found that, far from being Somocista mercenaries, "most of the soldiers said they had once supported the Sandinistas, until the revolution turned sour," and "they were all unpaid volunteers ranging in age from fourteen to sisxty-three. Their morale was remarkable."[43] Dickey added that:

> Although the Sandinistas say *contra* revolutionaries often kidnapped peasants and forced them to work with them, we saw no indication of coercion. . . . The troops showed high morale and appeared to be fighting voluntarily, often marching from dawn until nightfall through rough terrain, eating little more than a few chunks of beef or sugar cane.[44]

The *Contras* "moved through the countryside in broad daylight" appearing to count on "considerable and invaluable support" from peasants who "sold provisions to the troops with which we traveled, sheltered them and often provided them with intelligence about Sandinista movements."[45] LeMoyne observed "a surprising degree of local support" and that "most of the peasants seemed to welcome" the troops.[46] Dickey perceived "a pattern of support for the *Contras* by people with many grievances against the revolutionary government in Managua" and "the counterrevolutionaries seem to be doing everything they can to cultivate it [*i.e.*, 'popular support']."

> Again and again when peasants were asked why they were offering the "*con-tras*" food, sometimes bringing it unbidden to mountain tops for them, why they offered them shelter, why they told them where Sandinistas troops were moving and ambushes were laid or why they have joined the rebel army, they said nothing about fear. Instead they talked in terms of what they viewed as Sandinista threats to their economic, social and cultural survival.[47]

The *Contras* with whom Dickey and LeMoyne kept company, far from being a group of foreign adventurers, were "local country people for the most part," their contacts with the "peasant masses" often supplied by their own relatives.[48] The guerrilla column that Dickey visited was "commanded by tough professional soldiers from the old National Guard."[49] But the leadership had "been carefully selected to exclude those [Guardsmen] with close personal ties to the former dictator." Moreover, "as the fighting intensifies, new leaders are emerging."[50]

Contrary to the *Post*'s media frame which emphasized "the invasion-plan picture," Dickey wrote:

> The Nicaraguan government repeatedly has focused on the possibility of an invasion from Honduras. . . . But what has happened is a massive infiltration.[51]

As to the widespread impression that the *Contras* were militarily ineffectual, Dickey noted that "their forces were able to employ remarkably effective tactics."[52] Far from being mere cross-border marauders they operated "deep into the Nicaraguan interior."[53]

For three days running, Dickey's stories splashed across the front pages of the *Post*. The reports seemed to shatter the prevailing media frame. Later LeMoyne recollected that Dickey himself

> was very surprised by what we saw when we went in [to Nicaragua]. And the paper was very surprised by what he wrote. They had to print it, because there it was. But I know that Karen [DeYoung], who was the foreign editor, and other people were really shocked by what he saw.[54]

Karen DeYoung, the *Post*'s former Nicaraguan correspondent, now foreign editor, sent herself on special assignment to Nicaragua to look into the situation. On May 24 she filed the first major treatment of the *Contras* since the Dickey pieces. DeYoung depicted a rebel ambush of a Sandinista convoy including foreign journalists. The Sandinista officer in charge led the convoy into an ambush and was later reprimanded for panicking.[55] Though there are no interviews with *Contra* officials, DeYoung permits herself to "guess" that the ambush was aimed at the convoy with the journalists and to suggest that "the idea was to eliminate all of us." DeYoung's story focused on rebel violence against civilians and "how we Americans felt being shot at with guns our government had provided to the *Contras*."[56]

DeYoung employed the appellation "*Contra*" for the forces previously referred to in the *Post* as "former National Guardsmen," "anti-Sandinista rebels," "rightists," "exiles," or "counterrevolutionaries." As the Sandinistas understood, names counted for a lot in what had become a full-fledged propaganda war in the American media. The Sandinistas themselves had originally called themselves the "National Liberation Front," a name inspired by Vietnamese and Algerian anticolonial and Marxist revolutionaries. Several years later they attached "Sandinista" in order to add mystique and a nationalist cachet.[57] It was Sandinista government organizations who began calling the armed anti-Sandinista groups "*la contra*"—an abbreviation for counterrevolutionary. In an interview for this study LeMoyne of the *Times* commented on the name:

> The use of the term "*Contra*" was promoted by the Sandinistas and represented a great propaganda victory for the Sandinistas. There was little critical thinking on the use of the word on the part of editors. It is true that there were *Contras* who were "counter-revolutionaries". But there were many who were not. . . . Tagging them "*Contras*" was like branding the Sandinista government a "Marxist-Leninist government".[58]

After DeYoung's return from her visit to Nicaragua in May 1983, the term became standard in the *Post*. Rebel leaders, many of whom insisted that their object was not counterrevolution but to rectify a "betrayed revolution," complained bitterly that they were to be known by a term not only detrimental to their purposes but invented by their enemies.[59]

Nomenclature had been reversed since the time of Sheehan, Halberstam, and the other early Vietnam War reporters. They generally referred to the Vietnam National Liberation Front as the "Vietcong, "a derogatory nickname for the Vietnamese Communists invented by the U.S.-backed Saigon government. In Nicaragua the U.S.-backed rebels were baptized by the Communist-leaning Sandinista government.[60]

After DeYoung's visit and as the *Contra* military offensive deepened in rural areas, rebel human rights violations dominated *Post* coverage. Typical was a 1983 report by its Managua Bureau Chief Robert McCartney on Pantasma, "the rebels' most damaging attack on a single town." "The death toll was believed to be the highest in a single battle since the rebels began receiving CIA funds in December 1981," the *Contras* also "executed three unarmed men." The *Post* reporter cited residents claiming that local youths had been kidnapped by the *Contras*. And

> In brief informal interviews here, many residents said there was little support in the town for the guerrillas, although some people had sold them food. The town was considered particularly pro-Sandinista, with several farming cooperatives and a developed infrastructure, which may explain why the guerrillas chose it as a target.[61]

This picture of the sympathies of the residents of Pantasma is difficult to square with what the parish priest was to tell the *New York Times* in 1987: "They say there are no political prisoners, but there are 300 people in jail from my parish alone."[62] In 1989 the Sandinista counterinsurgency chief Wheelock told me that "the rising of Pantasma against the FSLN" was an example of local support for the *Contra* cause—"and these people were not the [National] Guard."[63] The Pantasma district voted overwhelmingly against the Sandinistas in 1990. The sources for the McCartney story were exclusively Sandinista officials and residents of a town under military control. His story contained no interviews with *Contras*—unless of course, they were the very same "residents [who] said there was little support in the town for the guerrillas."

"The rising of Pantasma" received similar coverage elsewhere. Julia Preston, who was to replace McCartney as the *Post*'s Managua bureau chief in 1985 wrote in the *Boston Globe* of "the blitz against Pantasma." Her report mirrored McCartney's in most essentials, with one minor but curious difference. "Manuel Rodriguez, 20, a farmer" was quoted as stating that the town "is very organized into cooperatives and it's been working all right."

> Asked if the *contras* received support in the town, Rodriguez said, "They didn't even ask us for water—and we didn't give it to them either."[64]

Preston's story noted that "300 Sandinista reserve troops arrived" after the attack. They were presumably in place when the "brief informal interviews" were conducted. Even under those circumstances, there were contradictions in what the townspeople told the reporters. These contradictions escaped comment in these newspaper accounts as well as in a similarly framed CBS television news report which presented the incident as part of the dire effect of U.S. *Contra* aid.[65]

Pantasma figures importantly in the memoir published in 1999 by Sandinista vice president, and novelist, Sergio Ramirez. He recounts that in 1984, the year after the events just described, "a group of small farmers from the town of Pantasma came looking for me, accompanied by the departmental delegate of the junta of government, Carlos Zamora, and the local representative of the land reform agency, Daniel Nuñez. . . ."

> They presented me with a list of complaints, of outrages and abuses to which dozens of peasant families in the town were being made the victim. One of them took off his shirt and displayed the scars from barbed wire with which for several days he had been lashed to a cot. He was charged with being a Somocista, together with others. In the course of telling of the story he wept, because the charge seemed to him both humiliating and unjust, more so than his torture. Carlos Zamora corroborated his accusations, as did Daniel Núñez, both helpless to do anything because the repression was being directed by the town's incipient party apparatus.

When I returned to Managua I succeeded in launching an investigation, and the facts turned out to be worse. The Sandinista political secretary in Pantasma, who was very young and a stranger to peasant life, had ordered not only tortures but executions. Ultimately he was sent to prison together with several of his aides in one of the exemplary trials of those times. However, by then it was too late, because the repression in Pantasma had caused hundreds of peasants to pass over to the side of the *contra*.[66]

In the *Post* and other news organizations the *Contras* whom Dickey and LeMoyne encountered rapidly disappeared under a sequence of stories concerning *Contra* atrocities perpetrated with U.S.-supplied weapons, the CIA mining of Nicaraguan ports, a CIA-produced instructional manual, and other American crimes. That stereotype of the *Contras* passed from the pace-setting pages of the *Washington Post*, *New York Times*, and *Newsweek* into television news and "news magazines" to the popular culture. In March 1985 Dan Rather introduced a segment purporting to show that though the "*Contras* are called 'freedom fighters' by President Reagan . . . , [they] are called murderers and terrorists by some civilians inside Nicaragua."[67] A few months later "*West 57th Street*" on CBS devoted a segment to "Nicaragua—the Dirty War." The "magazine" program featured a small boy who described how he watched the *Contras* execute his father after "pull[ing] the skin off his face and his feet."[68] The incident allegedly occurred in "a farming cooperative" of the sort that *comandante* Wheelock was later to describe proudly as "fortified cooperatives put to strategic use."[69]

A September 1986 episode of NBC's top-rated entertainment series "*Miami Vice*" opened with the eruption into a funeral in a peaceful "farming cooperative" of a *Contra* mortar attack led by two American mercenaries. An Indian girl is seen bearing a lifeless infant away from the flaming village in slow-motion—freeze framed, to evoke the renowned Vietnam photo. The remainder of the episode concerns the successful efforts of a CIA agent, played by G. Gordon Liddy (the convicted Watergate felon) to spike a story uncovering the atrocity. The end credits roll under a song which laments "the wars that are fought in places we can't even say their names."[70]

Such was the prevailing view of the *Contras* through the elections. As Branigan stated, the *Contras* were "portrayed for years as widely reviled in Nicaragua." Branigan himself had first-hand experience to the contrary when he participated in the first extended trip with *Contra* troops by a group of reporters from the major media since that of Dickey and LeMoyne. The CIA and the Honduran government discouraged newsgathering expeditions with the *Contras* after Congress suspended U.S. assistance in 1984.[71] The next major trip was not until the fall of 1987 when three American reporters accompanied a *Contra* patrol for three days in north-central Nicaragua. Upon their return Lindsey Gruson of the *New York Times* wrote that "the trip sharply contradicted the Sandinista argument that the *Contras* are little more than an appendage of the Reagan administration, relying on American financial and military support to survive."[72] Branigin wrote that his trek "through this area of seemingly solid support for the *Contras*" showed that "the *Contras* have built a network of informers, couriers, lookouts, food suppliers, and medical-support personnel in the area." Gruson noted that:

> The *Contras* can now apparently march undetected down Nicaragua's mountainous spine, aided by civilians and the thick canopy of jungle that stretches from Honduras down the eastern part of the country to Costa Rica.

The reporters accompanied the guerrilla column to some dozen mountain farms, where Branigin reported that the peasants "gave their reasons for supporting the rebels, describing what they said were killings, arrests, torture, rape, and forcible relocations at the hands of the Sandinistas." Gruson said that:

> One after another, peasants told similar stories. . . . They charged that the Sandinistas forcibly recruited children into the armed forces, brutalized civilians, and tortured rebel sympathizers.

Gruson added that the rebels were "exploiting . . . popular discontent to build what amounts to an underground civilian wing of this guerrilla movement" and were becoming "a politically astute, self-sufficient guerrilla army."

That same month Julia Preston of the *Washington Post*, in an article titled "Released American Says *Contras* 'Own' Vast Zone" quoted a volunteer from the anti-*Contra* "Witness for Peace" organization. The activist, who had been held captive by the rebels on maneuvers for two weeks in October, acknowledged that the *Contras* seemed to "own" a vast zone of central and eastern Nicaragua.[73] Several weeks earlier Clifford Krauss of the *Wall Street Journal* reported that

> in Chontales province less than two hours' drive from Managua in the center of the country, the *Contras* have won the active support of the peasantry . . . making for a convenient corridor between the *Contras*' northern and southern fronts.[74]

These direct on-the-spot reports diverged drastically from previous reporting on the *Contras*—with the exception of the direct April 1983 reports. It is worth noting how sharp the contrast was between direct reporting on the *Contras* and reporting on them filed from Managua or Washington, D.C.

Two books published after the conflict ended by reporters who had covered the *Contras* showed the same divergence. Like most journalists, Sam Dillon of the *Miami Herald* was a critic of the Reagan policy, the CIA, and the *Contras*. One of the few who sympathized was Glenn Garvin, of the conservative *Washington Times*. Nonetheless, the two reached arrestingly similar conclusions: the vast bulk of the *Contra* fighters and field commanders joined voluntarily as a result of Sandinista policies; the *Contras* were largely peasant volunteers who evolved into a genuine guerrilla army; and the military success of the *Contras* finally forced the Sandinistas, in Dillon's words, to "sue for peace."[75]

In 1999 Sergio Ramirez, Daniel Ortega's vice president and a veteran Sandinista wrote:

> many landless peasants went to war with [the *Contras*] or became their social base of support—resolved not to be corralled into the UPEs [agricultural collectives]. The same was true for other small and medium farmers who from the outset were frightened by the expropriations.

As the war drew on, Ramirez acknowledges:

> The ranks of the *contra* kept on growing, and by then moreover its field commanders were small farmers, many of them without any ties to Somocismo, who had supplanted the former National Guard officers.[76]

Thus, after the war reporters, and even the Sandinistas themselves, refuted their own presentation of the *Contras*.

***

Reporters covering the *Contras* from Managua repeated some of the errors of their counterparts covering the Chinese revolution from Chungking decades earlier, but they committed them for rather different reasons. More than forty veteran journalists and diplomats and a number of China scholars gathered to discuss China reporting in the 1930s and 1940s in Scottsdale, Arizona, in November 1982.[77]

Many of the reporters acknowledged that they were tougher on the Kuomintang than on the Communists. But it was not because they were prejudiced against a U.S. ally. Indeed, as a former *New York Times* correspondent stated:

> The mind set that we acquired in the United States before we came to China predisposed us to take a [negative] position regarding Communism, and that affected to some extent our views and subsequently our dispatches.[78]

Another former *New York Times* reporter explained:

> Much of the criticism of the Kuomintang was based on the fact that a lot of our people were living in Kuomintang areas and could see what was going on. What was happening in Communist areas we didn't know anything about. I went to Yenan . . . and it was the Camelot of China to the outward eye.[79]

In other words, as another reporter stated, "familiarity breeds contempt." She went on to explain:

The idiocies, the mistakes, in the KMT area were pushed upon you every day. You knew the battles between the factions, you knew the miseries and all the rest of it. On the revolutionary side we knew very little and certainly not the seamier side of the factional fights.[80]

In Nicaragua the situation was ostensibly the same. The reporters lived the "mistakes and miseries" of Sandinista rule in Managua. The *Contra* rebels operated in remote regions. Yet, it was the distant anti-Sandinista rebels who received the harsher criticisms. Did familiarity fail to breed contempt in the Nicaraguan case? Not exactly. It was the pro-U.S. *Contras* who were felt to be contemptible. Reporters disdained the well-dressed *Contra* officials they met in hotels in Miami and Honduras.[81]

The first *Contras* were actually Sandinista peasants; on this the Sandinista Bendaña, the conservative Garvin and the liberal Dillon all agree. But their ranks contained none of the ex-student activists who founded the Sandinistas and most modern revolutionary organizations. The task of establishing the *Contras'* organizational matrix and their foreign alliances fell to a former National Guard colonel named Enrique Bermùdez. Bermùdez brought with him a handful of National Guard cronies who monopolized the top posts. Eventually, tensions between Bermùdez' staff and the *Contra* peasants were to lead to open conflict and to the ouster of many of the former. But that was years after Bermùdez and company had soured the press on the *Contras*—in large part because their leadership corresponded perfectly to the reporters' preconceptions.[82] Nonetheless, it is a supreme irony that Latin America's largest peasant army since the Mexican Revolution took up arms not against a stereotypical U.S.-backed authoritarian junta but against a government extolled as progressive, anti-imperialist, revolutionary, and popular.

Notes

1. Juan Vasquez, *CBS Evening News*, February 26, 1990.

2. Richard Cohen, "Pipe Dream," *WP*, March 14, 1982, B1.

3. Richard Boudreaux, "Contras' Campaign Tactics Could Boost Sandinistas," February 17, 1990, A16.

4. For an elaboration of the foregoing version of the *Contras* by two influential American reporters see Roy Gutman, *Banana Diplomacy: The Making of American Policy in Nicaragua 1981-87* (New York: Simon & Schuster, 1988), chapters ii, v, vii, ix, xiii; and Christopher Dickey, *With the Contras: A Reporter in the Wilds of Nicaragua* (New York: Simon & Schuster, 1985), *passim*.

5. See Walter Lippmann, *Public Opinion* (New York: Macmillan, 1922; revised edition New York: Free Press Paperback, 1965), chapter vii ("Blind Spots and Their Value").

6. Sam Dillon, *Commandos* (New York: Henry Holt, 1991), xi.

7. See Robert S. Leiken, "The Revision Thing," *TNR*, August 31, 1982.

8. Charles Lane, "Who 'Won' Nicaragua?" *Newsweek*, March 12, 1990, 14.

9. "Interview with Comandante Luis Carrión: FSLN Takes a Deep Look Inward," *Barricada Internacional*, June 30, 1990, 6.

10. Orlando Núñez, "Pacts, Accords and Alliances," *Barricada Internacional,* June 14, 1990.

11. *Una Tragedia Campesina*, ed. Alejandro Bendaña (Managua: Edit-Arte, 1991), 13.

12. *Una Tragedia Campesina*, 50, 68-70, 122, 133, etc.

13. See for example *Una Tragedia Campesina*, 102, 139.

14. Marjorie Miller, "Election: A Truce for Families," *LAT*, February 22, 1990, A1, A12; also Jaime Wheelock in interview with author, see below. For "a very clear impression of peasant dissatisfaction with the government in 1987," as received on a tour of the central province of Boaco by a then top Sandinista military official, see Roger Miranda and William Ratliff, *The Civil War in Nicaragua: Inside the Sandinistas* (New Brunswick, New Jersey: Transaction, 1994), 243. Miranda terminated his tour "with the terrible feeling that he was regarded as the chief of an occupying military force in his own country."

15. "National Assembly of Sandinista Militants at El Crucero: June 16-17, 1990," in *Barricada Internacional*, July 1990 (Special Section).

16. *Comandante* Luis Carrión in Gutman, *Banana Diplomacy*, 299.

17. Author's interview with *comandante* Jaime Wheelock, Managua, April 21, 1989.

18. Author's interview with Wheelock.

19. See chapter 8, 119, fn. 485 *supra*.

20. Forrest D. Colburn, *Post-Revolutionary Nicaragua: State Classes and the Dilemmas of Agrarian Policy* (Berkley: University of California, 1986), Table 15, 114.

21. Colburn, *Post-Revolutionary Nicaragua*, 120.

22. The peasants belonged to the MILPAS, Anti-Somocistas Popular Militias. They kept the initials but changed the name to Anti-Sandinista Popular Militias in 1980. See *Una Tragedia Campesina*, 29, 68-70, 81, 96-97; Dillon, *Commandos*, 48-49; Glenn Garvin, *Everybody Has His Own Gringo: The CIA and the Contras* (Washington: Brassey's, 1991), 48 ff.; Robert Kagan, *A Twilight Struggle: American Power and Nicaragua, 1977-1990* (New York: Free Press, 1996), 148-49; Miranda and Ratliff, *Civil War in Nicaragua*, 234.

23. See appendix C for a quantitative content analysis of this coverage.

24. On the failure of the mission of Assistant Secretary of State Thomas B. Enders to Managua in August 1981 and its impact on U.S. policy, see Kagan, *Twilight Struggle*, 188-203. See also Gutman, *Banana Diplomacy*, 58-87; Shirley Christian, *Nicaragua: Revolution in the Family* (New York: Random House, 1985), 199; Don Oberdorfer, "U.S. in Secret Dialogue, Sought Rapprochement with Nicaragua," *WP*, December 10, 1981, A1; and Arturo J. Cruz, "Nicaragua's Imperiled Revolution," *Foreign Affairs* (Summer 1983): 1040-42.

25. See appendix C.

26. Dickey, "Anti-Sandinista Drive Grows, Exiles Say," *WP*, May 9, 1981, A1; Eddie Adams, "Cuban and Nicaraguan Exiles Train in Florida for Invasion of Homeland," *Parade* in *WP*, March 15, 1981, 5. See also Dickey, "Honduran Military Girds For War with Nicaragua," *WP*, May 5, 1981, A1; and a commentary by Philip Geyelin, "Ex-

iles in Training," *WP*, April 7, 1981, A17. No invasion was ever launched from Honduras.

27. *WP*, August 16, 1982, A1, A19; see also *WP*, May 9, 1981, A1-A18; August 16, 1981, A1; July 26, 1982, A1, A17; August 8, 1982, A12; January 1, 1983, A1-A10; January 2, 1983, A17; February 4, 1983, A25.

28. Dickey, "Anti-Sandinista Drive Grows," A1-A18; Adams, "Cuban and Nicaraguan Exiles Train in Florida."

29. *WP*, January 31, 1981, A1; see also March 17, 1981, A12 ("Economic Woes Fuel Discontent In Nicaragua . . . government economists readily concede: Nicaragua's economy is in serious trouble").

30. *WP*, March 16, 1981, A1.

31. *WP*, February 26, 1981, A26.

32. Dickey, "Sandinistas See New Violence: Escalating Clashes Spur Fears of Spreading Turmoil," *WP*, July 26, 1982, A17.

33. *Una Tragedia Campesina*, 16-17, 29, 31, 39-40, 81, 104, 139, 213, 227; Jaime Morales Carazo, *La Contra* (Mexico: Continental, 1989), 33-46, 277-79; Dillon, *Comandos*, 46-56, 58-60, 65-77; Garvin, *Everybody Has His Own Gringo*, 48-98; Arturo J. Cruz Sequiera, *Memoirs of a Counter-Revolutionary: Life with the Contras, the Sandinistas and the CIA* (New York: Doubleday, 1989), 127-30; Kagan, *Twilight Struggle*, 221-28 and Leiken, "Battle For Nicaragua," *NYRB*, March 13, 1986. Morales Carazo and Bendaña put the National Guard presence at 400 at its highest point, which is probably a very generous estimate. The total number of *Contras* exceeded 20,000.

34. *WP*, August 16, 1982, A1; May 9, 1981, A1; August 16, 1981, A1; July 26, 1982, A1-A17; August 8, 1982, A12; January 1, 1983, A1-A10; January 2, 1983, A17; February 4, 1983, A25.

35. Edward Cody, *WP*, December 20, 1982.

36. See *Una Tragedia Campesina*, 29, 81, 227; Dillon, *Commandos*, 290-91; Garvin, *Everybody Has His Own Gringo*, 48-51, 516; Kagan 1996, 223, 687-88 and Leiken, "The Revision Thing."

37. *See* appendix C for a quantitative analysis of this coverage.

38. See chapter 3, 23 *supra.*

39. Author's interviews with James LeMoyne, Miami, June 1989, and Dickey, Washington D.C., April 1984; see also Dickey, *With the Contras*, 175-76.

40. Cody, "Nicaragua Tour Suggests Fighting Is Modest." *WP*, March 25, 1983, A30.

41. Dickey, "Well-Armed Units Show Strongholds," *WP*, April 3, 1983, 1.

42. Dickey, "Well-Armed Units Show Strongholds," 1.

43. LeMoyne, "The Secret War Boils Over," *Newsweek*, April 11, 1983, 46-50.

44. Dickey, "Rebels Seek Peasants Support" *WP*, April 5, 1983, A1, 10.

45. Dickey, "Nothing Ragtag about Nicaraguan Rebels," *WP*, April 3, 1989, A14.

46. LeMoyne, "Secret War Boils Over," 48.

47. Dickey, "Rebels Seek Peasants Support," A1, 10.

48. Dickey, "Rebels Seek Peasants Support," A1, 10.

49. Dickey, "Well-Armed Units Show Strongholds," 1.

50. Dickey, "Rebel Odyssey," *WP*, April 4, 1983, A1, 22.

51. Dickey, "Well-Armed Units Show Strongholds," 1.

52. Dickey, "Nothing Ragtag About Nicaraguan Rebels," A14.

53. Dickey, "Nothing Ragtag About Nicaraguan Rebels," A14.

54. Author's interview with LeMoyne, Washington, D.C., June 7, 1989.

55. Author's interview with Major Roger Miranda Bengoechea, former Chief of the Secretariat of the Nicaraguan Defense Ministry, Washington, D.C., April 3, 1989.

56. Karen DeYoung, "Rebel Ambush on a Nicaraguan Road: A Fiery Rain of Death," *WP*, May 24, 1983, A1, A14.

57. See Tomás Borge, *La paciente impaciencia* (Mexico: Diana, 1989), 224; see also Donald C. Hodges, *Intellectual Foundations of the Nicaraguan Revolution* (Austin: University of Texas, 1986), 161-73.

58. Author's interview with LeMoyne, Miami, Florida, July 11, 1989.

59. Author's interviews with "Rigoberto," Miami, Florida, July 13, 1989; "Franklin" (Israel Galeano), Tegucigalpa, Honduras, April 1989; and Aristides Sanchez, Miami, Florida, July 14, 1989.

60. See William Prochnau, *Once Upon a Distant War: Young War Correspondents and Their Early Vietnam Battles* (New York: Vintage, 1996), 6.

61. Robert J. McCartney, "Guerrillas Devastate Nicaraguan Town," *WP*, October 21, 1983, A26.

62. Stephen Kinzer, "Few Contras Accepting Sandinista Amnesty," *NYT*, September 17, 1987, A10.

63. Author's interview with Wheelock.

64. Julia Preston, "Rebels Kill 46 in Nicaraguan Raid," *BG*, October 21, 1983.

65. *CBS Evening News*, November 6, 1983.

66. Sergio Ramirez, *Adiós Muchachos: Una memoria de la revolución sandinista* (Mexico City: Aguilar, 1999), 228-29; translation RSL.

67. *CBS Evening News*, March 7, 1985.

68. *West 57th Street*, CBS, August 20, 1985.

69. Author's interview with Wheelock. Sandinista militarization of cooperatives were described to me in detail by Major Roger Miranda Bengoechea, Washington, D.C., January 7, 1988, and Francisco ("Pepe") Matus, a former coordinator of Sandinista Defense Committees in rural Nicaragua, Tegucigalpa, Honduras, April 3, 1989. One of the rare U.S. media references to such practices states that "the Sandinistas are forming a defense cordon of militarized agricultural cooperatives in which peasant militiamen armed with assault rifles and mortars patrol the countryside" (Clifford Krauss and Frederick Kemple, "Managua Tightens Grip on Former Contra Strongholds," *WSJ*, February 6, 1987); see also Chris Hedges, "Nicaragua's Killing Fields: Co-op Farmers, Kin Live in Fear of Contra Attacks," *DMN*, September 20, 1987.

70. "Stone's War," *Miami Vice*, NBC, September 1986.

71. Author's interview with LeMoyne, who reported on the *Contras* for the *New York Times* during this period, Miami, Florida, July 11, 1989.

72. Lindsey Gruson, "For Contras in One Area, Growing Civilian Support," *NYT*, November 5, 1987, A1, A8.

73. Preston, "Released American Says Contras 'Own' Vast Zone," *WP*, November 3, 1987, A25

74. "Contras Find a Haven Inside Nicaragua," *WSJ*, August 3, 1987, A12.

75. Dillon, *Commandos*, 170; Garvin, *Everybody Has His Own Gringo*.

76. Ramirez, *Adiós Muchachos*, 227-28.

77. Stephen R. MacKinnon and Oris Friesen, *China Reporting: An Oral History of American Journalism in the 1930s and 1940s* (Berkeley: University of California, 1987), ix-x. For a discussion of similar errors in the coverage of the Soviet Union, see Whitman

Bassow, *The Moscow Correspondents: Reporting on Russia from the Revolution to Glasnost* (New York: Paragon House, 1989), especially chapters 3 and 4.

78. Bassow, *Moscow Correspondents*, 154-55

79. Bassow, *Moscow Correspondents*, 149.

80. Bassow, *Moscow Correspondents*, 150.

81. Interviews with Sam Dillon of the *Miami Herald*, Miami, July 11, 1989; and James LeMoyne, Miami, June 7, 1989.

82. See Leiken, "The Revision Thing."

Chapter 12
The System of Stereotypes

The pattern of stereotypes at the center of our codes largely determines what group of facts we shall see, and in what light we shall see them.

The stereotype precedes the use of reason; is a form of perception, imposes a certain character on the data of our senses before the data reach the intelligence. The stereotype is like the lavender window-panes on Beacon Street, like the door-keeper at a costume ball who judges whether the guest has an appropriate masquerade. There is nothing so obdurate to education or to criticism as the stereotype. It stamps itself upon the evidence in the very act of securing the evidence. That is why the accounts of returning travelers are often an interesting tale of what the traveler carried abroad with him on his trip.

—Walter Lippmann[1]

Lippmann offered "the idea of progress" as an example of "a fundamental stereotype" through which the early twentieth-century American viewed the world:

The country village will become the great metropolis, the modest building a skyscraper, what is small shall be big, what is slow shall be fast, what is poor shall be rich.

Moreover, "the immense physical growth of American civilization" seemed to substantiate the paradigm. But that pattern was partial and inadequate.

[The Americans] grew to be one of the most powerful nations on earth without preparing their institutions or their minds for the ending of their isolation. They stumbled into the World War . . . , and they stumbled out again, much disillusioned, but hardly more experienced.

165

The disillusion of the Vietnam War was more corrosive. After Vietnam, in the minds of many Americans, the United States was no longer a beacon of progress but an enemy of peace and justice. Progress was to be found not in expanding American civilization but in bridling it. Progress itself often gave way to relativity, as a "fundamental stereotype" within an alternative system of stereotypes.

Lippmann illustrates his idea of a fundamental stereotype with one that is very much to our purpose:

> When we use the word "Mexico" what picture does it evoke in a resident of New York? Likely as not, it is some composite of sand, cactus, oil wells, greasers, rum-drinking Indians, testy old cavaliers flourishing whiskers and sovereignty, or perhaps an idyllic peasantry a la Jean Jacques, assailed by the prospect of smoky industrialism, and fighting for the Rights of Man.[2]

Lippmann was writing in the aftermath of the Mexican Revolution. By the late 1970s the second image of "Mexico," or, in our case, of Nicaragua, had virtually displaced the first one in the American prestige press. The idyllic peasantry had acquired the luster of the "noble savage"—an ancient motif dating back to the ancients' Gardens of Eden and Hesperides and their Islands of the Blessed. The New World first evoked these sentiments in Columbus himself, whose first Indians were "gentle and do not know the meaning of evil, nor killing."[3] Exemplary peoples and paradises became staples of Western literature.[4] For many European postwar intellectuals, decolonization recast the "Third World" as the universal oppressed, the United States as global imperialist.

If alienated Americans could draw on a mother lode of cultural and political motifs, there was often something abstract in their allegiances. Regis Debray, the French journalist and former guerrilla theorist, wrote that "perhaps for the first time a whole generation is obliged to experience its age by proxy, in the form of ideas. . . . As an idea, the Third World is 'Third Worldism.'"[5] Absent an opportunity for direct encounters, the tendency was to transform the unknown into the personification of an abstract ideal.[6]

The new stereotype of Nicaragua was part of a system of stereotypes. That system cannot be ascribed to a single individual or text and its influence certainly extended far beyond journalism. It would be an exaggeration to attribute the turn in the American mind exclusively to Vietnam. When a great part of a whole generation of intellectuals, scholars, journalists, clerics, artists, political, and religious activists and other cultural leaders—not to mention "concerned" doctors, lawyers, and scientists—share a picture of the world, it must be comprehended as a cultural datum.

The system of stereotypes in question was not an aggregate of propositions, and the catalogue which follows is heuristic. Still, we can take David Halberstam's anguished conclusion that "we were on the wrong side of history" as one "tacit little theory."[7] Here are some of the others:

- History was on the side of Third World nationalism. The formerly colonial regions were experiencing a national awakening. Standing in the way were U.S.-backed authoritarian regimes. Thus, for a seasoned *Washington Post* correspondent covering Nicaragua:

  > Sandinista leaders and many of their followers . . . are encouraging a mood of national awakening after years of seeing their country take its lead from Washington during the rule of the Somoza family.[8]

- Partly because of an outdated "cold war vision," induced by an inordinate preoccupation with communism, the United States had been shoring up "colonial puppets" and "frustrating a widely supported national independence movement."[9] In the pursuit of this vision, the United States often found itself backing egregious violators of human rights. By the mid-1970s the Somoza dynasty, which a 1959 *New York Times* editorial had portrayed as enjoying "support from the peasants and workers," was considered one of the world's worst violators of human rights.[10]

- The United States deserved blame both for the particular neocolonial regimes it supported and for the general poverty of the Third World. The Lichter/Rothman 1979-80 survey of journalists working for the most influential newspapers found that majorities believed that the United States "exploits the Third World" and considered America's heavy use of its natural resources "immoral" and a major cause of its poverty.[11]

- Because colonial regimes maintained power through corruption and brute force, armed struggle was frequently the only route to liberation: hence the emergence of revolutionary movements led by national liberation fronts.

- As Halberstam learned, revolutionaries have a "sense of the people." Though some revolutionaries may be hard-line ideologues, most are principled but pragmatic patriots whose goal is national liberation and self-government.

- National liberation fronts may profess Marxism, but they are far more nationalist than Marxist. In any case, their Marxism is a local variety not to be confused with Communism. It represents the efforts of a stifled culture to secure its independence, not the embryo of a dictatorial or totalitarian regime.[12] For Thomas W. Walker, the Sandinistas' Marxism or Marxism-Leninism

  > simply meant that they—like an increasing number of Third World intellectuals—saw economics as the major determinant of social and political matters, believed in the reality of class struggle, identified imperialism as a major problem . . . and so on.
  >
  > The Sandinistas' nationalism was "as strong or stronger than their Marxism."[13]

- Owing to its past behavior the United States has no business attempting to "moderate" emerging revolutionary regimes, especially in Latin America. As a July 1979 *New York Times* editorial stated:

  > America's moral credit in Nicaragua is slim. It is a little late in the day, after four decades of involvement with the Somoza dynasty, for the United States to insist that any successor to President Somoza's regime must now meet Washington's test of moderate democracy.[14]

- The United States should change course and "befriend not the 'authoritarianism' of the oligarchs and generals but rather the nationalism of the people."[15] Practical as well as moral interests dictate that the United States should accommodate radical Third World nationalism, not oppose it. Communism itself was largely a reaction to Western intransigence—adopting a similar attitude to radical nationalism would only breed more of it. The United States should develop a new relationship with revolutionary movements such as the Faribundo Martí Liberation Front in El Salvador and revolutionary regimes like the Sandinistas. Such a policy shift would please European and Third World leaders. As Leslie Gelb argued in the *New York Times* when the Sandinistas came to power: "The world is looking on to see if . . . the United States has the political steadiness to try to establish a working relationship with a revolutionary government." The future *Times* editorial page editor warned that if Nicaragua requested, and the United States withheld, military aid,

  > it would mean an abrupt end to a policy shift of historic proportions: trying to work with and win over radical regimes rather than reflexively opposing them.[16]

- National liberation movements and fronts are diverse coalitions whose components range from conservative nationalists through Marxist-Leninists. Unless the front is radicalized by outside pressure, moderates tend to predominate. Encompassing as they do various political trends, such fronts constitute the main institutional form of democracy in the Third World. Thus, veteran *Post* correspondent Ed Cody described the Sandinistas in 1984 as

  > a kaleidoscopic mixture of Marxism, nationalism, Latin bravura, youthful zest and social welfare, with shifting patterns depending on which faction of the nine-member Directorate has prevailed on the problem in view.[17]

The argument was often made that national liberation fronts were a Third World revolutionary form of democracy itself, if democracy is not understood in a narrow "ethnocentric" manner. Democracy inevitably takes a shape different from " Western forms" in Third World countries. The revolutionary regime may not resemble Western democracy in all its particulars, but what counted was popular participation, even if within the structure of a single party. It could then even be argued that Third World "revolutionary movements . . . are the last wave of the democratic revolution that began in the West in the seventeenth and eighteenth centuries."[18]

• Popular nationalism and centralized authority render revolutionary regimes immune to attempts to encourage liberalizing them from the outside. Whether these efforts are political (assistance to political parties or labor unions), military (support for insurgents), economic (embargoes), or even cultural (assistance to opposition newspapers or external radio broadcasting), they are not only futile but counterproductive because they provide "a foreign devil to unite the country."[19]

• Movements of resistance to these regimes tend to be reactionary surrogates of foreign powers and cannot gain a popular following.[20] In those rare cases where they do, the support comes from pockets of traditional peoples highly susceptible to outside manipulation.

As with all stereotypes, these were a mixture of reality and fancy. Often the efficacy of a stereotype rests on its quantum of truth. Of course, not every American journalist who covered Nicaragua subscribed to every one of these propositions; and some would have demurred from certain of the preceding formulations without dissenting from their overall drift. But important here is not the catalogue itself or the views of an individual journalist but the general and hegemonic "pattern of stereotypes."

***

All the journalists who responded to our questionnaire opposed the war in Vietnam, with the exception of Karen DeYoung who answered "neutral or no opinion." Perhaps that response indicates that, as Julia Preston wrote of herself

> it is very hard to retrace the evolution of one's views of a period as long as a decade without some study,
> But in my case, you should remember that I was not entirely naive when I reached Central America. My dreamy, *circa* 1970 campus radicalism had been considerably dispelled [by] . . . close contact with . . . Peruvian radicals.
> Still I returned to the States in 1975 with much Martin Luther King and much anti-war movement bottled up inside. It was, you remember, a time when the Pinochet regime and the Argentine dirty war inspired legitimate shock and outrage.[21]

Such experiences appeared to have influenced most of the reporters.

But more varied, naturally, were the responses to questions about "early intellectual influences (books, thinkers, etc.) on your views of international affairs" as well as about "early influences on your views of Central America." Though few went as far as Karen DeYoung in claiming "none," as often as not the former Central American reporters cited a broad range of influences from "*The New York Review of Books, I. F. Stone's Weekly*" (Sam Dillon—both were publications strongly opposed to the Vietnam War), to "A. J. P. Taylor, George Kennan, Lenin, Clausewitz, Acheson" (James LeMoyne). Clifford Krauss named David Halberstam's *The Best and the Brightest* and "various Vietnam books"; Julia Preston mentioned, along with Harvard University's John Womack's *Zapata and the Mexican Revolution*, John Gerassi's *The Great Fear in Latin America*.

That last volume deserves separate attention. For one thing, it most nearly embodied what would become the entire pattern of stereotypes about Latin America. But it is also interesting because it was written by a journalist in 1962, that is, *before* the "cultural shift" associated with the Vietnam War. It represents another of the influences that contributed to the new paradigm: the ideas of European intellectuals.

John Gerassi reported from Latin America during the late 1950s and early 1960s for various U.S. publications including *Time, Newsweek,* the *Baltimore Sun,* and the *New York Times*. But neither his views nor his personal history had much in common with those of most of his contemporary colleagues. Gerassi grew up in Paris and Spain; his father, a close friend of Jean Paul Sartre and Simone de Beauvoir, had been a republican general in the Spanish Civil War and a model for Sartre's "committed" (*engagé*) intellectual.[22]

Gerassi's *Great Fear* argued that the misery of Latin America's common people derived from U.S. policies. The social inequities and economic underdevelopment of Latin American societies derived from the survival of a "medieval" and colonial structure inherited from Spanish imperialism and perpetuated by U.S. corporations, U.S. economic policies, and its support for the *ancien regime*.[23] Gerassi illustrated what he took to be the the Latin American masses' invariable hatred for the United States with a comment by "a small mildmannered man" who lived with two other families ("sixteen children") in a one room shanty in "one of those ugly Caracas slums surrounding gigantic ultramodern glass and steel skyscrapers":

> We began to stare with him at a fifty-foot wide Coca-Cola advertisement that stood out at the foot of the slum hill. "None of us in this house has ever drunk a Coca-Cola" he said softly. "One day we will kill those who make them."[24]

Gerassi believed:

> There is absolutely no doubt that Latin Americans, whose government and "ways" have so far been fashioned, mostly by us, in our image and too often for our profit, do not want our form of democracy.[25]

In 1963 when Gerassi's book appeared, two alternatives to the allegedly dominant Latin American "medievalist" regime were clearly apparent. One was presented by revolutionary Cuba and the other by the liberal democratic regimes founded by José Figueres in Costa Rica and Romulo Betancourt in Venezuela. Many observers believed that the future of Latin America would depend on which of these two models prevailed.[26] Robert J. Alexander wrote in 1964:

There is no doubt that the rivalry between the Cuban Totalitarian Revolution and the Venezuelan Democratic Revolution will go far to determine the future of the whole Latin America. Leaders of governments , political parties, labor movements, the business community of other Latin American countries, are observing very closely the results that are being achieved in the two Republics.[27]

In Gerassi's view:

Alexander and the other Liberal defenders of Latin American democrats are, unfortunately, very important.

If the argument [of such liberals] is meant as proof that democratic reformers are better than non-democratic reformers—that is, Castros—then one must compare Betancourt's "reforms" to Castro.

In such light, Betancourt's program becomes ludicrous. He could have closed all schools for one year, for example, drafted all students and teachers, sent them out to teach illiterates how to read and write. He did not.[28]

Gerassi believed "Latin America must radically change its whole structure." But it could not do so "without whole-scale nationalizations, enforced diversification, and rigid state planning" that required either "a nationalistic revolution" or making nationalizations, planning, and the rest a condition for receiving foreign aid.[29]

In his ideology, in his critique of contemporary mainstream reporting, and in his own reportorial methods, Gerassi was a harbinger of the new paradigm. Gerassi's colleagues at the Associated Press, United Press, and even the *New York Times* got their stories by reading the local newspapers, then putting in "a phone call to an official source to 'verify' what they have read, then filing it home." But the *engagé*, "participant" Gerassi interviewed "the extremes, Right or Left," walked through slums, talked with workers and peasants. "Occasionally, I had to travel by mule and sometimes by foot." Gerassi was not boasting: "never were the hardships so bad that my wife could not accompany me."[30] Instead, Gerassi's aim was to lambaste the physical and spiritual complacency of the U.S. press—"Generally the facts are not printed, just the news"—in order to make a more sweeping and systematic indictment of the United States:

If our press misrepresents the facts on Latin America, if our economic policies misrepresent Latin America's needs, if our political policies support Latin America's medievalists bent on profiting from such disregard, then perhaps we can understand why Latin Americans hate us.[31]

The Tenacity of the Stereotype

The pattern of stereotypes persisted even though neither the Sandinistas nor the *Contras*, nor other Central American groups, evolved in the direction anticipated by the stereotype. Events caused considerable evolution in the personal views of many of the leading correspondents, especially those, "with whom," in Julia Preston's words, "it is a matter of deepening vocation to set aside outright political conviction."[32] The tenacity of the stereotype in spite of this evolution of events, and of the correspondents' view of the region and of their role, suggests that we are dealing with something "structural."

Much of the rather slim body of investigative reporting conducted by reporters stationed in Managua during the mid-1980s was filed by Stephen Kinzer. At a time when, as Joe Klein wrote, Kinzer was "a reporter whose every adjective has political import," the *New York Times* bureau chief stubbornly defended his independence from partisan pressures.[33] Resisting the Managua social swirl which teemed with foreign Sandinista sympathizers and government officials, Kinzer industriously explored the country, immersed himself in its history, became a collector of its antiquities, and quietly developed relations with Managuans on both sides of the conflict.[34]

Kinzer's reporting reflected these virtues, which in 1988 won him the Columbia University School of Journalism's Maria Moors Cabot Prize for outstanding reporting from Latin America. By the same token, however, Kinzer's reporting also testifies to the tenacity of the "system of stereotypes." For all his resourcefulness and independence Kinzer's reporting evaded neither the "myths" recounted in chapter 6 nor the system of stereotypes established by his elders.

Before becoming a freelance journalist in 1976, Kinzer had been a campaign worker and political appointee of Massachusetts governor, and future presidential candidate, Michael Dukakis. Kinzer began reporting from Nicaragua as a freelancer in November 1976. By 1978 he was reporting occasionally for the *Boston Globe*. During the Sandinistas' final offensive Kinzer was in Managua "filing stories for the *Boston Globe* and the *Washington Post*." He shared a home with Alan Riding, Karen DeYoung, and Bernard Diederich that they called "the safe house" (after the Sandinistas' clandestine residences). Kinzer who was "by several years the youngest member of the household" forms a bridge between the first and second generation of American correspondents of the Nicaraguan revolution.[35]

In 1981 Kinzer became the *Boston Globe*'s Latin American correspondent, and in 1983 the *New York Times* invited him to open the first full-time office in Nicaragua of an American newspaper. By his own account what attracted Kinzer to the job was its "ability to help shape public discourse."[36] Kinzer's earlier hands-on, grassroots political experience was unusual for his generation of journalists, but his ambition to influence policy was not—nor were his policy aspirations. As we have seen, he relished the prospect of "ruining breakfasts in

Washington" and sparking "heated debate" in Congress over Administration *Contra* policy.[37]

His first *New York Times Magazine* feature in 1983 described the Sandinistas as radical nationalist populists who wished to "undermine the country's moneyed classes and isolate them from power." While "claiming the nationalist legacy of Sandino as their principal inspiration" the Sandinistas "readily acknowledge their debt to Castro-style Marxism." Kinzer cited Defense Minister Humberto Ortega's statement that "Marxism-Leninism is the scientific doctrine that guides our revolution," but quickly added that "in comparison with Cuba or the Soviet Union, Nicaragua today is quite an open society." But, of course, a more valid comparison would have compared this fourth year of Sandinista Nicaragua with Cuba at the beginning of 1962 or the Soviet Union in 1921, at the outset of the New Economic Policy.

Kinzer went on to state:

> Many Nicaraguans, most of them poor, say they feel freer now than they did under Somoza's rule. . . . Nobody, no matter how opposed to the Sandinistas, need fear soldiers or death squads bursting into his home and massacring everyone in sight.[38]

As we have seen, Kinzer and his colleagues encouraged expectations that revolutionary Nicaragua would install a democratic regime on the order of Costa Rica or a "system similar to that of the United States."[39] But as the promise of a democratic Nicaragua faded, the standard for comparison declined. Now pundits and reporters contrasted Sandinista Nicaragua to its authoritarian neighbors. By 1984 many reporters, though not Kinzer himself, were appraising the Sandinistas by what scholars and colleagues called "Central American standards"— that is to say, the standards established by authoritarian regimes such as that of Somoza. In fact, death squads and massacres had not typified Nicaraguan history. By this revised standard even the Somoza dynasty, which was not characterized until the very end by the routine savagery of El Salvador or Guatemala, was gentle. The idea that Nicaraguans had "no need to fear" its military or death squads received an appalling refutation when, at the end of the war, human rights organizations began discovering clandestine cemeteries, some dating from before the civil war, holding the remains of peasant and Miskito Indian civilians who balked at Sandinista policies.[40]

Kinzer evoked the old stereotypes most clearly in his discussion of political freedom. The Sandinistas maintained a "solid base of popular support," especially among the poor. If some of the poor were growing discontented, it was not because of the government's abridgement of civil and human rights:

> The loss of political freedom means little to people who never know it. . . . This disillusionment now setting in among ordinary Nicaraguans has more to do with chronic shortages, ration cards and long lines at stores.[41]

Kinzer leaves the impression that political freedom was a concern only of the well-to-do, whom he proceeds to associate with Somoza, whereas the masses worried only about their stomachs. For all their faults the Sandinistas were an authentic expression of Nicaraguan nationalism fending off "a foreign-supported attack." The correspondent explicitly warned Washington that after each past U.S. intervention "Nicaraguan nationalism reemerged more radical than before." Rather than pursuing current policy, "Washington must learn to live with revolutionary governments in its own hemisphere."[42]

How well did these notions survive five years in Nicaragua? Unlike some of his colleagues, Kinzer's political and ideological assumptions did not suppress his inquisitive instincts. As we have seen, he uncovered the vast clandestine draft resistance movement and found that the Sandinistas' 1984 elections were a "charade."[43] Several times Kinzer put himself in danger by venturing off-limits to the Atlantic Coast, the scene of fierce fighting between the Sandinista military and Miskito Indians. In 1985 Kinzer ignored a government ban to travel to the Rio Coco, the scene of a "cruel campaign of forced relocation that became the greatest collective trauma in Miskito history."[44] He found that the Sandinistas had uprooted "aboriginal" villages, "carpeting the lush countryside with 250- and 500-pound bombs."[45] Sandinista policies on the Atlantic Coast "devastated Miskito culture and cost the lives of many hundreds of Indians."[46]

In the spring of 1988, after the Sandinista government signed an agreement at Esquipulas, Guatemala, guaranteeing "democratic political processes" and respect for "freedom in all its forms," the civilian opposition was able to convoke rallies in several provincial capitals. Kinzer found the turnouts "surprisingly large."[47] So, evidently, did the Sandinistas. In a March 7 dispatch Sam Dillon of the *Miami Herald* reported that a Sandinista *turba* mob assaulted a group of Mothers of Political Prisoners as the Sandinista police stood by:

> hundreds of club-wielding Sandinista activists attacked an anti-government demonstration . . . , pelting outnumbered marchers with rocks and singling out panicked protesters for mob beatings[48]

On July 11 Kinzer reported from the town of Nandaime, forty miles southeast of Managua, that "Sandinista police used tear gas, rifle butts, and truncheons to break up a spirited opposition rally here today."[49] The police fired "volley after volley" of tear gas canisters "and soon all Nandaime was under a paralyzing cloud." Kinzer himself was clubbed by police and knocked unconscious, but still managed to meet his deadline.[50] The respected Nicaraguan intellectual and close associate of Pedro Joaquín Chamorro, Dr. Emilio Alvarez Montalván, told Kinzer "the Sandinistas are clearly on the defensive, and they have lost the base of support which they once had in the poorer classes."[51]

Kinzer surmounted physical challenges better than political and ideological ones. When, a year after the 1990 elections, Kinzer published his memoir of "life and war in Nicaragua" his basic tenets remained intact: the equity, relative openness, mildness, and popularity of the Sandinista regime; the authority and authenticity of their nationalism; the folly and futility of U.S. policy. Kinzer's verdict is that although the Sandinistas' "errors" were "enormous," their government "was moved always by patriotism, never by lust for money or power."[52]

These and other Kinzer conclusions contrast with his own experience and with his own newspaper's subsequent reporting. Earlier the former bureau chief attributed difficulties in finding quarters for the *Times* to the fact that "Sandinista leaders snatched up all the best homes, either for themselves or for government offices."[53] Later, even as he was completing his memoir, his newspaper was reporting on the vast Sandinista peculation which came to be known as "*la piñata*" (a vessel which is broken to dispense gifts at children's parties). Kinzer's successor Mark Uhlig reported that, after their election defeat, the lame-duck Sandinista legislators suddenly were moved to transfer to Sandinista leaders

> thousands of houses, buildings and other property, ranging from President Daniel Ortega Saavedra's own house, a sprawling, walled residence that was confiscated from an exiled banker, to state-owned protocol houses, military homes, political party offices, businesses, enterprises, radio stations, clubs, restaurants and even movie theaters.[54]

Government property, including vehicles, office machinery, and furniture, began disappearing from public buildings and reappearing in Sandinista homes and offices. The government's monetary reserves vanished. "They took over the government proclaiming that 'property is theft,' " observed a *La Prensa* editorial. "They are leaving proclaiming theft is property."[55]

The "*piñata*" also involved what Uhlig later described as "a wholesale revision of Nicaraguan laws to limit the new government's power." To protect their future status in the opposition, the outgoing government also reestablished the very laws of university autonomy and media independence "that the Sandinistas themselves had abolished" and provided immunity for all "unprosecuted crimes committed since July 1979."[56] The outgoing government also guaranteed the jobs of all state employees, thus attempting to assure that Sandinista appointees would continue to staff the bureaucracy of the new government. Soon after the election, "in small towns throughout the country, well-organized Sandinista crowds began systematic harassment and intimidation of local opposition leaders."[57] The attackers were sometimes armed with recently distributed weapons.[58] By threatening a "chaos" in which the Sandinistas themselves would "rule from below," the Sandinistas coerced President-elect Chamorro into retaining Daniel's brother Humberto Ortega as the head of the country's armed forces.[59]

Kinzer had learned from his years covering Nicaragua that the Sandinista leaders had brought off "a masterful deception" about their Marxist-Leninist ideology and that their "ultimate goal" was always "to make Nicaragua the second revolutionary Marxist state in the hemisphere."[60] Nonetheless, the reporter still took at face value Sandinista democratic professions and considered that they deserve a "place of historic honor" for providing "a basis on which a genuine democracy could be built."[61] The belief in the Sandinistas' democratic vocation was a theme which ran from 1977, when Alan Riding first described the Sandinistas' objective as being to "establish democracy," through the 1990 elections. In August 1993, in reply to a query from the author, Kinzer commented:

> As to whether my final characterization of the Sandinistas in my book requires updating, I guess the answer is obvious. I would only note that my book takes the story only up to the date of the Chamorro-Ortega election.[62]

Yet in 2001 when given the opportunity to "update," Kinzer reprised the stereotypes that afflicted his reporting on Nicaragua, proving just how tenacious these protocols remain.[63] The anti-Sandinista rebels remain "Reagan's *Contras*," the Sandinistas as a "corps of young patriots" who stayed "idealists" throughout their tenure in government. The vast peculation at the end of their reign, the *"piñata,"* was an isolated event that cast no shadow behind it. If we are to believe this "updating," the Sandinistas would be the first group to have been corrupted by *losing* power!

***

Most of the journalists interviewed or responding to my questionnaire reported a marked shift in their views. Chris Hedges, who reported for the *Christian Science Monitor* and the *Dallas Morning News* writes that, "Everyone in the press had signed on for the great crusade, when this all started." But by the mid-1980s many of "the real reporters," as opposed to the sympathizers with press credentials

> began to have second thoughts. . . . The repression of the Sandinistas, with the breaking of labor unions and suppression of the press, [was] obvious enough to . . . make people feel uncomfortable. Although I always found most the press willing to give . . . the Sandinistas the benefit of the doubt.

By the end, however:

> Most serious reporters left Central America very skeptical of liberation movements. We had gone down to Central America believing, or at least sympathizing, with the left. We were used, lied to . . . by these movements in the end.[64]

The questionnaire asked reporters to respond to Clifford Krauss' statement:

> There is a socialization process in journalism, just as in all professions. There are codes, ethics and an ethos of critical nonpartisanship to be learned and upheld. The same reporters who came down to Central America to prove that the

Contras commit atrocities (which they do) and that Washington still lies (which it does), found out that the FMLN guerrillas also murder innocent civilians and that the Sandinista *comandantes* can lie with the best of them.[65]

James LeMoyne responded: "This is the A-B-C of journalism. Krauss is right; it's just sad it took so many reporters so long to learn this basic lesson." And Julia Preston said: "This says it all."

It does not quite say it all. For despite this process of "socialization" and education, the paradigm survived into the 1990 election, influencing reporters and framing copy. True, many of the faces had changed, although Preston herself still filed occasionally from Managua. The tenacity of the stereotype, despite the pull of events, of professionalism and "deepening vocation," and personnel changes, reinforces the conclusion that it had become part, to borrow Noam Chomsky's terms, of "the deep structure" of post-Vietnam American culture and that the reportage was, in some sense, "structure-dependent."[66]

Notes

1. Walter Lippmann, *Public Opinion* (New York: Macmillan, 1922; revised edition New York: Free Press Paperback, 1965), 125, 98.

2. Lippmann, *Public Opinion*, 110, 68.

3. Christopher Columbus, *The Voyage of Christopher Columbus: Columbus's Own Journal of Discovery*, ed. and trans. John Cummins (New York: St. Martin's, 1992), 116, see also 152, 154.

4. See for example Montaigne's description of the Brazilians in "Of Cannibals," *The Essays of Montaigne*, trans. E. J. Trechmann (London: Oxford University, 1927), 206-8, 210-15.

5. Regis Debray in *Le Debat* (January 1981), cited in Pascal Bruckner, *The Tears of the White Man: Compassion as Contempt* (New York: Free Press, 1986), 177.

6. Cf. Bruckner, *Tears of the White Man*, 26.

7. See chapter 3, 30 and 37 *supra*.

8. Edward Cody, "Despite Problems, Many Support Sandinistas," *WP*, October 22, 1984, A16.

9. Townsend Hoopes, "Legacy of the Cold War in Indochina," *Foreign Affairs* (July 1970): 604-5.

10. "Editorial," *NYT*, June 16, 1959, 34.

11. S. Robert Lichter, Stanley Rothman, and Linda Lichter, *The Media Elite* (Bethesda, Maryland: Adler and Adler, 1986), 29-32. This tendency to hold the United States responsible for the poverty of the developing countries coincided with the rise in Latin America of "dependency theory." The latter viewed Latin America's misery and inequality as a part of a structure of international economic exploitation which the United States had inherited. Many Sandinista intellectuals endorsed dependency theory. See for example Jaime Wheelock Román, *El Gran Desafio* (Managua: Neuva Nicaragua, 1980), chapter iii.

12. Francis FitzGerald's prize-winning *Fire in the Lake* is a *locus classicus* for this notion as well as some of the others here summarized (FitzGerald, *Fire in the Lake* [Boston: Little, Brown, 1972]).

13. "Introduction," in *Nicaragua: The First Five Years*, ed. Thomas W. Walker (Westport: Praeger, 1985), 23. "Accordingly," to Walker "the overriding concern of the young revolutionaries who governed Nicaragua . . . was to reconstruct the country, defend its hard-won sovereignty and dignity and uplift the condition of its popular masses (*Nicaragua: First Five Years*, 23-24). So inclusive and catholic was the amalgam that Walker conceived to be the ideology of the Sandinistas that he found in addition to being Marxists, many of the Sandinistas were also devout Catholics (*Nicaragua: First Five Years*, 24).

14. *NYT*, July 11, 1979, A20.

15. Robert S. Leiken, "Reagan Ought to Befriend Latin Americans' Nationalism," *NYT*, July 1, 1982, A19.

16. *NYT*, August 29, 1979, A23.

17. Cody, "Despite Problems, Many Support Sandinistas," A16.

18. Leiken, "Eastern Winds in Latin America," *Foreign Policy* (Spring 1981): 106.

19. Robert G. Kaiser, "Yankees are a Sandinista's Best Enemy: Our Little War in Nicaragua is Providing Excuses for Authoritarian Controls," *WP*, January 16, 1983, B1, B3.

20. See for example Richard Cohen's "Pipe Dream," cited in the epigraph to chapter 11.

21. Julia Preston, letter to author, August 11, 1993.

22. Cf. Jean Paul Sartre, *Literature and Existentialism* (New York: Citadel Press, 1962); see Sartre, *Les Chemins de Liberte* (Paris: Gallimard, 1945), 3 vols. John Gerassi wrote a biography of Jean Paul Sartre, see *Jean Paul Sartre: Hated Conscience of His Century*, vol. I of *Protestant or Protester?* (Chicago: University of Chicago, 1989). He also wrote a biography of Fidel Castro, see Gerassi, *Fidel Castro, A Biography* (New York: Doubleday, 1973).

23. Gerassi, *The Great Fear in Latin America* (revised edition New York: Collier Books, 1965), chapter I and *passim*.

24. Gerassi, *Great Fear in Latin America*, 39.

25. Gerassi, *Great Fear in Latin America*, 409.

26. For Jose Figueres and Costa Rica see Manuel Rojas, *Lucha social y guerra civil en Costa Rica* (San José: Editorial Porvenir, 1980); John Patrick Bell, *Crisis in Costa Rica: The 1948 Revolution* (Austin: University of Texas, 1971); Rosendo Arguello, *Quienes y como nos traicionaron* (Mexico: [s.n.], 1954); Rodolfo Cruz Cerda, "Costa Rica since 1930," in *Central America Since Independence*, ed. Leslie Bethell (Cambridge, England: Cambridge University, 1991).

27. Robert J. Alexander, *The Venezuelan Democratic Revolution* (New Brunswick: Rutgers University, 1964), 4.

28. Gerassi, *Great Fear in Latin America*, 165.

29. Gerassi, *Great Fear in Latin America*, 31.

30. Gerassi, *Great Fear in Latin America*, 43.

31. Gerassi, *Great Fear in Latin America*, 42, 47.

32. Preston, letter to author, August 11, 1993.

33. Joe Klein, "Our Man in Managua," *Esquire* (November 1986): 104.

34. Information on Kinzer's Managua lifestyle comes from author's direct observation in August 1984 when he was Kinzer's houseguest, and interviews with reporters James LeMoyne and Clifford Krauss.

35. Stephen Kinzer, *Blood of Brothers* (New York: Putnam, 1991), 45.

36. Kinzer, *Blood of Brothers*, 92.

37. See chapter 2 above and Kinzer, *Blood of Brothers*, 110-13.

38. Kinzer, "Nicaragua: The Beleaguered Revolution," *NYTM*, August 28, 1983, 67.

39. Kinzer, *BG*, July 11, 1979; see chapter 9, 125 *supra*.

40. Since the Nicaraguan Army remained under Sandinista leadership during the Chamorro government, the number of clandestine cemeteries remains unknown. However, the Nicaraguan Association for Human Rights (ANPDH) has estimated those missing to be 1,000, a number proportionately equivalent to the "disappeared" in Argentina's infamous "dirty war." (See Asociación Nicaragüense Pro-Derechos Humanos, "Los Cementerios Clandestinos en Nicaragua," Managua 1991; see also Paul Berman, "Neckties and Mass Graves, *The Village Voice*, March 5, 1991; Ambrose Evan Pritchard, "The Nicaraguan Killing Fields," *National Review*, April 29, 1991; Nina Shea, "Uncovering the Awful Truth of the Sandinista Killing Fields," *WSJ*, August 24, 1990, A11; and Leiken, "The Revision Thing," *TNR*, August 31, 1982, 49.) Human rights organizations found that Sandinista assassinations usually were carried out selectively, the bodies deposited in the cemeteries. "The methods of torture most commonly reported by former detainees," according to one human rights group, "have been physical and psychological abuse that is nonbloody, often called 'white torture' by former victims because of its characteristics of not leaving scars" (Puebla Institute, *Nicaragua, Civil Liberties and the Central American Peace Plan* [Washington, DC: Puebla Institute, 1988], 96). The author heard similar descriptions in Chinandega in August 1984 and April 1986 and while on a human rights mission for the International League for Human Rights (see International League for Human Rights, *Report on Human Rights Defenders in Nicaragua* [New York: July 1986], 189-96). Repression was more overt the farther from the capital, especially on the Miskito coast where many of the mass graves were discovered after the war.

41. Kinzer, *NYTM*, 1983, 26.

42. Kinzer, *NYTM*, 1983, 67.

43. Kinzer, *Blood of Brothers*, chapter xv.

44. Kinzer, *Blood of Brothers*, 261.

45. Kinzer, *Blood of Brothers*, 281.

46. Kinzer, *Blood of Brothers*, 253.

47. Kinzer, *Blood of Brothers*, 378.

48. Cited in Clifford Krauss, *Inside Central America* (New York: Summit, 1991), 168-69.

49. Kinzer, "Sandinistas Halt a Protest Rally," *NYT* (Late City Edition), July 11, 1988, A2.

50. Kinzer, *Blood of Brothers*, 383.

51. Kinzer, "Sandinistas Lash Out," *NYT*, July 13, 1988, A1.

52. Kinzer, *Blood of Brothers*, 394.

53. Kinzer, *Blood of Brothers*, 134.

54. Mark Uhlig, "Sandinistas Move To Claim Property and Gain Immunity," *NYT*, March 9, 1990, A1; see also Uhlig, "Sandinistas Have Trouble Accepting Defeat," *NYT*, March 11, 1990, IV, 3; "Sandinistas Enact a Bipartisan Amnesty," March 12, 1990; "Sandinistas' Booty Sets Off a Bitter Battle in Nicaragua," *NYT*, June 25, 1991, A1. For more on the *"piñata"* see also Richard Boudreaux, "Sandinistas Legalize Property Sei-

zure," *LAT*, March 29, 1990, A10; Lee Hockstader, 'La Piñata' Stirs Bitter Controversy in Nicaragua," *WP*, June 23, 1991, A1; Joquín Ibarz, "Piñata Theology," *Crisis* (September 1991): 31-34; Jonas Bernstein, "How to Loot a Nation," *Insight* (July 8, 1991): 11-19; Leiken, "Old and New Politics in Managua," *Journal of Democracy* (Summer 1990).

55. Cited in Pablo Antonio Cuadra, "Reclaiming the Revolution," *Journal of Democracy* (Summer 1990).

56. Uhlig, "Nicaragua's Permanent Crisis: Ruling from Above and Below," *Survival*, vol. xxxiii, no. 5 (September/October 1991): 405; see also "Sandinistas to Retain TV Outlet," *WP*, March 7, 1990, A31.

57. Uhlig, "Nicaragua's Permanent Crisis." See also Uhlig, "In Nicaragua, Victors Are Menaced," *NYT*, March 8, 1990.

58. See Mary Speck, "Sandinistas With Guns Hold Farms," March 27, 1990, A16; Uhlig, "Embargo's End Praised by Sandinistas and Foes," *NYT*, March 14, 1990; Uhlig, "Shocked Sandinista Police Chief Hints He'll Accept the Turnover," *NYT*, March 2, 1990, A1.

59. Daniel Ortega, "Speech at Omar Torrijos Plaza of the Non-aligned, Managua," Radio Sandino, February 27, 1990 in *FBIS*, FBIS-LAT-90-040, February 28, 1990, 12; Daniel Ortega, "Comments on Defending FSLN Revolution," Managua, Radio Sandino, March 1, 1990 in *FBIS*, FBIS-LAT-90-042, March 2, 1990, 19-22. See Uhlig, "Sandinistas Demanding Control of the Military," *NYT*, March 6, 1990, A1; "Ortega Pledges Party Will Block Major Changes, *BG*, February 28, 1990, A1.

60. Kinzer, *Blood of Brothers*, 66, 60, 77. See chapter 11 *supra*.

61. Kinzer, *Blood of Brothers*, 394.

62. Kinzer, letter to author, August 15, 1993.

63. Kinzer, "Country Without Heroes," *The New York Review of Books* (July 19, 2001).

64. Kinzer, letter to author, August 8, 1993.

65. Kinzer, letter to author, August 8, 1993.

66. See Noam Chomsky and Morris Halle, *Sound Patterns of English* (New York: Harper & Row, 1968).

Chapter 13
Fear and Crowds in the 1990 Campaign

> When a system of stereotypes is well fixed, our attention is called to those facts which support it, and diverted from those which contradict.
>
> — Walter Lippmann[1]

"When foreign observers or journalists asked me what were the main factors in the triumph of democracy," Pablo Antonio Cuadra, the poet and *La Prensa* editor, wrote after the elections, "I pointed first and foremost to the Nicaraguan people's loss of fear."[2] From the beginning, we recall, UNO leaders argued that their objective was getting the people "to lose their fear" of the government.[3]

One of the most diligent of the American journalists, Julia Preston, acknowledged subsequently that it was not until "the night before the balloting" that she realized that the Sandinistas were going to lose. Preston's illumination ostensibly came after a ten-minute conversation with a young Sandinista policeman who was hitchhiking back from the hospital where he had visited his desperately ill infant daughter. The child's life was in danger for lack of medicine at "the seedy emergency room at the state-run hospital." Her father needed a ride because no public transportation was available. He was serving as a policeman because, forced into army service, he eventually had been able to wangle a transfer to temporary police duty in Managua where he was "treated 'like filth' because he was not a career policeman or a Sandinista party activist."

> The only time his voice brightened was when I asked him what he thought about the elections. He carefully limited himself to saying he was confident that the presence of hundreds of international observers would ensure a secret vote. But by the time he had climbed out of my car after a ten-minute ride, I was certain that he was one Nicaraguan who looked like a Sandinista, but who was going to cast his vote for . . . UNO.[4]

For Preston it was after those ten minutes that she "finally understood that the Sandinista National Liberation Front was likely to lose the national elections." One supposes she is speaking synecdochically. The ten-minute conversation with the disaffected policeman topped off many other interviews.[5] But equally symbolically, the ten-minute ride might be said to have marked

> the point where the stereotype and the facts that cannot be ignored definitely part company. . . . There comes a time, therefore, when the blind spots come from the edge of the vision into the center.[6]

For the sake of the *Washington Post*'s coverage, it is regrettable that Julia Preston's revelation did not come sooner. Nevertheless, in acknowledging her failure, Preston, along with Clifford Krauss, was a rare exception. Reporters who made the same, or worse, mistakes refused to acknowledge them.

Ten minutes of confidentiality with a Nicaraguan appears to have been another rarity. Whether because of the daily grind or because they did not consider it germane, few reporters appeared to pursue or value such opportunities. That seems to have been a major reason why, in a decade of intense media coverage, so many Nicaraguan stories remained untold. Because reporters seemed to depend so much on their eyes, rather than their ears, they could perceive mayhem but not a less perceptible dread, disclosed usually only in confidence. Of course, *confianza* was the last thing many Nicaraguans felt toward the foreign press.

Such confidences were not sought, or, when offered, not prized. Press and pollsters alike failed to notice or to appreciate what came to be called the "fear factor." They often mistook the content of the election race for a popularity contest between the candidates rather than a war of nerves between government and populace. Because reporters did not follow the opposition campaign or—disregarding the repressive side of Sandinista tactics—did not see the point of UNO strategy, they also failed to discern the moment when Sandinista tactics began to fail, although that moment was plainly marked by large, vocal crowds. The "blind spot" had moved to the center of their vision. Nicaragua's 1990 elections were not "American-style elections," but neither were they simple "demonstration elections"—such as those staged previously in Nicaragua (by both the Sandinista and the Somoza regime) and in some other parts of Latin America and in Eastern Europe.[7] For one thing there was a genuine, if harassed, opposition. Moreover, various external monitors compensated, to some extent, for the absence of internal institutional safeguards. Sandinista repression was not visible and gross, but selective and discrete. Documented repression would risk censure from the international observers upon whose approval hinged all that was to be gained by holding supervised elections. Consequently, the Sandinistas, as one official observer, the former Democratic governor of Arizona Bruce Babbitt, articulated it, "played this election like a pinball machine, shaking and jiggling it to improve the score, but never quite enough to light up the 'tilt' sign."[8]

The good offices of neighboring countries (especially Costa Rica and Venezuela) and the pressure of the *Contras*, the United States, and, to a much lesser extent, Mikhail Gorbachev's Soviet Union, helped to secure a preelection procedural accord between the government and the opposition.[9] Even if flawed and often violated, the agreement established a standard. Demarches from observer groups of the Organization of American States, the Council of Freely-Elected Heads of Government, led by former U.S. President Jimmy Carter, and the Washington-based Center for Democracy on various occasions succeeded in persuading the government to respect the accord and to discontinue abusive practices. More than 2,000 observers, including large official missions from the OAS and the United Nations, monitored election-day proceedings, and many were in the country throughout the campaign.[10] The vote-counting and "quick-count" procedures established or monitored by these organizations, together with unprecedented attention from the international media, seriously reduced opportunities for abuse, even if they did not eliminate them.

These interventions helped to create an atmosphere in which elections originally intended as a device to secure international legitimacy became a meaningful test of the popular will—even if the exam questions were slanted. If, to shift metaphors, the "playing field" was not "level," the slope was reduced to where it was obvious neither from the box seats nor the press box. Only rarely was there repression visible to official observers and to the media, such as the violent suppression of opposition rallies or the banning of a prominent opposition candidate.

In effect, the contest was conducted under two distinct, indeed antithetical, regimes. The contradiction produced a hybrid perhaps unique in the annals of political science: a liberal democratic process combined with a popular revolt against a dictatorship. This complex event presented a challenge to the journalists' imagination and ingenuity, a challenge not met by affirmations that "the election process has been relatively free and fair by Central American standards."[11]

As might be imagined the press had an easier time documenting the reassuring and diplomatic statements of official observer delegations. Exposing abuses was left chiefly to the reports from organizations critical of the Sandinistas—or for the back pages of official reports. As a consequence, neither the official nor the press reporting alerted readers to what, after the election, American public opinion analysts, seeking to explain polling inaccuracies, called "the fear factor."[12] But fear constituted the strategic substance of the campaign—which was not a popularity contest but a war of nerves. Without appreciating this factor, pollsters, analysts, and reporters would be unprepared to discern the moment when a Sandinista defeat came into view. But not to appreciate this factor was not to have lived or understood Nicaragua's history over the past decade.

***

In the election campaign the Sandinistas returned to the dual tactics that brought them to preeminence a decade earlier. Between 1977 and 1979 the FSLN, led by the Ortegas' "*Tercerista*" faction, had promoted a broad political front while running an armed insurgency; had united with the "bourgeois" anti-Somoza opposition but kept their own counsel; had presented a democratic public platform without wavering from private Marxist-Leninist principles; had reached out to democratic countries like Costa Rica, Panama, and Venezuela even while they tightened their intimate relations with Cuba. Similarly, during the election campaign the Sandinistas removed the word "socialism" from their party platform, allowed opposition parties to hold rallies, distributed land to individual peasants, loosened restrictions on the press, released political prisoners, allowed religious services on army bases and suspended conscription. The Sandinista government also accepted the international election monitoring called for in the Esquipulas agreements, though it restricted observation to the groups expected to be least rigorous.[13] At the same time Sandinista gangs disrupted opposition rallies, while opposition candidates, poll watchers, and organizers were beaten, jailed, or called up for military duty and government officials, from the president on down, made it clear that opposition voters would be punished once the observers were gone. Just as in 1977-79 the American media focused on the public, ostensibly democratic side of Sandinista conduct while virtually ignoring the covert and despotic side.

The Sandinistas' "American-style" media campaign was only one element of their tactical approach, and by no means the most vital one. The media campaign was aimed mainly at securing a large youth vote. Teenagers were the most likely to be wooed by the FSLN's modern campaign techniques. They were not generally burdened by family responsibilities and were thus less preoccupied by the economic hardships. Further, for the better part of a decade all Nicaraguan students had been instructed under a government-designed curriculum which had been imposed on private as well as public schools, over the strong objections of parent organizations and the Catholic church. Moreover, since 1983 those sixteen and above had been drafted into the Sandinista Popular Army where they received regular "political education." Accordingly the voting age was lowered, *comandante* Ortega exchanged his fatigues for hip-huggers, and the formerly drab official media ran FSLN advertisements showing nude teenagers locked in an embrace and proclaiming that "doing it for the first time is beautiful."

But all was not hugs and kisses. The FSLN had developed quite a different set of tactics for those less likely to be favorably disposed to their candidate. Sandinista media and candidates made clear from the outset that electoral politics were a continuation of the war by other means. President Ortega told a news conference in September: "The economic and military struggle now has a political expression: the election process. . . . A mercenary force in the political field has been organized."[14]

In this war the Sandinistas, who had no chance of losing, would know how to reward their enemies.

> The people are not going to vote for a loser. The people know who the winner is and the people will vote for the winner—the Sandinista Front. . . . They will not vote for the United States, and this is what our opponents represent.[15]

The Sandinistas, wrote Pablo Antonio Cuadra, "set about to keep fear alive during the election campaign." Mindful of the presence of an augmented press corps and "of an army of extraordinarily agile and efficient international observers," the FSLN "mounted a series of small-scale assaults all over the country—here today, there tomorrow—that were difficult to verify. [It was] scatter-shot terror, designed to numb the electorate."[16]

In part because of its selective character, this coercive underside of the Sandinista campaign, unlike their attempts at persuasion, or seduction, received negligible coverage in the American media. The only first-hand reports by a major American reporter did not appear in the press at all. Clifford Krauss, on leave from the *Wall Street Journal* to write a book on the region, accompanied both Chamorro and Ortega on the campaign trail. The few pages his book devotes to the campaign are more illustrative than anything in the American press reporting.

Krauss describes in some detail both an Ortega rally and a Chamorro rally. At the Sandinista candidate's rally in Masaya, a market-town half an hour's drive from Managua, the crowds were "large and young, mostly from local high schools." Older residents "generally didn't come out." Krauss noticed "twenty parked buses" showing "that the Sandinistas had brought people in from around the countryside." The President "didn't make any promises about improving the country's social and economic problems." Instead Ortega concentrated on linking UNO with Washington:

> The Yankees invented the National Guard and the Nicaraguan people destroyed them, and now the Yankees invented UNO—and the Nicaraguan people will destroy them too.

Observing that his "message was mixed with a threat," Krauss quotes the next portion of Ortega's remarks:

> Don't mix yourself up with the UNO, or you'll fall. Defend Nicaragua against the Yankees! Remember, on one side is Bush and on the other is Daniel. A vote for UNO is a vote for Bush and a treason committed against Nicaragua.

The official slogan of the Ortega campaign was "Everything Will Be Better" [*Todo Sera Mejor*], but the subtext was "everything will stay the same." The audience did not need to be reminded how "traitors " were treated in Nicaragua.

This was the darker side of Ortega's "authentic expression of Nicaraguan nationalism," designed less to inspire patriotism in his supporters than to instill fear in prospective opponents. Mrs. Chamorro believed that the main burden of the Ortega campaign was to intimidate:

> To frighten the people, President Daniel Ortega has called us "traitors" and "mercenaries" and "CIA agents," and has declared that a vote for us is "a vote for the enemy of the people." Pronouncing the Sandinistas "sure winners," he has emphasized that people would "not be so foolish as to vote for a loser"—darkly intimating that after a Sandinista victory opposition voters will be treated as traitors. Our jails are filled already with "enemies of the people."[17]

Not surprisingly, the secrecy of the ballot was the burden of the Chamorro rally which Krauss attended:

> As Chamorro spoke in the city of Camoapa, in the middle of the pro-*Contra* province of Chontales, a Sandinista army helicopter flew around the rally threateningly. The crowd of 8,000 shook Nicaraguan flags at the helicopter and chanted. . . . Chamorro had quickly understood that the helicopter buzzing was an attempt at intimidation. "Don't forget," she screamed. "The ballot will be secret ."[18]

Indeed, according to the Chamorro campaign spokesperson: "The main task of the campaign was to give the people confidence that their vote was secret."[19]

On October 27 President Ortega announced his intention to renounce a nineteen-month-old cease-fire agreement with the *Contras* and resume offensive military actions. The *New York Times* reported that the Nicaraguan armed forces "had already begun what appeared to be a coordinated offensive against the *Contras*."[20] "Increased military activity by the *Contras*, aimed at subverting the electoral process" was President Ortega's reason for ending the cease-fire.[21] But Ortega's claim that *Contra* attacks were "endangering the electoral process" did not convince many observers, even those not unsympathetic to the Sandinista perspective. A *Christian Science Monitor* report datelined Mexico City noted:

> Even some Latin observers are beginning to say that Ortega, the presidential candidate, is playing electoral politics. The Sandinistas, faltering slightly in the latest opinion polls, would not be hurt by a militarized election—nor by a campaign that focuses more on security issues than on the devastated economy.[22]

During the month of October 1.74 million Nicaraguans had registered to vote, close to 95 percent of those eligible. Throughout the cease-fire period there had been skirmishes between Sandinista and *Contra* units, but U.S. military aid to the rebels had been canceled twenty months earlier. The *Contras* posed no threat to a Sandinista army which continued to be well equipped by the Soviet bloc and Cuba.[23] Nearly out of ammunition, the rebels were subsisting on no-lethal "humanitarian aid," which carried a Congressionally imposed ban against offensive action. A few thousand *Contras* had indeed reinfiltrated, not to fight but to campaign. From Matagalpa the *Post*'s bureau chief Lee Hockstader reported:

> The *contras* have infiltrated into Nicaragua from their base camps in Honduras at a rate of about 200 a week since late August. In this area, they have been campaigning actively for UNO, encouraging people to register to vote and generally singing the praises of opposition presidential candidate Violeta Chamorro.[24]

The *New York Times* editorial page, no friend to the *Contras*, commented: "It is not a waning insurgency that appears to be Mr. Ortega's real target but a swelling United Opposition Union [*sic*]."[25]

* * *

In late October Sandinista authorities stepped up their harassment of UNO candidates, activists, and supporters, sometimes beating or detaining them. As in 1984, "*turba*" mobs attacked opposition rallies in rural areas—as at the towns of Matagalpa, Muelle de Los Bueyes, and Pantasma.[26] In the only mention of such activities on American television, NBC's Ed Rabel reported in late October

> it seems to be open season on Ortega's political opposition, which has been gaining ground in the campaign. Sandinista supporters confronted opponents at a rally yesterday in Jalapa, the most serious incident in the campaign.[27]

In December "a bipartisan group of American observers" happened to witness one of the acts of the "divine mob" at an UNO rally in Masatepe. The observers told *New York Times* bureau chief Mark Uhlig that a confrontation "was deliberately provoked by Sandinista mobs" wielding machetes, stones, and other weapons. Among the observers was a well-known and influential veteran Democratic Party activist, Bob Beckel, who had managed Walter Mondale's 1984 presidential campaign. Beckel, who had "stood just a few feet away as a Sandinista youth slashed an opposition demonstrator from throat to waist with a machete," told the *Times* "what we saw was an outrage. . . . There was no doubt among any of us at the scene that the violence was instigated by the Sandinistas."[28] After this notoriety, wholesale attacks on UNO rallies suddenly ceased, suggesting that such incidents were hardly as spontaneous as the Sandinistas claimed.

UNO officials and many Nicaraguans resented the foreign media for providing the Sandinistas a "free ride" by "minimizing the repression."[29] But certainly Masatepe could be cited as a major charge against the Sandinista account. The UNO campaign spokesperson held that by provoking the incident at Masatepe the Sandinistas were "testing whether the international community would react to repression" of the opposition.[30] That reaction proved "pivotal":

> The upshot of Masatepe was that Sandinista repression became less overt, more sophisticated and selective. Now violence had to be employed more judiciously. But, of course, they still were able to detain our funds and equipment, or cut off our electricity.[31]

After Masatepe the Sandinistas generally resorted to more veiled forms of intimidation and harassment. By early January, according to a report commissioned by the National Democratic Institute of the U.S. Democratic Party, numerous UNO poll watchers had resigned due to "pressures put on them by anonymous elements presumably pro-Sandinista" as well as more overt "pressure from the military."[32] Later that month observer missions from the OAS and the United Nations reported resignations of as many as 350 local and national opposition candidates.[33] The nongovernmental Nicaraguan Permanent Commission on Human Rights reported at least seven opposition officials and candidates assassinated, twelve "disappeared," twenty arrested, and thirty assaulted. Scores had their property confiscated or their homes or campaign locales sacked.[34] A group of former heads of state led by former President Jimmy Carter lodged an official complaint. Though the matter was not taken up in other media, the *Atlanta Journal and Constitution* carried Carter's warning that if the "margin of victory" were small and many UNO poll watchers absent out of fear, "I would declare that the results of the election were not certifiable."[35]

Military conscription had been suspended officially in September after protests that it was targeting UNO activists. The *Los Angeles Times* reported in December the government

> kept its word in the cities and towns while continuing to draft young men in remote rural areas. Opposition leaders also complain that men aged 25 to 39 are still being called for reserve duty.[36]

Then, on December 22, President Ortega declared a "State of Maximum Alert" in response to the U.S. intervention in Panama. His brother, Defense Minister General Humberto Ortega, ordered the mobilization and deployment throughout the country of troops and tanks. A communiqué followed calling up reserves and militias and instructing "all permanent and reserve military units, Sandinista militia and military counterintelligence agencies, in close cooperation with state security agencies" to prepare for a "Yankee intervention." At such time the units were to carry out plans for neutralization, isolation and execution of all the most recalcitrant traitorous ['vendepatria"] elements who have both overtly or covertly encouraged Yankee intervention.[37]

These were the terms regularly employed to describe UNO. The following day Chamorro reported that she and other UNO members received numerous telephonic death threats by callers citing General Ortega's order.[38]

Again, if in the capital the authorities threatened, in the provinces, where press and official observation was sparse, the army was more emphatic. In late January the regional observer mission of the OAS in Matagalpa reported that a Sandinista military convoy had attacked four truckloads of UNO sympathizers returning from a rally. The soldiers beat the demonstrators with rifle butts and stones, injuring women and children.[39] In provincial areas such as Matagalpa Sandinista state security and military forces continued to make their presence felt right through election day when Carter group observer Governor Babbitt was "met by two unlikely 'get out the vote' workers" at the Sandinista election headquarters: "a uniformed *comandante* of the security policy and an armed Sandinista colonel."[40]

Where international supervision was more constant, the Sandinistas were more discreet. In the public arena they counted more on residual fear, braced from time to time by thinly veiled threats or organized rumors. Government press and ubiquitous wall posters declared GN–UNO, asserting an equivalence between the civic opposition and Somoza's National Guard (Guardia Nacional or GN). "GN" was also another Sandinista term for the "*Contra*."

At an Ortega rally in Matagalpa the candidate indicated how UNO voters might expect to be treated:

> The GN-UNO are traitors. The people of Matagalpa are patriots. The GN-UNO are Somocistas! The people of Matagalpa are Sandinistas. What for the GN-UNO? [Crowd answers: "Death"][41]

Sandinista victory was assured: "Who doubts that the Matagalpan people have already voted? . . . All of us here already know who Nicaragua's president-elect is."[42] *Le Monde* found that "national radio, which is totally committed to the Sandinistas . . . proclaims unceasingly . . . 'we've already won' and 'the vote is only a formality.'" In the opposition's view the purpose of such declarations, reported *Le Monde*, was to discourage as useless the risky proposition of a UNO vote.[43] And for those unwise enough to ignore the warning, Ortega warned at Matagalpa that after the election,

> we will send you the full bill. . . . Let them go without a newspaper, that will be paid in full. Let them go without a press, that will be paid in full. We will turn the lady's home [Chamorro] into a CDS.
>
> We have already won the elections . . . shouts, groans and cries will come later.[44]

Ortega's threats and others like them were backed up by what the *Washington Post*, in an uncharacteristic passage, called the Sandinista "lock on the levers of government."[45] The *Post* was presumably referring to the Sandinista control not only of the military, police, and security apparatus but also "mass organizations," neighborhood block committees, the judiciary and educational systems, and the electoral apparatus itself.[46] This monopoly of power allowed the FSLN "to harass the opposition in unusual ways."

> An example came during UNO's campaign finale last Sunday, a rally in downtown Managua. The Sandinistas suspended public transit in and around the city, shut down two opposition radio stations, blocked a sound system from entering the country, changed train schedules and put "Batman" and the Mike Tyson-James 'Buster' Douglas fight on television.[47]

All this resourcefulness fell short of its objective. The *Post* described the UNO windup as "the most dramatic public display of civic opposition" to the Sandinista regime. UNO's largest crowd "flooded a downtown plaza today to cheer Violeta Chamorro." Moreover, according to the *Boston Globe* the candidate

> accused the Sandinistas of preventing truck loads of supporters from reaching the plaza on time. Enraged supporters then accosted Sandinista police officers at the gathering.[48]

In *La Prensa*'s account the climax of the rally came when a young UNO supporter, Fernando Moya Jiménez, to the wild cheering of the crowd, scaled the National Cathedral and planted the UNO banner.[49] That night the teenager "went out and did not return," his mother told the *Post:*

> About 5 a.m. Monday, three policeman came to the house asking for Jiménez, his mother said. A little while later, she said, they told her her son was dead.

The Sandinista police captain stated that the boy was killed when he became "aggressive" in a police station and "tried to flee."[50] For his public audacity, revenge was exacted privately, but in such a way that the lesson could not be lost on the public. Headlines in Managua, the standard-bearer was buried in the back pages of the *Post*.

After the election American pollsters and journalists alike recognized that fear had played a central role in the campaign, distorting poll results and expectations.[51] That recognition, as the *Post*'s Branigin wrote, "shattered another myth: that the Sandinistas were not associated with widespread repression."[52] But before the elections that myth was sustained by reporters and election observers. For example, two days before the close of the opposition campaign Branigin's newspaper headlined a Hockstader report from Managua: "Nicaraguan

Campaign Seen As Relatively Free and Open: Observers Find Most Threats, Violence to Be Minor." The report featured statements to that effect by chief United Nations observer Elliott Richardson and by the Sandinista-appointed Nicaraguan election administrator:

> "Go around and see if you see any sign of widespread fear," said Mariano Fiallos, chairman of the government's Supreme Electoral Council, which oversees the election. "You see demonstrations, people putting flags everywhere, painting the walls. You don't see signs of electoral fear in Nicaragua."[53]

Hockstader asserted that "the vast majority of UNO workers have campaigned without interference," though he did not indicate how many of those workers he had interviewed. The piece did acknowledge that "a substantial number of instances of intimidation . . . have been reported," yet Hockstader concluded

> there is little evidence that they have affected the campaign. In many cases, the incidents appear only to have stiffened the opposition's resolve.[54]

The number of resignations of opposition candidates and poll watchers would not seem to bear out this conclusion. Hockstader's response to the paradoxes of this hybrid campaign was to assert that there was little repression but that what there was made the race not less but more competitive! In fact the opposition's confidence indeed was rising with each passing day—though one would not have learned this from the *Post* reporting, and the source of UNO's "stiffened resolve" was neither Sandinista repression nor its supposed absence.

The UNO "Surge"

"On three successive weekends, UNO rallies came alive with an enthusiasm that opposition leaders are at a loss to explain," the *New York Times* reported two weeks before the election on February 9.[55] UNO leaders had their explanations; it was the press that was caught off guard. That brief retrospective note, three weeks after the shift of tide or "*repunte*," was as much as American readers and viewers would learn of the decisive chapter in the campaign.

Until the third weekend in January the UNO campaign was in the doldrums. Though at the outset UNO had attracted growing crowds and enthusiasm, its momentum was slowed by the militarization of the campaign—the Sandinista termination of the cease-fire with the *Contras*, the "*turba*" attacks on opposition rallies, Defense Minister Ortega's threats following the invasion of Panama—and then paralyzed when first U.S., and then Sandinista, red tape held up delivery of campaign funds and equipment. As if these obstacles were not enough, at the end of the Christmas holiday, Chamorro, who suffered from osteoporosis, shattered her kneecap. On January 2 she flew to Houston for medical treatment, leaving her poorly organized campaign in disarray.[56]

Her return to the campaign was scheduled for Saturday, January 20, in Granada, her husband's birthplace and the Conservatives' historic citadel. During the week preceding the rally, the government media and the Sandinista press featured stories on the resignations of local UNO candidates and acknowledgments of defeat imputed to local UNO leaders as well as rumors that UNO was planning to withdraw just as the opposition was alleged to have done in 1984.[57]

The government went to remarkable lengths to discourage attendance at a rally that, by its own account, should hardly have attracted a pigeon. According to *La Prensa*, Sandinista police dispensed tear gas and overhead warning shots at a small crowd which had begun to form hours before the scheduled start of the event. *La Prensa* characterized those actions as "a mini-reprise of Nandaime 1988."[58] The nongovernment human rights officials and UNO campaigners claimed that several local organizers were jailed in the days before the rally, but freed when international observers arrived in Granada for the rally.[59] That same day local bus drivers were called to an "urgent" compulsory, and as it turned out, protracted assembly. Deprived of public transportation, as was generally the case for UNO rallies, most demonstrators, as in other opposition rallies, came on foot or horseback, in sharp contrast to the government-transported crowds at Sandinista rallies.

The Sandinistas sought ingeniously to distract as well as deter. Sports authorities rescheduled the country's big baseball game from Rivas to Granada, and added the unprecedented enticement of free tickets and refreshments to the "home field advantage." If baseball is America's national pastime, it is Nicaragua's national passion. But for those indifferent to the sport, the authorities reopened a major tourist park, offering free admission and food and beer at a bargain price. A capacity crowd entered the stadium, but Sandinista maneuvering had only succeeded, so to speak, in loading the bases for Mrs. Chamorro. As her cavalcade proceeded from the outskirts to the town's cathedral, it passed by the stadium, whence the spectators promptly poured out of the stands to join it. When the throng arrived at the amusement park, the visitors, tossing back their complimentary refreshments, fell in too.[60]

A high point of the rally was Chamorro's descent in her wheelchair from the back of a pick-up truck over three large planks which formed a path to the podium. Via a makeshift sound-system, powered by a sputtering gasoline-fueled generator, she launched into her new stump speech: her crutches symbolized not the UNO campaign, as asserted by the Sandinistas media and echoed in U.S. reports, but Nicaragua itself—"broken and limping under the Sandinistas." She recalled that Granada had led the national resistance to the American filibusterer William Walker:

> and that heroic spirit still lives. In all our struggles for liberty, Granada has always taken the lead. Now the struggle is civic. Now the secret ballot is the arm of the liberator.

Patriotic Nicaraguans should vote to "end an international dictatorship and begin a truly national republic, one not managed by Cubans or Russians." She received a booming ovation when she called for an end to the draft. And when she urged the crowd to vote without fear, it answered: "We're not afraid."[61]

Earlier that day Chamorro was greeted by similarly doughty crowds in two other southwestern towns. The following day she traveled to the northwest where she spoke in Ocotal in Nueva Segovia and Somoto in Madriz, departments where the *Contra* war had raged. At Ocotal an official from the American embassy reported:

> A crowd of 2 to 3,000 people, mostly poor campesinos in bare feet and rags, walked three kilometers alongside the UNO candidates.
> Of note was the obvious poverty of the vast majority of rally attendees—a marked contrast to FSLN crowds. One man in a tattered cap, torn shirt, ragged pants but sturdy boots told us that he had ridden and walked for three days . . . to get to the rally. When asked why, he went into a lengthy description of Sandinista abuses. Two of his sons were forcibly conscripted into military service. His third son is in hiding to avoid it. He recounted how one man from his town was hauled off in handcuffs for trying to get out of service.[62]

In her stump speech Chamorro urged her supporters not to let anyone seize their voter registration card "nor to let yourselves be intimidated."[63]

The following Saturday, January 27, thousands turned out for a large Chamorro rally in Estelí, considered the Sandinistas' principal provincial stronghold. On Sunday Chamorro spoke at spirited rallies in the villages south of Managua. The following Saturday, February 3, *La Prensa* reported from Chontales, a central region which had been the scene of some of the fiercest fighting in the war: "Thousands of peasants who, on foot or horseback, left their own districts to come to St. Domingo and Los Chinamos," had then waited through "an unrelenting rain" to greet the UNO caravan.[64] That Saturday Chamorro spoke at a large rally in her native city of Rivas in the southwest. The next day trucks brought crowds of peasants from the surrounding countryside to Chinandega, along with workers from the port of Corinto and the adjacent sugar mills. The crowd, which waited several hours to greet her, filled the town square and the surrounding streets, where residents opened their doors and offered water to UNO supporters. Later in León, another reputed Sandinista stronghold, a crowd of several thousand gathered to cheer the candidate as she passed through the city.[65]

The campaign visited virtually every major town and department, and the crowd numbers continued to mount with each succeeding weekend until the campaign closed in Managua on Sunday, February 18.[66] Major UNO events nearly always were held on weekends, as was customary given the long work days and weeks. As noted by *Le Monde*, but not by American news organizations, that was another contrast with Ortega rallies:

"The Front does not hold its biggest rallies on weekends" [a government employee told the paper]."They have them on working days, because they have to round people up from their workplaces."[67]

Ernesto Palazio who functioned as the campaign's press spokesperson and later became the Chamorro government's first ambassador to the United States, testified to the growth of the UNO crowd. When the campaign began in the fall "Violeta, the driver, Pedro Joaquín [son], Antonio [Lacayo, son-in-law and campaign manager], and I would visit small towns to try out her speech." Those meetings would usually be held *inside* houses.

> The crowd would only be large enough to fill a single room. But . . . at Chichigalpa [near Chinandega and a large sugar refinery] suddenly there was a large crowd. People climbed trees to hear us. That was when we began to gain 'momentum'.

The "momentum" was lost with the militarization of the campaign, the detention of funds and equipment, and Mrs. Chamorro's injury. But after the candidate returned to the hustings, Palazio and his associates were back on the campaign trail with a "motorcade" of five cars. Palazio developed a fluid standard for measuring the growth of the UNO crowd. When they reached the outskirts of a scheduled campaign stop, the "motorcade" would pause to allow the passengers to relieve themselves "because otherwise the next four hours would be impossible."

> Violeta would go behind a bush. . . . But at each succeeding rally we'd have to stop farther from the town. We'd see up ahead crowds of campesinos walking to the rally. . . . Each time we'd run into the crowd farther from the town.

What impressed Palazio most "was the courage of those who lived in those towns. I would say to myself: 'we'll be going home to Managua, but these people have to survive here after we're gone.'"[68]

UNO campaign officials considered the sequence of rallies and marches that began in Granada to have marked the "*repunte*" (turning point) of the campaign. Opposition organizers stated that when they saw the "chain reaction after Granada" they became confident of victory and that their main task, "overcoming fear," had been accomplished.[69] The UNO strategy of simply getting the candidate "to as many towns as possible" was working.

American Press Coverage of the UNO "Surge"

In September 1978 a string of spontaneous urban insurrections which spread from Matagalpa and Masaya to Chinandega, León, Carazo, and Estelí signaled the beginning of the end of the Somoza regime.[70] The "chain reaction" after

Granada, involving many of the same cities as 1978, bore a similar relation to the electoral revolution of 1990, a *repunte*. While the earlier turning point received prolific coverage, the latter went virtually unreported. This disparity is especially remarkable when one takes into account the large contingent of American journalists on hand for the 1990 elections. By contrast, in the summer of 1978 Nicaragua had only begun to attract the attention of the American media. Moreover, the chaotic, undirected urban uprisings presented serious perils for those covering them, especially since Somoza responded with heavy artillery and bombing raids. Nonetheless, television and print carried detailed descriptions of the urban uprisings, featuring lengthy interviews with teenage rebels and their parents.[71] The hazardous events of 1978 were covered far more fully than the nonviolent opposition rallies of 1990.

Television's notorious predilection for violence does not explain the discrepancy. The 1990 election campaign received ample coverage, but the decisive UNO rallies did not. And in September 1978 there had been were plenty of stories without scenes of violence, such as those focusing on the Somoza regime and its relations with the United States.[72] Moreover, television's penchant for violence cannot explain the same discrepancy in the print coverage.

Historians will have no press reports to study, no "first, rough draft of history" when they treat the turning point in the campaign, and in Nicaraguan history.[73] U.S. reporting on the opposition rallies, despite the extensive coverage of the elections, was negligible. What attracted press attention was not the Chamorro tour of Nicaragua but Daniel Ortega's new "rock star" image. There was no television reporting of the Chamorro *repunte* and next to nothing in the print media. Neither the *New York Times* nor the *Washington Post* filed reports from these rallies, though both mentioned them in later pieces.

For the most part the U.S. press registered the opposition "surge" only in retrospect, and sometimes only to discount it, as when Juan Walte reported from Managua two days before the election in *USA Today* that:

Many here believe Ortega will win Sunday's voting, despite an apparent surge by Chamorro. The most recent poll, an ABC/*Washington Post* survey, puts the incumbent ahead, 48 percent to 32 percent.[74]

Also retrospectively Uhlig reported that:

In recent weeks the opposition has seemed to surge, drawing large and often euphoric crowds in provincial towns.[75]

Two days earlier, as we have seen, he had written that "opposition leaders are at a loss to explain" the UNO surge.[76] But the press itself, skeptical of opposition explanations, appears to have been even less capable of accounting for the phenomenon.[77]

Another retrospective piece by Richard Boudreaux of the *Los Angeles Times* did succeed in capturing the elán of a Chamorro campaign that had been "propelled forward, in spite of itself, on a tide of popular enthusiasm." The recap of the UNO campaign was filed after its final rally in Managua:

> since her comeback in the wheel chair on January 20, [Chamorro] has drawn thousands of people on foot, bicycle and horseback to see her all over the country. Although her rallies are fewer, the turnouts rival those of Ortega, whose party delivers many of its crowds in state-owned trucks.

At an earlier Chamorro rally in Masaya:

> For three hours, they had converged on the tiny plaza, thousands of Nicaraguans eager for a glimpse of the gray-haired widow.

Boudreaux added that "the large turnout at such [Chamorro] rallies belies most of the polls." But the reporter seems to attribute much of the UNO dynamism to Chamorro's personal popularity, even as he continued to emphasize her "regal bearing."[78] In a similar retrospective piece the *Boston Globe*'s Philip Bennett reported after UNO's closing rally that "the opposition has gained momentum in recent weeks."[79] That same day a *Washington Post* report observed that:

> In recent weeks the opposition has seemed to surge, drawing large and often euphoric crowds in provincial towns.[80]

But on-the-spot reportage in the *Post* from Chamorro rallies was confined, paradoxically, to an "op-ed"—by a pair of conservative columnists.[81]

A rare direct report from an earlier UNO rally was filed by Boudreaux from San Rafael del Sur, where Chamorro spoke immediately before the Granada rally. On Monday, January 22, he reported in the *Los Angeles Times* that Chamorro's

> comeback from surgery, welcomed by enthusiastic crowds in three towns Saturday, and two on Sunday, is being overshadowed by delays in the delivery of U.S. aid.[82]

Despite the hopes of the Bush administration, Boudreaux added, "her campaign has yet to take off." Like so many of the election reports, this one was directed at Washington. The article pointedly concluded with a Nicaraguan intellectual's complaint: "The paradox of your [American] system is that you could give money to fight the *Contra* war but not to fight an election the way it ought to be fought." Similarly, three days later the *Post* correspondent, even as he acknowledged "wildly enthusiastic crowds in the city of Granada and two smaller towns," described the UNO campaign as "lacking momentum, tangled in red tape, beset by squabbles, and paid for by Washington."[83] That same day the *San Francisco Chronicle* reported "the U.S.-backed Chamorro candidacy has recently slumped badly."[84] Two days later NBC's Rabel predicted that "Daniel

Ortega will win the presidency by a wide margin," mainly because of opposition to the invasion of Panama.[85] These reports seemed to be inspired more by partial polling data and a desire to embarrass Washington than by directly sampling popular sentiments.

As Chamorro's crowds grew larger and braver, a headline in the January 28 *Miami Herald* declared "Chamorro campaign faltering." Correspondent Christopher Marquis found that "in contrast to Ortega, who seems to be everywhere, [Chamorro] appears only on weekends and leaves few traces."[86] On January 29, after UNO enjoyed its second weekend of encouraging rallies, the *Dallas Morning News* asserted:

> A glum defensiveness permeates the atmosphere within . . . UNO. "Day by day they (UNO) becomes weaker," said Mauricio Diaz, head of the anti-Sandinista Popular Social Christian Party.[87]

Mauricio Diaz was a frequent source for American journalists. Though known to make anti-Sandinista statements, he was also anti-UNO and widely suspected of cooperating with the government.[88]

On January 30 the *Christian Science Monitor* reported that UNO "appears to be losing momentum." The evidence:

> Sandinista propaganda seems to be everywhere in the capital . . . UNO propaganda . . . is barely visible. . . . Its candidates . . . make fewer appearances than their opponents, and supporters at rallies, while enthusiastic are far fewer.[89]

If in Vietnam the American press was preoccupied with "body-counts," here the numerology tracked candidate appearances, rallies, posters, and polling data. All of these stories featured a survey conducted in mid-January by the Greenberg-Lake organization which found Ortega leading by a margin of better than two-to-one.[90] The safest, easiest but most cursory manner of covering this election was simply to tally such data, as superficial and illusory as they may have been. Since these methods produced no results which conflicted with the journalists' own preconceptions, they activated no alarms. There was something indolent and remote about much of the American election reporting.

American reporters did attend Chamorro rallies.[91] However, direct reporting on them was rare. Fleeting images of Violeta Chamorro in a white dress appeared in televised reports. Uhlig once quoted a paragraph from Chamorro's speech at Granada in a *New York Times Magazine* feature.[92] Like the *New York Times*, the *Washington Post* mentioned the rallies only weeks later and carried nothing from Chamorro rallies, notwithstanding the paper's extensive election coverage and a lengthy profile of the candidate in the Style section which focused on her "aristocratic" breeding. Boudreaux of the *Los Angeles Times* filed a dispatch from the Chamorro rally at San Rafael del Sur. But, unlike his retrospective piece at the end of the campaign, the article gave no clues as to the mood or makeup of the crowds or the motives that brought them to the rallies.

At the time Boudreaux found the Chamorro crowds "similar to those drawn by
the president." The only "difference is that Ortega is campaigning more often
and spending more money."[93]

The *Le Monde* correspondent, who depicted the UNO rallies in greater detail than his American counterparts, reported other differences. At the Sandinista
rallies there was "a great apathy except among young militants"; at the opposition rallies "one notes, on the contrary, a great deal of emotion, especially an-
ger." Those attending

> inveigh against repression, military service and the generalized Sandinista ar-
> gument which accuses the United States of originating the economic crisis pro-
> voked by the activities of the *Contra* guerrillas.
>
> Occasionally UNO partisans take out after the foreign press—"Tell the
> truth"—whom they reproach as having taken the side of the Sandinista gov-
> ernment. . . . They have no more confidence in the international observers . . .
> who "minimize the repression." . . . One senses that many opponents of the re-
> gime no longer have anything to lose and now want to confront the Sandinistas.
> "If the government does not recognize our victory," affirms an accountant,
> "we'll take up arms, and unlike Panama, we won't need a U.S. intervention be-
> cause we are used to guerrilla war." The people around him applaud and sev-
> eral interrupt. The women are the most militant and the most violent, adding
> that it is necessary to overthrow the Sandinistas just like the Somoza dictator-
> ship.[94]

The militance of women against the Sandinista government, a theme likely to
have been struck in another context, received no attention from the American
media.

The Campaign Crowds

Crowds for the UNO rallies "would appear suddenly," wrote Pablo Antonio
Cuadra, who often traveled with the campaign, "like swarms of ants that draw
strength from their numbers." Modest groupings of demonstrators could be dispersed by the police, as at midday in Granada, but the larger the crowd the
greater the safety, perhaps in no small part because large crowds attracted international observers. But the primary protection was in the numbers themselves,
even if the safety was contingent and temporary.

In different ways fear conditioned the varying crowds that the election campaign brought out in Nicaragua, and the crowds themselves neutralized the fear,
also in different ways. The Ortega crowds were, for the most part, mandatory.
There would be repercussions if a state employee did not attend, if a worker or
peasant did not board the bus leaving from factory, cooperative, and barrio.
Safety lay in joining and melting into the crowd. The crowds traditionally
bussed and trucked in by authoritarian Latin American governments for rallies

and "elections" are sometimes called "*acarreados*" (portable). Young demonstrators at the Ortega rallies sometimes could appear euphoric, much like those who file past Fidel Castro in Havana on May Day or on the 26th of July to celebrate the Revolution.[95] But election day would dramatically reveal that the merriment was illusory and forced.

Precisely the opposite was the case of the UNO crowds described by Cuadra, Krauss, and the *Le Monde* correspondent. In joining them lay danger, yet also a kind of safety. The UNO rallies acted as a catalyst. The presence of a few encouraged the presence of more. When the *Granadino* saw his neighbor or the baseball fan sitting next to him join in, he felt prodded to do likewise. By the same token, word of Granada and Ocotal emboldened Estelí the next week, which encouraged Chinandega, and then León, and so on until the finale in Managua.

Nothing quite like the UNO crowd can be found in the typology of Elias Canetti's magisterial anthropological study *Crowds and Power*. The crowd brought forth by the UNO campaign is most like Canetti's "reversal crowd" which "comes into existence for the joint liberation of a large number of people from the stings of command they cannot hope to get rid of alone."[96] A reversal crowd is composed of those who have been "subject for a long time to the commands of the other group."[97] As isolated individuals their only recourse was to dissipate "the sting" by passing it down the chain of command, down what Giovanni Sartori calls "the arch of fear."[98] But "people who are habitually ordered about" absorb the stings of perpetual command. They would dearly love to "extract" those stings by avenging their sufferings on their superiors. "One man alone, weak, and helpless" gets an opportunity to do so only on the rarest occasions. On the other hand, "if many men find themselves together in a crowd, they may jointly succeed in what was denied them singly."[99]

As an example of the "reversal crowd" Canetti offers the throng which stormed the Bastille—a crowd which rages and razes, rises "against the king's justice" and metes out its own justice.[100] The UNO crowds appear to have possessed such an ire. "What impressed [Clifford Krauss] most about the incident" at Masatepe

> was the anger of the crowd. Young boys broke stones and handed them to older boys who threw them at Sandinista supporters to protect Chamorro's rally. There was pure hatred in their young faces. As they left the rally, they descended on a local Sandinista party headquarters, looted it, and burned it to the ground. I came away feeling Nicaragua was in another pre-insurrectionary moment similar to 1977 or 1978.[101]

In another sense the UNO crowd differed from the Bastille crowd, which Canetti describes as an "open" crowd: "there are no limits whatever to its growth; it does not recognize houses, doors, or locks, and those who shut themselves in are suspect."[102] Except at Masatepe UNO crowds were contained, did not and could not, storm and raze. Confined within the closed framework of Sandinista power and the electoral campaign, the UNO crowd was the descendant of those that welcomed Cardinal Obando y Bravo in June 1985 and that filled the churches and squares at his open-air masses in the following months. The opposition crowd was an expression of the ambivalent conditions that nurtured it: the closed nature of Sandinista power combined with the demands for space that surrounded it. Spontaneous and angry like Canetti's reversal crowd, but schooled over the years to curb its rage and to limit itself to certain spaces. The special circumstances of the elections—the pent-up hostility, the opportunity offered by the international observation, the wariness still mandated by Sandinista domination—shaped an historically unique crowd. That crowd was not "contagious and insatiable" like fire, one of Canetti's crowd metaphors; but like gas—or air—expanded to the boundaries of its receptacles.[103] It gave rise to that most special and splendid of the Nicaraguan crowds, the silent, national congregation that formed in rathe, orderly, interminable lines at the polls on election day.

The Election Day Crowd

Senator Larry Pressler, a Republican member of the Carter delegation, was "not prepared" to find at a small village polling place "150 people . . . lined up to vote in the early morning hours. Some had arrived at 3 a.m." What Presser saw was typical. "All across Nicaragua," CBS reported, "the voters were so eager they stood in line for hours before the polls opened."[104] The *Washington Post* reported that "long lines of people, many dressed in their Sunday best, formed at polling places starting before dawn Sunday for the 7 a.m. opening of the polls."[105] Throughout the day CNN showed "deep, long lines."[106] NBC's Rabel described voters "jammed into long lines, struggling to get to the ballot box . . . some of them had waited in line since midnight. . . . In rural Nicaragua entire towns lined up to vote."[107] Senator Pressler's "amazement turns to astonishment" as the day proceeds. In the mountains

> another incredible sight greets us. In the midst of a pasture at an old school house stand some 200 voters moving slowly through a line. All have arrived on foot or on horseback. Horses are tied to fence posts. Some people have walked several miles to vote. Mothers carry their babies. Some have brought food, anticipating an all-day wait.[108]

At Zapote, Matagalpa, Governor Babbitt found a similar scene:

> There is not a single motor vehicle in sight, and just a handful of scrawny horses. . . . Most of these voters have walked in from the hills. Some arrived at 3 a.m. Others began walking last evening, slept by the roadside, and resumed their pilgrimage at daylight.[109]

Members of the observer mission from the Puebla Institute were likewise "struck by the long distance many voters had to travel in the countryside" generally without benefit of public transportation. One voter the delegation interviewed "was afraid to register and vote in his hometown" because his brother had been imprisoned by Sandinista authorities. He had walked three days to a distant village in order to cast his ballot. Returning to Managua at nightfall the group saw voters on their return journey,

> scores of people with candles sitting in the open by the roadside, preparing to rest until morning. Other observers reported they saw men *en route* sleeping out in the open by the roadside the night before the election.[110]

After long predawn waits outside urban polling booths, impatient young voters "burst inside like race horses at the starting bell."[111] The contrast with the 1984 "first free elections in Nicaraguan history" could hardly have been sharper. In November 1984 "the Nicaraguan election mood was one of indifference." *Time* found the low turnout in 1984

> a surprise since the government had made it clear that it considered failure to vote a counterrevolutionary stance. In the days prior to the election, members of Nicaragua's neighborhood Sandinista Defense Committees carried that message door to door.[112]

The voters' earnestness and alacrity in 1990, their extraordinary exertions to get to the voting places, in contrast to their reluctance or apathy in 1984, constituted a verdict on the 1984 elections from an incomparable source.[113]

If people were eager to cast their ballots in 1990, and willing to exert themselves to do so, their mood could hardly have been called upbeat. Contrary to the holiday mood that often prevails on election day in Latin America, there was no merriment. Voters encountered by an American labor union delegation "weren't 'festive';" and refused "to give us any clues about their intentions."[114] Similarly those interviewed by the Puebla Institute delegation "would not tell us whom they had voted for."[115] In Matagalpa several are happy to chat with Governor Babbitt about other matters, "but no one wants to talk about the candidates or speculate about the outcome of the election, much less disclose how they are going to vote."[116] In Juigalpa "the entire town arose well before sunrise today to ask for divine guidance before casting [their] vote."[117] In Somotillo *Newsweek*'s Charles Lane described "the dignified hush" in the schoolhouse where peasants waited to vote on the "creaky porch."[118] In similar terms, foreign observers and Nicaraguans described the reverent mood of the crowd, "as if on a pilgrimage."[119] Election day, in the words of former president Jimmy Carter, was "solemn like a mass."[120]

The act of voting on February 25, 1990, was ceremonious and participatory and yet intimate and confidential. The dichotomies individual/collective and private/public usually go together. That they did not do so in the Nicaraguan election campaign may help to explain why the American canvassers and press failed to fathom what was happening. On election day Nicaraguans behaved in an almost uniform manner—"All across Nicaragua the voters were so eager they stood in line for hours before the polls opened." In a sense the vote was collective, a crowd act. But it was also scrupulously private: voters refused to "give us any clues about their intentions." In the end the collective will, much invoked by the authorities, could be expressed solely in private acts. On the other hand Nicaraguans seemed to regard responding to opinion surveys as a public, not a private act. Lastly, the UNO rallies were public and collective, offering a measure of safety in numbers. Those numbers strengthened the collective will for a private vote.

In theory, and in the general practice of liberal democratic regimes, the voters' deliberative process is both individual and private. The voter weighs the merits of the candidates. His response to a poll is uncoerced. He or she is willing to disclose his preference to an outsider. The pollster elicits an individual and public expression. Even in democracies the society at large, the "climate of opinion," influences the individual voters. Studies of "the bandwagon effect" reveal that undecided voters tend to support the candidate that they perceive to be winning as election day approaches.[121] The German sociologist and polling analyst Elisabeth Noelle-Neumann has shown that voters backing the eventual winner are more outspoken: "those confident of winning speak up, while the losers tend toward silence."[122] In Nicaragua, however, it was the winners who "tended toward silence." And the "late surge" was not, as the term usually suggests, the result of undecided voters shifting to the eventual winner, but rather of the committed determining that it was safe and meaningful to vote their preferences—"your vote will be secret."[123]

The decisive "deliberation" in Nicaragua concerned not the merits of the candidates but the propriety of expressing one's will. In that sense, deliberation itself was collective, a crowd act as well as a private one. The collective formation of the UNO crowd "empowered" the private will.

The most widely publicized public opinion surveys did not support the idea that Chamorro was the likely winner. The growing UNO crowds surely helped to produce an opposition vote. But the Ortega crowds were even bigger. Crucial was the assurance that the vote would be secret. When observers from the United Nations and the OAS affixed posters adjacent to polling places affirming the presumably innocuous and nonpartisan principle that "*Tu voto es secreto,*" they were unwittingly consummating the work of the UNO campaign. Less unwitting, and equally important, was the repeated recommendation of Nicaragua's most influential citizen Cardinal Miguel Obando y Bravo to "vote your conscience." It was an injunction to overcome fear.

Or to disregard it—for, judging from the mood of the election day crowd and subsequent interviews, many opposition voters went to the ballot box dubious of victory, with their hearts in their mouths. In Masaya after the election a market woman told the *New York Times*:

I knew all along I was going to vote for UNO, but I thought I was going to be in the minority. . . . I thought it was going to be just like 1984, when the vote was not secret and there were not all these observers around.[124]

But the election was not like 1984 or any of those held prior to 1984 in Nicaragua. Nor, for that matter, is it easy to find a precedent elsewhere. The pollsters have been stumped before, though perhaps never by such an enormous margin.[125] But when had a party so ubiquitous, enjoying such a "lock" on the levers of power and patronage, been defeated—and in a landslide to boot? The day after the election the *Post*'s Managua bureau chief wrote: "It was believed to be the first time that a revolutionary government had been turned out of power by free elections."[126] Pablo Antonio Cuadra was more definitive: "In an achievement that not even the brave peoples of Eastern Europe can claim, we became the first nation ever to defeat and displace communism through the electoral process."[127]

Notes

1. Walter Lippmann, *Public Opinion* (New York: Macmillan, 1922; revised edition, New York: Free Press Paperback, 1965), 119.

2. Pablo Antonio Cuadra, "Reclaiming the Revolution," *Journal of Democracy* (Summer 1990): 44.

3. See chapter 5, 62 *supra*.

4. Julia Preston, "The Defeat of the Sandinistas," *NYRB*, April 12, 1990, 25.

5. In her response to the author's questionnaire, Preston chose "1988" and not "1989-90" as the time when she began "to think that the Sandinistas no longer enjoyed popular support."

6. Lippmann, *Public Opinion*.

7. On "demonstration elections," see Edward S. Herman and Frank Brodhead, *Demonstration Elections: U.S.-Staged Elections in the Dominican Republic, Vietnam and El Salvador* (Boston: South End Press, 1984). For a discussion and debate on Nicaragua's 1984 election as a "demonstration election," see Robert S. Leiken, "The Nicaraguan Tangle" and "The Nicaraguan Tangle: Another Exchange," *NYRB*, June 26, 1986.

8. Bruce Babbitt, "Poll Position: An Observer's Observation," *TNR*, March 19, 1990, 17.

9. See Robert Kagan, *A Twilight Struggle: American Power and Nicaragua, 1977-1990* (New York: Free Press, 1996), 648-52.

10. Lee Hockstader, "Nicaragua Awash in Observers," *WP*, February 26, 1990, A14.

11. John Goshko, "Baker Sets Conditions on Nicaraguan Relations," *WP*, February 23, 1990, A19; Hockstader, "Nicaraguan Campaign Seen as Relatively Free and Open," *WP*, February 17, 1990, A1.

12. For example, the comments of Robert Schroth of Bendixon-Schroth, who did the poll for Univisión: "We simply underestimated the fear factor even with secret ballots," Price, *WT*, February 27, 1990.

13. As with the international press, the Nicaraguan government sought to exclude observer groups most likely to be critical. Several observer groups were barred or saw their access limited after issuing critical reports. A journalist in *The New Republic* commented sardonically:

> Never has a government invited so many international observers to observe an election process, Jimmy Carter correctly told a press conference before the election. He might have added that never has a government denied visas to so many international observers, either (Martin Weiss, "Managua Diarist," *TNR*, March 26, 1990).

See also "Nicaragua to Deny Visas to Hill's Poll Watchers," *WP*, December 1, 1989, A45; William Branigin, "Opposition Campaign Focuses on Nicaragua's Sagging Economy," *WP*, January 8, 1990, A19; "U.S. Observer Team Disbands before Nicaraguan Elections, Sandinistas Bar at Least 3 U.S. Lawmakers," *WP*, February 8, 1990, A1; "End to Official U.S. Observer Role in Managua Vote Raises Debate," *NYT*, February 9, 1990, A6.

Members from two observer groups which exposed abuses were later denied permission to observe the elections. One group, the Puebla Institute, sent a small delegation which was able to enter through Costa Rica on previously issued visas (Telephone interview with Nina Shea, director of the Puebla Institute, March 1, 1990). The Center for Democracy was also able to send a reduced group (see below). The government barred several foreign journalists as well (see Mark Uhlig, "Nicaragua, Altering Policy, Keeps out Some Journalists," *NYT*, January 16, 1990).

14. Foreign Broadcast Information Service (FBIS), "Ortega Holds News Conference 26 Sept.," FBIS-LAT-98-187, September 28, 1989, 9-10.

15. FBIS, "Ortega Holds News Conference," 15.

16. Cuadra, "Reclaiming the Revolution," 44.

17. Violeta Chamorro, "Keep Watch on Our Elections," *WP*, November 8, 1989, A23. Mrs. Chamorro's daughter, an official in the Nicaraguan foreign ministry, replied to her mother's commentary (Claudia Chamorro, "Taking Exception: A Chamorro for the Sandinistas," *WP*, November 19, 1989, D9), but she did not address this point.

18. Clifford Krauss, *Inside Central America* (New York: Summit, 1991), 173.

19. Author's interview with UNO Press Officer Ambassador Ernesto Palazio, Washington, D.C., June 18, 1993.

20. "Nicaraguan Leader Will Halt Truce with the Contras," *NYT*, October 28. 1989, 1; "Nicaragua Begins a Sweep Against a Contra Stronghold," *NYT*, October 28, 1989, 5.

21. Daniel Ortega Saavedra, "Why I Ended the Cease-Fire," *NYT*, November 2, 1989, A31.

22. Brook Larmer, "Ortega's Big Gamble," *CSM*, November 3, 1989, 1.

23. On October 13, 1989, Reuters reported from Washington, "The Soviet Union has cut direct arms shipments to Nicaragua in half this year, but increased shipments from Eastern Europe, North Korea, and Cuba have made up the shortfall, the Defense Department said yesterday," *WP*, October 13, 1989, A30.

24. "In Rural Nicaragua, War Dominates Politics," *WP*, November 12, 1989, A35.

25. "Mr. Ortega's War," *NYT*, November 3, 1989, A34.

26. United States Department of State, "Sandinista Harassment of the Opposition," Report prepared by the Nicaragua Desk of the Bureau of Inter-American Affairs (undated), 1-2.

27. *NBC Nightly News*, October 30, 1989.

28. Uhlig, "Nicaraguan Melee Darkens Peace Talks," *NYT*, December 12, 1989, A3. See also Mary Speck, "One Killed in Nicaraguan Election Riot," *WP*, December 11, 1989, A25. For a fuller personal account by another member of the bipartisan group of American observers, which was organized by the Washington-based Center for Democracy, see L. Brent Bozell III, *Murder in Masatepe* (Washington, D.C.: World Freedom Foundation, 1990). On January 8 the *Post* reported that the Nicaraguan government

> has issued a warning to a private American group, the Washington-based Center for Democracy.
> The center's president, Allen Weinstein, said he was told by a top Sandinista official that a report blaming Sandinista mobs for the violent disruption of an opposition rally in Masatepe on Dec. 10 was unacceptable. He said the official hinted that the group might not be allowed to observe the elections (Branigin, "Opposition Campaign Focuses," A19).

More than a third of the Center's delegation was refused visas to observe the elections (see "Nicaraguan Election Council to Delay Releasing Results to Prevent Violence," *WP*, February 22, 1990, A26).

29. Author's interview with Ernesto Palazio, June 18, 1993; and Bertrand de la Grange, *Le Monde*, February 20, 1990, 4.

30. Author's interview with Ernesto Palazio, June 18, 1993; and de la Grange, *Le Monde*, February 20, 1990, 4.

31. Author's interview with Ernesto Palazio, June 18, 1993.

32. Interworld Consultants, "Memorandum to Executive Vice-President, National Democratic Institute," January 9, 1990.

33. OAS, "Third Report on the Observation of the Nicaraguan Electoral Process," 7; "The Third Report to the Secretary-General by the United Nations Observer Mission to Verify the Electoral Process in Nicaragua," January 31, 1990 (A/44/917), annex I; see also "Carter Wins Nicaraguan Pledge to Free U.S. Funds Sent to Back Opposition Races," *AJC*, January 29, 1990, A3.

34. Comisión Permanente de Derechos Humanos, "Informe," February 1990.

35. "Carter Wins Nicaraguan Pledge," A3.

36. Richard Boudreaux, "Issue of Military Draft Exploited by 2 Sides in Nicaragua's Campaign," LAT, December 15, 1989, S7.

37. Office of the Chief of Staff, Sandinista Popular Army, Ministry of Defense, Managua, Nicaragua, December 27, 1989.

38. Author's interview with UNO campaign official Humberto Belli, January 18, 1990.

39. Grupo de Observadores, O.E.A., VI Región, Matagalpa, January 29, 1990.

40. Babbitt, "Poll Position."

41. FBIS, "Ortega Holds Election Rally in Matagalpa," FBIS-LAT-90-032, February 15, 1990, 18.

42. FBIS, "Ortega Holds Election Rally in Matagalpa," 19-20.

43. de la Grange, "Le Front sandiniste mobilise ses partisans," *Le Monde*, February 23, 1990, 6.

44. FBIS, "Ortega Holds Election Rally in Matagalpa," 20-21.

45. Hockstader and Branigin, "Sandinistas Seen Changed by Election Campaign," WP, February 25, 1990, A1.

46. Four of the five members of the Supreme Electoral Council (CSE), including the president, were selected by the FSLN or its satellite parties. The CSE's staff, including its

executive director, named by the Council's president, was composed predominantly of Sandinista supporters. "All nine regional electoral councils are dominated by Sandinistas who control each council by a 2 to 1 margin" (John McAward, *Mission to Nicaragua: The First Stage of the Electoral Process* [New York: Freedom House, 1989]).

47. Hockstader and Branigin, "Sandinistas Seem Changed," A1. The *Post*'s Branigin also reported another "unusual" use of government resources—the distribution of United Nations and Canadian food aid as campaign gifts (Branigin, "Sandinistas Give Out U.N. Food Aid," *WP*, February 25, 1990, A19).

One example of a not so veiled threat was reported in *Le Monde*. CDS block committees were charged with the task of "intimidating those who displayed blue and white flags on their houses." Nonetheless, "in one of the poorest quarters of Managua, . . . opposition banners were numerous." One family reported that the CDS "told us to take them down if we didn't want to get into trouble" (de la Grange, "Le Front sandiniste," 6).

48. "Nicaraguan opposition gains a voice," *BG*, February 19, 1990, 1.

49. Cristiana Chamorro B., "La marcha que cambió a Nicaragua," *La Prensa*, February 19, 1990, 3.

50. Hockstader, "Activist's Death Raises Tensions in Nicaragua," *WP*, February 21, 1990, A17.

51. See comments of the *Washington Post*'s polling director, Richard Morin, in Don Podesta, "Pollsters Try to Explain Failure to Spot Result," *WP*, February 27, 1990, A17; and Rob Schroth of Bendixen-Schroth (Univisión) in Fiedler, "For Pollsters Upset Carries a Btter Sting," *MH*, February 27, 1990, 13A. Scroth made a similar observation to the *Washington Times*: Price, *WT*, February 27, 1990.

52. "Election Shattered Many Sandinista Myths, *WP*, March 2, 1990, A26.

53. *WP*, February 17, 1990, A1; see also Podesta, "Elliott Richardson Predicts Fair Nicaragua Vote," *WP*, January 16, 1990.

54. *WP*, February 17, 1990, A1; see also Podesta, "Elliott Richardson Predicts."

55. Uhlig, "Opposition Gaining a Bit in Nicaragua," *NYT*, February 9, 1990, A6.

56. "Candidate Chamorro Sidelined with Broken Leg," *WP*, January 3, 1990, A25; see also Boudreaux "Delays in U.S. Aid Hamper Opposition in Nicaragua," *LAT*, January 22, 1990, A1.

57. "Doce mas renunciaron ayer: A 102 ascienden las bajas electorales del UNO," *Barricada*, January 13, 1990, 1; "Absención sería 'profundo error,'" *Barricada*, January 16, 1990, 1; "El posible retiro de la UNO," *Barricada*, January 16, 1990, 3; "Jefe UNO seguro de que perderan," *Barricada*, January 18, 1990, 1.

58. Ana María Ruiz, "Granada celebró el triunfo de la UNO," *La Prensa*, January 22, 1990, 3.

59. Interviews with Marta Patricia Baltodano of the Nicaraguan Human Rights Association, Washington, D.C., December 1992; Lino Hernández, director of the Nicaraguan Commission of Human Rights, Managua, March 1990; and Pedro Joaquín Chamorro Barrios of the UNO campaign, Managua, March 1990.

60. Ana María Ruiz, "Granada celebró," 3; Pedro Joaquín Chamorro Barrios, manuscript "Granada, 20 de enero," Special for *El Diario Las Américas*; also interviews with Pedro Joaquín Chamorro Barrios, January 26, 1990 (telephone), March 7, 1991 (Managua); Ernesto Palazio, February 10, 1990; and Marta Patricia Baltodano, June 12, 1993 (telephone).

61. "Violeta: 'Mis muletas son el símbolo de Nicaragua,'" *La Prensa*, January 22, 1990, 1. Details on the Granada rally from Pedro Joaquín Chamorro Barrios, manuscript "Granada, 20 de enero," Special for *El Diario Las Américas*; Ana María Ruiz, "Granada celebró," 3; United States Embassy, Managua, "UNO rallies, January 20-21," Reports

unclassified and undated (obtained from the Embassy); also interviews with Marta Patricia Baltodano, June 12, 1993 (telephone); Pedro Joaquín Chamorro Barrios, January 26, 1990 (telephone), March 7, 1991 (Managua), Roger Guevara Mena, January 25, 1990 (telephone), Ernesto Palazio, January 25, 1990 (telephone), Francisco Mayorga, March 7, 1991 (Managua), Virgilio Godoy, March 8, 1991.

62. United States Embassy, Managua, "UNO Rallies Jaunuary 20-21."

63. "Violeta vuelve," *La Prensa*, February 22, 1990, 1.

64. Roger Suarez Martinez, *La Prensa*, February 3, 1990, 1.

65. Ana Maria Ruiz, "Occidente selló la victoria," *La Prensa*, February 5, 1990: 1; interviews with Roger Guevara Mena and Ana Guadalupe Gutierrez, Managua, March 1990.

66. Author's telephone conversations with various Nicaraguans including UNO campaign officials Roger Guevara Mena, Antonio Lacayo, Alfredo Cesar, Silvia Cesar Lacayo, and Ernesto Palazio and with Violeta Chamorro (November 8, 1989, February 7, 10, 20, 21, 25, 1990); author's conversation with *Le Monde* correspondent Bernard Legrande, February 20, 1990; see also Leiken, "The Sandinistas Might Lose . . ." *NYT*, February 12, 1990.

67. de la Grange, "L'hostilité au régime s'accentue," *Le Monde*, February 20, 1990, 4

68. Interview with Ernesto Palazios, May 4, 1993, Washington, D.C.

69. Interviews with Roger Guevara Mena, Alfredo César, and Pedro Joaquín Chamorro, March 1991; Silvia Cesar Lacayo, February 25, 1990; and Ernesto Palazio, June 18, 1993.

70. See Julio Lopez C., Orlando Nuñez S., Carlos Fernando Chamorro Barrios, and Pascual Serres, *La Caída del Somocismo y la Lucha Sandinista en Nicaragua* (Managua: EDUCA, 1980), 185, 193-214.

71. For examples see DeYoung, "Nicaragua: Troops vs. Teen-Age Rebels," *WP*, September 1, 1978, A1; *CBS Evening News*, September 1, 1978; *NBC Nightly News*, September 18, 1978.

72. For example see *ABC World News*, September 7, 1978; *NBC Nightly News*, September 14, 1978.

73. Though the dictum that a newspaper is "the first rough draft of history" usually gets attributed to Benjamin C. Bradlee, executive editor of the *Washington Post* from 1968 to 1991, Bradlee himself attributed it to Philip Graham, former publisher of the *Washington Post* (See Bradlee, "Second Annual Theodore H. White Lecture" [Lecture delivered at the Joan Shorenstein Barone Center, Harvard University, 1991], 9, 12). Graham is cited as the author of the parase by Chalmers Roberts, the veteran *Post* correspondent (Roberts, *First Rough Draft* [New York: Praeger, 1973], 2.

74. Juan Walte, *USAT*, February 23, 1990, 4A.

75. "For the Devoted Sandinista, An Item to Fit Every Mood," *NYT*, February 11, 1990, 28.

76. Uhlig, "Opposition Gaining a Bit in Nicaragua," *NYT*, February 9, 1990, A6.

77. Ernesto Palazio, the UNO press spokesperson, says he described his reasons for believing that Chamorro would win over a long lunch with Lee Hockstader of the *Post* in early February. According to Palazio, Hockstader was dismissive: "You don't expect me to believe any of this, do you?"

78. "Political Novice Winding Up Bid to Dislodge Ortega," *LAT*, February 19, 1990, A1.

79. "Nicaraguan Opposition Gains a Voice," *BG*, February 19, 1990, 1.

80. Hockstader, "Crowds Cheer Opposition," *WP*, February 19, 1990, A1.

81. Rowland Evans and Robert Novack, *WP*, February 19, 1990, A19.

82. Richard Boudreaux, "Delays in U.S. Aid Hamper Opposition in Nicaragua," *LAT*, January 22, 1990, A1.

83. Hockstader, "Nicaraguan Opposition: Outsmarted and Outspent," *WP*, January 25, 1990, A29, A34.

84. Robert Collier, "U.S. Firm's Nicaragua Poll Gives Ortega Wide Lead," *SFC*, January 25, 1990.

85. *NBC Nightly News*, January 27, 1990.

86. Christopher Marquis, "Sandinista hits election stride as foe falters," *MH*, January 28, 1990, A1; continued on A17 under headline "Chamorro Campaign Faltering."

87. Peter McCormick, "Sandinista Foes Struggle," *DMN*, January 29, 1990, 1A. UNO organizers did not regard Díaz as anti-Sandinista but as one who sought to divide and weaken the anti-Sandinista vote.

88. Interviews with Ernesto Palacio and Roger Guevara Mena.

89. J. D. Gannon, "Sandinista Foes Lose Momentum," *CSM*, January 30, 1990.

90. Stanley Greenberg was later to argue the doubtful proposition that the Chamorro "surge," and not his own polling methodology, was responsible for his survey's wide variance from the final outcome. According to Greenberg, the poll results were correct, but the Nicaraguans changed their minds. But the Greenberg-Lake findings were reproduced by subsequent American polls, notably the ABC/*Washington Post* survey. Meanwhile the polls conducted by Costa Rican, Venezuelan, and Argentine firms all showed a consistent UNO edge throughout. Greenberg's excuse fails to address the main problem: the discrepancy between private beliefs and public manifestation, and the failure of his and other American polls to reveal the former. The late January Chamorro "surge" did not signify a shift in private attitudes but in the willingness to express them publicly.

91. Interviews with Ernesto Palazio, UNO media spokesperson.

92. Mark Uhlig, *NYT*, February 11, 1990, 35; for television see for example *ABC World News Tonight*, February 21, 1990; *NBC Today*, February 22, 1990.

93. See Boudreaux, "Delays in U.S. Aid Hamper Opposition in Nicaragua," *LAT*, January 22, 1990, A1.

94. de la Grange, "L'hostilité au régime s'accentue," 4. A U.S. embassy official who attended the rally at Ocotal reported: "The people held banners that were handwritten: 'Cuba Sin Fidel Y Nicaragua Sin Daniel' [Cuba without Fidel and Nicaragua without Daniel]. The most popular chant was 'Que dice la gente? Que se vaya el Frente' [What do the people say? The Front has to go]. The chants were mostly unorganized and spontaneous" (de la Grange, "L'hostilité au régime s'accentue," 4).

95. I was on the podium at one such display in Havana on the morning of May 1, 1984. Interviews in workers' barrios that afternoon revealed a very different state of mind. See Leiken, "Inside the Revolution," *NYRB*, October 11, 1984.

96. Elias Canetti, *Crowds and Power* (New York: Farrar, Straus & Giroux, 1984), 328.

97. Canetti, *Crowds and Power*, 59.

98. On election day *La Prensa*'s literary supplement reprinted an essay by the Italian political theorist, Giovanni Sartori entitled "La Boveda de Miedo,"—"The Arch of Fear"—(*La Prensa Literaria*, February 25, 1990: 4-5). *La Prensa* like other Nicaraguan newspapers, and many Latin American ones, is casual in its use of previously published sources. In this instance there was no attribution beyond the name of the author. After a futile search for the original in the Library of Congress, I consulted Sartori directly. Sartori, who is the Albert Schweitzer Professor in the Humanities at Columbia University, remembered using the term previously to distinguish between the "fear" of everyday

totalitarianism and the state of "terror" induced at certain moments in totalitarian regimes, for example, Stalin's purges, or Mao Ze Dong's "Cultural Revolution." Sartori could not identify the extract reproduced in *La Prensa*, but directed me to his usage of the term "vault of terror" in his *The Theory of Democracy Revisted* (Giovanni Sartori, *The Theory of Democracy Revisited* (Chatham, New Jersey: Chatham House Publishers, 1987), 99-100; see also 193-203). Sartori remarked that "fear" was a more accurate term in this context than terror.

99. Canetti, *Crowds and Power,* 58.
100. Canetti, *Crowds and Power,* 59.
101. Clifford Krauss, *Inside Central America* (New York: Summit, 1991), 173-74.
102. Canetti, *Crowds and Power,* 16.
103. Canetti, *Crowds and Power,* 76.
104. *CBS Evening News*, February 25, 1990.
105. William Branigin and Lee Hockstader, "Opposition Claims Upset Win in Nicaragua," *WP*, February 26, 1990, A1.
106. *CNN Headline News*, February 25, 1990.
107. *NBC Nightly News*, February 25, 1990.
108. Larry Pressler, "A Lesson for Us All," *WP*, March 4, 1990, C7.
109. Bruce Babbitt, "Poll Position: An Observer's Observation," 17.
110. Puebla Instititute, "Nicaraguan Election Report of the Puebla Institute Observer Delegation," Washington, D.C. (March 20, 1990), 4.
111. *CBS Evening News*, February 25, 1990.
112. George Russell, "First Trip to the Polls" (November 19, 1984), 102.
113. Nicaragua's 1990 election turnout appears to challenge the efforts of political scientists to explain voting patterns on the basis of "rational choice theory" and "game theory." Rational choice theorists originally emphasized the "free rider" phenomenon in elections. They held that turnouts would tend toward nil since any individual voter would have an infinitesimal impact on the outcome and therefore take a "free ride" on other voters, receiving the benefit of their participation. Though voter turnout has declined in the United States, the historical tendency has been for voters to go to the polls in numbers far above what the "free rider" theory would suggest. Accordingly, rational choice theorist John Aldrich argued that voting decisions are of "low cost, low benefit" and therefore exempt from rational choice theory. But as Donald Green and Ian Shapiro ask: "Can it be said of Latin American elections, in which voters spend hours in polling lines, sometimes amid threats of violence, that turnout is a low-cost activity?" In the case of Nicaragua, as we have seen many voters also spent hours and even days getting to registration and voting booths and the costs with which they were most concerned were not merely time and trouble. See Green and Shapiro, 1994; and John A. Aldrich, "Rational Choice and Turnout," *American Journal of Political Science* 37: 246-79; for the classical account of free riding, see Mancur Olson, Jr., *The Logic of Collective Action* (Cambridge: Harvard University, 1971).
114. David Jessup, "Nicaragua—A Civics Lesson in Democracy," *AIFLD Briefs* (March 9, 1990): 1.
115. Puebla Institute, "Nicaraguan Election Report," 12.
116. Babbitt, "Poll Position: An Observer's Observation."
117. *CBS Evening News*, February 25, 1990.
118. Charles Lane, "Who 'Won' Nicaragua?" *Newsweek*, International Edition (March 12, 1990): 14.
119. Author's interview with Dr. Emilio Alvarez Montealván, director of *El Nicaragüense*, Managua, March 8, 1991. Also interviews with Roger Guevara Mena,

March 3, 1990; Ernesto Palazio, June 18, 1993; Marta Patricia Baltodano, Director, Nicaraguan Association for Human Rights, Managua, March 6, 1991; Pedro Joaquín Chamorro, Managua, March 7, 1991; Sergio Ramírez, former Vice-President, Washington, D.C., May 11, 1993; and Nina Shea, telephone interview from Managua, February 26, 1990. Cf. Babbitt, "Poll Position."

120. Lane, "Who 'Won' Nicaragua?" 14.

121. Cf. Paul Lazarsfeld, Bernard Berelson and Hazel Gaudet, *The People's Choice: How the Voter Makes Up His Mind in a Presidential Campaign* (3rd edition, New York: Columbia University, 1968).

122. Elisabeth Noelle-Neumann, *The Spiral of Silence* (Chicago: University of Chicago, 1984), 21.

123. Paul Oquist, the Sandinista campaign spokesman (see chapters 5, 6, and 14), basing himself on a survey by a Sandinista research institute, affirms:

> The analysis of the evolution of the electoral campaign demonstrates that the FSLN had effectively lost the election well before the campaign started. The reduction of support after 1984 constituted an erosion difficult to reverse for a party that was confronting adverse economic, political and international conditions. Indeed, 87.7 percent of FSLN voters had decided how to vote before the campaign (Oquist, "Sociopolitical Dynamics of the 1990 Nicaragua Elections," in *The 1990 Elections in Nicaragua and Their Aftermath*, ed. Vanessa Castro and Gary Prevost [Lanham, Maryland: Rowman & Littlefield, 1992], 30).

Oquist, a Sandinista official, proceeds from the assumption that the 1984 election returns were a valid sampling of opinion. Thus, the FSLN's "reduction of support" must have begun "after 1984." Otherwise, his conclusions about FSLN voters are credible— *i.e.,* this was a captive voting bloc made up of militants, government employees, and sympathizers identifying with the regime.

But we must be more careful with a Sandinista survey of UNO voters. Oquist believes, somewhat inconsistently, that the election was decided by "a group of swing voters." His survey found that 23 percent of UNO voters made their choice of candidates during the campaign and that another 13 percent decided at the moment of voting. Even assuming these figures to be accurate, what were the vacillating UNO voters deciding? Were they choosing between campaign "messages" or whether it was safe to vote their preferences?

124. Larry Rohter, "Ortega Spurned in Old Stronghold," *NYT*, March 5, 1990.

125. Americans will think of the 1948 Truman upset. But the polls, though inaccurate, were far closer to the mark than in Nicaragua. The final Gallup poll showed Governor Thomas Dewey with a five-percentage-point lead. President Truman was re-elected by a four-point margin. That made for a nine-point margin of error. In Nicaragua the American polls missed the mark by more than 30 points. [See David McCullough, *Truman* (New York: Simon & Schuster, 1992], 703, 710-11).

126. Hockstader, "Chamorro Issues Call for Reconciliation," *WP*, February 27, 1990, A1.

127. Pablo Antonio Cuadra, "Reclaiming the Revolution," *Journal of Democracy* (Summer 1990): 42.

But if it had not happened before, it did happen again. Before the May 1993 United Nations supervised election in Cambodia, it was a generally assumed that the ruling Hun Sen regime would win. The only question was whether the Khmer Rouge guerrillas would succeed in disrupting the voting and rendering the election meaningless. But the vote was massive, and the Hun Sen regime was defeated. The voters had defied both the Khmer Rouge guerrillas and the repressive Communist government.

And the resemblance was even more faithful. William Shawcross reported that:

> The Cambodian people kept their counsel, and went to the polls in their best clothes. As they waited patiently in line, they seemed to me and to others visibly pleased at the chance to express their views in a secret ballot.
>
> A writer . . . called the election Cambodia's St. Crispin's Day. Certainly it was one of the most moving events I have ever witnessed. . . . In spite or perhaps because of the Hun Sen regime's powerful and often brutal apparatus of control—its secret police and its ability to dispense patronage—people had voted against it. . . ." ("A New Cambodia," *NYRB*, August 12, 1993.: 37).

Chapter 14
Polls, Press, Professors, and "Americo-Centrism"

> The commission's Bollinger agrees. " . . . Somebody is terribly wrong in these polls . . . somebody's going to have a lot of egg on their face come the 26th."
>
> —*Washington Post*, news item[1]

> Dr. Peter Marchetti, the Jesuit priest, who supervised the canvassing for the Central American University . . . that showed that the FSLN would win with 70 percent of the vote, has been contracted by Harvard University to direct the school of population studies. Harvard had to fight fiercely with Yale to gain Marchetti's services, such is the Jesuit's reputation after his Nicaraguan electoral prognostications.
>
> —*La Cronica*[2]

Let us return to the surveys of American coverage of the 1990 elections mentioned at the outset. The study conducted by the Center for Media and Public Affairs found no news story, and only a single opinion piece, which cited polls predicting a Chamorro victory. The survey conducted for this study, whose starting point is several months earlier, found only two news stories, out of forty-nine, which cited polls to suggest that the Sandinistas might lose.[3] Those news stories (one by *Chicago Tribune* staff reporters, the other by Juan Walte of *USA Today*) both occurred at the end of October when President Ortega announced his intention to renounce the truce with the *Contras*.[4] If this brief, isolated show of skepticism reflected anything more than the predilections of a conservative newspaper and a reporter raised in El Salvador, it was the widespread puzzlement as to Ortega's motives for breaking the cease-fire.

Of the forty-two subsequent news reports citing polls to predict an outcome, not one suggested a Chamorro victory. Forty indicated a likely Sandinista victory and two that the election was too close to call. One of the latter appeared on election day, when some news organizations seemed to sense that the race was "tightening." The other "too close to call" came from the *New York Times*, whose correspondent Mark Uhlig was consistently leery of the polls.[5]

With the exception of Richard Harwood's ombudsman column in the *Washington Post*, the daily press carried no *postmortem* on its performance in Nicaragua.[6] But there were several lengthy pieces devoted to the errors of the pollsters.[7] In one of these the *Miami Herald*'s political editor explained that:

> The effect of the three major U.S. polls was to establish a conventional wisdom, echoed by much of the American media, about an impending Ortega victory.[8]

As we have seen, however, the assumption of Sandinista victory rested on a conventional wisdom not "echoed" but established and promulgated by the press. The prevailing stereotypes were propagated by a journalism of exposure whose favorite target was the U.S. government, that all-purpose villain who had earned the enmity of most Nicaraguans, an indignation which was to be expressed in the elections.

Moreover, if the American polls are to be held culpable, the American reporting on them deserves at least equal blame. Before the elections ABC *Nightline*'s Forrest Sawyer maintained that "every independent poll shows [Ortega] far ahead." Announcing the election results NBC's Tom Brokaw claimed that: "*All* the preelection polls showed Ortega ahead."[9] But, as the *Washington Post* more accurately observed the next morning:

> Slightly more than half of the 27 preelection surveys . . . indicated President Daniel Ortega . . . leading.
>
> In all, 14 of the polls conducted in Nicaragua in 1989 and this year for which results were released showed the Sandinistas ahead; 13 gave the lead to UNO. . . . Of the last nine polls, five showed the Sandinistas leading.[10]

Taken as a whole the pre-election polls were split, not unanimous. Moreover, in contrast to the American coverage, *Le Monde* ran a major piece which cited even-handedly polls with opposite results, pointing out that

> surveys are not at all reliable in Nicaragua because of the polarization of the society after ten years of a revolutionary regime and the fear of the people interviewed towards pollsters who are often suspected of being government agents.[11]

The press did not passively echo the pollsters but ostensibly exercised its own judgment in choosing to feature certain surveys and certain results but not others.

As it happened the polls featured were invariably by American and those neglected by Latin American firms—Argentine, Costa Rican, and Venezuelan.[12] The Latin American pollsters insisted that they had made every effort to bring their research to the attention of the U.S. media. Two Costa Rican pollsters, Carlos Denton and Miguel Gomez, who conducted some of the more accurate preelection polls, claimed that their company, CID-Gallup (part of the Gallup International Federation) had sought unsuccessfully to interest American news organizations in its findings.[13] Likewise, the Argentine pollster Felipé Noguera, whose survey results matched the election totals almost exactly, complained that: "Most Latin American print media reported the outcome of our [poll]. U.S. media that received our results decided not to carry them."

A story in the *Los Angeles Times* was one of the few U.S. press reports which mentioned the existence of conflicting polls:

> President Daniel Ortega's chief rival in the Feb. 25 election has lost ground in all five voter opinion polls published in recent weeks, and three of the surveys give the Sandinista leader a huge advantage.
>   Violeta Barrios de Chamorro, the challenger, is ahead by smaller margins in the other two polls, conducted by her United Nicaraguan Opposition (UNO). But those results are questioned by independent analysts because their polling methods have not been fully disclosed.[14]

Contrary to the impression left here, most of the surveys which favored Chamorro were not sponsored by UNO.[15] But more to the point—the *Times* was obviously aware of discordant polls but chose, apparently on the advice of "independent analysts," to discount them.[16]

Though the *Los Angeles Times* correspondent did not choose to identify those on whom he apparently relied for such a crucial judgment, an educated guess may be hazarded. The triumphant but disgruntled Costa Rican pollsters claimed that the Commission on Nicaraguan Pre-Election Polls, established by William Bollinger, an American professor critical of U.S. policy, steered the media away from their surveys.[17]

The *Washington Post*, in the front-page piece announcing the results of the *Post*/ABC preelection poll, also relied on Commission members to evaluate the accuracy of the conflicting polls. Likewise Commission members, who again raised doubts as to the methodology of polls showing Chamorro ahead, were described as independent "experts." The article added that:

> The commission and its head, William Bollinger, director of the InterAmerican Research Center at California State University at Los Angeles were accused by *La Prensa* of being agents of the Sandinistas. . . . "We tried to stay out of the limelight when we got down here," Bollinger said. "But we were immediately caught in the crossfire."[18]

The Commission challenged the Argentine, Costa Rican, and Venezuelan surveys that had UNO leading because each of these polling organizations refused
to allow the Commission "to investigate their methods" or to allow Commission
members to "accompany interviewers."[19] The Costa Rican firms objected that
disclosing the identities of interviewers could subject them to Sandinista pressure and that divulging survey methodology would reveal trade secrets to their
competitors.[20]

There was more to it than that. From the outset the Nicaraguan preelection
polling was enmeshed in politics. Well before the elections Sandinista supporters began to fear that if the preelection surveys conflicted with what they confi-
dently expected to be a Sandinista victory, the polls could be used to justify a
Bush Administration claim of fraud and thus evade normalizing relations with
Nicaragua. They recalled that when in 1984 the Sandinistas had hoped elections
would undermine support for the *Contras*, the Reagan Administration had labeled them fraudulent. On the other hand opposition leaders had hoped that the
canvassing could serve as a safeguard against fraud.[21] They saw Panama as a
precedent. In May 1989 preelection and exit polls supported opposition claims
that Panamanian strongman, and firm Sandinista ally, General Manuel Antonio
Noriega had stolen the election.

By the summer of 1989 two camps of preelection pollsters had begun to
form in Nicaragua—those affiliated with Managua's Jesuit-administered Central
American University (UCA), which even the liberal *Boston Globe* conceded was
"widely considered sympathetic to the Sandinista revolution," and two private
Costa Rican firms widely viewed as pro-opposition and pro-U.S.[22] The govern-
ment-controlled media trumpeted the polls that had the Sandinistas ahead, while
La Prensa did the same for the UNO-leading polls. In the midst of a polarized
and sometimes violent campaign, there was little middle ground in what came to
be known as "the war of the polls."

Into this setting William Bollinger's Commission on Pre-Election Polls arrived—as a professedly neutral and scientific "monitor." It was as "independent
analysts" that the Commission members were cited in the American media. Yet
none of the disputants viewed Bollinger as a neutral. Sandinista publicists repeated his view that

> the most reactionary opposition groups, of which *La Prensa* is the spokesper-
> son, wish to use the polls to demonstrate that the Sandinistas have little support
> and cannot win a fair election. Any Sandinista victory would have to be seen as
> a fraud.[23]

The Costa Rican pollsters complained that Bollinger had forfeited any claim to
neutrality or independence by virtue of his association with one camp of pollsters and his previous writings attacking the other. In June 1988 Bollinger's Interamerican Research Center cosponsored the first nongovernment poll permitted by the Sandinista authorities since they banned the 1981 *La Prensa* survey.

The poll's Nicaraguan sponsor was the UCA in Managua, and it was conducted by a think tank called Itztani composed of UCA professors. Bollinger regularly praised the work of Itztani and the other UCA offshoots in the publication of the Interamerican Research Center. Moreover, the respected Costa Rican pollster Victor Borge considered Bollinger's August 1989 criticisms of his Nicaraguan polling tendentious and unfair.[24] Borge was Oscar Arias' personal pollster and one source of the Costa Rican president's conviction that the Sandinistas would lose "a free and fair election."

For their part, Denton and Gomez of CID-Gallup charged that in the previous year Bollinger had orchestrated an attack on their credibility by American academics opposed to the Reagan Administration Central American policies. Bollinger had coauthored a piece in the radical weekly *The Nation* which cited "independent polls" conducted by "scholars" which "cast severe doubts on the reliability of the Gallup affiliate in Central America." The article charged the Costa Rican CID/Gallup firm of colluding with the United States Information Agency (USIA) to produce survey results supportive of Reagan Administration policy.[25] The USIA-CID/Gallup polls had found broad grassroots anxiety about the Sandinistas in neighboring Central American countries.[26]

Prompted in part by those USIA polls, Bollinger and a Salvadoran researcher, who was later assassinated by the Salvadoran military, organized PROCADOP (Central American Public Opinion Program) to coordinate the "independent polls." Bollinger described PROCADOP as "a network of university-linked polling institutes" from Mexico, Central America, and the United States whose aim was to combat "the abuses of opinion polling by certain governments and commercial firms."[27] In turn, PROCADOP fathered the Commission on Nicaragua Pre-Election Polls.[28]

As might be expected Bollinger's initiative was not exactly welcomed by those Central American "commercial firms." Denton and Gomez of CID/Gallup, both tenured university professors, were not gratified by Bollinger's suggestion that his was a mission on behalf of academic standards versus a crass and even corrupt commercialism. They considered Bollinger "a dedicated polemicist" and observed that

> most of the research firms in Central America are peopled by academicians from one field or another. It was with some bemusement that the Central American researchers viewed the arrival of a group of United States professors to the region to defend the principles of good research and to establish . . . a linkup between three or four universities . . . to conduct polls that were more in accordance with their view of the world.

"Resentment" rather than "bemusement" might better characterize the reaction of Denton and Gomez, who only recently had helped persuade nine major Central American firms to adopt the principles of the Code of Ethics of the European Society for Opinion and Market Research (ESOMAR). They clearly were affronted by Bollinger's efforts to "put together a new code of ethics [which] . . . violated basic norms of the ESOMAR code and which he insisted all Central American research firms sign." After the elections Commission member Peter Miller acknowledged that the Commission "was viewed by pollsters in the UNO 'camp' . . . as having a political agenda, instead of a methodological interest." Miller believed this to be a major reason why the Commission "received little or no cooperation from UNO-lead pollsters."[29]

That contentious background and Bollinger's embattled position went unmentioned by the *Los Angeles Times* or the *Washington Post*, or any of the other outlets which carried the Commission's assessments. Neither did they note that the Commission's disclosure criteria were based on a code of ethics which the Commission's founder himself had devised to replace the current code; nor that the code had been signed by the groups whose polls the Commission approved, while those they deplored had signed the other. Furthermore, those stories, and others citing the Commission's findings, failed to indicate that Professor Bollinger was a member of the Advisory Board of Hemisphere Initiatives which sponsored one of the polls finding the Sandinistas far in front—the Greenberg-Lake poll which produced results similar to the ABC/*Post* survey. Nor did the stories mention the intimate ties between Bollinger's Interamerican Research Center and UCA/Itztani, which had conducted the ABC/*Post* survey.[30] Had they mentioned any of this their readers might have been in a better position to determine whether Professor Bollinger had been "caught in the cross fire" or had brought arms and ammunition to one camp.

UNO leaders had their own reasons to doubt Commission claims of neutrality. Several Commission members had helped draft the Latin American Studies Association (LASA) report that found Nicaragua's 1984 elections to be "a model of probity and fairness." UNO could hardly be expected to regard as impartial the report's view that Arturo Cruz's banned *Coordinadora Democratica*, to which most of them had belonged, commanded only a negligible "mass base" and that "no major political tendency in Nicaragua was denied access to the electoral process in 1984."[31]

The *Boston Globe* editorial page, which strongly disapproved of U.S. policy and admired the Sandinistas, appreciated the Commission:

> The Commission on Nicaragua Pre-Election Polls, which is based at California State University and supported by the Ford Foundation, will evaluate the pollsters' methodology and make it possible to tell which polls are biased.[32]

The imprimatur of the Ford Foundation, California State University, and the inclusion of several reputable academic public opinion specialists would lend the Commission's appraisals, and the press reports which embraced them, an aura of respectability.

Nancy Llach contends that Bollinger's Commission sought to influence international media coverage of the elections in a direction favorable to the Sandinistas:

Convinced by the findings of their own people that Ortega would win, Bollinger, the Interamerican Research Center and the Pre-election Commission (if not all members) were apparently laying ground work for a tenable defense of an Ortega victory in the event that the U.S. government accused Ortega of fraud . . . . The conclusion of the Interamerican Research Center's report on the July 1989 Borge poll is illustrative: "By presenting an exaggerated picture of Sandinista political weakness, *La Prensa* hopes to persuade the international media that the Sandinistas could not win a clean election. The objective is to discredit, in advance, any FSLN victory on February 25th."[33]

Whatever Bollinger's motives, he could hardly be designated, any more than Llach, a public opinion researcher at USIA, an "independent analyst."[34]

Bollinger's activities merit attention beyond their role in the press's misreading of the signals from preelection Nicaragua. They also provide an example of the often sophisticated endeavors to influence Nicaragua press coverage. Those efforts arose from both camps on this controversial issue. The Reagan State Department's Office of Public Diplomacy for Latin America and the Caribbean and the White House Central American Task Force both concentrated on publicizing Sandinista malfeasance. But a number of correspondents and editors, always off-the-record, have told this writer of far more intensive, extensive, and effective lobbying efforts from the opposite camp. These ranged from religious, human rights, professional, and university-based organizations to peace and anti-intervention groups and solidarity and support networks. Such groups do not fit the customary profile of media-managing "special interests"—such as the National Rifle Association or the Tobacco Lobby.[35] Our case history suggests that the press may be more vulnerable to manipulation from less publicized, more "virtuous," sources—especially to the degree that they share the journalists' own values, predilections, and social background. The most influential interest groups were those which could present themselves plausibly as well-informed but non-aligned, such as ostensibly bipartisan groups, or human rights organizations which could claim activity on both sides of the Cold War divide, or groups of university scholars and teachers, like LASA and the Commission on Nicaragua Pre-election Polls. The intimate ties between many American academic groups and the Sandinistas, or fellow travelers like the UCA, were not generally appreciated or acknowledged.

Paradoxes of Ethnocentrism

Clearly, American news organizations were well aware of conflicting poll results—one *Washington Post* article even referred to "poll wars"—but discounted or dismissed them.[36] That is to say, they ignored or cast doubt on precisely the surveys which proved to be reliable while reporting and defending those which proved specious.

"Ethnocentrism" would seem an improbable source for this predilection for U.S. over Latin American companies. The press had consistently called on U.S. policymakers to heed "the views of the Latin Americans themselves"—when those views seemed to corroborate their own and contradict those of the administration. Nevertheless, in our case American news organizations, and a number of American pollsters, banked on the judgment of a group of American professors who presented themselves, and were presented as, nonpartisan. The press did not trouble itself to examine the *bonafides* of their "independent analysts." The professors, after all, were validating surveys whose results already seemed plausible, that is to say consistent with the news organizations' own notion of where the Nicaraguans stood. If our case implicates any *"ethnos,"* that could not be the United States as a whole—there were a range of views on Nicaragua— but a segment or subculture of it: a grouping which would include journalists as well as professors and pollsters.

After the election the Costa Rican pollsters, on a panel entitled "Poll Wars," told a meeting of American public opinion analysts that the American surveys contained a faulty premise:

> The premise . . . reflected in questionnaire design . . . was that the international issues and the contra war were major determinants of voting behavior.[37]

The Argentine pollster Noguera likewise concluded that the American polls included "what I like to call 'Americo-centric' questions."[38] The United States Congress had only recently, in February 1989, gone through the last of several bruising debates over whether to approve aid to the Nicaraguan rebels—debates which eventually were swallowed up by the notorious Iran-*Contra* affair. The controversy about the American role in Nicaragua barely engaged the attention of the general public, except when Lt. Colonel Oliver North—depending upon one's perspective, Iran-*Contra*'s villain or hero-victim—testified before the joint congressional committee investigating the matter. Yet it was a dispute that engrossed the media, the academy, and the political class. Politicians were divided, but most intellectuals, journalists, professors, and pollsters strongly opposed funding the *Contras*. The Congress voted to end military funding to the *Contras* in February 1988.[39]

The Latin American pollsters were referring to the numerous U.S.-centered queries in the American pollsters' questionnaires. They asked, for example, if "[Chamorro will] take most of her directions from the United States or . . . become an independent leader" (ABC/*Washington Post*); others were directed at the prospects of a U.S. invasion, or were about the "*Contra* war" (Greenberg-Lake, Bendixen-Schroth). All the American-designed surveys referred casually to "the *Contras*," apparently aware neither of the large number of Nicaraguans who called them by the name they preferred ("the Resistance"), nor that the usage of the term *Contra*, in Nicaragua's highly charged environment, could convey a value judgment, or even an allegiance.[40]

Stanley Greenberg, who directed the Hemisphere Initiatives/Greenberg-Lake survey widely cited by the U.S. media, and who later became President William Jefferson Clinton's chief pollster, was Robert MacNeil's other guest on the evening Congressman Steven Solarz maintained that the Sandinistas would lose because of their economic policies and despotism. Here is how Greenberg responded:

> I think the Congressman highlights really the central contradiction. . . . The question is . . . why, if there is such discontent, why are not voters turning out the Sandinistas. . . . The reason . . . the opposition has failed to capitalize . . . is the Contras. The Contras are enormously unpopular. . . . That is the single biggest doubt that the voters have against the opposition, the principal reason why they are holding back is that they are too close to the Contra rebels, too close to the United States. . . . The Panama action was opposed by an overwhelming majority of Nicaraguans. In our polls Daniel Ortega's popularity went up ten points after the invasion and the voters began to give more credence to externalized explanations, that is the U.S. was responsible for conditions in the country.[41]

These very same opinions, as we have seen, were shared by many journalists. Ours is decidedly not a story of American news organizations having been led into error simply by reporting scientific surveys in good faith. The journalist, the pollster, and the analyst, their eyes fixed on the clouds, walked arm-in-arm over the precipice.

They may have been steered in that direction by some friendly Nicaraguans. There was an important difference between the pollsters for the UNO-leading Latin American and the U.S. firms. The Argentine, Costa Rican, and Venezuelan organizations utilized their own supervisors and trained *ad hoc* teams of interviewers. On the other hand, the Americans, without exception, entrusted Nicaraguan organizations with the fieldwork.[42] The Americans may have been drawn to the Nicaraguan firms by the recommendations of the Commission on Nicaraguan Pre-Election Polls.[43] But they could also have acted on the innocent, if abstract, assumption that Nicaraguan subjects would be more comfortable with Nicaraguan interviewers, who would likewise be more familiar with their own countrymen.

The problem was that many Nicaraguans regarded the subcontracted firms as friendly to the government, and they had reasons for thinking so. The Nicaraguan polling organization Itztani was subcontracted for fieldwork by the firms responsible for two of the three major American surveys: Greenberg-Lake (Hemisphere Initiatives) and Belden & Russonello (ABC/*Washington Post*). Marvin Ortega, the founder and director of Itztani, together with UCA, created the Nicaraguan Institute of Public Opinion (INOP) which in turn established Itztani. In November 1981, when it banned nongovernmental public opinion surveys, the Sandinista government assigned public opinion polling to INEC, the National Statistics and Census Institute, a government agency. In June 1988 INEC authorized INOP/Itztani to conduct the first public opinion survey not undertaken by the government or the FSLN in nearly seven years. The report of the survey's U.S. cosponsor (Bollinger's Interamerican Research Center at California State which later organized the Commission on Pre-Election Polls) states that the governmental INEC

> provided the UCA and Itztani with comprehensive and up-to-date demographic data on household and neighborhood size as well as access to maps of all neighborhoods in Managua.[44]

The CID-Gallup pollsters add that "it was not unusual for INEC employees to moonlight at INOP."[45] The Costa Ricans also claim that "all efforts to obtain permission from the INEC on the part of other Central Americans were rebuffed."[46]

At the time of the June 1988 INOP survey the research director of another research institute was arrested. The Costa Rican pollsters recount that: "It was known in scholarly circles in Managua that this research institute was contemplating public opinion polling sponsored by right-wing opposition groups."[47] The research director of UCA at this time was Peter Marchetti, another kind of illustration of the close ties between American academia and one sector of Nicaraguan politics.[48] Marchetti's qualifications for supervising impartial surveys may be gleaned from an article he published three years earlier celebrating the Sandinistas' "successful agrarian reform," Nicaraguans' rising nutritional levels, "a 13 percent increase in productivity" and "thousands of new cooperatives free to profit as they want in the market."[49] Even Sandinista officials now acknowledge that at the time these remarks were published Nicaragua was suffering a severe agricultural crisis as a result of sharply fallen productivity, food shortages were commonplace, peasant complaints of state coercion widespread, and agrarian reform based on state cooperatives had proved an economic and political disaster, forcing major revisions in this very period.[50]

As might be expected, the preelection polls sponsored by UCA—which were carried out by Itztani and another offshoot—ECO (*Estudios y Consultas de Opinión*), which also conducted internal polls for the Sandinistas—showed the most lopsided margins in favor of the Sandinistas.[51] The June 1988 INOP/Itztani/California State survey was assuredly one of the "three independent polls in the last year" which suggested to the *Washington Post*'s correspondent "that Ortega is . . . at least three times as popular as any single opposition figure."[52]

Along with those conducted by INOP/Itztani, the fieldwork for a third major American survey, designed by Bendixen-Schroth for Univisión, was fielded by Logos. Nancy Llach asserts that Logos is "an offshoot of the same group [INOP-Itztani], organized by three UCA professors."[53] However, Bollinger insists that its director, Marvin Saballos, claimed "total independence" from the government.[54] The Chamorro campaign, nonetheless, considered Logos "part of the same network."[55]

Llach also claims that INOP and UCA "were the regular pollsters for the Sandinista campaign." She describes Marvin Ortega as "a long-time Sandinista and one-time member of the Ortega government."[56] That was the view of the Chamorro campaign which claimed that Ortega preserved links with the Sandinista party. Bollinger depicts Ortega as an "heretic leftist" who was jailed by the Sandinista government for his association with a subsequently banned radical leftist newspaper called *El Pueblo*. According to Bollinger, Ortega joined the FSLN and worked at a think tank associated with the Agrarian Reform Ministry, but he became "disenchanted over the lack of internal democracy" and left the organization. There was no disagreement that Marvin Ortega once had been a Sandinista. The controversy centered on his current relationship with the government. Luis Sanchez, the leader of the Socialist Party which belonged to the UNO coalition, stated that he possessed a copy of a letter instructing Sandinista poll watchers to provide information to Ortega's Itztani.

Ortega's profile in the *Washington Post* story on its preelection survey closely matches Bollinger's account:

His work is well regarded by academic researchers and private pollsters in the United States, and he is considered a leftist critic of the Sandinistas by foreign journalists in Nicaragua. Although he was once jailed briefly by the Sandinistas, he has repeatedly been accused of being a Sandinista sympathizer by Chamorro's supporters.

The *Post* then added that:

A State Department official questioned his impartiality. "Everything in Marvin Ortega's background indicates that he is a long time Sandinista supporter and a self-proclaimed leftist," he said. "It is perplexing, to say the least, how he could be considered a credible party to conduct an election poll in Nicaragua."[57]

Nevertheless, the article which frequently cites the American "academic researchers" of the Commission, leaves the impression that those questioning the *Post*'s polltakers are partisans. After the elections Marvin Ortega told Branigin of the *Post*, in a statement that undermines both the notion that he was still a Sandinista and the judgment of those who endorsed his surveys: "'I think people were scared'. . . . They thought we were Sandinistas.'"[58]

The paradoxical relationship between U.S. polling firms and Nicaraguan subcontractors shines another light on contemporary "ethnocentrism." In subcontracting with the Nicaraguan firms American polling organizations may have made the understandable, but hazardous, assumption that institutions associated with Nicaraguan universities, and also with U.S. universities, could be relied upon to be independent. Following another customary U.S. practice the American firms were careful to withhold the name of their sponsors and to attribute sponsorship to "an independent research firm." However, Llach points out, this terminology was identical to that used by at least one prominent Nicaraguan firm . . . in polling reports which were widely distributed by the Sandinista media. Rather than mitigating respondent fears, it linked the U.S. surveys even more closely to the Ortega government.[59]

Finally, the Nicaraguan subcontractors shared a common pool of interviewers. Those interviewers were described after the elections by the *Los Angeles Times'* polling director I. A. Lewis as mostly "middle-class college students sent out from Managua." Lewis emphasized the "disparities of class, age, education, and locality between interviewer and respondent." Simply by virtue of these disparities, Lewis argued, many respondents might assume their interviewer to be "pro-Sandinista."[60] That was quite apart from the opposition rumor that the interviewer pools may have been infiltrated by members of Sandinista youth.[61] After the elections, Marvin Ortega told the *Los Angeles Times* that

> he and other pollsters underestimated how much fear the Sandinistas had instilled among Nicaraguans. He said many voters thought his pollsters were Sandinistas and mouthed support for Ortega, then voted against him.[62]

When Does *Güegüense* Tell theTruth?

Nicaraguans were apparently even afraid to admit they were afraid. Ninety-two percent of the Nicaraguans who by a three-to-two margin told Bendixen-Schroth (Univisión) that they intended to vote for Ortega also said they felt "personally free to participate openly in any of the presidential campaigns on behalf of any candidate I choose"![63] After the elections the *Washington Post's* polling director, Richard Morin, acknowledged "the apparent reluctance of Nicaraguans to answer poll questions directly," and Rob Schroth of Bendixen-Schroth concluded "we greatly underestimated the fear people have to respond to polls."[64] Morin told *Campaign Industry News:*

> Our polls were wrong because the people perceived the pollsters as representatives of the government. They, as a result, tailored their answers to what they thought we wanted to hear.[65]

Morin believed that Nicaraguan respondents "assume you are a part of the government or a part of the opposition canvassing team."[66] Professor Miller of the Commission on Nicaragua Pre-Election Polls wrote after the elections that:

> It is clear in retrospect that respondents were saying one thing to one group of polling organizations and the opposite to another group.[67]

During the campaign another Commission member, Professor Howard Schuman of Michigan University, directed a test poll in which one-third of the interviews were conducted with pens with Sandinista colors, another third with UNO pens, and a third with neutral pens. Only the surveys with UNO pens proved accurate, while both the Sandinista pens and the neutral pens yielded results similar to those in the American polls. Schuman concluded that "the 'neutral' poll was not believed to be neutral."[68]

Commission member Miller was left to wonder at "how respondents determined the political affiliation of the polltakers." Occasionally, the explanation was "straightforward, as when interviewers for Borge y Asociates [sic] introduced themselves as doing polling for *La Prensa*."[69] The CID-Gallup pollsters explained that their interviewers "conducted their work wearing a large identification [badge] prominently displaying the Costa Rican flag and stating CID-Gallup Costa Rica."[70] It was widely understood in Nicaragua that the Costa Rican government supported Chamorro's candidacy. ECO fieldworkers told respondents that their sponsor was UCA.[71] But in remaining cases, only rarely, Miller believes, could affiliations have been so widely aired by the partisan press.[72] Like many other visitors, he failed to take into account just how much was communicated by word-of-mouth in Nicaragua's still predominantly oral culture. Aside from the fact that for the last decade public opinion polls not authorized by the government had been banned, it should have come as no surprise that independent and impartial surveys were tramontane where state power has usually been a prize won violently, where allegiance came first, the rule of law last, and where numeration customarily had been a gambit for defrauding the unschooled.

Nonetheless, culture and tradition cannot explain, or explain away, everything. Marvin Saballos of Logos, the Nicaraguan subcontractor who conducted the Univisión/Bendixen-Schroth poll, put forth what proved to be a popular "cultural" explanation for the fiasco. The pollsters had run afoul of traditional "Nicaraguan social-psychology." Saballos invoked the comic folk hero *El Güegüense* who foils the "colonial authority" by responding to his demands with feigned deafness, ironic puns, and double entendres, seeming to obey without actually complying. In the same fashion:

> Sectors of the population distrusted the companies carrying out the polling, identifying them with the authorities and thus responded in a manner which confused the pollster and at the same time guaranteed what respondents considered to be their personal security.[73]

ABC's Peter Jennings also invoked *El Güegüense*.

> If you have followed our Nicaraguan coverage carefully over the last couple of weeks, you know that the ABC News-*Washington Post* poll has turned out to be terribly wrong. The only consolation may be an item in the *Economist* magazine which points out Nicaragua's Mayan mythology, including a character named the *Güegüense*. It wears a mask, it never lies, but never tells the truth.[74]

Other American journalists, along with professors and pollsters found this explanation felicitous.[75] *El Güegüense* appeared to provide a "cultural" explanation which had the additional merit of absolving press and polls from responsibility (by placing it squarely on the shoulders of perfidious Nicaraguans). It allowed one American pollster/professor to conclude that "there was little [the pollsters] *could* do to counter the effect of perceived affiliation."[76]

These interested parties failed to notice an inconsistency: their *Güegüenses* dissembled discriminately. If the Nicaraguans had distrusted all the polling firms, the *Güegüense* factor ought to have produced similar deviations in every survey. The Ortega voters would have equivocated to the Latin American pollsters, thus skewing those results. The UNO-leading polls then should have had a significant pro-UNO deviation to account for frightened Ortega voters counted as pro-Chamorro. Before the vote, expecting an Ortega victory, that is precisely what the Commission's Bollinger thought was happening.[77]

Yet, far from forecasting an exceedingly lopsided Chamorro victory, all but one of the UNO-leading polls came within the margin of error. The *Güegüense* factor does not show up on the UNO-leading polls. On the other hand, "the fourteen published FSLN-leading polls . . . differ[ed] from the eventual election results by no less than 11 percentage points and by as much as 29 percent."[78] Thus the pro-FSLN voters never felt the need to equivocate, while the pro-UNO voters equivocated only with the neutral and FSLN-inclined pollsters. In other words, the Sandinista voters consistently felt confident while those favoring the opposition were apprehensive. Such a picture squares with the other data we have presented.

El Güegüense lied only to interviewers thought to belong to the government and told the truth to interviewers displaying Costa Rican flags, openly working for a U.S. affiliate or displaying opposition pens. Since the number of pro-Sandinista responses in the Latin American polls approximated the outcome, even Sandinista voters evidently felt that they had nothing to hide from the "pro-Americans."

If Nicaraguans were candid only with UNO-leading polls (the ones questioned by the U.S. journalists) and if they viewed the U.S. Ortega-leading pollsters with suspicion, then how did they view U.S. journalists? Recall the journalists who "encountered hostile shouts of 'tell the truth'" at the return of Cardinal Obando y Bravo in 1985. Were Nicaraguans any more open with the journalists than with the pollsters? If they were not, what was the impact on U.S. reporting over the years?

Peter Jennings's remarks may be regarded either as "self-criticism" or as an attempt to evade responsibility for ABC's mistakes by blaming the Nicaraguans. As an editorial in *La Prensa* pointed out during the campaign, the comedy of *Güegüense* "was created to mock with the highest courtesy those who want to trample on the national pride."[79] The modern *Güegüense*, following the analogy, had cast the American interviewer as the "colonial authority"—certainly not the role the modern American journalist has assigned himself in the great drama of Third World liberation.

***

Nancy Llach, the USIA researcher, puts a reasonable question:

> How could such highly professional firms as Bendixen and Schroth and Belden and Russonello have made critical errors in the selection of their fieldwork contractors and the attribution of their survey sponsorship?[80]

Her answer suggests that the mistakes of the U.S. pollsters, like those of their compatriots in the press corps, were not isolated instances of poor judgment but reflected their view of the Sandinista regime:

> U.S. pollsters clearly underestimated the level of intimidation and fear felt at expressing opposition support by many Nicaraguans. Consequently, the import of interviewer associations with the Sandinista regime escaped notice. Instead, there was general concurrence with William Bollinger's assertion that "most opponents of the government freely express[ed] anti-Sandinista views."[81]

Llach contends that the Americans "were misled by the apparent willingness of Nicaraguans to discuss socio-political issues and by the ubiquitous sight of FSLN graffiti, flags, and slogans."[82] In this, of course, the pollsters were of a piece with the journalists. By contrast, the Argentine pollster Noguera concluded after four preparatory trips to Nicaragua that "the Sandinista Front was conducting a low-key campaign of intimidation to 'convince' people to attend rallies, wear party T-shirts and caps, etc."[83] Noguera's firm therefore structured its fieldwork in such a way that "interviewees could be made 100 percent comfortable and confident."[84]

The American pollsters and the Commission found unprofessional the practice of the Latin pollsters to place questions as to candidate preference after, rather than before, "background" questions. Since these background questions naturally alluded to the country's economic difficulties, the Americans regarded them as prejudicial and likely to elicit anti-Ortega responses. But the Latin pollsters responded that general uncontroversial questions were needed in Latin America in order to put diffident respondents at ease, and were especially necessary under the tense Nicaraguan circumstances. They would permit the interviewer to establish rapport by gradually easing the respondent into more controversial issues.[85]

Evidently, the Latin American and U.S. pollsters had different mental pictures of Nicaragua. If the U.S. pollsters entrusted their fieldwork to organizations which had earned the approval of the relevant government agency, to do so may have seemed quite natural—and might have been appropriate in a country in which public administration enjoys a degree of independence from the "incumbent" party. Besides, they might have reasoned, the only Nicaraguans with recent polling experience had exercised their trade with the blessing of the government—other polling being proscribed.

Dan Rather's inclusion of "the U.S. government" among those "stunned" by the election return was questionable.[86] A majority of government officials interviewed said they thought Chamorro might well win, although there was apparently a "constituency" in the State Department who thought otherwise.[87] But Rather was unquestionably right to include "American journalism" among the stupefied. For it was above all the *American* journalists—and pollsters and area specialists—who failed to see the signs of the impending debacle. The intentions of most of these professionals were irreproachable, and they went about their business professionally. Their reports and surveys were flawed, but they were not usually fraudulent. Yet these Americans proceeded with a kind of "innocence abroad" that recalls archetypes from the novels of Henry James and Graham Greene. The Quiet American was "impregnably armored with his good intentions and his ignorance." On his rather more vocal descendants, who had prided themselves on having shed "ethnocentric stereotypes," we find a similar carapace, though of superior resilience.

Stereotypes, Analogies, and Frames

The system of stereotypes which had come to regulate American perceptions of Latin America proved treacherous in Nicaragua. U.S. journalists, area specialists, and pollsters were familiar with traditional authoritarian governments. (All the pollsters had conducted polls in other Latin American countries.) These professionals were certain that Sandinista Nicaragua was different, but because they thought it more free, not even less so.[88]

Costa Rican pollsters at the American Association for Public Opinion Research postelection "Poll Wars" panel contended that the American pollsters failed to recognize that public opinion researchers faced problems under the Sandinista regime every bit as severe as those presented in neighboring right-wing authoritarian regimes. The statements of the coordinator of the Commission on Nicaraguan Pre-election Polls would seem to bear out the Costa Ricans. In 1988 Bollinger and his colleagues in PROCADOP found that while 65 percent of respondents in Tegucigalpa "said they believed Hondurans were afraid of expressing their political views in public" and "a significant number of Salvadorans told us they do not discuss politics, period, even with close friends or relatives." In Nicaragua "77 percent of some 1,129 respondents in Managua answered poll questions without apparent fear or distrust."[89]

One American pollster expressed "puzzlement" to Commission member Howard Schuman because in a neighboring country that both considered "even more repressive" than Nicaragua his polls had proved far more accurate. Schuman's analysis was that voters in the unnamed other Central American country had no expectation that the vote would be fair. On the other hand, Nicaraguan voters "were convinced that the election itself would be fair—probably based on the visible presence of large teams of outside observers—but not that poll organizations were impartial."

In this view it was the discrepancy between voters' distrust of pollsters and their trust in the ballot that produced the polling fiascoes. Schuman's implication was that in the other Central American country voters dissembled both to pollsters and in the voting booth. The variance in Nicaragua was due to the "large teams of outside observers."[90] But during Nicaragua's 1984 elections "large teams of outside observers" were also present, without any election surprise. Schuman should have added that the 1990 observers were perceived as impartial by Nicaraguans.

The presence in Nicaragua of neutral outside observers did make a crucial difference, but Schuman provided no evidence that polls diverged so radically from election returns in any "neighboring country." El Salvador appears to be the neighboring country in question (it had been the scene of polling by organizations belonging to Bollinger's PROCADOP and by Greenberg-Lake). But El Salvador conducted successful elections in the face of armed guerrilla boycotts—boycotts which many Salvadoran guerrilla and opposition leaders came to regard as a strategic error. Salvadoran opposition leaders accepted the Nicaraguan election results as reflective of the Sandinistas decline in popularity.[91]

Under the Sandinista regime citizens vigorously discussed politics, but at the same time dissembled; public opinion canvassers who presented themselves as "independent" were assumed to be covertly working for the government; and the ruling party turned out countless, cheering, T-shirted supporters who voted devoutly for the opposition as soon as they got the chance. After the elections several journalists related tales of Nicaraguans who, without the slightest intention of voting for him, wore Ortega T-shirts and sun visors simply because they were too destitute to be choosy about their clothes.[92] The reporters' implication here was that economics outweighed politics. But the Sandinistas did not lose solely because of economics. In the privacy of the voting booth the Nicaraguan voter shed his or her political disguise and terminated a regime, which is something more than deciding an election.[93]

That the meaning of citizens' behavior varies with their political system is no recent discovery. Aristotle observed that "the virtue of a citizen must necessarily be relative to the regime to which he belongs."[94] The same activity undertaken by citizens under one regime may carry a different political meaning in another. In Sandinista Nicaragua attending a political rally, cheering the President, wearing a campaign T-shirt, responding to a "neutral" pollster all carried different meanings from similar actions in Costa Rica or the United States. The similarity in form concealed a radical difference in content.

But the prevailing "system of stereotypes" prevented journalist and pollster alike from seeing beyond the similarity of forms. It led them to assume a different difference: Nicaraguans would vote for the Sandinistas because they did not want, as Swarthmore College professor Kenneth Sharpe wrote, "our political system, our economic system, our way of life."[95] The new paradigm had been born out of a perception of differences from the West. That perception, however, hardened into a barren stereotype.

The big international stories leading up to the Nicaraguan elections concerned *glasnost* and *perestroika* in the Soviet Union, the crackdown in Beijing, elections in Poland, the opening of Hungary's border, the fall of the Berlin Wall: that is to say, the crisis of most of the world's totalitarian regimes. The citizens of those countries were demonstrating their opposition not simply to a particular ruler or policy but to "the system in which we live" in Vaclav Havel's words.[96] Dissidents often publicly identified themselves with Western democracy and even with the United States.

Spokesmen for the Polish and Chinese regimes explicitly sought to represent their challengers as "puppets of the CIA." Nonetheless, the American media framed those stories not in terms of intervention and nationalism but as a contest between democracy and tyranny or "totalitarianism."[97] That was the frame for Solidarity's campaign against the Polish Communist Party's slate in the spring of 1989. Just before the elections the *New York Times* ran prominently an interview with an elegant woman running for Senate on the Solidarity ticket from a southeastern district of Poland which included Cracow:

> Probing the soul of this southern Polish region . . . , she talked of Cracow's patrician past as the seat of kings, and an intelligentsia grouped around the tradition-laden Jagellonian University.
> "In Cracow there is . . . an established intelligentsia, and naturally anti-Communist, linked to the aristocracy on the one hand and with the Catholic Church," she said. . . . "The working class was the most anti-Communist. And the mountain people, well, they are always the most contrary, the most independent. . . . " But the most vigorous force behind the campaign, in a deeply religious region, was the church.[98]

The manner in which American media covered their election campaigns was decidedly not among the many similarities between the outspoken Polish senator and Violeta Chamorro.

The journalists also ignored precedents and parallels closer to home. In the midst of the campaign Mrs. Chamorro appealed in a *Washington Post* op-ed to American elected officials, human rights organizations, labor unions, and "news and polling organizations" to "keep watch" so as to prevent Nicaragua from being "doomed to elections in the style of the Sandinistas' ally General Noriega."[99]

Six months earlier Noriega had refused to accept his overwhelming defeat by an opposition coalition in Panama's presidential elections. During the campaign government-organized gangs repeatedly attacked opposition supporters. Noriega was opposed by a coalition that closely resembled Violeta Chamorro's UNO. The most conspicuous Panamanian opposition leader in the U.S. media was the crusading publisher of an independent newspaper, coincidentally, named *La Prensa*! The pro-Noriega gangs, or "Dignity Battalions," which attacked opposition rallies, were modeled on the Sandinista *Turbas Divinas*, the "Divine Mobs," which performed similar functions during the Sandinistas' 1984 and 1990 elections. According to opposition leaders, the organizers of the Dignity Battalions were trained by Nicaragua and Cuba, Noriega's closest allies.[100] Noriega's main campaign strategy was to label his opponents "tools of U.S. imperialism," opposed to the authentic "Panamanian nationalism" which he embodied. Though confident of victory, Noriega was defeated by a three-to-one margin. His refusal to concede defeat was part of the chain of events which led to the U.S. invasion of December 1989. The invasion, though denounced by Noriega and his domestic and international supporters as an imperialist occupation, was acclaimed by an overwhelming majority of the Panamanians, according to the U.S. media.[101]

Throughout the campaign Chamorro repeatedly drew analogies with Eastern Europe and Panama as well as with the Philippines and Chile. She accepted her nomination by comparing herself to Corazon Aquino then declaring: "We're fighting for democracy, just like people in Poland and all over the world."[102] Her running mate claimed that Nicaragua's election was a "plebiscite" exactly like Panama.[103] Chamorro's *Washington Post* commentary began with the assertion that from "Manila to Mexico, from Budapest to Berlin to Beijing a great gale of democracy is blowing."[104] In January a Chamorro spokesman insisted, "This is not an election in the real sense of the word. . . . This is a plebiscite on Sandinista rule. It's pretty much the same as in Chile."[105] Chamorro's February stump speech proclaimed:

All across the world people like you are burying Communism and proclaiming democracy. So set your watches . . . to the same hour as Poland, as Bulgaria, as Czechoslovakia, as Chile![106]

At the final UNO rally in Managua Chamorro proclaimed that "the winds of change blow around the world and blow strong in Nicaragua. Somocista and Marxist-Leninist dictatorships are over."[107]

This view of the election remained outside of the American media frame. The U.S. invasion of Panama was cited by pollsters and press alike as having "played right into Ortega's hands"; it never evoked a comparison between Noriega's rule and that of the Sandinistas. Chamorro's insistently drawn analogy to Eastern Europe was ignored when it was not derided.[108]

A story by Juan Vasquez of CBS was a rare exception. It was the only report to present the Chamorro perspective on the relationship between the "economic issue" and the political. Vasquez correctly noted that the main theme of the Chamorro campaign "is that Daniel Ortega is a traitor who betrayed Nicaragua by turning a successful nationalist uprising into a communist revolution that has destroyed Nicaragua's economy."[109]

How would the coverage, polling, and scholarly analysis of Nicaragua turned out had an "Eastern European" rather than a "post-Vietnam" frame been "hegemonic?" Such a frame easily would have encompassed the Sandinista abuse of power, the totalitarian aspects of the regime and the widespread resistance to it.

The utility of an "Eastern European frame" can be illustrated by a front-page story by Mary Speck of the *Miami Herald*. The three paragraphs printed on page one contained conventional material about "Ortega . . . making over his image Madison Avenue style." But on page three the piece continued:

> But despite the hoopla there are signs that the Sandinista campaign may be a well-oiled machine that is better at mobilizing the masses than at convincing them to vote for the government ticket.
>
> "The Sandinistas have run a great campaign," said a Latin American diplomat who is following the election closely. "But great organization does not necessarily translate into great support. We've learned that lesson from Eastern Europe."[110]

Few of the Americans in Nicaragua had learned any such thing, at least until after the elections when the East European analogy suddenly, and briefly, became popular.[111] Far more representative of the general attitude toward the Eastern European analogy was the somewhat sardonic observation of ABC's David Ensor, who had recently returned from an extended assignment in Moscow. Chamorro had "presented her campaign as freedom's crusade against a new dictatorship, a crusade the United States has supported with words and with money."[112]

U.S. journalists, pollsters, and professors all believed the Sandinistas would win the 1990 elections because Ortega spoke the language of anti-U.S. nationalism. For these Americans the invincibility of radical nationalism had become an article of faith ever since Vietnam. In their minds the UNO opposition was tainted precisely by its association with the United States and the U.S.-supported *Contra* rebels.[113]

The Sandinistas ran an "American-style campaign" which the American media, pollsters, and academics found highly effective. The Chamorro coalition campaigned in a more traditional Nicaraguan style and got the majority of its countrymen's votes—to the astonishment of the American experts.

The majority of Nicaraguan voters must have found the American-style campaign of the Sandinistas inappropriate or worse, but they supported UNO's American-style message of democracy versus communism. The message of radical anti-Americanism, so seductive to the American reporters, pollsters, and professors in Nicaragua, had lost whatever charm it had for Nicaraguans. The Americans, for all their militant sensitivity to ethnocentrism, to "the Latin American viewpoint," were preoccupied by something else—the putative U.S. role in the Third World. They were unprepared for actual Nicaraguans.

For sheer tenacity the laurels go to the quixotic postelectoral analysis of Commission member Barnes who contends that the Ortega-lead polls revealed a "deeper truth" than the elections.[114] From those surveys Barnes concluded that "the broad ideals of the Revolution remain hegemonic, the election results notwithstanding," and that Nicaraguans should look to "a new Third Worldism . . . which the Sandinista movement . . . will help to formulate."[115]

Unfortunately for resolute Third Worlders and for Daniel Ortega, who had attributed his first defeat to U.S. economic and military pressure, Ortega suffered another rout in 1996. With U.S. hostility a thing of the past, the Sandinista's second re-election bid was overwhelmed by a virtually identical margin (51 to 37.7 percent). Moreover, on that subsequent occasion Ortega did not face a united opponent, as the UNO coalition had splintered. Nor did Ortega have to contend with the "advantages of incumbency," since Mrs. Chamorro chose not to run again. She endorsed the splinter-party candidacy of her son-in-law and Chief Minister Antonio Lacayo, whom voters held responsible for the widespread corruption during the Chamorro years. The *New York Times* observed that: "In contrast to the February 25, 1990, election . . . today's vote was remarkably free of political tension and fears of fraud or voter intimidation."[116]

Notes

1. Richard Morin and Lee Hockstader, "Pre-Election Poll Shows Ortega Leads: Surveys Influence Nicaraguan Politics," *WP*, February 21, 1990, A1.

2. "Charla de cronistas," *La Crónica*, Managua (March 8-14, 1990): 10.

3. Our computerized survey utilized the sixteen major news outlets available on NEXIS, an online computer service. It was restricted to news stories which appeared during the six months up to and including election day. The survey included news stories datelined after August 25, 1989 through February 25, 1990. The sixteen news outlets were *ABC-Television News*, the *Boston Globe, Chicago Tribune, Christian Science Monitor, Los Angeles Times, MacNeil-Lehrer News Hour, New York Times, Seattle Times, San Francisco Chronicle, USA Today, Washington Post, Wall Street Journal, Newsweek, Time, US News*, and UPI.

In order to establish an objective criterion for article selection, the computer search was designed to call up only articles citing preelection polls and was confined to a fixed six-month time period. Thus, for example, a February 16 *Wall Street Journal* article stated that "it is too soon to predict who will win the election." Since it did not cite public opinion surveys, it was not counted in the tabulation. Editorials and opinion pieces were also excluded.

Steven Kaplitt of Georgetown University Law Center provided indispensable technical counsel. Leslie Cintron of the Harvard University Department of Sociology double-checked the findings for accuracy.

Differences in time period and content explain the slight disparities between our survey and that of the Center for Media and Public Affairs. Our survey excluded editorials and opinion pieces and covered the period August 26, 1989 to February 25, 1990. The

Center's survey encompassed the period February 1 to March 31, 1990, and included editorials and commentaries as well as news stories.

According to the Center's Research Director Daniel Amundson, the two items which failed to cite the Sandinistas as likely winners were a February 26, 1990, *Time* magazine article and a *New York Times* "op-ed."

The *Time* magazine article fell outside the period of our survey which ended on election day, but since news magazines are predated, it appeared before the elections and thus constituted a kind of prediction. However, the article did not actually predict a Chamorro victory. The piece merely observed that "opinion polls project wildly conflicting results." The item noted astutely that: "The discrepancy confirms a suspicion that Nicaraguans, unused to honest elections and chary of speaking their minds to strangers, say whatever they think a pollster wants to hear" (John Moody, "The Odd Couple Plays Managua" *Time* [February 26, 1990]: 25). Moreover, our time frame also excluded a February 26 *Newsweek* piece which stated: "Ortega is the favorite. Recent opinion polls show his Sandinistas ahead" (Charles Lane, "Voting on the Revolution," *Newsweek* [February 26, 1990]: 48).

The opinion piece forecasting a Chamorro victory in the Center for Media and Public Affairs survey was dated February 12, 1990, and stated that the opposition "seems poised to win the February 25 elections" ("The Sandinistas Might Lose," *NYT*, February 12, 1990, A21.) It was written by Robert S. Leiken. On February 21 the *Times* balanced that commentary with one of the same length and placement. "Nicaragua: The Sour-Grapes Brigade" by Ralph I. Fine and Kenneth E. Sharpe rebutted the earlier op-ed and foresaw "an imminent Sandinista victory at the polls" based on surveys "by the most reliable pollsters," *NYT*, February 21, 1990, A25.

Several other opinion pieces divined Sandinista defeat. In his syndicated column Ben Wattenberg's "guess from far away" was "that the Sandinistas are going to lose" ("Betting on an Upset", *WT*, February 14, 1990). Carlos Alberto Montaner, a social democratic Cuban exile and an editor of Miami's *El Nuevo Heraldo* deduced a Chamorro victory "from common sense and historical experience." He specifically cited the Costa Rican and Venezuelan opinion polls ("Don't Predict the Nicaragua Vote," *MH*, February 21, 1990). The *Wall Street Journal*'s David Asman also cited conflicting surveys to question the U.S. poll results in "Nicaragua's Through-the-Looking-Glass Election," *WSJ*, February 22, 1990; Jean Kirkpatrick speculated in "Can the Sandinistas Steal the Elections?" *WP*, January 22, 1990, that "Daniel Ortega just might lose the election anyway, much in the way Communist candidates were swept to defeat in Poland"; Rowland Evans and Robert Novak foresaw a Sandinista defeat in "Chamorro Surging as Vote nears," (*New York Post*, February 16, 1990) but then seemed to change their minds in their next piece: "In Nicaragua, Too Little Too Late," *WP*, February 21, 1990.

4. The *Chicago Tribune* ran an Associated Press wire service report quoting "a senior State Department official," who claimed that Ortega's decision would be "a pretext to end the election process." The report then added: "Recent polls show Ortega to be trailing the U.S.-backed presidential candidate, Violeta Chamorro, in campaigning for February's elections ("U.S. Keeps up Attack on Ortega over Cease-Fire," *CT*, October 31, 1989, C4). In a similar context Juan Walte reported in *USA Today* that "a Gallup Poll in Nicaragua last week gave the opposition an 11-point edge" and cited Susan Kaufman Purcell, a Latin American specialist who attributed Ortega's action to a possible fear of losing the election ("Ortega 'Looking for a Way Out,'" *USAT*, October 30, 1989, 4A).

5. The election day too-close-to-call report was Storer H. Rowley and Nathaniel Sheppard, Jr., "Close Race Expected in Nicaragua," *CT*, February 25, 1990, 1. The *Los*

Angeles Times and UPI of that day both seemed to step back from earlier suggestions that the Sandinistas were sure winners (see Marjorie Miller and Richard Boudreaux, "World Keeps Watch as Nicaragua Polls Open," *LAT*, February 25, 1990, A1; Douglas Tweedale, "Nicaraguans Vote in Ortega-Chamorro Showdown," UPI, BC Cycle, February 25, 1990).

The *Times* would seem to have its correspondent to thank for its prudence. In early September the newspaper ran a front-page article citing public opinion surveys which "showed that voters prefer the Sandinista Front to the opposition by nearly 2 to 1" (Steven Kinzer, "Anti-Sandinistas Choose Candidate," *NYT*, September 4, 1989, 1). In several respects the article was unusual. It was written not by the current *Times* correspondent Mark Uhlig who was on vacation but by his predecessor, Steven Kinzer. The latter was on an extended leave of absence from the *Times* writing his memoir on Nicaragua before taking up assignment in West Germany in 1990. Kinzer had been the *Times*'s Managua bureau chief from 1983 to January 1989 when Uhlig succeeded him. Kinzer's article was drafted in Boston where Kinzer was engaged in writing his book (Kinzer, *Blood of Brothers* [New York: Putnam, 1991], 388-89).

Three surveys were conducted in Nicaragua during the summer in which the article appeared. Two had Ortega in front by a large margin but one favored Chamorro. The Chamorro-leading survey was conducted for *La Prensa*, *La Nación* of Costa Rica, and *El Nuevo Heraldo*, the Spanish-language counterpart of the *Miami Herald*. The results were reported in the July 15, 1989, *Miami Herald*. Kinzer cited polls showing Ortega with a large lead but ignored a poll which showed Ortega trailing by a similar margin. This suggests that he departed Nicaragua with the sense that the Sandinistas retained much of their popularity, though his book, published after the elections, suggests otherwise (Kinzer, *Blood of Brothers*, 385).

Kinzer's article was the only occasion on which the *Times* was to cite public opinion polls to predict a winner in the Chamorro-Ortega race. The *Times* "too close to call" citation came in an article datelined Atlanta mentioning the first Univisión poll "showing a virtual dead heat" ("Carter Says Sandinistas are Trying to Smear Foes," *NYT*, November 15, 1989, A11).

All this suggests that the *Times* took the lead from its correspondents for its policy on the preelection polls.

Distance from Nicaragua, as in Kinzer's case, could not have been the explanation for the *Washington Post*'s reportage. Reporting on the very same polls Kinzer had employed, the *Post*'s bureau chief Lee Hockstader wrote in October: "Polls taken during the summer, before Chamorro was nominated, suggest that the Sandinistas start the campaign with a substantial advantage." (Hockstader, "Nicaraguan Opposition Operating on a Shoestring," *WP*, October 13, 1989, A1).

6. Conservative journals carried most of the critical articles on the media coverage of the elections. See Arturo J. Cruz and Mark Falcoff, "Who Won Nicaragua?" *Commentary* 89, no. 5 (May 1990); and Terry Eastland, "Press Watch: Peter and the Wolves," *The American Spectator* (May 1990). *The New Republic*, a liberal weekly, carried Robert S. Leiken, "Oops," *TNR*, March 19, 1990.

7. Examples of articles criticizing the polls include: Don Podesta, "Pollsters Try to Explain Failure to Spot Result," *WP*, February 27, 1990, A17; Tom Fielder, "For Pollsters, Upset Carries a Bitter Sting," *MH*, February 27, 1990, 13A; Norman Ornstein, "Why Polls Flopped in Nicaragua," *NYT*, March 4, 1990, A25; Howard Schuman, "3 Different Pens Help Tell the Story," *NYT*, March 7, 1990, A25; Jim Hoagland, "Dictators, Beware Those Good Polls," *WP*, March 1, 1990, A25. See also, an article by the late

Los Angeles Times polling expert I. A. Lewis, "'Poll Wars' and Poll Debacle in Nicaragua," *The Public Perspective* (May/June 1990).

8. Fiedler, "For Pollsters Upset Carries a Bitter Sting," 13A.

9. *ABC Nightline*, February 21, 1990; and *NBC Nightly News*, February 26, 1990 (Brokaw's emphasis).

10. Podesta, "Pollsters Try to Explain Failure," A17.

The Interamerican Research Center of California State University/Los Angeles was able to obtain results from 28 preelection surveys conducted in Nicaragua in the twelve-month period before the elections. Of these fourteen favored the Sandinistas and fourteen the opposition.

Peter V. Miller, a professor of Communication Studies and Journalism at Northwestern University, who was a member of the Commission on Pre-Election Polls, analyzed a similar but not identical list in his article, "Polls—A Review: Which Side Are You On? The 1990 Nicaraguan Poll Debacle," *Public Opinion Quarterly* 55, no. 2 (Summer 1991): 281-302.

The *Post* did not get it quite right even after the fact. According to both Miller and the Commission five of the last nine polls had UNO in the lead, not the Sandinistas. The *Post* may have been misled by a press release from the Commission which carried a table erroneously showing the Sandinistas in front in five of the last nine polls.

11. Bernard de la Grange, "La guerre des sondages prend de l'ampleur," ("The Poll War Widens") *Le Monde*, February 20, 1990, 4.

12. The Latin American firms were Borge and Associates and CID-Gallup of Costa Rica, DOXA of Venezuela, and Mora y Araujo of Argentina.

A rare nondisparaging mention of a Latin American survey in the news columns of a U.S. newspaper during 1990 was printed in the ninth paragraph of a January 25, 1990 Reuters story ("Ortega increasing preelection lead, latest poll shows," *Seattle Post-Intelligencer*, January 25, 1990.

Three opinion pieces gave some favorable attention to the Latin polls favor and questioned the U.S./Nicaragua surveys: Montaner, "Don't predict the Nicaragua vote;" Asman, "Nicaragua's Through-the-Looking-Glass Election;" and Leiken, "The Sandinistas Might Lose."

Le Monde featured both a Venezuelan poll and the Univisión polls of mid-February in its article on the poll wars and gave prominence to the Costa Rican polls in its article on the closing of the campaign (see de la Grange, "La guerre des sondages"; and "Le Front sandiniste mobilise ses partisans," *Le Monde*, February 23, 1990).

13. Carlos Denton and Miguel Gomez, "Public Opinion Polling in Central America: Looking at Nicaragua and Beyond" (paper presented at the 45th annual meeting of the American Association for Public Opinion Research (AAPOR) panel "Poll Wars: Observers Discuss the Pre-Election Polls in Nicaragua," May 1990), 10. The initials CID signify Interdisciplinary Development Consultants (Consultoria Interdisciplinaria en Desarrollo, S.A.). William Bollinger and Daniel Lund ("Mixing Polls and Propaganda: Gallup in Central America," *The Nation* [May 7, 1988]: 635-38) describe Denton as "a U.S. political scientist who has resided in the region on and off since 1945."

14. Boudreaux, "Chamorro Losing Ground in Nicaragua," *LAT*, February 15, 1990, A9.

15. See Miller, "Polls—A Review," 283-85, table 1.

16. The *Times*'s claim that Chamorro had "lost in all five voter opinion polls published in recent weeks, and three of the surveys give the Sandinista leader a huge advantage" is more difficult to explain. According to the tabulations both of Peter V. Miller and

the Commission, three of the five most recent polls before the *Times* article gave UNO the advantage.

17. Denton and Gomez, "Public Opinion Polling in Central America," 3, 10, 13-15.

18. Morin and Hockstader, "Pre-Election Poll Shows Ortega Leads," A1.

19. Phone interview with Commission Coordinator William Bollinger, February 23, 1990.

20. Miller, "Polls—A Review," 301; Nancy C. Llach, *The Nicaraguan Pre-Election Surveys: Rights and Wrongs* (Washington, DC: United States Information Agency, Office of Research, American Republics Branch, April 1991), 12-13.

21. Author's conversations with Violeta Chamorro, Antonio Lacayo, and Virgilio Godoy, Managua, April 19-20 1989, and with Antonio Lacayo, Violeta Chamorro, Pedro J. Chamorro, Jr., and Ernesto Palazio, New York City, November 6, 1989.

22. Phillip Bennett, "Poll: Managuans Oppose Contra and Are Split on Leaders," *BG*, July 1, 1988.

23. Bollinger as cited in Instituto para el Analisis de los Medios, "El Fracaso de la Intervention de Estados Unidos en las Elecciones de Nicaragua," *Quien Es Quien*, no. 4: 11. The citation is somewhat muddled, but it is apparently taken from a report by Bollinger for the Interamerican Research Center dated February 8, 1989.

24. Bollinger, *"La Prensa* Poll #1," *Interamerican Research Center Public Opinion Series*, no. 10 (August 1989).

25. Bollinger and Lund, "Mixing Polls and Propaganda," 635-38. See also James C. Coleman and Lee Siegelman, "Poll Review: 1985 USIA Central American Surveys," *Public Opinion Quarterly* 52 (Fall 1988): 552-56; William J. Millard, "Poll Review Response: The USIA Central American Surveys," *Public Opinion Quarterly* 53 (Winter 1988): 134-35.

26. For example, USIA public opinion surveys conducted by CID/Gallup in 1987 found that between 75 and 90 percent of those polled in El Salvador, Guatemala, Honduras, and Costa Rica had unfavorable views of the Nicaraguan government and between 70 and 75 percent wished to see a *Contra* military victory. See United States Information Agency, Office of Research, Research Memorandum M-5/7/87.

27. Bollinger, "Taking the Pulse of Social Justice in Central America," *Interamerican Public Opinion Report* (January 1990): 7; telephone interview with Bollinger, February 23, 1990.

28. Miller, "Polls—A Review," 299-300.

29. Miller, "Polls—A Review," 300.

30. A previous *Post* story (John M. Goshko and Al Kamen, "U.S. Accused of Overstating Managua Election Offenses," *WP*, January 25, 1990, A29) which reported the results of the Greenberg-Lake poll (Ortega leading Chamorro by 51 to 24 percent) described the poll's sponsor Hemisphere Initiatives as "a Boston-based American group whose polling and monitoring in Nicaragua is regarded as objective by many observers." The *Post* did not name any of these observers. John MacAward, the former Human Rights director of the liberal Boston-based Unitarian-Universalist Service Committee, described the group leaders as "Sandinista sympathizers" (Telephone interview January 31, 1989). Hemisphere Initiatives did much of its informational work on the Nicaraguan elections in conjunction with the Universalist-Unitarian Service Committee as well as the better-known Washington Office on Latin America and the Center for International Policy (see for example its information packet "Nicaragua's Elections . . . a step towards democracy," Boston 1990). All of these groups have been spirited critics of U.S. policy in Central America.

In a February 23, 1990 telephone interview with the author, Professor Bollinger acknowledged that he belonged to the Board of Hemisphere Initiatives, and conceded the group's partisan profile, but maintained that he had not been involved in their recent Nicaraguan polling efforts. However, Hemisphere Initiatives names Bollinger, along with Stanley Greenberg, president of Greenberg-Lake, as its polling consultant in its list of "Media Contacts." Besides Bollinger, two other members of the Commission belonged to the Advisory Board of Hemisphere Initiatives.

None of the newspaper reports on the Greenberg-Lake poll examined the credentials of Hemisphere Initiatives, the poll's sponsor. The *San Francisco Chronicle*'s report described Greenberg-Lake as "a highly professional firm" (January 25, 1990). *USA Today* ran a large graphic embodying the "Survey of 901 voters for Hemisphere Initiatives; sampling error is 4 percent" accompanying its article which described Ortega as "a crowd-pleaser" and "wildly popular" (February 1, 1990), but the article did not characterize Hemisphere Initiatives. The *Los Angeles Times* (January 29, 1990) report on the poll mentioned "Hemisphere Initiatives, a Boston-based group monitoring the Nicaraguan election," but added that opposition leaders had alleged that Itztani, "the Nicaraguan polling firm working with Greenberg-Lake is biased toward the Sandinistas." The *Miami Herald* (January 28, 1990) and the *Boston Globe* (Reuters, January 25, 1990) reported the results with no comment. An op-ed in the *Christian Science Monitor* (Brad R. Roth, "What if the Sandinistas Win Fairly?" *CSM*, January 25, 1990) characterized Itztani as "independent."

Subsequent fundraising appeals for Hemisphere Initiatives featured prominently the *Post* account of its "objective" polling and monitoring (*e.g.,* fundraising letter of February 6, 1990).

31. Latin American Studies Association (LASA), *The Electoral Process in Nicaragua: Domestic and International Influences* (report of the LASA Delegation to Observe the Nicaraguan General Election of November 4, 1984), 32, 18.

The Latin American specialists on the Commission on Nicaraguan Pre-Election Polls were all outspoken opponents of U.S. policy towards Central America and warmly sympathetic to the Sandinista regime. The three Latin Americanists on the Commission who participated in the writing of the report were John A. Booth (University of North Texas), Lars Schoulz (University of North Carolina, Chapel Hill), and Thomas Walker (Ohio University). Walker was cochair of the LASA delegation and Schoulz was president-elect of LASA at the time of the 1990 elections. Of the Commission's other Latin Americanists, one was Tommie Sue Montgomery (Agnes Scott College), an outspoken supporter of both the FSLN and the Salvadoran guerrillas. See for example her *Revolution in El Salvador: Origins and Evolution* (Boulder, Colorado: Westview Press, 1982). The other was William A. Barnes who wrote in January 1990 that the Hemisphere Initiatives poll of the previous month which gave Ortega a 17-point lead was "probably a more accurate indicator of current voting intentions among most likely voters than any other poll." Barnes thought its disparity with other polls likely to continue "if only because powerful groups are willing to ensure that there are at least some polls showing Chamorro no worse than tied." But such efforts would not avail because "most Nicaraguans are too nationalistic to simply be bought by a lavishly financed UNO campaign" (Barnes, "U.S. Media and Government Ignore Nicaraguan Public Opinion," *The Central American Bulletin* [January 1990]: 6-7).

Not all members of the Commission, which included several reputable academic public opinion analysts, were publicly associated with pro-Sandinista views. As is usually the case with such enterprises, the Commission included members who may very well have been genuinely neutral.

At least one invitation to participate on the Commission was spurned. Norman Webb of Gallup International wrote to Bollinger to decline his invitation, complaining: "the nature of [your] attacks [on CID and Gallup] reveals serious shortcomings in what you regard as evidence. So how independent, nonpartisan, etc. can this Commission be?" (Webb's letter to Bollinger is cited in Llach, *The Nicaraguan Pre-Election Surveys*, 13.)

32. "Nicaragua Election Forecasts," *BG*, January 27, 1990, 14. The editorial was written by Randolph Ryan, whose signed columns were strongly supportive of the Sandinistas and assumed an easy Sandinista victory (*e.g.,* "Nicaragua Testing Time," *BG*, February 21, 1990, 19). On the basis of the polls, Ryan predicted a landslide Sandinista election victory on the Boston CBS television talk show *Boston Common* on Sunday, February 18, 1990.

33. Llach, *The Nicaraguan Pre-Election Surveys*, 14.

34. This is not intended to impugn the integrity of Llach's work simply because she is a public servant.

35. For an analysis of this kind of manipulation see Stephen Klaidman, "Blowing Smoke," 1989 Essay Contest Winner, Wilson Center Competition in Media Studies, Washington, 1989.

36. Morin and Hockstader, "Pre-Election Poll Shows Ortega Leads," A1, A17.

37. Denton and Gomez, "Public Opinion Polling in Central America," 10.

38. Felipe Noguera, "South Polls," *Campaigns & Elections* (April-May 1990), 36.

39. For a discussion of the press' reaction to Oliver North and Iran-*Contra*, see Leiken, "The Making of a Mock Epic," *Times Literary Supplement* (February 10-16, 1989).

40. Examples of the use of the term "*Contra*": question #19 in the Bendixen-Schroth (Univisión) poll released February 12, 1990, and questions #24 and #25 in the Greenberg-Lake poll, January 1990.

There seems to have been some recognition that "*Contra*" was a loaded term, oddly enough, in a previous poll conducted by the same pollster who later directed the field work for both the ABC/*Washington Post* and the Greenberg-Lake poll, "the term '*Contras*' was dropped from early questionnaire drafts in favor of 'Nicaraguan Resistance'" (Interamerican Research Center, 4).

41. "Focus—Vote on Change," *MacNeil-Lehrer NewsHour*, February 23, 1990.

42. The procedure was that the American firms would design the surveys (Greenberg-Lake for Hemisphere Initiatives, Belden and Russonello for ABC/*Washington Post* and Bendixen-Schroth for Univisión) and then subcontract a Nicaraguan firm for the fieldwork.

43. Bollinger praised them highly in a telephone conversation with the author on February 23, 1990.

44. Interamerican Research Center, 5.

45. Denton and Gomez, "Public Opinion Polling in Central America," 8.

46. Denton and Gomez, "Public Opinion Polling in Central America," 8.

47. Denton and Gomez, "Public Opinion Polling in Central America," 6.

48. After the elections the independent Nicaraguan weekly published the acerbic commentary cited at the outset of this chapter. The item suggests how that publication saw the ties between American academia and Nicaragua as reflected in the person of Peter Marchetti.

49. Peter Marchetti, "The Disenchanted Liberal Stereotype," *In These Times* (March 13-19, 1985). The article was a criticism of the present author's "Nicaragua's Untold Stories," *TNR*, October 8, 1984.

50. See for example *Una Tragedia Campesina*, ed. Alejandro Bendaña (Managua: Edit-Arte, 1991), 38-51; and Forrest D. Colburn, *Post-Revolutionary Nicaragua: State Classes and the Dilemmas of Agrarian Reform* (Berkeley: University of California, 1986), especially chapters iv-v.

51. See Miller, "Polls—A Review," 283-86. See also Hemisphere Initiatives, "Nicaragua's Elections."

52. Julia Preston, "Nicaragua's Rulers Live By Revolution," *WP*, July 2, 1989, A1; her comment about the campaign is cited at the beginning of section III.

53. Llach, *The Nicaraguan Pre-Election Surveys*, 4.

54. Author's telephone interview with Bollinger, February 23, 1990.

55. Telephone conversation with Ernesto Palazio from Managua, February 21, 1990. The *Washington Post* reported dismissively that *La Prensa* considered the fieldworkers for the February Univisión poll (which showed Ortega with a commanding 18-point lead) "had been infiltrated by the Sandinistas" (Morin and Hockstader, "Pre-Election Poll Shows Ortega Leads," A1).

56. Llach, *The Nicaraguan Pre-Election Surveys*, 4.

57. Morin and Hockstader, "Pre-Election Poll Shows Ortega Leads," A1.

58. William Branigin, "Election Shattered Many Sandinista Myths, *WP*, March 2, 1990, A26.

59. Llach, *The Nicaraguan Pre-election Surveys*, 5.

60. I. A. Lewis, "Poll Wars," 15. Commission member William Barnes acknowledged that "such people . . . probably were . . . the most pro-Revolution, pro-FSLN demographic group" (Barnes, "Rereading the Polls," in *The 1990 Elections in Nicaragua and Their Aftermath*, ed. Vanessa Castro and Gary Prevost [Lanham, Maryland: Rowman & Littlefield, 1992], 85).

61. See Llach, *The Nicaraguan Pre-Election Surveys*, 4; and Noguera, "South Polls." Commission member Barnes twice states that he found "no evidence" for the charge (Barnes, "Rereading the Polls," 79, 85).

62. Miller and Boudreaux, "Sandinistas Conclude They Lost Touch With Populace," *LAT*, March 4, 1990, A12.

63. News release, Bendixen-Schroth (Univisión), February 12, 1990.

64. Podesta, "Pollsters Try to Explain Failure," A17; Fiedler, "For Pollsters Upset Carries a Bitter Sting," 13A; Scroth made a similar observation to the *Washington Times*: Price, *WT*, February 27, 1990.

65. Christian K. Foreman, "Danny: Yank Polls Stank!" *Campaign Industry News* (April 1990): 11.

66. Fiedler, "For Pollsters Upset Carries a Bitter Sting," 13A.

67. Miller, "Polls—A Review," 295.

68. Schuman, "3 Different Pens."

Schuman's experiment was the subject of curious interpretations by Commission members. Before the elections, when he was expecting a Sandinista victory, Commission coordinator Bollinger cited the experiment as evidence that subjects lied not to the Sandinistas but to UNO. Bollinger assumed that the "neutral" poll would be in line with election results. Bollinger's assessment of Schuman's experiment (an assessment he claimed was identical to that of Schuman) was that Nicaraguans were reticent only with pollsters bearing the UNO pen. Our independent analyst went on to explain this behavior as a result of the fact that Nicaraguans "feared the consequences" of divulging their true preferences to those associated with the "pro-American opposition" (Interview with Bollinger, February 23, 1990).

Another commissioner, Northwestern's Peter V. Miller later disclosed that one reason why Schuman's "'neutral' polltakers were viewed as probable government representatives or sympathizers' was because they associated themselves with the UCA which "may have been perceived as Sandinista affiliated" (Miller, "Polls—A Review," 297). Miller himself suggested that since the FSLN-leading polls were sponsored by U.S. groups, "respondents may have tended to give support to the Sandinistas out of a sense that they should show a united front against the U.S. pressure" (Miller, "Polls—A Review," 297). By this account we would have to conclude that Nicaraguans' antiimperialism influenced their replies to pollsters but not their voting. Stereotypes die hard.

69. Miller, "Polls—A Review," 297.

70. Denton and Gomez, "Public Opinion Polling in Central America," 11.

71. Miller, "Polls—A Review," 297.

72. Certainly literacy rates were highly exaggerated thanks to the much advertised but short-lived Sandinista "literacy campaign" of 1980. However, fellow Commissioner Barnes notes that Sandinista television boosted the Ortega-lead polls and "radio talk show hosts of all political persuasions commented and joked about the poll war." (Barnes, "Rereading the Polls," 86).

73. Marvin Saballos' commentary in *Interamerican Public Opinion Report* (Spring 1990): 5; see also Lewis, "'Poll Wars,'" 15.

UNO supporters had employed the *Güegüense* analogy earlier in attacking the Ortega-leading polls. An editorial in *La Prensa* compared the "false polls" to the ploys of "colonizers" who "exchanged gold for glass beads and mirrors." *Güegüense* was created "at the time of the Colony . . . to mock with the highest courtesy those who want to trample on the national pride" ("El pueblo no se engaña con falsas encuestas," *La Prensa*, January 26, 1990, 2).

The character *El Güegüense* is the protagonist of the folk comic-ballet "El Güegüense o el Macho Ratón," transcribed probably in the middle of the seventeenth century in a Nahuatl/Spanish dialect. To this day the play sometimes is performed at festival time in the plazas and atria of Diriamba, Diriomo, Catarina, and other Nicaraguan villages and towns.

The picaresque *mestizo el Güegüense*—whose name seems to be both a play on the Nahuatl for "*viejecito*" (old guy) and on the Spanish for Nicaraguan (*Nicaragüense*)—responds to the colonial governor's demands with flattery, calculated misunderstanding, feigned deafness, double entendres, and other verbal slapstick. He professes obedience but never complies, finally appropriating what is dearest to the governor, his daughter, for his son's bride.

The text of the original comic ballet may be found in Alvarez. For commentaries on "the preeminent character of Nicaragua literature" and the historical importance of the character, see also Pablo Antonio Cuadra, "El Primer Personaje de la Literatura Nicaragüense: El Güegüence," in *El Nicaragüese* (Managua: Pez y Serpiente, 1981), 90-97; and Jorge Edcuardo Arellano, *Panorama de la literatura nicaragüese* (Managua: Nueva Nicaragua, 1982), 22. For a modern American journalist's perspective on the Latin American tradition of *obedecer pero no cumplir* (obeying without complying—formally respecting authority without actually executing its commands), see Christopher Dickey, "I obey but I do not comply," in Leiken, *Central America: Anatomy of Crisis* (Washington: Carnegie Endowment for International Peace/Pergamon, 1984).

74. *ABC World News Tonight*, February 26, 1990.

75. For example Preston in "Looking Back at the Revolution," *NYRB*, July 18, 1991; Peter Jennings, *ABC World News Tonight*, February 26, 1990; and Miller "Polls—A Review," 297, 298, fn. 18.

76. Miller, "Polls—A Review," 297

77. Phone interview with William Bollinger, February 23, 1990.

78. The average deviation in half (seven) of the FSLN-leading polls taken closest to election day was over 20 percent. On the other hand, "the average absolute deviation from the actual UNO vote share for all 14 [UNO-leading] polls is 5 percent, about the same as the average deviation noted by [Irving] Crespi [in his *Pre-Election Polling: Sources of Accuracy and Error*] in his examination of 430 U.S. preelection polls" (Miller, "Polls—A Review," 28).

79. "El pueblo no se engaña," 2.

80. Llach, *The Nicaraguan Pre-Election Surveys*, 7.

81. Llach, *The Nicaraguan Pre-Election Surveys*, 7.

82. Llach, *The Nicaraguan Pre-Election Surveys*, 8.

83. Noguera, "South Polls," 36.

84. Llach, *The Nicaraguan Pre-Election Surveys*, 9.

85. For an account of one instance of the benefits of a considerable get-acquainted period with a resident of Monimbo, Nicaragua, see Leiken, "Nicaragua's Untold Stories," 19.

86. See chapter 1, 2 *supra*.

87. Officials interviewed by the author cited cables from the U.S. embassy in Managua predicting a Chamorro victory. *Miami Herald* columnist Carlos Alberto Montaner apparently spoke to some of the same officials. "The U.S. State Department," he wrote, "shared this opinion" of the Venezuelans and Costa Ricans "that Violeta will sweep the elections if they are honest" ("Don't Predict Nicaraguan Vote"). A *Washington Post* reporter found a State Department official who claimed to represent a "constituency" in the department which seemed to foresee a Sandinista victory (James M. Dorsey, "U.S. Officials View Fair Vote as Chance to Close Old Issue," *WP*, February 26, 1990, A7, cited in Robert Kagan, *A Twilight Struggle: American Power and Nicaragua, 1977-1990* [New York: Free Press, 1996], 699). One State Department official also indicated to me off-the-record that he believed the CIA expected a Sandinista victory.

88. They assumed it was different because it was less repressive, not because Sandinista repression was of a more "modern" and "scientific" character. For a discussion of this point, see Leiken, "The Nicaraguan Tangle: Another Exchange," *NYRB*, June 26, 1986.

89. Bollinger and Lund, "The Perils of Polling," Pacific News Service, undated, but distributed over PNS wire in August 1988.

90. Schuman, "3 Different Pens."

91. Author's interview with Ruben Zamora, Presidential Candidate of Convergenica Democrática, San Salvador, March 23, 1990; and *comandante* Ferman Cienfuegos of the Faribundo Martí National Liberation Front, March 30, 1990, Mexico City.

92. For example, see Larry Rohter, "Ortega Spurned in an Old Stronghold," *NYT*, March 5, 1990; Ana Puga, "Visions of Nicaragua's Future Vary," *HC*, March 4, 1990, 27A; Preston, *NYRB*, April 12, 1990.

93. For a discussion of the ideological and manipulative character of People's Democracy, see Vaclav Havel, *Living in Truth* (London: Faber and Faber, 1989); and Leszek Kolakowski, "Totalitarianism and the Virtue of the Lie," in *1984 Revisited*, ed. Irving Howe (New York: Harper & Rowe, 1984), 127-28. Kolakowski argues that "the

great cognitive triumph of totalitarianism," resided in "abrogating" the idea of truth independent of the regime.

94. Aristotle, *The Politics*, trans. Carnes Lord (Chicago: University of Chicago, 1984), book III, chapter iv, 30. See also Baron de Montesquieu, *The Spirit of Laws*, trans. Thomas Nugent (Berkeley: University of California, 1977), book III, chapter 3. For a more recent discussion of political systems, see Samuel P. Huntington, *Political Order in Changing Societies* (New Haven: Yale University, 1968), 18-21, 80-82, 148-53. See also Harvey C. Mansfield, Jr., *Machiavelli's New Modes and Orders: A Study of the Discourses on Livy* (Ithaca, New York: Cornell University, 1979), 34-40, 97.

95. Sharpe, "Monitoring Nicaragua," *BG*, February 13, 1990, 15.

96. Havel, *Living in Truth*, 37.

97. The term "totalitarianism" fell out of favor after the U.S.' involvement in Vietnam. As the Soviet Empire began to crumble, the term experienced a revival. A computer search conducted on NEXIS/LEXIS for this study showed that the number of articles in which the terms "totalitarian" or "totalitarianism" appear at least once in the *New York Times, Washington Post, Los Angeles Times, Newsweek*, and *Time* rose from 172 in 1980 to 788 in 1991. The most dramatic increase was between 1988 (461) and 1989 (665), the year of the great events in Eastern Europe.

98. John Tagliabue, "Warsaw Journal; How to Be Big Winner: Just Make No Promises," *NYT*, June 23, 1989, A4.

99. Violeta Chamorro, "Keep Watch on Our Elections," *WP*, November 8, 1989, A23.

100. Author's interview with Roberto Eisenmann, publisher of *La Prensa*, in Cambridge, Massachusetts, April 13, 1988.

101. See "Troops in Panama Report Gains in Restoring Order," *NYT*, December 24, 1989, 1; "Amid Ruin, Residents Cheer GIs," *BG*, December 24, 1989, 1; "He Goes to Embassy: Citizens Celebrate," *BG*, December 25, 1989, 1; "In the Battered Capital, People Are Celebrating," *NYT*, December 26, 1989, A10; "Dictator's Dodge: Legalities Are Murky but Panama Cheers Noriega's Downfall," *WSJ*, December 26, 1989, 1; "'Our Liberation Has Finally Come'—Panamanians Embrace GI's with Outpouring of Gratitude," *WP*, December 27, 1989, A1.

102. Hockstader, "Nicaraguan Coalition Finds Unity Difficult," *WP*, September 4, 1989, A18; Kinzer, "Anti-Sandinistas Choose Candidate," 1.

103. Mary Speck, "Violeta Chamorro is Picked to Run Against the Sandinistas," *MH*, September 3, 1989, 18A.

104. Chamorro, "Keep Watch on Our Elections," A23. Chamorro clearly had the Bejing events of Spring 1989 in mind.

105. Christopher Marquis, "Sandinista Hits Election Stride as Foe Falters," *MH*, January 28, 1990, A1.

106. Uhlig, "Her Husband's Murder Sparked a Revolution . . . ," *NYT Magazine* (February 11, 1990): 35.

107. *La Prensa*, February 19, 1990, 2.

108. For an example of the latter see Goshko and Kamen, "U.S. Accused," A1.

109. *CBS Sunday Morning*, February 25, 1990.

110. Mary Speck, "Ortega Makes Over Old Image," *MH*, February 20, 1990, A1.

111. In the opening paragraph of his postelection report Uhlig wrote that: "The vote prepares the ground for the first democratic transfer of power that this country has known, a turnover that parallels to some degree the changes in Eastern Europe . . . ("Chamorro Elected: Ortega Pledges He Will 'Respect and Obey' Voters' Mandate," *NYT*, February 27, 1990, A1). The *Washington Post* "News Analysis" described Nicara-

gua as "a country that had just fallen out of [Moscow's] orbit," though the *Post* had never previously depicted Nicaragua as being in the Soviet "orbit" ("Defeated Sandinistas Retain Institutional Strengths," *WP*, February 27, 1990, A1). The *San Francisco Chronicle* reported: "The Sandinista loss. . . follows. . . the movement toward democracy in several Soviet-aligned nations of Eastern Europe and democratization in the Soviet Union itself (Robert Collier, "Chamorro Wins, Pledges Unity: Ortega Says He Accepts Voters' Decision," *SFC*, February 27, 1990, A1).

112. *ABC World News*, February 25, 1991.

113. After the elections Sandinistas dropped the view that Chamorro was crippled by U.S. support and adopted the position that voters backed Chamorro because the U.S. did. In postelection speeches Daniel Ortega claimed that: "The United States succeeded . . . in influencing a large sector of the population" with a policy of "blackmail, pressure, aggression, and death." "We held elections with a gun, with a gun barrel pointed at the head of the Nicaraguan people" (FBIS, LAT 90-042 [March 2, 1990]: 21, 24).

114. Barnes, "Rereading the Polls," 51.

115. Barnes, "Rereading the Polls," 98, 99.

116. Larry Rohter, "In Nicaragua, Showdown between Left and Right at Polls," *NYT*, October 21, 1996, A3. In November 2001 Ortega and the Sandinistas lost their third consecutive election by a margin similar to previous defeats, this time to an overtly pro-American businessman.

Chapter 15
Who Failed the Test?

> The authors have proceeded without animus against the *Times*, and with much admiration for its many excellent qualities. They trust that the readers of this report . . . will not regard it as an "exposure" of the *Times*, but as a piece of inductive evidence on the problem of the news.

> —Walter Lippmann and Charles Merz[1]

There is little dispute that the press failed Nicaragua's "test of the news." One journalist who for many years accepted the media account observed that the 1990 elections "cast a very unflattering light on the U.S. press corps, which after years of intense reporting somehow failed to notice the fatal decline in Sandinista popularity."[2] As we shall discuss below, the analysis found in the influential media studies we have reviewed cannot explain that oversight. Nor do the explanations suffice that have been offered for the inadequacies of foreign coverage in general and of Latin American coverage in particular.

A traditional complaint has been that Latin America attracts the notice of the U.S. press only in the event of "natural disasters, coups, revolutions, or imbroglios with the United States."[3] But this time misapprehension cannot be blamed on inattention. Even if induced by revolution and counterrevolution, and by American involvement, the U.S. media gave Nicaragua sustained, extensive, and intense coverage for more than a decade.[4] Nor can the media's failure be laid to an absence of resources of the sort that, it has been argued, were responsible for defects in the coverage of the Vietnam War.[5]

Was the Central American U.S. press corps itself callow or substandard? If a number of journalists got their start in Nicaragua, there was no paucity of veterans like Peter Arnett of CNN, Bernard Dietrich of *Time*, Ed Cody and Loren Jenkins of the *Washington Post*, Juan Vasquez of CBS, David Ensor of ABC, and Ed Rabel of NBC. Alan Riding went on to become the *New York Times* bureau chief in Paris; Cody became the *Post*'s deputy foreign editor. A number of correspondents who were inducted on the Central American beat were promoted to prestigious posts elsewhere. They include many of those who have attracted our primary attention. Stephen Kinzer became the *New York Times* bureau chief in Berlin, Chris Hedges in Cairo and Bosnia. Clifford Krauss later covered Congress for the *New York Times*. Lee Hockstader became the *Post*'s man in Moscow and then in Israel, Julia Preston its United Nations correspondent and later, along with Sam Dillon, part of a *New York Times* team that won a Pulitzer prize for reporting on Mexico. Karen DeYoung went from Managua correspondent for the *Post* to foreign editor, later to national editor, and then to assistant managing editor for national news.

Hedges, who with the *Christian Science Monitor* and the *Dallas Morning News* acquired in Central America a reputation for candor, and later reported on the Gulf War for the *New York Times*, wrote me that:

> I consider that the press in Central America to have been made up of some of the most courageous and hard-working reporters I have ever seen. Few of them would have stood for Gulf war press restrictions.
> In the end I have great respect for many of these reporters, . . . even if they were a little too ideological. They got out. They risked their lives and many died doing their job. They generally wrote the truth. If they lied, it was the lie of omission.[6]

Certainly the common American practice of moving correspondents to new assignments after relatively short periods, of two or three years, did sometimes subtract know-how and experience—though, in the case of Kinzer's replacement by Uhlig, fresh perspective was to prove beneficial. But Central American tours tended to be much lengthier than, for example, Vietnam War assignments. There was a good deal of continuity: Riding stayed for a decade, and by switching to different news organizations Kinzer, Preston, and Krauss stayed even longer. When he returned once more to cover the 1990 elections, Rabel had been visiting the region for NBC regularly since 1978. Yet Rabel's perspective hardly differed from that of Ensor, who arrived after stints at the State Department and in Moscow.[7]

Long duration can increase know-how, but it can also jade. A new arrival may bring fresh perspective or only received truth. Whether veterans or novices, an open and independent mind seemed to serve journalists best—a healthy skepticism about one's own assumptions and a professional ethic of impartiality—along with exposure to ordinary Nicaraguans. Fresh ground was broken both by newcomers like Charles Krause and Mark Uhlig and by old-timers like Alan Riding, Steven Kinzer, Chris Dickey, and James LeMoyne, as well as by those who filed from Nicaragua only on occasion, like the *Washington Post*'s William Branigin and ABC's Peter Collins, not to mention Marcel Niedergang and Bernard de la Grange of *Le Monde*.[8] But individual breakthroughs never seemed to disturb the established pattern of stereotypes.

In Nicaragua the press tended to stand and fall together. With few exceptions, it uncovered Somoza's blemishes together and ignored those of the Sandinistas together. Except for those who actually traveled with the *Contras*, it uniformly colored the latter pitch-black. The American news organizations unanimously disregarded the Latin American preelection polls. The pressure of the consensus was such that at election time even the best of journalists were unable to trust their own "observations from almost any set of random interviews."

In our case that consensus was formed not only by journalists but indirectly by pollsters, academic experts, and interest groups, as well as the host government. But often very porous membranes separated the reporters from outsiders seeking to influence them. Several journalists enjoyed warm relations with the Sandinistas, relations which the latter did their best to encourage. Press passes were issued to sympathizers who were referred to by the government as "internationalists," and by the ever-jocose Nicaraguans, adverting to their attire, as "*sandalistas*." Many of these simulated journalists served as "correspondents" for their Alumni News or for small radical newsletters. These exerted peer pressure at news conferences and elsewhere. They were joined by numerous "internationalists" from other walks of life in the highly politicized Managua social scene. According to several reporters it was not uncommon to encounter known members of the East German *Stasi* and Cuban-trained Sandinista state security agency socializing with journalists, along with "internationalists" and other interested parties.[9]

"Peer pressure," the opinion of one's colleagues, mattered a lot—as has often been the case in contemporary journalism.[10] If good reporting was the exception rather than the rule, it often seemed to come from those who socialized less with their colleagues. American correspondents in Central America tended to congregate—sometimes, as we have seen, sharing living quarters and even apportioning work. The best "on-the-record" account was provided by Peter Collins of ABC.

> Every time that you go into a [Central American] city on a big story, you find all the journalists staying at one particular hotel. They all gather in the morning over breakfast. . . . It's a sort of ritual, especially when a story is continuing, or "hot."
>
> One comes into the coffee shop and looks around to see who's there. There's a lot of preening, lot of comparing of notes and gloating or, on the other hand, moaning about having been beaten on this particular subject or not.
>
> The press corps consists of little circles and eddies of friends who work together and drive out to the field together. . . . It's very common for three or four journalists who work for ostensibly competing organizations like the *New York Times*, the *L.A. Times*, the *Washington Post* or one of the news weeklies, to rent a car or two cars together and go out in the field and compare the story and then compare notes over supper that night. Then a dominant voice among

the group will establish a common perception for them all. That's how a pack line gets established.[11]

Of course, it was quite natural for nationals sharing the same profession to mingle in a foreign country. Reporters derived obvious professional benefits from swapping sources and impressions. But beyond a certain point their fraternization made it more difficult to avoid the temptations of "pack journalism"— temptations which were reinforced, rather than discouraged, by competitive pressures from home.

Like cooperation, competition seemed unfailingly to produce uniformity. Home offices were aware of the problem. *Washington Post* foreign editor Karen DeYoung explained in 1985 that despite additional resources

> we're still lacking in people and space . . . to write about what is going on inside the Nicaraguan government, aside from who blew up what bridge. We've looked inside that government and have tried time and time again. We send people down there; they are there two days, then something happens in El Salvador, and they rush off. Some of our people here say: "we spend $150,000 per year on this bureau, so why should we have to do fifty-eight pieces on El Salvador everytime something happens?" That kind of internal allocation of time and money and personnel and space takes a long time to sort out. . . . We focus so much on the one story of the moment.[12]

But sometimes the home office was the problem. Julia Preston of the *Post* did not forget

> one or two singularly unpleasant evenings in Managua when I received phone calls from the *Post*'s foreign night editor informing me that Kinzer had this or that story on the front page of the *Times* and asking me if, in the eighteen minutes remaining until our second edition deadline, I could "match" it.[13]

Bryna Brennan of the AP has recounted similar torments inflicted by the home office, as have other correspondents.[14] Attending every press conference and covering all the standard events was a safeguard, but that solution penalized those who wished to depart from the beaten track, to get outside the capital for more than a few hours.

If in the old days a lone wolf in Managua, like Henry Giniger, with no competitors around to scoop him, had little incentive to visit "the northern mountains," in revolutionary Nicaragua reporters felt constrained to hang around the capital so as to avoid "unpleasant evenings." They traveled safely only with the pack. Both the old and the new structures placed artificial barriers between the journalist and something as central to his subject as the experiences and views of ordinary Nicaraguans. There was double irony in that the new journalism prided itself on embracing the previously neglected views of the masses. It was the views of workers and peasants and other ordinary Nicaraguans that got left out—and that broke through in the 1990 elections.

The failure cannot be blamed solely on the Central American press corps. Sandinista Nicaragua was not an open society. Access to official thinking and public records was centralized and limited and was used to discipline reporters. Beat reporters in particular had to be wary of what they wrote and with whom they associated.[15] Ordinary citizens did not often speak what was on their minds. Indeed, most of the constraints which dogged coverage of revolutionary regimes, from Soviet Russia to Saddam's Iraq, functioned in Nicaragua.[16] Should this come as a surprise to the reader, it may be because the press corps was not often candid or explicit about these constraints, when they were conscious of them.

In this respect reporters were facing a perplexity of twentieth-century international reporting: how to indicate to the reader that a political regime is limiting coverage without further limiting access. Steven Kinzer of the *New York Times* mixed puff pieces and "human interest" stories with his harder-hitting reports. Though that distorted the overall picture, it at least allowed Kinzer to score occasional bulls-eyes. But the tolerance afforded to the *Times* could not be assumed by most correspondents.

One disappointing feature of the reporting was the failure of the journalists, grappling on a daily basis with a closed regime, to give their readers a sense of that government—despite supposedly having, in DeYoung's words, "looked inside that government and . . . tried time and time again." As we saw in chapter 9, within two weeks of taking power, the FSLN delivered on national television a basic course on the nature of the Sandinista regime. The screening demonstrated that the Sandinista National Directorate controlled the government apparatus, and had dictated a program of government that it expected would be carried out by all administrative organs. The *comandantes* announced that the party would monopolize television and that the press would have to "support the revolution."[17] Yet not only did the story receive scant coverage, the U.S. media continued to report for a decade that the regime was a heterogeneous medley of radicals and pragmatists feeling its way toward democracy.

The television sessions coincided with the readily available Sandinista literature, the views of former members of the FSLN, and the group's acknowledged political lineage. The sessions were also consistent with the way the regime operated on the ground. Too often the reporters relied on FSLN sources, their own predispositions, or the demonstrations manifestly organized by the government. The problem was less a refusal to understand Nicaraguan culture, which changed very slowly, than a failure to grasp the nature of the political regime and of the revolutionary group that headed and staffed it.

Conditions in the field did not primarily mould the U.S. Central America press corps in as an institution. That press corps was but a branch of the U.S. media, subject to the conditions of existence, the pressures and the prejudices of the home office. Before setting out for the region the reporter did his background reading, consulted area specialists and officials, debriefed his predecessors and other knowledgeable journalists, thus bathing himself or herself in the U.S. conventional wisdom.[18] That they carried to Nicaragua, even when, as in the case of Mark Uhlig, James LeMoyne, Clifford Krauss, Chris Hedges, and Julia Preston, their views were decisively altered by what they encountered.

A few journalists have recounted, "off-the-record" of course, heterodox stories discouraged or "killed" by producers, editors, and other middle managers. But these incidents appear to have been rare. Moreover, neither the editors nor the correspondents were solely responsible for a "system of stereotypes" which screened the perceptions and opinions of virtually everyone in the news chain—from the lowliest staffer to the most exalted anchor.

In addition, there were the competitive pressures, the "unpleasant evenings," issuing from the home office. That competition ran along a narrow groove. One thousand flowers did not bloom in the press corps. Competition took the form of getting the story first or more fully, and—especially on television—competing in style of presentation, but not in diversity of viewpoint or of "paradigm." One of the most dismal features of the reporting on the Nicaraguan conflict was its homogeneity—the same subjects were chosen—here Kinzer made occasional exceptions—with the same frame, the same perspective, and the same sources, with very rare exceptions. Differences among news organizations were dwarfed by their broad homogeneity of frames, sources, approaches, conclusions and stereotypes. Here again there was a failure of "imagination," or imagination was throttled by political inclinations and the system of stereotypes. The competition was confined within the system of stereotypes. The formation of that system is also the story of how rebellious trailblazers were pressed, in Harold Rosenberg's phrase, into "a herd of independent minds."[19]

Pack behavior reinforced the homogeneity inherent in a system of stereotypes. The ideas of the pack were not created out of thin air nor were they the special property of the bearers. Indeed one thing that comes across powerfully in reading the coverage is how slowly, if at all, assessments changed even in the face of direct reporting to the contrary. The "myth of Sandinista popularity" withstood reporters' direct perception of coercion and fraud during the 1984 election. Notwithstanding this direct reporting, the very same reporters and their colleagues later suggested that the 1984 elections had been free and fair. Reporters in 1990 knew that demonstrators for Ortega intended to vote for the opposition, but they failed to let their readers in on the secret. For more than six years reporters who got the opportunity to travel with the *Contras* almost invariably filed reports that contravened the conventional wisdom. Yet that wisdom, or those stereotypes, held up with a remarkable resilience. Such resilience is one sign that we are dealing with "hegemonic ideas"—presuppositions which characterize not so much individual journalists as an era and a culture.

It will be argued that this analysis of the Nicaragua reporting is but a single "case study." Insofar as the Nicaragua story concentrated the energies and resources usually devoted to several major stories, it was something more than an isolated case. But comparative studies surely would test the scope, range, and tenacity of the system of stereotypes—the "post-Vietnam paradigm"—I describe. A comparable study must include a longitudinal component so as to be able to record the effect over time of changing political and cultural conditions on frame, approach, sources, outlook, and product. Second, that study should be latitudinally extensive: it should analyze not just one or two news organizations but the major national television and print outlets. Third, it should focus on a sequence of events that attracted the sustained attention of the major media for several years. By these criteria, a broad study of the U.S. media reporting of the Persian Gulf War would meet the second criterion but not the first or third. Studies that would meet all three criteria might include: U.S.-Iran reporting 1957-80, U.S. reporting of the Arab-Israeli conflict from 1967 to 1991, and U.S.-China reporting 1965-90.

News Activism and Media Studies

In chapter 2 Leon Sigal argued that a progovernment media was a structural inevitability because *"the routine channels for newsmaking . . . constitute mechanisms for official dominance of national and foreign news . . .*[20] (italics Sigal). Gaye Tuchman described the organization of newsgathering as a "strategic ritual" whose end is to "legitimate the status quo."[21]

Official sources do influence coverage, and, in specific circumstances, may "dominate the news," as Sigal contended, or even "manufacture" it, in Lippmann's famous phrase.[22] But the circumstances always demand examination. Since the late 1960s official dominance appears to have been more the exception than the rule.

Sigal's lineal proposition does not survive a cursory review of the media treatment of major foreign and domestic crises between 1968 and 1998. Consider how the Washington press covered the 1968 Tet offensive, the "Christmas bombings" of Hanoi and Haiphong in 1972, the 1973-74 Watergate scandal, the neutron bomb debate, the 1982 war in Lebanon, the Iran-*Contra* affair, the Bork hearings, and the multiple Clinton scandals.[23] If official Washington manufactured news, through official spokespersons, press releases, news conferences, authorized leaks and "spin," in each of these instances Washington proved unable to "dominate the news" or to prevent the coverage from undermining its policies and preferences. To put it in the manner most kindly to Sigal's thesis, in the "interaction" of the government and news bureaucracies, the media prevailed. Of course, one can also cite cases where the government did dominate— the Granada and Panama invasions and the Persian Gulf War, for example. But in Granada, an initially skeptical press was swayed by the reaction of Granadians. The press also greeted the Panama action with suspicion, but after Panamanians welcomed U.S. troops and Noriega was captured, the coverage turned favorable.[24]

Had Sigal confined his conclusions to Washington reporting, they would have been more persuasive, though dated. However, he claimed more broadly that "*the routine channels for newsmaking thus constitute the mechanisms for official dominance of national and foreign news*" (italics Sigal) and that "information from officials and conventional wisdom in official circles dominate press coverage of events."[25] In the Nicaraguan case we have provided one extensive illustration of the limited and circumstantial character of Sigal's calculus. Were his assertions generally applicable, we would expect the Nicaraguan news to have been pro-Somoza, anti-Sandinista, and pro-*Contra*. That coverage would have conformed to the policy of the incumbent administration. However, in general, the press maintained adversarial not fraternal, and certainly not docile, relations with policymakers.[26] When administration policy changed, in the case of the Carter Administration in 1978-79, it took a direction staked out by the press. When a Republican Administration reversed that change in 1981, it faced broad and fierce media hostility that it was unable to gainsay.

Sigal, like Gans, and the others, was looking at the news through the rearview mirror. Gans in particular failed to recognize that after "the mid-1960s," as Martin Linsky has observed, "a substantial evolution in the press-government relationship" occurred. The central consequence of this change has been to challenge the preexisting convention that the job of the press was more or less to report what officials said and did.[27]

To his credit Sigal noticed that "among young reporters, discontent with old practices is endemic."

> Advocacy journalism, organized opposition to editorial policy, demands for promotion of women and blacks—all manifest the rise of a new generation of reporters as a self-conscious occupational class pressing for changes within the industry and outside it.[28]

However, Sigal, with the conservative assumptions about cultural change of a dyed-in-the-wool radical, took it for granted that "the routines and conventions of newsmaking will be grafted onto the attitudes" of the "latest recruits." As a result change was "likely to be glacial."[29]

Certainly in Central America the ice melted far faster. Indeed, at the very moment Sigal's book was published reporting from that region and Mexico was undergoing a sea change. The shift was precipitate and ardent, but after a decade and a half in the tropics, many correspondents reverted part way to the "professional" ethics of an older, cooler era.

In the Nicaragua case we have inspected the milestones. Henry Giniger, a solid representative of the old order of reporting, was accustomed to traveling to Managua for spot stories, for which he would talk to a few U.S. and Nicaraguan government sources. Slowly, as the opposition gathered force, he began consulting their public leaders. By 1968, of all years, for the first time the viewpoint of the civic opposition "dominated" the news. But throughout the sixties, we hear of revolutionaries only through hostile official sources.

Especially as their sympathies shifted—*principally due to developments outside Nicaragua and mainly internal to U.S. culture*—journalists turned to revolutionaries and what used to be called "fellow-travelers." But at the same time these and all sources were subordinated to the active journalist's own sense of things.

"The participant journalist" figured in Sigal's typology of Washington journalists. He was likely to "rely less heavily on the formal channels of information than the neutral observer." Sigal's dominant type—"the chronicler" in Pollock's taxonomy—is rendered "susceptible to use by his sources." The participant decides "more consciously" whether "to be used or not."[30] Sigal is describing unwittingly the kind of journalist who was coming to dominate news coverage.

In 1971 Alan Riding arrives in Mexico for the *New York Times*. There and in Costa Rica he can conduct "secret interviews with leaders of the Sandinist Liberation Front." In Nicaragua he talks quietly to "doctors, lawyers, and priests who regularly visit the mountain areas and enjoy the trust of the peasants"—*i.e.* Sandinista sympathizers or cadre. He travels outside Managua to report on government repression in the countryside, relies on unidentified sources of his own choosing, and draws the ire of the Somoza government. In 1978 he introduces a "democratic" Sandinista as his principal source.

Riding blazed a new path, but it quickly became crowded. Moreover, to shift metaphors, Riding mounted the same post-Vietnam *zeitgeist* that Sigal, Gitlin, Gans, and Tuchman rode when attacking news "objectivity." Furthermore, Riding, DeYoung, Kinzer, and the others who followed represented news organizations who could afford their correspondents the time and freedom to travel in-country and to dig up new sources. These print journalists were now competing with television which, after Vietnam, is especially eager to cover breaking revolutions in Third World countries and increasingly able to do so with videotape and satellite connections. Their activism reflects a burgeoning and confident media.

Sigal also adumbrates another phenomenon that would date his own conclusions. "The spread of bureaus around the country and overseas," he writes, "counterbalances somewhat the dominance of U.S. official sources." While reporters in foreign bureaus may also "get their stories from officials," most of these "are officials of foreign governments, with perspectives on the world that might be at variance with those of American officials."[31] When it came to governments as hostile to Washington as the Sandinista, such an observation embrangles Sigal's larger claim about "official dominance of national and foreign news."

With the advent of correspondents like Riding, DeYoung, and their cohort, Sigal's view that "the sources a newsman talks to largely shape what he reports" also came in need of revision.[32] Since the new foreign correspondent was a "participant," he (or she) felt free to choose his or her foreign sources, official, opposition, or revolutionary. The new correspondent also decided whether to allow himself "to be used or not" by them. Alan Riding demoted official sources when the government was led by Somoza, relied on unnamed pro-Sandinista sources and chose to make a Sandinista dissident his primary source (without acknowledging his dissidence), an orthodox Leninist *Tercerista* program notwithstanding. In choosing to be used by him, the Sandinistas used Riding for their own purposes. The same was true of DeYoung and the others who made similar "use" of Eden Pastora and other "moderate" Sandinistas.

With the Sandinistas in power, Nicaraguan official sources recovered their influence. Indeed, their potency waxed, in part, because official sources were not often acknowledged as such. The manner in which the term "*Contra*" was adopted is one example. The same could not be said of U.S. official sources which exercised little or no influence—and less as American policy grew more hostile to the Sandinista government. Often U.S. government sources were cited to "balance" the prevailing view or to stigmatize by association, as in "the U.S.-backed *Contras*." Reporters' tacit and myopic reliance on Sandinista government sources and residents of a town under military occupation converted "the rising of Pantasma" into "the blitz against Pantasma," a Sandinista into a *Contra* human rights atrocity.

Media that accentuated the Sandinista opposition during the fall of 1978 discounted the anti-Sandinista opposition in the winter of 1990—so much so that they missed the turning point of the election campaign.

Not only the frame changed in the aftermath of the turbulent 1960s but the sources, the reporters' relation to his or her sources, and their blindspots. Once these circumstances are acknowledged and the "friction" produced by media activism is taken into account, to borrow an example from mathematician John von Neumann's study of turbulence, Sigal's linear equations become nonlinear, and the "character of the equation . . . changes simultaneously in all relevant respects. . . . Hence bad mathematical difficulties must be expected."[33]

Government dominance of the news depended on a "correlation of forces," as the Marxists called it, which began changing in the 1960s. Social and technological changes put television at the hub of the household, and of mass communication, and diminished "intermediate institutions" as against both the government and the media. The media gains were more durable. At the same time public confidence in government began its thirty-year decline.[34] The suddenly prestigious profession of journalism started demanding and attracting a type of newsman not content with chronicling, "a self-conscious occupational class pressing for changes within the industry and outside it."

As the journalist became more active, more "participant," the kind of news coverage upon which Sigal, Gans, and Tuchman had trained their sights fell out of favor. The journalist—reporter and editor—became more active, ready and willing to play one source off against another, and to decide, by his own lights, which to stress and which to ignore. Under these circumstances the relationship between sources and reporter underwent a revolution of its own. Sources often were subordinated by the journalist. Objectivity gave way to "interpretation."

Not just a view of the world entered the scene but a new "participant" approach to sources, methods, and products.

The doctrine that the government dominates the news presumed the relative docility of the media. That thesis loses validity in an era of aggressive media and active journalism. The post-Vietnam ideological critique of objectivity, whether bureaucratic as in Sigal, or structuralist as in Tuchman, becomes, along with its other failings, obsolete.

The new journalist is not only a participant: He is a critic, often an adversary. The cozy ethnocentrism—Gans's "small-town pastoralism"—was becoming a thing of the past even as Gans denounced it. The "liberal internationalism" of the post-World War II era had given way to an anti-imperialist paradigm. "The problem of the news" was less official domination, government manufacture of news, though that remained a problem, than media manufacture of the news.

Sigal criticizes explanations of news content that focus on the journalist and thus lead "to a concentration on the personal beliefs and social origins of the newsmen as the primary explanation for news content." Such perspectives overlook the fact that newsmen work "not as individuals on their own but in large-scale bureaucratic organizations."[35] Lippmann, Sigal, Tuchman, and Gans properly called attention to the structure of newsgathering. But change became possible when, as a result of changes in society and the media, new correspondents with new beliefs—or belief systems—arrived on the scene and began relying on different sources. Yet the primary explanatory variable was not the origins or attitudes of individual reporters. What counted was not individual belief but the force of the shared paradigm. That force was social, political, and cultural.

The U.S. media coverage of the revolutionary struggle against Somoza was unprecedented in immediacy, intensity, and scope. The American public was brought directly onto the battlefield by daring photojournalists and television cameramen. One television reporter lost his life at the hands of a resentful National Guard officer. News organizations exhibited a fresh sensitivity to the human rights violations of an authoritarian Latin American regime traditionally allied with the United States. Nicaraguan workers, peasants, slum-dwellers, and students occupied the media frame and journalistic sources expanded well beyond the usual government and opposition spokespersons. In many of these respects the coverage marked an advance. But looking carefully at that coverage, we have seen once iconoclastic frames "hardening into the taken-for-granted conventional wisdom, the hegemonic definitions of how things are."[36]

What Nicaragua "tested" and found wanting was not so much the journalists or even the media as a whole; what was found wanting was a paradigm, "a system of stereotypes." The "test of the news" administered by Nicaragua's 1990 election revealed that the paradigm was obscuring more than it illuminated. The new system of stereotypes had spawned fresh and more fertile "myths" which were to be refuted by the elections. Before the elections a few liberal mainstream journalists such as LeMoyne, Krauss, Hedges, Preston, and Dillon had begun to work their way free from the dogma. In the aftermath of the elections, but only in the aftermath, several journalists acknowledged their former captivity.

The system of stereotypes, in effect, did the thinking for many of the reporters, and for many political and social scientists as well. The stereotypes did the perceiving and conceptualization of Sandinista Nicaragua, usually conceptualizing before perceiving. If, as Thomas Kuhn argued, paradigms institute what he called "normal" scientific investigation, in the case of Nicaraguan analysis, reporting and polling, the post-Vietnam paradigm became a proxy for investigation.[37]

Lippmann's solution to the press's propensity to stereotyping was typical of the positivism of the progressive era. He wished to replace the reporters' proverbial nose by "a system of intelligence that is also a check upon the press."[38] He looked to the development of the research institution, "an independent, expert organization for making the unseen facts intelligible." These organizations would be staffed by analysts "not personally involved, who control enough facts and have the dialectical skill to sort out what is real perception from what is stereotype, pattern, and elaboration."[39]

Research institutions, now often located at universities, hardly fulfilled Lippmann's hopes in the Nicaraguan "test of the news." If anything, the postmodern experts compounded the difficulties. Whether they were area specialists or "scientific" pollsters, they often proved to be more "involved" and partisan, more closely tethered to the paradigm, than the new correspondent himself.[40]

The paradigm with which the new correspondent emerged from the transformed university, his "pattern of stereotypes," cannot be ascribed to a single individual or text or even to a war, and its influence clearly extended well beyond journalism. As we have said, when the better part of the cultural mass of an entire generation share a picture of the world, it must be comprehended as a social datum.[41]

That they were not the authors of their fatal assumptions does not absolve the media from blame. Failure in the biggest foreign news story since Vietnam suggests that the media's growth has been confusing for the profession itself as well as for society. Such failures have helped stimulate rival media—cable news channels, talk radio, the Internet, critical media journals. They have also provoked a search within and around the profession about accountability. Juvenal's ancient question haunts: *Quis custodiet ipsos custodies* (How to guard against the guardians)?

Notes

1. Walter Lippmann and Charles Merz, "A Test of the News," *TNR*, August 4, 1920: 3-4.

2. Paul Berman, "Neckties and Mass Graves," *Village Voice*, March 5, 1991, 33.

3. Waltraud Queiser Morales. "Revolutions, Earthquakes and Latin America: The Networks Look at Allende's Chile and Somoza's Nicaragua," in *Television Coverage of International Affairs*, ed. William C. Adams (Norwood, New Jersey: Ablex Publishing, 1982), 79. One of the earliest observations of this sort was made by President Calvin Coolidge in 1926: "readers of our newspapers might have imagined revolution and volcanic disturbances were the chief product of Latin America." Herbert Gans believed "this remark remains true fifty years later and applies as much to television and the newsmagazine as to the daily press" (Gans, *Deciding What's News* [New York: Vintage, 1980], 32).

4. See chapter 2, 12.

5. See chapter 2, 10.

6. Chris Hedges, letter to author accompanying questionnaire, August 8, 1993.

7. In Vietnam "a year to eighteen months was the standard stay for newspaper and news magazine reporters, in deference to the demands of family life." Television "bureau chiefs were assigned to Vietnam for one year, the reporters came turns varying from one to six months" (Peter Braestrup, *Big Story: How the American Press and Television Reported and Interpreted the Crisis of Tet 1968 in Vietnam and Washington* [Garden City, New York: Anchor Press, 1978; reprint, New Haven: Yale University Press, 1983], 12). Average Central American tours for print journalists were three or four times as long; proximity to the United States somewhat alleviated the "demands of family life"—and it was not uncommon for spouses to accompany journalists or to commute from Miami. Televison bureau chiefs stayed for several years. Television reporters came for as little as a week, or even less, though sometimes for much longer. Some, like Peter Collins of ABC, were regularly assigned out of Miami. (Author's interviews with James LeMoyne, Sam Dillon, Chris Dickey, Shirley Christian, Peter Collins, Elena Caldera [NBC], George Russell [*Time*], and Clifford Krauss.)

8. In the absence of a study of French reporting, the explanation for *Le Monde*'s relative success must be a matter of speculation. The stereotypes which animated U.S. journalists came into and went out of fashion earlier in France (see Pascal Bruckner, *The Tears of the White Man: Compassion as Contempt* (New York: Free Press, 1986), 37-38 and Tony Judt, *The Burden of Responsibility* (Chicago: University of Chicago, 1998), 87-135). Niedergang has a reputation for accuracy in Latin America. La Grange would later buck the tide in covering the guerrillas in Chiapas, Mexico (see Bertrand de la Grange and Maite Rico, *Marcos o la Genial Impostura* [Mexico: Aguilar, 1998]).

9. Clifford Krauss remembers a wedding attended by members of the American press corps where one guest was Lt. Nelba Blandon, the Interior Ministry official charged with censoring the Nicaraguan press.

10. For other illustrations of peer pressure in the contemporary press, see Larry Sabato, *Feeding Frenzy: How Attack Journalism Has Transformed American Politics* (New York: Free Press, 1991), 59-61.

11. Peter Collins, interview, Miami, July 12, 1989.

12. *Reporters Under Fire: U.S. Media Coverage of Conflicts in Lebanon and Central America*, ed. Landrum R. Bolling (Boulder: Westview, 1985), 114.

13. Julia Preston, "Looking Back at the Revolution," *NYRB*, July 18, 1991, 11.

14. Bryna Brennan, "'The First Casualty'—Covering Central America," (Occasional paper no. 3 of the Media Studies Project, Woodrow Wilson International Center for Scholars, Washington, D.C.), 53 ff.; and author's interviews with James LeMoyne of the *New York Times*, Sam Dillon of the *Miami Herald*, and Chris Dickey of the *Washington Post*, 1983 and 1989.

15. Author's conversations with Steven Kinzer, August 1984, October 1984, and November 1984.

16. On the former see Whitman Bassow, *The Moscow Correspondents: Reporting on Russia from the Revolution to Glasnost* (New York: Paragon House, 1989), chapters 4, 6-7; Andrew Nagorski, *Reluctant Farewell* (New York: Holt, Rhinehart & Winston, 1985); and Eugene Lyons, *Assignment in Utopia* (New York: Harcourt Brace, 1937), 135.

17. See chapter 9.

18. Author's interviews with Chris Dickey, Lee Hockstader, William Branigin, Scott Wallace, April Oliver, Charles Mohr, Peter Collins, Sam Dillon, and Julia Preston.

19. See Harold Rosenberg, *The Tradition of the New* (New York: Knopf, 1966).

20. Leon V. Sigal, *Reporters and Officials: The Organization and Politics of Newsmaking* (Lexington, Massachusetts: D. C. Heath, 1973), 125.

21. Gaye Tuchman, "Objectivity as Strategic Ritual," *American Journal of Sociology* (January 1972): 669.

22. Sigal, *Reporters and Officials*, 70, 124, 190; for a less nuanced version, see Mark Hertsgaard, *On Bended Knee: The Press and the Reagan Presidency* (New York: Farrar, Straus & Giroux, 1988).

23. On Tet, see Kathleen J. Turner, *Lyndon Johnson's Dual War* (Chicago: University of Chicago, 1985), 217-20; and Braestrup, *Big Story*; on the Christmas bombings, Martin F. Herz, *The Prestige Press and the Christmas Bombings, 1972* (Washington, DC: Ethics and Public Policy Center, 1980); on the neutron bomb, Martin Linsky, *Impact: How the Press Affects Federal Policymaking* (New York: Norton, 1986), 23-35; the war in Lebanon, *Reporters Under Fire*, 17-93; Iran-*Contra*, Suzanne Garment, *Scandal: The Culture of Mistrust in American Politics* (New York: Times Books, 1991), chapter 8; Robert Kagan, *A Twilight Struggle: American Power and Nicaragua, 1977-1990* (New York: Free Press, 1996), chapter 47; Robert S. Leiken, "The Making of a Mock Epic," *Times Literary Supplement* (February 10-16, 1989); and Ethan Bronner, *Battle for Justice: How the Bork Nomination Shook America* (New York: W. W. Norton, 1989); Clinton press, Ken Auletta, "Inside Story: Why Did Both Candidates Despise the Press," *New Yorker* (November 18, 1996). Larry Sabato dates the rise of "attack journalism" and the "feeding frenzy"—the reiterative journalistic pursuit of the foibles of public figures—to the years 1968-74 (see Sabato, *Feeding Frenzy*, 26, 45-46).

24. In Panama the media first anticipated a "Third World Quagmire" (R. W. Apple, Jr., "Big Obstacles to Victory" (News Analysis), *NYT*, December 22, 1989. Reporters thought that Noriega would mobilize the population against the U.S. invaders (Joseph Treaster, "US says Noriega Seems to Direct Attacks in Panama," *NYT*, December 23, 1989). They initially mistook Noriega's bands of looters, organized in "Dignity Battalions," as representing Panamanian "nationalist feeling" (Lindsey Gruson, "Cities Are Looters' Jungles as Chaos Consumes Panama," *NYT*, December 23, 1989). The tenor of the news soon shifted when reporters began to fan out into the country. They witnessed Panamanians greeting U.S. soldiers and discovered that Panamanians themselves were resisting Noriega's Dignity Batallions and supporting U.S. troops (Gruson, "Troops in Panama Report Gains in Restoring Order," *NYT*, December 24, 1989, 1; William Branigin, *WP*, December 24, 1989, A1; Walter V. Robinson and Phillip Bennett, "Amid Ruin, Residents Cheer GIs" and "Progress Cited in Calming Panama," *BG*, December 24, 1989). Even so, some journalists ignored the Panamanian popular reaction and continued to see the action as the big power invasion of a "pygmy" (Strobe Talbot, "Operation Mismatch," *Time*, January 22, 1990).

In both Granada and Panama reporters chafed under Pentagon restrictions and complained about them in print. (See "How Reporter Missed the War: On a Tight Leash, Journalists Assail the Pentagon's Pool System," *Time* [January 8, 1990]).

25. Sigal, *Reporters and Officials*, 70, 125.

26. That did not mean that dissident policymakers in the State Department, the Pentagon, or the Joint Chiefs of Staff failed to supply a thirsty adversarial press with leaks. Opponents in Congress did so as well, of course, as did officials who supported the policy.

27. Linsky, *Impact*, 40, 68.

28. Sigal, *Reporters and Officials*, 192.

29. Sigal, *Reporters and Officials*, 192.

30. Sigal, *Reporters and Officials*, 78.

31. Sigal, *Reporters and Officials*, 125.

32. Sigal, *Reporters and Officials*, 2.

33. John von Neumann, "Recent Theories of Turbulence," in *Collected Works*, ed. A. H. Taub (Oxford: Oxford University, 1963), vol. VI, 437; cited in James Gleick, *Chaos: Making a New Science* (New York: Viking, 1987), 24: "Without friction a simple linear equation expresses the amount of energy you need to accelerate a hockey puck. With friction the relationship gets complicated. . . . Nonlinearity means that the act of playing the game has a way of changing the rules."

34. See "Americans Losing Trust in Each Other and Institutions," *WP*, January 28, 1996, A1, a report on a 1996 survey by Harvard University and the Kaiser Family Foundation. See also Seymour Martin Lipset in *A New Moment in the Americas*, ed. Robert S. Leiken (New Brunswick: Transaction Publishers, 1994).

35. Sigal, *Reporters and Officials*, 179.

36. Todd Gitlin, *The Whole World Is Watching* (Berkeley: University of California, 1980), 303.

37. Thomas S. Kuhn, *The Structure of Scientific Revolutions* (Chicago: University of Chicago—Phoenix edition, 1964), 24-25.

38. Walter Lippmann, *Public Opinion* (New York: Macmillan, 1922; revised edition, New York: Free Press Paperback, 1965), 364.

39. Lippmann, *Public Opinion*, 31, 402.

40. News organizations are "constantly buffeted by the data war, much of it waged by think tanks," wrote the *Washington Post*'s media reporter Howard Kurz in 1997 ("Media Notes: Stop the Presses! Please!" *WP*, April 14, 1997).

41. On "cultural mass," see appendix B and also Daniel Bell, *The Cultural Contradictions of Capitalism* (New York: Basic Books, 1976), 33-34, 123.

Epilogue

Nicaragua as a concrete, knowable place disappeared in the stereotyped reporting of the revolution and counter-revolution. The country was supplanted by a system of stereotypes: of embattled revolutionary peasants (in fact, the Sandinistas were radicalized students; they had no peasant, or even proletarian, roots to speak of) and puppet "contras" (the anti-Sandinista rebels did have a considerable peasant base). After the election defeat of the Sandinistas which shattered the prevailing myths, even "Nicaragua," that fiction of a place, vanished.

According to a survey of five major news sources on LEXIS-NEXIS, from 1981-90, 8,983 stories mentioned Nicaragua. In the decade 1991-2000 that number fell to 839, less than one-tenth of the previous coverage.

In short, as far as the American reader was concerned Nicaragua disappeared. It vanished despite the fact that Nicaragua was "the most controversial" and "the single most divisive foreign policy issue since Vietnam."[1] How was it that the country faded from American journalism, politics, and culture, leaving barely a trace?

A variety of explanations spring to mind. The Cold War ended, consigning to the back pages erstwhile hot spots like Angola, Afghanistan, Cambodia, and Nicaragua. And Central America in general can be said to have been a victim of America's notoriously short attention span. If interested in foreign affairs at all, Americans moved on to South Africa, Somalia, Bosnia, Rwanda, Kosovo, Indonesia, and the Middle East. Then again, when America turned inward in the 1990s, foreign policy, as in most peaceful times, became a specialty.

But Nicaragua was more than a foreign policy topic; it was an issue, a bitter domestic controversy at a time when Americans were sharply divided, not least, over the international conduct of the United States.

Most of those divisions were still with us in the 1990s, but they rarely involved the question that made Nicaragua so absorbing: the role of U.S. power. For those who regarded the exercise of U.S. power as a negative force in world affairs, as an evil, Nicaragua was archetypal, a story of humble heroes striving for justice against reactionary puppets whom everyone loathed. Unlike Afghanistan or Rwanda, Nicaragua became a cause, it became for the 1980s what the Spanish Civil War was for the 1930s. For sympathizers Sandinista Nicaragua was the equivalent of the Bolshevik Revolution in the 1920s and 1930s or Cuba in the 1960s.

However, those crusades sustained followings for a generation. With the Sandinista election defeat, overnight Nicaragua became a lost and forgotten cause. When Nicaraguans opted for the American candidate, the archetype, which was also a worldview, became obsolete. It is hard to argue with a democratic election.

Moreover, the debate over the moral status of U.S. power has evolved substantially since the 1980s. Many of those who backed a nuclear freeze and deplored aid to the *Contras*, endorsed U.S. military intervention in the Balkans. After September 11 patriotism even became respectable.

But Vietnam, just as much as Nicaragua, was a Cold War issue and represents an equally antiquated picture of the world. Why, then, did the "obsession" of the 1980s, vanish while Vietnam remains the subject of countless essays, articles, books, special issues, and other commemorations? Of course nearly 3 million American troops fought and 50,000 died in Vietnam, none in Nicaragua. Yet like Vietnam, Nicaragua, was not merely a fleeting Cold War hot spot.

No, the reason no major article or book has been published on Nicaragua in English for several years seems to involve embarrassment as much as irrelevance. Certainly journalists and professors have little wish to recall their great indiscretion. And that is what our Nicaraguan obsession feels like today; an excess of youth or of zeal.

Nicaragua wrote a kind of epilogue to Vietnam. As we have seen a post-Vietnam paradigm governed much of the reporting on Nicaragua. Journalists perceived in Nicaragua another example of a deluded U.S. foreign policy thwarting a country of peasants pursuing freedom; another dictatorship, hated by the people, installed and propped up by the United States; another National Liberation Front falsely portrayed by the U.S. government as Communist; one more newly independent country, led by a broad national movement, resisting the colossus of the North and its proxies. Eventually several reporters dug their way down to the actual Nicaragua, but not before a dogged belief in Sandinista popularity had settled in, part of a climate of convictions which left journalists, and others with a similar mind-set, radically unprepared for Daniel Ortega's February 1990 landslide election defeat.

That upset ended an argument, but it also ruined a good story. What would have happened had the Sandinista triumphed against the U.S.-backed opposition? Would Nicaragua have disappeared from the news, from *belles lettres,* from the publishers' lists, and the college courses? Defeat was "an orphan," though in this case victory never found its fathers.

The 1990 elections sucked all the glamour from Nicaragua; no one came to call, no missions, no political tourists, no reporters. Once again, it became an ordinary small country. It was as if, after the heady, but bruising, adventure of being larger than life, Nicaragua, like Alice, suddenly became minute.

There is another way in which Nicaragua was like a forbidden drug. One journalist used the Spanish word *hartazgo,* to describe her current indifference to Nicaragua: a satiety, as in a glut or overdose. We overdosed on Nicaragua; as in a youthful indiscretion.

In the many memoirs of Vietnam journalists, the reporter is typically cast as the truth-seeker, the dispeller of myths, the teller of truth to power. Few journalists could aspire to such a role in recounting the story of the Nicaraguan revolution. The reporter was more often the reporter of lies. The Nicaraguan performance of the scholar, the pollster, and the policy analyst seldom shined any brighter. To all of these, far from self-congratulation, recollection might bring more than a twinge of shame. Those wishing to understand why Nicaragua vanished, may rest here.

Note

[1]See chapter 2, page 12, and footnote.

Appendix A
Questionnaire on Nicaragua Reporting

Please circle letter or write in answer when appropriate. Fuller responses are more than welcome, sc please feel free to append any additional comments.

Basic data
Age _____ Gender _____

Birthplace
A. Northeast-Mid-Atlantic
B. Mid-West
C. South
D. Far West
E. West Coast
F. Other (specify)

Early environment (1-18)
A. Urban
B. Rural
C. Suburban
D. Other (specify)

Parents
A. Wealthy
B. Poor
C. Upper-middle-class
D. Lower-middle-class
E. Middle-class
F. Other (specify)

Education
A. High school
B. College
C. Postgrad
D. Years of Postgrad _____
E. Military service
    Yes   No

Employment history
When did you begin working in the news field?

Assignments before Central America:

Background

1. Most influential experience that led to journalism:

2. Early intellectual influences (books, thinkers, etc.) on your views of international affairs:

3. Early influences on your views of Central America:

Please circle the letter indicating the description which most closely approximates your views at the time or when the issue emerged. Feel free to write in an answer if you prefer.

1. U.S. involvement in Vietnam
      A. Supported   B. Opposed   C. Neutral or No Opinion

2. At the time you began covering Nicaragua, how would you have characterized U.S. relations with the Third World?
      A. Exploitive   B. Constructive C. Other (specify)

3. What was your general view of national liberation movements?
      A. Communist fronts
      B. Nationalist coalitions
      C. Other (specify)

4. Did you consider U.S. policy toward Third World regimes to be:
      A. Too soft   B. Too hard   C. Other (specify)

5. Would you have regarded armed opposition to radical or communist regimes as likely to be:
      A. Foreign surrogates
      B. Popular movements
      C. Other (specify)

At the time you began covering Nicaragua:

1. How would you have characterized the Somoza regime?
      A. Repressive dictatorship
      B. Moderate authoritarian
      C. Other (specify)

2. How would you have characterized the U.S.-Nicaragua relationship under the Somozas?
      A. The Somozas were American puppets
      B. The Somozas were relatively independent of United States
      C. Other (specify)

3. How would you characterize your predisposition to the Sandinistas?
     A. Favorable   B. Unfavorable   C. Neither/Other (specify)

4. Did you initially regard the FSLN as:
     A. A group dominated by Marxist-Leninists
     B. A moderate coalition of nationalists, democrats, Marxists, etc.
     C. Other (specify)

5. Did you look favorably or unfavorably on Cuban foreign policy in the late 1970s?
     A. Favorably   B. Unfavorably   C. Other (specify)

6. How would you have characterized relations between the FSLN and Cuba circa 1978?
     A. Comradely
     B. Initially close, but now only proper
     C. Other (specify)

7. What were your expectations for the revolutionary government?
     A. Liberal regime of national unity to establish democracy
     B. A transition to Marxist one-party rule
     C. Other (specify)

8. Were your expectations borne out more or less?
     A. Yes   B. No   C. Neither (specify)

9. Roughly when did you start to think the Sandinistas no longer enjoyed preponderant popular support?
     A. 1980   B. 1982   C. 1984   D. 1986
     E. 1988   F. 1989-90   G. After Feb. 25, 1990
     H. Other (specify)

10. How would you characterize your predisposition to the *Contras*?
     A. Favorable   B. Unfavorable   C. Neither/Other (specify)

11. How did you initially view U.S. aid to the *Contras*?
     A. Interference in internal affairs of sovereign nation
     B. Support for a just cause
     C. Other (specify)

12. How did your views toward the *Contras* evolve?
     A. More favorably   B. Less favorably
     C. Unchanged   D. Other (specify)

13. Clifford Krauss has written that he and most of his colleagues:

> brought new and critical assumptions that the vast majority of our older colleagues would have found unacceptable. We had grown up with the Kennedy and King assassinations, the Tonkin Gulf incident, the secret bombing of Cambodia . . . Watergate. Our first assumption was to doubt the word of U.S. officials and the justice of the American cause. Many . . . came to Central America to help stop the next Vietnam.

How well does this characterization fit you and/or your colleagues? (*Please comment*)
>   A. Well   B. Poorly

14. Could you describe more extensively the evolution of your views of Nicaragua? You might wish to comment on another observation of Clifford Krauss (use back of sheet if you like):

> There is a socialization process in journalism. . . . There are codes, ethics and an ethos of critical nonpartisanship to be learned and upheld. The same young reporters who came down to Central America to prove that the *Contras* commit atrocities (which they do) and that Washington still lies (which it does), found out that the FMLN guerrillas also murder innocent civilians and that the Sandinista comandantes can lie with the best of them.

15. How much did the evolution of your personal views affect your reporting
>   A. Not at all   B. A little   C. A lot

Working conditions. (Please describe more fully if you care to)

1. How would you characterize the influence of your editors?
>   A. Very interventionist
>   B. Acquiescent
>   C. Other (describe)

2. How many of your stories did your editors "spike"?
>   A. None   B. One or two (extremely rare)   C. Several

3. How often did the editors alter the substance (as opposed to style) of your stories?
>   A. Never   B. Rarely
>   C. Occasionally   D. Often

4. What were their motives? (Check more than one if you wish. Please elaborate if you care to)
>   A. Personal/political disagreement
>   B. Felt pressure from U.S. government

C. Felt pressure from supporters of U.S. policy
D. Felt pressure from opponents of U.S. policy

5. Were you aware of individuals or groups approaching your news organization seeking to influence your coverage?
    A. Never   B. Rarely   C. Occasionally
    D. Often   E. Continually

6. Were you approached by those seeking to influence your coverage?
    A. Never   B. Rarely   C. Occasionally
    D. Often   E. Continually

7. Did pressures derive more often from supporters or critics of U.S. policy (indicate roughly what percentage if you can)?
    A. Supporters   B. Critics   C. Both equally

8. Did you feel pressure from the government or from groups inside Nicaragua? (comment)
    A. Never   B. Rarely   C. Occasionally
    D. Often   E. Continually

9. Did you feel pressure from other members of the press corps in Managua?
    A. Never   B. Rarely   C. Occasionally
    D. Often   E. Continually

Name and address if you wish (include conditions for use)

Appendix B
Postindustrial Society and the New Foreign Correspondent

What are the broader economic, social, and cultural sources of the new foreign correspondent and his ideology? The enhanced status and prestige of the journalist, the heightened power and influence of the media, and the university-reflected changes in the socioeconomic structure, as well as in the cultural and political world, changes which many believed marked a new epoch or age. In 1973 Harvard sociologist Daniel Bell proclaimed the coming of "post-industrial society" while other contemporary theorists annnounced "the information age," "the knowledge society," "the technetronic age," "the cybernetic era," "the second industrial revolution," "the third scientific revolution," and "postmodernism."[1]

Postindustrial society or the information age or, less dramatically, "advanced capitalism" involved three major shifts involving several dimensions of change.[2] The first major shift was the information revolution itself: the increased "centrality of theoretical knowledge" to the productive process.[3] The new intellectual technology based on linear (and now nonlinear) programming, stochastic processes, and cybernetics influenced virtually every enterprise from construction to health care to weather forecasting. The new technology transformed and expanded industries such as chemistry, pharmaceuticals, finance, entertainment, and telecommunications, and spawned vast new ones such as electronics, petrochemistry, nuclear energy, biogenetics, synthetics, aerospace, polymers, optics, computers, and robotics.[4] That technology was based on a "codified theoretical knowledge" developed at universities and industrial laboratories. The information society multiplied instruction, research and development in universities, private and government laboratories, and research institutions. New corporate information giants arose such as IBM, Xerox, Time-Warner, and Microsoft.

Secondly, as capitalism, contrary to most Marxist expectations, expanded and "structurally differentiated," to use Emile Durkheim's term, the "service" sector (consumption, finance, marketing, and state sectors) grew more rapidly than the industrial.[5] The expansion of consumption, services, and government together with the more intellectual character of work gave rise to or brought to prominence many occupations and professions. "Human services" such as law, medicine, journalism, and social services burgeoned, as well as technical services such as research, evaluation, computers and systems analysis.[6] The supplying of services rather than the production of goods had become the principal occupation of the new age, employing as much as two-thirds of the workforce by the mid-1970s.[7]

The combination of the information revolution and the shift from goods to services produced a corresponding change in the character of work: from "blue" to "white collar," from physical to mental labor. The shift in the character of work meant that those who manipulated symbols—language, math, ideas—rather than tools, came to occupy the central place in the economic structure of society. The typical skilled worker in postindustrial society utilizes acumen rather than strength, and his or her workplace depends on communication of information rather than physical cooperation.[8]

In *The Cultural Contradictions of Capitalism*, Daniel Bell argued that the capitalist work ethic, of deferred gratification, sobriety, etc., meets resistance as capitalism develops and begins to deliver an immense array of consumer goods. The ethic of deferred gratification, the ethic of production, is challenged by an ethic of consumption: self-expression or self-gratification. In the later twentieth century these changes created the conditions for the emergence of a "cultural mass" for *avant-garde* and adversary ideas that had gestated in industrial society for 150 years.

With the advent of mass readership in the industrializing, democratizing early nineteenth century, the coterie of artists and intellectuals around the court gave way to a dissident intelligentsia whose sources of financial support were less regular and, by and large, divorced from the political establishment. The classical court painter or poet gave way to the romantic *avant-garde* of the garret, the disaffected artist and intellectual appalled by the ugliness and inequities of industrialization. This new strata of artists and intellectuals dates from the late eighteenth century in Europe, though the seventeenth-century Puritan Anne Hutcheson could be considered the founder of the American dissident tradition that reached high water marks with Henry David Thoreau and the transcendentalists ("Things are in the saddle/And ride Mankind," R. W. Emerson) or with early twentieth-century exiles such as Gertrude Stein, Ernest Hemingway, and Ezra Pound. The alienated intellectual came to reject the values and institutions of capitalist society, in favor of a radical utopianism and varieties of socialism in politics, nihilism in philosophy, hedonism in values, and "modernism" in art.

Until the coming of postindustrial society a relatively small disaffected subsector of the elite incarnated this "cultural contradiction of capitalism." The development of capitalism into postindustrial society, with its consumerism, its enormous service sector, and its greatly broadened intelligentsia creates social strata, a "cultural mass," receptive to an ideology adverse to the productive ethic. In postindustrial society, Bell wrote, "[t]he adversary culture has come to dominate the cultural order" though the productive ethic continues to dominate the socioeconomic structure."[9] Bell considered the "deep tension" between a social structure "ruled by an economizing and technocratic mode" and "an anti-institutional and antinominan" culture to be the "most fundamental problem of postindustrial society."[10]

The spread of antibourgeois values in the 1960s and 1970s went "hand in hand with the expansion of a new intellectual class huge enough to sustain itself economically *as* a class . . ."[11] Bell later would consider the category of class (as in "new class" or "knowledge class") inappropriate to characterize the varied social strata created or strengthened by postindustrial developments.[12] Indeed, as the Lipset and Ladd study of the late sixties' university showed, these social strata can be deeply divided in their political and social views and in their economic interests. But Ronald Inglehart has found in Western postindustrial societies a "preponderance" of what he calls postmaterialism (an "adversary culture" view on issues) "among young professionals and managers."[13] Moreover,

By 1980, a Postmaterialist outlook had become more common than a Materialist one among young technocrats, professionals and politicians in Western countries. As experts, congressional staffers and members of ministerial cabinets, Postmaterialists had direct access to the command posts of the sociopolitical system.[14]

The impact of the adversary culture was no longer symbolized by the student with a protest poster but "by the public interest lawyer or the technocrat with an environmental impact statement."[15] As for the United States, Steven Brint has observed that by the 1980s "liberal professionals" had become numerous and influential enough "to play a more or less autonomous role as seedbed of liberal politics. . . ." Moreover, the character of liberal politics was now determined in good part by postmaterialist "liberal zones of the professional stratum" and "the declining significance of organized labor."[16] This is one reason for emergence of the post-Vietnam liberalism first associated with George McGovern.

Though postindustrial society and postmaterialism are common to all advanced industrial countries to varying degrees, as we have seen this does not mean that a reporter from *Le Monde* would cover Nicaragua in the same way as an American or a Swede. National political or cultural developments, the anti-communist new philosophers movement in France for example, as well as a host of other pertinent factors such as press traditions, may shape the approach of an individual journalist. Our generalizations rest on safer ground when the sample is large enough to constitute a press corps.

Cultural and political change is not a simple biproduct of socioeconomic change. Indeed, for Bell changes in the cultural, political, and socioeconomic realms are entirely independent of one another. What Bell terms the "axial principle" of the economic realm is linear: continuous improvement. "[T]he axial principle of modern culture," however, "is the expression and remaking of 'self' in order to achieve self-realization and self-fulfillment." Moreover, "in culture there is always a *ricorso*, a return to the concerns and questions that are the existential agonies of human beings. . . .Boulez does not replace Bach."[17]

Certainly not, but none of the above signifies that the socioeconomic and the cultural (or for that matter the political) realms are airtight. *Relative* independence seems a more accurate characterization of their relationship: with one sphere decisively influencing another under certain conditions.[18] For example, the political sphere has a determinant influence at the time of the foundation of a regime; the socioeconomic during technological revolution—the industrial revolution for example. The cultural sphere may be decisive in an era that seeks to consolidate or institutionalize political and economic systems, as today in many post-Communist countries or at the time of the consolidation of the first empire in China when "[t]radition displaced charisma."[19]

In our case developments in both the cultural realm and the social structure contributed to the prominence and resilience of the post-Vietnam paradigm among that layer of white-collar professionals we can call "intellectuals." The information revolution had created demands for mental labor, converting the university into a mass institution. Intellectual skills were rewarded with relatively high-paying jobs; their possessors became a social force. But at the same time, the historical "cultural contradictions of capitalism" meant that the cultural realm was predisposed to anticapitalist and anti-imperialist positions. The interplay of these two phenomena created a cultural mass for the adversary ideas of the sixties. From this cultural mass came the new correspondent who covered Nicaragua's revolution and counterrevolution with such mixed results.

Bell wished to segregate the political, socioeconomic-technical, and cultural realms in reaction to the more typical and vulgar custom of merging or muddling them—as in the view that economic growth inevitably produces a democratic transition or workers must support socialism. But this effort produced its own contradictions. When studying the technical, economic changes associated with postindustrial society Bell spoke of a knowledge class. But after writing *The Cultural Contradictions of Capitalism* he changed course and denied the class character of these strata—reducing the phenomenon to a "mentality" restricted to the cultural realm. In the first instance the cultural "class" is a direct outgrowth of economic development. In the latter the economic, cultural, and political spheres are separated by chasms—or Chinese walls, disregarding the role of the technico-economic transformations Bell explored earlier.

The distinctions among realms, while important, can become reified. The realms can be mistaken for actual social phenomena as opposed to sociological concepts designed to explicate those phenomena. That is, they can be mistaken for external reality when in fact they are only representations of that reality—part of Bell's elaborate system of representations.[20]

The media, which Bell does not analyze directly, straddle three spheres. Journalists derive from and often feel loyalty to the cultural realm, aspire to influence the political, but must serve the socioeconomic. Correspondents such as Chris Hedges, Clifford Krauss, Julia Preston, and James LeMoyne who recognized the impact of "the socialization process in journalism" and "an ethos of critical nonpartisanship" were, among other things, indirectly acknowledging the demands and discipline of the socioeconomic sphere (see the discussion of "the media's objective role" in chapter 4, 49-51). In that sphere what counts is information.

Notes

1. See for example, Herbert Kahn and Anthony J. Weiner, *The Year 2000* (New York: Macmillan, 1967); Alain Touraine, *Societe post-industrielle* (Paris: Denoel, 1969); Zbigniew Brzezinski, *Between Two Ages: America's Role in the Technetronic Era* (New York: Viking Press, 1970); Ramond Aron, *The Industrial Society* (New York: Praeger, 1967); and Amitai Etzioni, *The Active Society* (New York: Free Press, 1968).

Bell's work was preceded by or coincided with several others. Theorists coined terms like "the knowledgeable society" (Robert Lane), "the technetronic age" (Zbigniew Brzezinski), "the active society" (Amitai Etzioni), and "the information society" (various). Other influential works which coincided to a greater or lesser degree with Bell's analysis included Aron's *The Industrial Society* and W. W. Rostow's *Stages of Economic Growth* (Cambridge: Cambridge University Press, 1960) which spoke of a "postmaturity" economy.

Ralf Dahrendorf's *Class and Class Conflict in an Industrial Society* (Stanford: Stanford University, 1959) discussed "postcapitalist society" and sustained that the labor question had been "encapsulated" and no longer generalized as polarizing division. David Reisman in *Mass Leisure* (Glencoe, Illinois: Free Press, 1959) spoke of post-industrial society but only in reference to patterns of leisure, not of production. George Lichtheim held that "contemporary industrial society is 'postbourgeois'" (in *The New Europe: Today and Tomorrow* [New York: Praeger, 1963], 194). Both writers stressed the diminution in importance of private ownership and the independence of political authority from ownership. Amitai Etzioni's "postmodern" society was characterized by the "radical transformation of the technologies of communication, knowledge, and energy" (*Active Society*, vii). Kenneth Boulding thought the advanced countries at the start of a "postcivilized" era were characterized by the primacy of the noosphere (Teilhard), the sphere of social knowledge or the social direction of society (Boulding, *The Meaning of the Twentieth Century, The Great Transition* (New York: Harper & Row, 1964). Peter Drucker wrote of the growth of "knowledge work" as a central component of the new age (*The Age of Discontinuity* [New York: Harper & Row, 1969]).

Also in 1969, in the epilogue to *British Politics in the Collectivist Age* (New York: Vintage, 1969), Harvard historian Sam Beer stated that "postcollectivist" politics were replacing the traditional party politics. Sydney Ashlstrom in "The Radical Turn in Theology and Ethics" (*The Annals*) described the U.S. religious scene of the 1960s as "post-Puritan, post-Protestant, and post-Christian." And Daniel Bell himself wrote of the "end of ideology." In some respects Bell's work was preceded by Fritz Machlup's exhaustive volume *The Production and Distribution of Knowledge in the United States* (Princeton: Princeton University, 1962). Bell recognized Machlup's "heroic effort to compute the proportion of GNP devoted to the production and distribution of knowledge" (Bell, *The Coming of Post-Industrial Society* [New York: Basic Books, 1973], 212). But to regard Machlup's volume as "the empirical backdrop to subsequent work by Daniel Bell" as does Marc Uri Porat in his update of Machlup, *The Information Society: Definition and Measurement* (Washington, D.C.: U.S. Department of Commerce, 1977), 44, is to overlook not only the conceptual flaws of Machlup's work but the sociological, historical, and philosophical breadth of Bell's. Machlup's groundbreaking but pedestrian survey has none of Bell's theoretical rigor or his encyclopedic range. Moreover, Machlup's work was flawed by an imprecise and exuberant definition of "knowledge." Machlup's communications media includes greeting cards, stationery, and office supplies; his "information machines" include microphones, musical instruments, address plate embossing, and "check-handling machines"; his information services include stock brokerage and investment counseling, insurance carriers, real estate agents and "jobbers, dealers, and traders in wholesale agents and brokers." His admittedly "wide concept of knowledge industries" derives from a concept of knowledge which embraces everything from science to "small talk." (See Machlup, *Production and Distribution of Knowledge*, 295, 22.) Porat's own endeavor to update Machlup found other problems of a more technical and methodological nature (Porat, *Information Society*, 44-46).

2. The term postindustrial society can be misleading because, as Bell pointed out, industry does not disappear anymore than agriculture vanished in the passage to industrial society.

3. Postindustrial society is distinguished by the "primacy of theory over empiricism" and the "codification of knowledge into abstract systems of symbols." The great inventors of the industrial age (Bessemer, Edison, Bell, *et al.*) were "inspired tinkerers indifferent to science." They produced key industries such as steel, telephone, and electric light. On the other hand, developments in postindustrial fields such as petro-chemistry, chemistry, nuclear, polymers, optics, electronics, and cybernetics depend directly on advances in theoretical work, on codified theoretical knowledge (Bell, *Coming of Post-Industrial Society*, 20, 26).

4. See Bell, *Coming of Post-Industrial Society*, xvi, 27-34.

5. For a discussion of "services," see Ronald Kent Shelp, *Beyond Industrialization* (New York: Praeger, 1981), chapter ii.

6. Bell, *Coming of Post-Industrial Society*, xvi, 133

7. Bell, *Coming of Post-Industrial Society*, xvi, 129. Bell expected the proportion to rise to 70 percent by 1980 and to continue to rise (Bell, *Coming of Post-Industrial Society*, 127-36). In a book that Bell singled out for special praise in a 1995 review, Theodore Caplow observed that "contrary to a widespread belief, the proportion of service workers remained unchanged" between 1970 and 1986. But the (minor) discrepancies here are mainly terminological. Caplow also noted that between 1970 and 1986 there was a 57 percent rise in managerial, supervisory, and administrative occupations, and a 76 percent rise in clerical and technical workers. Both agree that the "shift from blue collar to white collar" jobs marked "an historic turning point" (Theodore Caplow, *American Social Trends* [San Diego: Harcourt Brace Jovanovich, 1991], 87; and Daniel Bell, "The Disunited States of America," *Times Literary Supplement* [June 9, 1995]: 16-17).

As Bell recognized "the term 'services' disguises different things such as personal services (restaurants, travel, hotels, automobile services, entertainment, sports, etc.), the expansion of medical services, of the educational system, and of government" (Bell, *Coming of Post-Industrial Society*, 127-28). Analysis by Porat factors out those he considers "information workers" from noninformation workers (in a two-sector aggregate by percent) and from those engaged in services, industry, and agriculture (in a four-sector aggregation). His two-sector analysis shows that "the information workforce in 1860 comprised less than 10 percent of the total. By 1975, the information workers [under his inclusive definition influenced by Machlup—see *infra*] surpassed the non-information group." His four-sector series shows information workers outstripping service workers in the early 1960s (Porat, *Information Society*, 119-21, and figures 7.1 and 7.2).

8. For summary of changes in the American labor force between 1970 and 1986, see Caplow, *American Social Trends*, 88-98. For statistical updates of the various aspects of Bell (and Machlup's) analysis, see also Porat's *Information Society*; *Public Employment in Western Nations*, ed. Richard Rose (Cambridge: Cambridge University, 1985); Frederick Williams, *Measuring the Information Society* (Beverly Hills: Sage, 1988); Shelp, *Beyond Industrialization*; and Steven Brint, *In an Age of Experts* (Princeton: Princeton University, 1994).

9. Bell, *The Cultural Contradictions of Capitalism* (New York: Basic Books, 1976), 40.

10. Bell, *Coming of Post-Industrial Society*, 44.

11. Bell, *Coming of Post-Industrial Society*, 478.

12. It is not within the scope of this thesis to investigate this question deeply. Readers interested in the theory of the "new class" should consult the works of Bell, *Coming of Post-Industrial Society*, 34-36, 86-99, 232; *The New Class?* ed. B. Bruce-Biggs (New Brunswick, New Jersey: Transaction Books, 1979); Steven Brint, *In an Age of Experts*, 13 ff.; Thomas Edsall, *The New Politics of Inequality* (New York: W. W. Norton, 1984), 49-61; Kevin P. Phillips, *Mediocracy: American Parties and Politics in the Communications Age* (Garden City, New York: Doubleday, 1975), 29; and Irving Kristol, *Two Cheers for Capitalism* (New York: Basic Books, 1978), 23-28. For the origins of the "new class" idea, see Bruno Rizzi, *The Bureaucratization of the World* (New York: Free Press, 1985); Milovan Djilas, *The New Class: An Analysis of the Communist System* (New York: Harcourt, Brace & World, 1969); and Max Schactman,

The Bureaucratic Revolution: The Rise of the Stalinist State (New York: Donald Press, 1962).

13. Inglehart conclusions are based on a "massive number of surveys from nine Western nations" and corroboration by two major studies of American data. Both Jennings and Markus (1984) and Delli Carpini (1986) have traced the generation that came of age during the 1960s into the 1980s—and have found that this group as a whole, and its upper-status segment in particular, remain "politically and socially more liberal than preceding generations" (Ronald Inglehart, *Cultural Shift In Advanced Industrial Societies* [1990], 320). The studies are M. Kent Jennings and Gregory Markus, 1984 and Michael X. Delli Carpini, 1986.

14. Inglehart, *Cultural Shifts*, 331.

15. Inglehart, *Cultural Shifts*, 331.

16. Brint, *In an Age of Experts*, 95-96.

17. Bell, *Cultural Contradictions of Capitalism*, 13. The same point has been made by Ludwig Wittgenstein and Frederick Engels in relation to the great philosophical debates between materialism and idealism (Searle, 196; Engels, *Feuerbach and the End of Classical German Philosophy*, in Marx and Engels, 195, vol. II, 370-76).

18. On the concept of relative independence see "Engels to Schmidt," in Marx and Engels, 1958:492; see also Althusser (1971), 135.

19. "The Chinese Literati," in *From Max Weber*, 420; see also, Francis Fukuyama, "The Primacy of Culture," *Journal of Democracy* (January 1995): 7-8.

20. See chapter 4, 43 *supra* on conceptual relativity and external reality.

Appendix C
Comparative Quantitative Analysis: News Depiction of the Sandinistas and the *Contras*

Quantitative surveys of the coverage of the *Washington Post* and the *New York Times* were conducted. News articles surveyed included the Nicaragua coverage of the *Washington Post* from July 1978 to June 1979 and from January 1983 to April 1984 and the Nicaragua coverage of the *New York Times* from July 1978 to June 1979 and January 1983 to August 1984.

Findings

The first survey compared the news treatment of popular support for the Sandinista National Liberation Front (FSLN) in 1978-79 with the treatment of popular support for the Contra rebels in 1983-84. All thirty-two articles referring to the issue characterized the Sandinistas as enjoying popular support. In the case of the *Contras*, only eight articles raised the question of popular support, of these two stipulated popular support, while six indicated an absence of popular support.

The second survey compared references to the organizational composition of the two groups. Of the twelve news articles which discussed the organizational composition of the FSLN, five highlighted their peasant composition, five the involvement of students, and one the role of Christians. Only one news article mentioned that the FSLN contained Communists or Marxists. Of the seventeen news articles which discussed the organizational composition of the *Contra* rebels, one mentioned their peasant origin, two their *Somocista*, affiliations and fourteen their National Guard background.

The third survey monitored news articles for their political characterization of the Sandinistas and the *Contras*. Twenty-three articles characterized the Sandinistas as leftist, four as a heterogeneous mix, and in only two (7 percent) as Marxist-Leninist. The *Contras* were depicted as U.S.-backed in twenty-four articles, in seven as CIA-backed, in four as rightist, and in one as representing the National Guard.

The final survey appraised the depiction of the military forces that fought the FSLN and the *Contras*, respectively. The army fighting the Sandinistas was described seventy-six times as the National Guard, ten times as Somoza's army and only five times as the army of Nicaragua (6 percent). Conversely, the army which fought the *Contras* was called the Nicaraguan army thirteen times (65 percent) and the Sandinista army seven times (35 percent).

Summary and Analysis of Findings

The question of popular support figured much more prominently in news articles dealing with the FSLN than in those dealing with the *Contras*. The articles surveyed conveyed unanimously that the Sandinistas enjoyed popular support, a perception which was borne out by the course of events. On the other hand, the issue of popular support rarely appeared as such in *Contra* articles. In the eight articles which specifically treated the question, six of them found the *Contras* to lack support. This treatment was not borne out by 1990 election returns from the provinces in which the *Contras* operated.

Though the Sandinistas bore only a meager peasant presence, the news articles surveyed portrayed the Sandinistas as composed mainly of peasants and students. Their Communist background was mentioned only once. The *Contras* were composed overwhelmingly of peasants, but their peasant composition was mentioned only once in the news articles surveyed. Cited nearly universally were the *Contras'* National Guard and Somoza connections.

Only 7 percent of news articles characterized the Sandinista Front as Marxist-Leninist, which was the burden of the Somoza government disparagement of it. On the other hand, the press tended to echo the Sandinista government charges against the *Contras*, that they were U.S.- and CIA-backed intruders.

Though the army which fought the *Contras* was called the Sandinista Popular Army, it was usually referred to in the press as the Nicaraguan Army, suggesting that it was not partisan but represented the nation as a whole. By contrast, the equally partisan army that fought the Sandinistas was called the Nicaraguan Army only 6 percent of the time and was usually referred to as the National Guard.

Stephen Kaplitt, a research assistant at the Harvard University Center for International Studies, helped conduct the statistical survey.

Index

La Crónica, 213
Ladd, Everett C., 28
Lane, Charles, 78–79, 80, 81, 201
Lapham, Lewis, 40
La Prensa (Nicaragua), 96, 97, 98, 139,
    181, 219, 225, 226, 231;
    censorship of, 133, 137;
    circulation of, 64–65; coverage of
    pre-election polls in, 216; election
    coverage in, 64–65, 190, 192–93;
    survey conducted by, 132
La Prensa (Panama), 231
LASA, 47, 134–35, 218, 219
Lasch, Christopher, 43
Latin America, reporting on, 27
Latin American Studies Association.
    See LASA.
League of United Latin American
    Citizens (LULAC), 134
Le Monde, 4, 247; election coverage in,
    189, 193–94, 198, 199, 214
LeMoyne, James, 153–55, 157, 170,
    177, 246, 250, 255
Lenin, Vladimir Ilyich, 121, 123, 170
Levi-Strauss, Claude, 43
Lewis, I. A., 224
Liberal Party, 74, 109
Lippmann, Walter, 7, 8, 11, 30, 50, 52,
    77, 141, 148, 165, 181, 245, 255,
    256
Lipset, Seymour Martin, 28
Linsky, Martin, 252
Llach, Nancy, 218–19, 222, 223–24,
    227
Logos, 222, 225
Los Angeles Times, 25, 247; coverage
    of pre-election polls in, 215, 218,
    224; election coverage in, 65, 72,
    73, 133, 135, 136, 139, 188, 195,
    196, 197; portrayal of the Contras
    in, 147
Lovler, Ronnie, 3

MacNeil, Robert, 66, 221
Mailer, Norman, 44
manufacture of consent, 7–8, 47, 49
Marchetti, Peter, 213, 222
Markel, Lester, 41, 51
Marquis, Christopher, 197
Marx, Karl, 88, 121, 123

Marxism, 41, 123, 167
Marxism-Leninism, 48, 49, 66, 120–21,
    123, 125, 150, 167, 173, 175
Massachusetts Institute of Technology,
    46
Matthews, Herbert L., 88, interview
    with Fidel Castro by, 89–90, 112,
    114, 117–18
McCartney, Robert, 137, 155, 156
media, 3; as academic field, 37; as
    advocates of policies, 46; as
    business, 8–9, 49–51; ascendance
    of, 29–30; coverage of 1984
    Nicaraguan elections in, 9, 47–48,
    132–41; coverage of 1990
    Nicaraguan elections in, 1–4, 7,
    48, 61–68, 78–81, 181–82, 245–
    47; coverage of anti-Somoza
    struggle, 7, 255; coverage of Cuba
    in, 89–92; coverage of draft
    resistance in, 139–40, 174;
    coverage of earthquake in, 108–
    10; criticism of, 10, 47, 117, 121–
    22, 127; ideology in, 10, 11, 49,
    51–52; objectivity of, 39–42, 45,
    49–52, 125; portrayal of the
    Contras in, 147–60, 247; portrayal
    of Sandinistas in, 111–14, 117–27,
    168, 245, 249–50; relationship
    with government of, 45–46; role
    of, 29, 30, 45; studies of, 3, 13,
    37–39, 41–51, 124–25; technology
    in, 11
media frame. See news frame.
media studies, 37
Merz, Charles, 7, 8, 11, 245
methodology, 13–14
Mexican Revolution, image of, 114,
    166
Miami Herald, 2, 117, 148; coverage of
    the Sandinistas in, 174; election
    coverage in, 62, 135, 197, 214,
    232; portrayal of the Contras in,
    148, 158
Miller, Peter, 218, 224
Millett, Richard, 123
MILPAS, 152
Miskito Indians, 173–74
Mohr, Charles, 15
Morin, Richard, 224

About the Author

Robert S. Leiken is the director of the Immigration and National Security Program at the Nixon Center in Washington, D.C. He is also a nonresident senior fellow at the Brookings Institution. Previously, he was a senior associate at the Harvard Center for International Affairs, the Carnegie Endowment for International Peace, and the International Forum for Democratic Studies of the National Endowment for Democracy. Leiken worked for a decade in Mexico where he was professor of economic history at CIDE (Center for Economic Investigation and Instruction) and at the National Agricultural University.

Other books by Leiken include: *The Melting Border: Mexico and Mexican Communities in the United States, Enchilada Lite: A Post-9/11 Mexican Migration Agreement, Central America: Anatomy of Conflict, The Central American Crisis Reader,* and *A New Moment in the Americas.* His articles on Nicaragua have been nominated for the Overseas Press Club award and republished in several anniversary issues. His commentaries have appeared in major newspapers and his reports and essays in *Foreign Affair, Commentary, New Republic, New York Review of Books, Times Literary Supplement, Washington Post Outlook, National Interest,* and *Journal of Democracy* among others. He has also appeared as a guest commentator on many television news programs and talk shows.

Leiken graduated from Harvard College Magna Cum Laude and Phi Beta Kappa and received his doctorate from St. Anthony's College, Oxford University.